David & Suzanne's Big Frickin' Canadian Motorcycle Adventure

David P. Moore

Cover design & artwork:

Erick M. Lingbloom

David P. Moore
press@bigfrickinadventures.com
http://www.bigfrickinadventures.com

Published in the United States of America

LIBRARY OF CONGRESS CONTROL NUMBER: 2011905330

ISBN-13: 978-1456352424
ISBN-10: 1456352423

Printed in the United States of America

Bulk purchases, please contact bulk_sales@bigfrickinadventures.com

For my two Amazons.

And especially my Sweet Baboo.

Thank you for my life.

Foreword

I had an agent read this book and comment, "Sure, you hate Canadians, but . . . ".

Which made me laugh out loud. Because the person couldn't have *really* read the book and come away with that opinion. Agents. Don't get me started.

Hate Canadians? Nothing could be further from the truth.

Canada, for me, is like a brother. I can tease, laugh, and cajole the Canadian people for two reasons:

One, they are family. I can say what I want about family. That's the way it works. But don't you dare say something or there will be an ass kicking in order.

Two, unlike most Americans in our oh-so-easily offended nation, Canadians are smart enough to get the joke.

You, dear reader, should know I wrote this as a series of letters to my daughter as she completed Navy Officer Candidate School in Rhode Island. I did this as a distraction, something to get her through the days as she completed one of the hardest programs around. OCS is no picnic. If you don't know the particulars I suggest that you take a moment and do a bit of research. It puts things in perspective. Fast.

And yes, she graduated and got her wings.

David P. Moore

David & Suzanne's Big Frickin' Canadian Motorcycle Adventure

September 8, 2008

Dear Amber,

Mom says that you made it to your Navy Officer Candidate School in Rhode Island and that I should fulfill a hasty yet heart-felt promise and tell you about our trip to Canada.
Fine.
I almost killed your mom last week.
Talk to you later.

Love,
Dad

*   *   *

September 9, 2008

Dear Amber,

Mom says that was a horrible letter and I should elaborate to soothe your nerves.
Fine. I almost killed your mother last week --- multiple times.
Feel better?

Love,
Dad

P.S. Was your bedroom always full of water?

*   *   *

September 10, 2008

Dear Amber,

Mom says I am an awful father and to tell you what really happened. I would argue that I'm an adequate father but a horrible husband.

I came to this conclusion as I sat on a wet gravel road, high in the Canadian Rockies, in the dying light of one weird, weird day. Hungry, hypothermic, lost, full of remorse, Grizzly spittle drying on the back of my neck, and alone. Horribly and utterly alone. Well, except for your mother sitting behind me, gently weeping and describing my character in what I think are very unflattering terms. She could at least have used words with more than four letters and some hyphens.

Oh, there was a moose there too. Did I tell you that?

Anyway, as I sat there, shivering, shaking, highly paranoid that we were going to be eaten at any moment I promised myself one thing: I promised myself should I live I would tell the complete, unvarnished, absolutely true tale to my daughters as a cautionary fable full of insight, wisdom, and delicious, delicious meats.

Since your sister, being the first-born, can smell my BS a mile away and is pretty quick to run I guess you're the lucky one.

It's okay. You can thank me later.

So, did I tell you we bought a new motorcycle? No?

Okay, I'll start at the beginning. I have it on the highest authority that this is a very fine place to start. But do me a favor. Hold your opinion until the end.

Love,
Daddio

*   *   *

Chapter 1

The Journey Begins . . . Sort of

Since you've forsaken us and left us to wander alone in our twilight years while you're off getting all Navy-a-pated - we did what most 'recently elderly' people do and bought a new motorcycle. She's a 2008 Victory Vision. This beauty is like nothing you've ever seen. The styling on this bike is revolutionary. She is an ode to art deco. She is a sonnet of line and form and function with a bass note of devil-may-care intensity. Cherry Red. 106 cc's and 96 hp. Cruise control. Stereo. GPS. Heated seats. Heated hand-grips. Electric adjustable windshield, and enough computer chips to build a robot.

I admit, I'm smitten. I may, if pressed, leave your mother for this bike - she's just that hot. Not that your mother isn't hot - she is. But Mom doesn't cruise from 0 to 60 in 4.5 seconds. Well, unless she's mistaken the caffeine pills for breath-mints again. How best to sum up the Vision? She's a big-ass Buck Rodger's lookin' rocket-ship that raises more eyebrows than a beauty-pageant contestant explaining the nuances of quantum physics. Needless to say, the bar-hopping motorcycle-fashion crowd gives us a wide berth. Evidently, and unbeknownst to us, it's entirely possible the Vision is a virus that may infect chrome. But you know us. You know how we are when it comes to other people's opinions . . . we could not care less. Oh yeah - we're rebels. We're trend-setters. We just roll like that. Plus, we're tired of sore butts and cold hands. And cold butts. And sore hands. That's been fixed because our new baby is a plush recliner on wheels that corners so well and accelerates so quickly it should come equipped with an extra pair of undies and an insurance policy as standard equipment. Zoooommmmmm!!!!!

So, what do you do when you have a big honkin' bike? Isn't it obvious? You take a big honkin' trip. And that's exactly what we intended to do. Go bust some blacktop, you know? Shred some twisties. Run afoul of the law if possible. Oh, the wild yonder called to us, begging us to explore, to investigate, to conquer its mysteries. You don't keep a thoroughbred locked in the barn, do you? Same with the Victory Vision. She may look like a cover-girl model but our baby is no garage queen. She's a debutante born to tour the world. The open road is her life-blood. She is an artist of speed and g-force with the countryside her canvas.

Did I mention I love this bike?

But where to go? That was the real question. A relaxed weekend on the coast? A nice day-long drive through the Cascades and around Mt. Rainier? An over-nighter down on the Columbia River Gorge?

Silly, silly Amber. This is us - these are your parental units of which we speak. Short trips are for the weak and feeble. Anything less than 300 miles a day is for sissies. We had the time. We had the equipment. We lacked common sense. All the cards were falling into place. This was our chance to really test the legs of the bike as well as our endurance. Possibly our marriage, but that would come later. So, in the fevered optimism that is our 'reason d'etre', we decided that a 2500 mile, week-long motorcycle excursion to the Canadian Rockies, and Banff National Park in particular, on a big-ass spaceship-styled road-eating motorcycle seemed like a good idea.

No, that's not quite right. This trip seemed like a GREAT idea.

Protip: Pay particular attention to the word "seemed". Funny word that. All kinds of interesting connotations.

In retrospect I'm sure this is how most ill-fated adventures start - thinking it's a good idea. The Donner Party probably thought racing the first snow to cross the mountains into California *seemed like a good idea*. The hundreds that boarded the gang-planks for the maiden voyage of the Titanic probably thought that being the first passengers on a state-of-the-art luxury liner *seemed like a good idea*. Hell, that whole Hitler and the Third Reich marching into Russia thingy probably looked like a cake-walk in the planning stages. Well, a cake-walk if you deliberately overlooked the pesky details of Russian winters. Yet, we all know where these adventures led - straight to the proverbial toilet and the pages of history books.

I make no claim that *our* trip should be listed amongst those haughty ranks, but upon reflection I believe that our journey did share something in common with those previously mentioned. That commonality would be an abstract and idle thought that blossomed for us all at a certain point in time. I believe that place to be somewhere between abject despair and intense regret. That tiny window when hope was fading but not yet entirely crushed. I believe it was summed up quite succinctly by General George Armstrong Custer moments before his untimely demise at the Little Big Horn. To wit: "What the Hell were we thinking and why didn't someone talk us out of it?"

Memorize those words. It may keep you from inadvertently annexing Poland some day.

You know how your mom and I are when it comes to planning road trips. We --- and when I say "We" I mean your mom --- started the logistical analysis of this particular foray into the depths of Hades somewhere before Christmas. Christmas 1995. Which just proves her foresight because back then we didn't own a bike, and had no plans to EVER own a bike, and, to put it bluntly, weren't particularly fond of Canada. Weird, huh? Is she psychic? A time traveler? Even though I love her to tears that woman frightens me.

I, on the other hand, am a bit of a free-spirit when it comes to travel. It's my Gypsy blood. My nomadic nature. My joie de vivre! I like to throw a few items in the saddlebags, make sure the bike is in good mechanical order, and I'm off for adventure. See, this is where your mom and I differ in our approach to life, and if you reflect on it for a moment you'll see that this is also symptomatic of our separate and distinct personalities. I believe that there's nothing like starting out a vacation ill prepared. It gets the blood pumping and adds to a heightened sense of excitement. Oh sure, I may have to turn around a few times to go back home and get the things I forgot, but isn't this is all part of the fun? Sort of a tease to the main show. The Prologue to the epic-ness that is to come. (It is so a word-don't give me that look. Even though you're 22 and almost a Naval Officer if you don't knock it off you're going straight to your room. Although I'll have to evict the transient we rented it to first.) I believe starting out at 6 AM, burning a tank of gas and never traveling more than 15 miles from the house by sundown is a day well spent. Needless to say your mom does not share my enthusiasm. Silly woman. Your mother, were she to live in a perfect world, would have an 18-wheeled semi following close behind us at all times, chock full of necessities that we may, or may not need but in her mind is a damn good idea to have on hand just in case. Things like extra clothes. A nice set of cutlery. Possibly the refrigerator.

So planning for a trip is a compromise. A delicate dance between two long-time partners, learning to share and cooperate. To communicate their needs, wants, and desires so that both come away from the process feeling fulfilled.

Or, to put it another way, I shut the hell up and do what I'm told. Contrary to the popular opinion floating about, I am not a stupid man.

Thus, we found ourselves two days before blastoff scurrying about like a late-arriving band of Orthodox Druids at the summer Solstice. I was nailing down the route with the aid of Google Maps, playing with the balance of travel times versus scenic routes. Where we would stay was taken care of and crossed off the check list. Weeks before I had booked us some fine looking lodging in Carnack, Alberta, breathtakingly close to the true wilderness of the Canadian Rockies. I could see it now - us in a postcard like setting, the wind flowing on our faces, the sun shining benevolently on our helmet-clad noggins as we wound our way through paradise. I hadn't told your mom, but If I could find a boat, and a Mountie Uniform, your mom could look forward to a serenade of "When I'm calling you-ew-ew-ew ew-ew ew. . . ." Because really, isn't that what Canada is all about? If old movies were any clue, it certainly is, and they haven't let me down thus far.

Now I will admit that I may have been a tad optimistic in the distances we were to cover each day, but I knew that the three of us - me, your mom, and the luxury that is the Victory Vision - could knock down the miles like a two-year old knocks down a canned pea display at the end of a supermarket aisle. That being stupidly fast followed by a lot of tears and possibly a tantrum. It was even better when I realized that we weren't talking about miles, we were talking kilometers! That fact sealed our schedule! True, my memory of the metric system was a bit hazy, but I was sure that it was something like 80 kilometers to the mile. Shoot, this was going to be an easy-peesey piece of cake! And a beautiful, seven-tiered butter-cream frosted Canadian cake at that! Oh! And since it's Canada - a beer. Mmmmm. . . cake and warm beer. The thought makes my teeth itch.

Your mom, whilst I was virtually navigating, was gathering the items deemed necessary for our adventure. I don't have to tell you that this had been going on for days. There was a pile of crap - I mean necessities - in the living room large enough that it threatened to touch the ceiling. Seriously. We had to split the pile in two in order to make a path to the door. I refrained from pointing out the reality that we had VERY limited space on the bike between the saddlebags and the trunk, because. . . well, there was no reason to put a damper on the party this early in the show. Plenty of time to play the spoiler later. Besides, while she was busy adding to the pile, it left me time to . . . to . . . well, I have no idea. Something. But she was occupied and for now that was enough.

I know people think I exaggerate but you know I speak gospel when it comes to this particular quirk in your mom's personality. Do you remember those car trips we took when you were a wee child? The one's where the trunk of the car would be so close to bursting that I would have to sit both you and your sister - sometimes the dog as well - on the lid and push down HARD to get the latch closed? And the back seat was piled with so many pillows and snack bags and games and sweaters and books and inflatable rafts that at times, not only could you not see out the windows, but for brief periods the entire contents of the backseat would shift, and we would become convinced we had left one of you at a rest stop, pull a U-turn at 80 miles an hour on the freeway, and rush back to your last known location only to hear you whimper quietly from underneath the complete set of Encyclopedia Britannica?

Yeah. Good times, good times. So when I speak of your mom's preparations you know exactly what I'm describing.

Mom walked up with a badminton set in her arms. She looked over my shoulder, studying the screen and the blue, highlighted path I had plotted. Our course blazed straight and true east-west across the map of Washington State before breaking into a squiggle as it snaked north across the border into the dark, dark heart of Canada.

"Oh cool! So, that's the route we're taking?"

"Yes," I answered, full of pride regarding my excellent navigational skills. "I think that this will be the prettiest route we can take that will still give us a taste of everything the region has to offer, and afford us ample time to reach the Lodge on schedule." I smiled, convinced that she would admire the brilliance of my planning and relish the fact that she bore my children.

She leaned close to the screen and studied the way-points and miles, (Whoops! Kilometers!), and estimated arrival times.

"Day number two looks like a long one."

"Yeah, but you have to remember that the numbers are in kilometers. Not miles."

"Hmmmm. . . still, that's a long day. 628 Kilometers. Do you think we can do that? Isn't that pushing it a bit?"

I gave her my best reassuring smile, and hoped it didn't look too patronizing. "Honey, please. Do I tell you how to pack? Trust me, I've got this covered."

Standing she said, "Actually, you tell me how to pack all the time."

This is true. "Well, maybe. But you have to admit you do have a tendency to go a bit over-board on the 'necessities'."

Here, I actually put in air quotes with my fingers. I immediately wished I could have taken it back, but the horse was out of the barn. The plane was down the runway. The fuse, so to speak, was definitely, and irrevocably, lit.

"Did you just air quote me?" she asked, narrowing her eyes.

I froze. Luckily, I was on top of my game that day, and an answer, one that I hoped would avoid disaster, sprang from my mouth like a bus load of little leaguers at free beer and pizza night.

"No. I wouldn't do that. Not air quotes." I jerked my hands around willy-nilly in the air. "Minor seizure. Nothing with which to concern yourself."

She stared at me for a moment, sighed, and with a shake of her head went back to looking for that combination panini-press and hair dryer for which she'd been searching these last two hours. Because, after all, you never know when a nice hot sandwich is going to save your life. And as any sane person would readily admit, if that occasion should arise you would want your hair to look it's best.

I tried to focus on the map again, just to make sure I hadn't made a mistake, but I hit the wrong button and became distracted by a new series of LOL Cats. Damn you barely literate felines! Must your antics amuse me so? Must your inability to conjugate a verb, or construct the correct tense send me into hysterics? Must you tickle the absurdity region that seems to be so prominent in my brain? I don't even try to squelch this passion anymore. All praise Ceiling Cat kthxbi! I make a mental note to donate a wad of cash to the 'Cheeseburgers 4

Kittehs Fund'. I think you'll agree in a nation as rich as ours, no LOL Cat should ever be without.

Right before I become completely immersed and stumble off into the dark reaches of the Interwebs, (By the by. . . did you know the Interwebs is a series of tubes? Who knew? Thank you Senator Ted Stevens for that bit of insight), Mom summons me downstairs. This can only mean trouble, and I think of hiding under my desk for a minute but I know that's just delaying the inevitable. Plus, there might be spiders under there. Ugh. So, like the good soldier I am, I trudge downstairs where your mom, with furrowed brow, is surveying her collection.

"I think," she says glancing about the room, "that we may need to get an extra bag to tie onto the trunk. I don't see how we are possibly going to fit everything in unless we do."

I want to tell her that everything she has assembled to take on the trip would overfill a 3/4 ton truck, but I hold my tongue. Why? Well, I smell an opportunity to go buy another piece of gear for the bike. As you are well aware, no REAL rider ever turns down the opportunity to add to their bike-related accessories. The paraphernalia of the motorcycling world is vast and varied, but it all shares one thing in common - that crap ain't cheap. Yet the mantra of a good rider is 'more is never enough'. Unless you're talking about road-rash. Or rain. Or insurance premiums.

"Oh goody!" I squeal, "let's go buy things! Shiny, shiny things! We can go to the bike dealer, then down to Tacoma to that place with all the gear, then ---"

Your mom cuts me off mid-sentence. "Not so fast cowboy. I was thinking something cheap. And non-leather. Let's just go to the sporting goods store in town. I'm sure we can find something there."

Non leather? What heresy is this? I study her for any hints of all things PETA-y. Had she gone vegan on me when I was occupied planning our route? Later I would have to tempt her with bacon just to make sure. But for now I had a different agenda.

I took a deep breath and said, "I don't think that we can put a piece of luggage on the bike that comes from a sporting goods store. It's not that I mind, you understand, but I believe it's a law. And not a State law, but a Federal law with long prison terms and vicious consequences. And at the end of the day a guy named 'Bubba', if you know what I mean."

"Yeah. I'm not buying that. I'm sure we can find a duffel bag, or nylon sack of some kind."

"But. . .", I stammer, "that will look . . ."

"Yes?" she asks.

"Well, it would look . . . ookie."

"Really?", she says and places one hand firmly on her hip. "This from the man that put neon green light-up valve stem caps on the bike tires because, and I quote, 'It looked real purty at night?'."

Your mother is a worthy adversary. Touche' woman, touche'.

Time to change tack. Brimming with confidence that we would find nothing suitable at the sporting goods store, I offered the enthusiasm of someone convinced that the other is completely and totally wrong, but more than willing to let them find out on their own and still look good for my steadfast unconditional support. "You have a point. I'm sure we can find something that will work. You ready to go now?"

Mom looks about the room. I know what she's up to - she's looking to make sure she has everything she needs. Third-world armies are less well supplied but I refrain from saying this because I really would like this to be a good vacation. Besides, the real battle will come later when we actually pack the bike.

"Seems like I'm forgetting something. . ."

She studies the piles and hesitantly prods the mountain of items closest to her with a tentative toe. You know - much like one would do should they stumble across a body in the woods and a pointy stick is nary to be found.

"Well, whatever it is I'm sure it will come to me. Yeah, let's go."

So, it's a jump in the truck and off to the Sporting Goods store we go! This will be fun! I love field trips!

We arrive at the store, "Buckshot - If it's alive we'll help you kill it!", and I instantly become distracted by the "Buckets of Bargains" lining the parking lot. You never know what treasure you'll find at a drastically reduced price. I once found an Electric Smoker designed specifically for Elk meat, with utensils, digital readouts, and a recipe book for $10! I brought it home and realized (with some strenuous prodding from your mother), that not only do I not like smoked Elk meat, but I've never hunted Elk in my life and barring the apocalypse, more than likely never would. I tried to explain to her that wasn't the point. The smoker was $10 marked down from $800! I had just saved her $790 and all she could do is criticize. (Later, we would get 50 cents for the whole kit-and-kaboodle at a yard sale - but that's a different story entirely.) So I suppose her irritation as I rummaged through each bucket was understandable. Still, the exercise satisfied the 'hunter/gatherer' instinct, that pervasive and primitive genetic memory so active in my soul.

"Look Suz! We could use one of these!"

"What is it?"

I pick a treasure from a bucket and hold it up for her to see. "It's a device for making potable water from just about any source! Isn't that amazing? And the best part is it's only $39.99."

"And why would we need potable water? We're not backpacking are we?"

"Well," I said as my brain scrambled, "no, but what if we were stranded in the desert? You'd thank me then."

"I'm not trying to be a wet-blanket here, but are there any deserts in the Canadian Rockies?"

Gah! I hate it when she gets all reasonable like that. However, that would not deter me. "Most of Eastern Washington is semi-arid."

"And," she said, "we will be through that part in about three or four hours. I don't think we will die of thirst in that time."

Ouch. A right hook.

"Fine. But when you're passed out from dehydration don't come running to me."

"Okay. That's a deal. If, on this trip, I'm comatose from lack of water I won't look to you for help."

I didn't much care for her tone, but I let it go. Evidently, this little shopping spree was going to be much more confrontational than I had imagined. So be it. I was up to the challenge.

"Come on, let's go find a bag," she said, grabbing my hand and dragging me through the sliding double doors into the store.

You ever notice how different stores have different smells? I mean of course there are the obvious ones like a candle store, or a Florist, or a mortuary, but I'm talking more about regular stores - office stores, hardware, you know what I mean. This store definitely had an odor. I couldn't quite place it but it smelled very . . . redneck-y. Kind of like chew and beer and bad cologne. Much like your Uncle Scott before a date. Or maybe it was latex and bug spray and gunpowder. Or, just stale air freshener. I would have wandered around, trying to quantify the odor, seeking out the source, but Mom, having learned her lesson, refused to let go of my hand and before you know it we are in the aisle for all things packy.

There were backpacks and daypacks and rucksacks. There were stuff bags and canteen holders and tackle boxes. There were camel packs and quivers and, what I thought at the time was a holder for unruly children but in actuality was a portable toilet. Guess it's a good thing you're not little anymore, huh? Mistakes like that can require extensive therapy later in life. Just ask your sister. Unfortunately, nary a motorcycle bag to be seen. This however did nothing to daunt your mother.

"This will do just fine," Mom said, picking up a duffel bag made of heavy canvas and approximately 92 feet long. You could have stored a torpedo in there. And the crew to fire it. Maybe the boat as well.

"Ummmmm. . . .", I say, as if I'm actually contemplating her selection of luggage but was in reality biding time so that I could point out the absurdity of her choice without getting smacked. Physically or mentally.

"I think, and I'm going out on a limb here, that it may be a bit big for the bike."

"Hmmmmm. . .", Mom paused, and sat the bag on the floor. "You may be right. But it would hold all of our stuff." She surveyed the length of the duffel. "I don't think it's that big."

I had a momentary vision of us going down the road with either the bag draped over the trunk and dragging on both sides, or your mom balancing it on her head along the axis of the motorcycle's length, like a canoe on a car-top. Neither was going to work. Yet, experience has taught me that I could not quell this idea without offering a suggestion of my own. Luckily I had something in mind, something for which I had been dreaming of for quite a while. I tried to contain my excitement. If I were to be successful it would have to be a slow and gentle journey to get your mom to come around and agree to what I was thinking. Would my ploy work? Only time would tell.

"What about this one," I said, holding out a camouflaged-colored tight mesh bag. If the pictures on the tag could be believed this bag was for your trophy fish. A bag in which to stuff your fish. Oh this modern world, what will they think of next?

"What about what?"

"What about this?" I asked, shaking the bag in front of her.

"What are you talking about?"

"This!" I said, and placed the bag in your mom's hand.

As you know, your mother's sense of humor can pop up at the oddest times. My radar went on full alert. I was being toyed with.

"Alright. If this is that same old joke about you not being able to see the bag because it's camouflaged, there's going to be trouble." I wrinkled my nose. "Big trouble."

"Okay," Mom says, "just trying to lighten the mood here." She studied the bag. "That's not going to work for several reasons."

"Oh," I said, "and why not?"

She sighed, just a little and said, "For one, it's a fishing bag. Do you hear me? A fishing bag. It's way to small. The only way to put it on the bike would be to glue it to a saddlebag or hang it from the handlebar, but mostly," she took a mighty sniff of the air, "it's a return. You don't want a return."

"What's wrong with a 'return'?" I asked. As you know, I'm a huge fan of Refurbs, (or RoXoRs, as the cool kids say). You and your sister were Refurbs. Look how well you turned out.

"Usually nothing. But this one stinks of dead fish. It must have been put back on the shelf by mistake. Once the August heat hits, that thing is going to reek."

Typical roadblocks and weak logic erected by the desperate. Obviously she was unconvinced and suspicious that I was causing a problem because I wanted a leather bag. While this was true, it hurt me that she would think such a thing. My mind raced looking for an excuse that made sense, and would get me one step closer to that $9000 touring bag with the buckles and chrome and built in computer screen/DVD recorder/espresso maker and axle and duel tires for which I had been lusting lo these many days.

"I think that the smell of dead fish would be a good way to distract bears. We are going to the mountains you know, and if we run into trouble we could huck that baby a good ways away and the bears would run for it instead of making lunch of us. You don't want to be eaten by a bear, do you dear?" I purred.

This made her pause again, but only for a moment. "Do you really think we have to worry about bears? Really? I seriously doubt that bears attacking us on a motorcycle should be at the top of our worry list. You're just being difficult because you have something you want, and you think that you can wear me down."

See, this is the problem with a 30 year marriage. She knows me. I mean, really, really knows me. That's just . . . well, that's just unfair.

I change tactics like a true warrior and appeal to her sense of thrift. "This bag. . . ", I flipped the tag over to show her the price, "it's only $10."

"That may be, but for crying out loud it's a fishing bag! There are," and here she looked up and down the aisle, "about 30 other things that would work. And wouldn't stink. With a little effort on your part, I'm sure we'll find something. So quit dragging your feet like a three-year old and help me."

"Well," I sing-song, "I'm not sure we can find something. At least not here. Now, if we went down to the bike dealer. . ."

"Oh stop it. You're not getting whatever it is you have stuck in that head of yours. Now let's get serious. We have a ton of stuff to do before Tuesday. We need a bag. A simple bag to hold our clothes." She turned her back and muttered a string of words that were inaudible. I did pick out "fishing bag", and "wanker", then I stopped listening.

Fine. I walked half-way down the aisle and grabbed the first large storage device I came across. "What about this? It's big enough to hold everything we need." My voice was even, dead-flat and dangerous.

"You're kidding, right? It's a 50 gallon Styrofoam cooler. Not only is it obscenely large, it has a picture of a bikini-clad woman on the side. Why don't I just carry a garbage can on my lap? It would work better than that thing."

Point taken.

"Well," I said trying to keep the satisfaction out of my voice, "it's obvious we've run out of options. Let's go to the bike shop, bite the bullet, and get the 'UberBitchin' Tote 9000. It might be a little pricey, but as you've so often said, you get what you pay for."

Ha! I have turned her own words and philosophy against her! Escape this intellectual trap mon petite dewdrop!

"We," Mom said, dropping her voice somewhere into the baritone range, "are definitely not buying that god-awful thing. It's not even a piece of luggage. It's a trailer. A trailer for your bike. Think about that for a moment."

Now we all know that for a biker, the line between 'wild and wicked King of the Road' and 'old-fartism', is a motorcycle trailer. Really, when you get to that point just buy a car. (Lest you think ill of your dear old Papa, let me take a moment to offer my apologies to all my bro's with trailers. But you're all old-farts and will never read this anyway.) However, appearance or not, I lusted for the 'UberBitchin' Tote 9000' like an Atkin's dieter lusts for a crusty, warm, sweet loaf of bread. And a potato. Ummmm . . . potatoes. . .

"You know, you could take all the gear you wanted in the Uber Tote with room to spare." I knew that was hitting low, but I feared I had tipped my hand too early so it was worth a shot. It was sneaky and manipulative to appeal to her minor obsession in such a manner, but . . . but . . . well I got nuthin', I just really, really wanted the damned Uber Tote. It was now in my blood. It was a mental itch that needed to be scratched.

Ignoring me completely, your mom placed a hand to her brow and slowly massaged her temple, "You know, I don't even think they made it as a real product. I think they made it to see what kind of an idiot would buy something like that." Her eyes drew to slits, challanging me, demanding a response.

Oh, two can play at this game. "Must I remind you, dear lady, that I **AM** that kind of idiot?"

"I know exactly what kind of idiot you are, but I married you anyway. So give it up Chuckles. There is no espresso maker/DVD recorder for the bike in your future."

"Did I tell you it pops up into a fully contained sleeping compartment with a queen-sized bed?"

"No. Uber. Anything. That's final."

Your mom had said that in a tone that left no room for discussion. I could see that this was one battle I was not going to win, so I let it go. For now. All I needed to do was orchestrate some situation during the vacation where the concept of a tent/DVD recorder/espresso maker would be an undeniable boon to the trip. It shouldn't be that difficult. I began to scheme immediately. She forgot to mention the computer screen. This may just be the 'in' I was looking for. I filed that tidbit of knowledge away for future reference.

Ignoring me for the moment, Mom turned her attention to a display at the end of the isle.

"What about these? This looks like it could work. Not as much storage as I'd like, but I think we can manage with this," she said, and picked up a nylon bag, about 2 and a half feet long and a good 14 inches high. Soft sided, blue, strong seams - it would work perfectly. I could see it bungee-corded to the luggage rack on the trunk. Of course, I couldn't say this to your mom.

"It's even waterproof," Mom said holding out the tag proclaiming 'New and Improved! Now 50% more waterproof!', for me to read.

"Why would we need waterproofing? It's not going to rain. It's August."

Mom was fast losing her patience with me. "You mean to tell me that it CAN'T rain in August?"

"Well of course I'm not saying that. That would be stupid. What I AM saying is that it's not going to rain on US."

"And why would that be, Mr. Weather Wizard?"

"Because," I said with a smug smile, "I've been monitoring the extended weather forecasts for every town between here and Carnack. No rain. Nothing but blue skies and clear sailing. As you can see, I am in touch with the Digital Gods. The word has been spoken in 0's and 1's and I have taken it to heart. No rain. So, the purchase would be pointless."

A noise escaped your mother's mouth similar to a punctured tire going flat. "No, we're getting this one. It will be fine."

"No, we are going to keep looking. Even if we have to go out of town." I fold my arms across my chest. I'm making a stand as I am still holding out a slight hope for the Uber Tote.

"No," Mom said, cocking her head almost imperceptibly, "we are getting THIS one. Now. It's only $19.99."

It went on like this, back and forth, fore and back. Neither one of us budging. There may have been a head-lock involved. I can't remember, I think I blacked out. Your mom has one wicked sleeper hold.

Finally, the afternoon ended with your mother and I standing about 10 feet apart, pointing at each other viciously and shouting "NO YOU!!!". Because of the commotion, we were asked to leave the store. People are so picky about a middle-aged couple having a small spat that involves screaming and biting and rolling around on the floor. I mean, get a life people! Like the security team that ushered us out of the place had never had a public argument with their spouse? At one point I asked them, "Are you telling me that some of your most heated 'in-store' discussions, and possible criminal records, never stared out with, "I don't know. What do *you* want for dinner?" As you know that one can deteriorate into weapons. Quickly. Unconvinced, we were quite un-glamorously shown the door, but not before your mom bought that bag. That big, blue, waterproof, 'perfect for the back of a motorcycle' nylon bag.

With your mother victorious and I a defeated husk of a man, we went home to pack. Perhaps she had taken round one in a unanimous decision, but round two was approaching, and this round was mine.

I had a plan.

Sort of.

*　　*　　*

September 12, 2008

Dear Amber,

Quick note about life on the home-front before we continue the story. What's been happening since our return . . . not much. Couple of small fires. A trip or two to the emergency room. Scrambling to come up with bail money for cousin Molly. Same old, same old. As you can see our routine hasn't changed much since you've forsaken us to become a Navy Pirate.
L8R G8R!

Love you,
Daddio

P.S. Almost forgot . . . your cat died and we rented out your room to transients. Hope you're having a great day Princess!

*   *   *

Yes, it was now 24 hours 'till blast-off. The excitement level in the household had reached a fevered pitch. It was Christmas Eve. It was Carnival in Rio. It was the night before a root canal sans novocaine.

Let me just state for the record that I was a cucumber. In a bowl of ice. Sitting in the refrigerator. Meditating. It was your mother, poor soul, that had lost it and had become - well, there's no other way to put it - a complete whack-job.

As you know I have certain responsibilities pre-trip. I know what most of them are and Mom tells me the others. I check the bike over quite thoroughly. I change the oil. I make sure the tires are good and full to the proper pressure. Nothing quite like an under inflated tire on a bike. You may be able to get away with it on a car, but on a bike each tire constitutes 50% of your contact with the road. Since I like to be able to steer - I know, picky me - proper inflation is imperative. I also check the lights, the turn signals, the exhaust. I wash the beast, and make her shiny. Probably until the next trip - aren't dead bugs considered decoration in some cultures? A badge of honor? Well, they should be. What? Not so much in certain Hindu sects? Oops. My bad. There goes the bike trip through India. Anyway, I look for loose hoses, cables, nuts, bolts and check all things dangley. I fill her with premium fuel. I confirm that the gauges, gizmos, and doo-dads are in proper working order.

Which is a polite way to say I try to keep busy and stay the hell out of your mom's way while her psychosis runs its course.

As for packing I wanted to start with a clean slate. I took all of the junk - wait . . . I didn't say junk. I meant to say 'necessities' - out of the saddlebags, out of the trunk, out of the various nooks and crannies and arranged them on the ground next to the bike. When I was done, I stepped back and looked at the array. Astonishing. It appeared that the bike had suddenly become ill, and regurgitated an eclectic collection of items that had been clogging its gullet. Think of those cartoon images of the inside of a whale after they've swallowed the hapless hero. Much like that minus the rowboat. The sheer volume and range of crap amazed me. I rarely pay attention to what your mom has in the bags, and most of the time I don't really care. That's her domain. Usually. But we were going to be gone for seven days, it was time to pare back on the 'essentials'. The time had come to show your mother how a man would pack. (She's not looking over my shoulder is she? Good.).

So here is a brief run-down of what I found:

A pair of binoculars, a huge bag of rags and various cleaning products, a waffle maker, a first Aid Kit, 7 individual gloves, 2 sweaters, 2 sets balaclava and silkies, a crushed pop can, and 3 maps all full of mildew and in various states of disintegration. 1 gallon bag of over the counter meds, a thermos of congealed something, a panini press/hair dryer (there it is!), 2 broken flashlights, various magazines from 2001, a feather duster, an inflatable pillow, 1 bag with two rolls of flattened toilet paper, a set of helmet-to-helmet intercom systems that we had used once, and 4 pair of sunglasses - two with missing lens. Also, a deck of cards that had 'drawn moisture', a cribbage board, a notebook, 35 ink pens - only 2 with caps, a nerf football (although that might have been on the ground before I unpacked), a calculator, a stapler sans staples, a bag of 'feminine products', 2 hair brushes, 2 umbrellas, 12,000 paper napkins stolen from every fast-food joint we had ever visited, a house plant, durable power of attorney, road flares, a hammer, and a flute.

Then there were the bags of food. Bags and bags and bags of nuts and cheeses and jerky and cookies and candy and power-bars and . . . and God knows what else. We could have opened up a convenience mart at any rest stop we visited.

I stood back to examine the cargo. I was mightily impressed. I mean honestly, how could you not be? I had not the slightest clue your mother even played the Flute.

I called to your mom who was inside the house adding to her 'absolute necessities'. "Hey babe, wanna come out here for a minute?"

The poor thing walked out of the house with a wild look in her eye. I say 'eye', not 'eyes' because for some reason one eye was open quite wide, and the other was clenched shut. 'Scrinched' I believe is the proper descriptor. I would have asked why, but it didn't seem appropriate. I knew this was the most stressful time for her.

"What do you want?", she asked, "I'm kind of busy in here."

"Ummm. . .", I stammered, "I took everything out of the bike so we could pack. I think," I said, as calmly as I could, "that we need to be a little more spartan in what we take." I pointed to the stuff laying on the ground. I've seen yard sales with less inventory.

Mom looked over the driveway filled with debris. She turned to me - or on me - I couldn't tell, and said, "What about it?"

I didn't much care for her challenging tone, but I would let it pass because I'm a coward. "Well, I just think that we need to conserve as much space as possible. Surely we can leave some of this stuff at home?"

To your mom, them there is fightin' words.

"We need that stuff", she said as if she were explaining to a small child.

"All of it?"

I swear to God she rolled up her sleeves, clenching and unclenching her fists. Well, maybe not. I might have imagined that part.

"You have stuff in there too, it's not just me so don't act like I'm being unreasonable."

I shook my head in the positive, agreeing. "I would never suggest that you were being unreasonable. However, let's look at what you have, and lets see what I have, shall we? You," I said, and swept my arm towards the contents spread on the ground, "have all of this. While I," I said and reached down and picked up a small bag with Allen wrenches, a Phillip's-head screwdriver, a standard screwdriver, needle-nose pliers, 10 zip ties, 3 short bungee cords, a tire gauge, and a roll of duct tape, "have this." Except for the duct tape it fit quite well in a small baggie.

She looked from me to the disgorged contents of the bike, to the bag I held in my hand, then back to me. "And your point is what?"

"My point is that there is no way we can take all of this AND our clothes AND the extra stuff we're going to need."

"Oh," she said, "you mean like the laptop you want to bring along?"

Gah. She had me there. You know how I get to Jonesin' if I don't have my Interwebs. I had to think quickly. "Well, I'll admit that may seem like a luxury, but we need it to plan routes and look up . . . things."

"And for you to check email, the forums for the bike, Woot, and LOL Cats?"

Damn you LOL Cats! There you are again! You will be my downfall yet!

"Among other things," I answered. "But look, we're getting off the point here. Really, can't we do without some of it? I mean, do we need a hammer?"

She looked like maybe she would like to use the hammer now. Upside my noggin. "Fine. Yes, that we can do without. We can leave the hammer."

My knees felt weak, I hadn't expected her to acquiesce so quickly. It threw me off my game plan. She's a crafty woman, perhaps this was part of HER plan.

"Oh! Well . . . good! How about the space blankets, and the other items for cold weather riding?"

"What if we're stuck out in the middle of nowhere with a broken down bike on a deserted road with no hope of rescue and it's late at night and we're freezing?"

Sometimes I'll catch a glimpse of what really goes on in your mother's mind. Tres disturbing. It's almost as if she doesn't fully trust me. As gently as I could, I explained. "Well, for one it's summer. Two, we are not going to be riding at night. Or dusk. I've planned the trip to the 'T'. We will be stopping each day by 4 PM. That still gives us a good 4 hours of light. We're not going to be riding deserted roads, all of the places we're going are heavily traveled, and if worse-comes-to-worse we always have our cell phones. I think your fears are unfounded my dear."

HA! Take that woman! That's right - I've thrown a logic-bomb your way! Your reasoning is crumbling faster than a 5 year-old's cotton candy in the shower.

"Fine."

Did I hear her correctly? If so, I don't think I like where this is going. "Fine?"

She put a hand to the bridge of her nose, her fingers gently pinching the juncture, "Yes, fine. What else?"

Okay, now we were making progress. "What about the waffle maker? Do you really think we're going to use that?"

"What if we want waffles?"

In your mother's world, this seemed like a perfectly reasonable question. I was miles ahead of her though, and had already crafted an appropriate response.

"What," I said cocking my head and smiling as if I'm pointing out a completely foreign thought, and a rather clever one, "if we **don't** want waffles?" That is some fine thinking right there. I was very proud of myself.

She started to rub her temples in slow, circular motions. "Have it your way. The waffle maker stays. Is that it?"

"Well, what about all that food? I mean, we aren't going camping. Can't we just take a couple of things to snack on?"

She looked at me like I had lost what little of my mind I had left. "We need that stuff! You don't know what we're going to run into. What if we are stuck in the middle of nowhere, and it's dark and cold and we get hungry?"

I'm beginning to notice a pattern here. Evidently most of your mother's reasoning centered around the idea that we were going to be stranded in the middle of nowhere for an extended period of time. At night. This, I'm sorry to say, was part of her delusional state. Poor, poor Mom.

Now before you think that I'm being too hard on her, I'm willing to admit that over the years, there may have been a couple of times when we found ourselves in just such a predicament. You know, you were there for some of them. We've run out of gas a couple of times. Well, maybe more than a couple. Certainly not more than twenty - twenty-five tops. Then there was the time we popped a fan belt, and sat on the side of the road for about 7 hours because I said "We don't need to carry tools. It's a new car." There was the fact that we had been in the ditch a few times, usually in a place that we had no business trying to drive a car. I, on rare occasions, have been known to lock the keys in the vehicle at the most inopportune moments. There were a few incidents with a pesky carburetor on a 1975 Ford Courier. In case you don't know the Ford Courier was the smallest truck ever made that didn't have "Hot Wheels" stamped on the side. It's true we'd been lost - a bunch. We've had to sleep in the car from time to time. And of course there had been the flat tires, the blown engines, the occasional small fires. Pretty typical stuff. You know, no different than anyone else and certainly nothing over which I had the slightest bit of control.

"Babe," I said, "trust me. We're not going to be stranded in the middle of nowhere. We'll take a couple of snacks and call it good. Why, I bet we won't even use those! You'll see, everything will be fine." I saw an opportunity here, and I went for it. "You know - and I'm just sayin' - that if we had the UberBitchin' Tote 9000 we could take everything. Ev - Re - Thing." I drug the word out long and slow then inserted a moment of silence for effect. "Just think about that. If we had the UberBitchin' Tote we could take all you desire . . . all you desire and more!"

This caused her to pause. I saw the conflicting emotions roll over her face like a cold spring wind in a field of wheat.

"You are horrible. Absolutely, positively horrible. Do you know that?"

"Sweetie, I'm just looking out for you."

"I seriously doubt that. Listen and listen close. This is the last time I'm going to say this - we, under no circumstances, are buying that Uber thing."

I could see that her resolve ran deep. Crap. "That's fine. But if we can't buy the UberBitchin' Tote 9000 with the computer screen/dvd recorder/espresso maker/queen-sized bed, then most of this stuff is gong to have to go." I walked around the stuff on the ground, giving a quick poke here and there with the tip of my cane. "Now, what shall we leave. Hmmm?"

She took a heavy breath and massaged her temples again, only this time much more vigorously, "Look, tell you what. You've obviously got it all planned out in that head of yours. So YOU do what you think is right. Take or leave whatever. I'm going to go back inside and pack the clothes and the other stuff." She started to walk into the house and paused, not turning around yet addressing me all the same. "Just don't screw it up."

I thought about replying, I really did. But I realized that no good could come of that, and besides, I WON! Sort of. True, there was no Uber Tote in my immediate future but I could live with that. For now.

Mom walked back into the house muttering to herself. I hoped she was being kind, but somehow I doubt it.

Ha ha! Victory is mine, sayeth the David. I rubbed my hands together in anticipation.

Well, if my travels had taught me anything, we needed the tools. So those went in the 'take' pile. Binoculars would be good for the few days we were spending at the Lodge, and you never knew when you were going to see an animal or a waterfall or a UFO or a bikini-clad supermodel that made you want to grab a better look. We would take one rag, and one bottle of windshield/screen cleaner. First Aid Kit, of course. I would allow one pair of gloves, in addition to what we were wearing, each. Sweaters, silkies, hoodies - into the 'leave' pile. Crushed pop can was small and flat, and you never knew when the ground or asphalt would be too soft to support the weight of the bike on the kickstand, so that was a necessity. Didn't need no stinkin' maps. The medicines could be pared back significantly and fit well in a baggy - decongestants and pain relievers would suffice. Medical histories probably weren't a bad idea, but I could carry those in the pocket of my coat. The power of attorney was troubling - I made a note to talk to your mother about this later.

Out went the space blankets, candle, fork, and thermos. The food - dear God, we were not feeding the Roman army. I took one package of peanut butter crackers, more as a token of peace than anything. If we were hungry or thirsty it would force us to stop and take a break. That's a good thing. Sometimes when we had the devil asphalt pumping through our veins we would push on way past our limits. So hunger, thirst, bathroom breaks - these were just nature's way of saying 'get the hell off the bike for a bit before your entire body cramps into a pretzel.

What else? There was no way I was taking a wad of napkins that would choke a Hippo. The flashlights were out, I mean, we wouldn't be in the dark so that was just wasted space. No old magazines, no feather duster. The toilet paper. . . I learned that lesson long ago. The toilet paper was a definite 'take'. The intercoms were useless, and should be sold on Ebay. I wear photo-gray glasses, so I was limiting your mother to one pair of sunglasses. I hoped she choose a pair with both lenses because if she didn't - well that would just look sad.

She could take a single handkerchief for her neck, and that she could wear or keep in her pocket. The cards were hopelessly fused together, so unless we planned on using them as a weapon they would be better left at home. If we had no cards, the traveling cribbage board made no sense. A stapler? Really? Out it went. Same with the printed maps, umbrellas, hammer, potted plant and flute. The make-up and feminine products would go along for the ride as a peace offering along with one of the hairbrushes.

I stepped back and took a look. Now that was some fine, fine packing right there. I had whittled down the contents into one, I repeat ONE, zip-lock bag. This was going to be easier than I thought.

It was then that Mom began hauling bags out of the house. Garbage bags, paper bags, cloth totes from bookstores, and a brand-spanking new nylon bag stuffed so full it looked like a sausage on a dare.

I started to say something. To point out the inevitable failure brewing. I realized the sane thing to do was to leave. Leave and never look back. I would let your mom pack the bike. Whatever she could fit in the bags and the trunk was fine with me. I felt bad for her and I had lost all enthusiasm for the battle.

As I began to slink away, your mom called out to me, "Where do you think you're going?"

"Ummm . . . thought I would take a little break and go grab some coffee. Can I bring you something? Can of pop? Bottle of water? Anesthesia?"

She looked around at the various bags and bundles. "No, I'm fine."

"Okay sweetie, well you just call me when you need me."

"Mm-hmm," Mom murmured, and I could see the gears in her brain calculating the spatial puzzle spread before her.

In the meantime I went to look up some prices online. Perhaps, with the aid of teh internets I could find the UberBitchin' Tote 9000 on sale. You never know.

*　　*　　*

I looked at the clock on my desk and realized that 2 hours had passed and I had heard nary a peep from your mother. Where did the time go? I started out checking prices for the Uber Tote, and somehow wound up memorizing the lyrics to "Chocolate Rain" as performed by Chad Vader, Darth's younger brother. Da Netz is a vast resource of obscure knowledge. It is because of things like Chad and "Garfield minus Garfield" and epic fails that I needed to bring the laptop on vacation. What if I fell behind? What if I lost my edge? That was a risk I could not take.

I found your mom, sitting against the house with her hair hanging in her face, and sweat beading on her forehead like the sheen on the outside of a cool, cool tasty drink on a hot, hot summer's day. Or much like the forehead of our accountant Fred.

"It's not all going to fit," she said, somewhat dejectedly, "and before you even start in we are not getting the Uber monstrosity."

Nicely played fair lady.

She looked so sad, so forlorn that it broke my heart. I walked over and offered my hand to pull her upright. "It's okay sweetie. Let's see what we can do."

As you know, the flip-side to your mother's little tic was that I had learned to squeeze things into an allotted space that should not be allowed by our current understanding of matter. I walked over to the bike, and looked at what she had done. The saddlebags were close to bursting, so I let them be. The trunk, on further inspection, and with some minor rearranging, could take in a bit more before it popped the hinges. You want to know what love is? Right there in the bottom of the trunk was the laptop. She'd abandoned the Panini press/hair dryer and packed my laptop. Further evidence of the many, many reasons that your mom is the love of my life and my best friend. I mean really . . . who else would put up with my crap?

"You know, you've actually done a pretty good job here tiger. I can move some things around a little, and maybe squeeze some more room. What couldn't you fit in that you really, and I mean REALLY, need?"

Mom paused for a moment. It's hard to watch someone's dream die right before your eyes. Unless that person is a former member of the Bush Cabinet or a Fox reporter, then it's a hoot. "I guess just these pairs of tennis shoes. I thought it would be nice to get out of our boots at night. I have no idea how to get your cane in there so you can reach it easily." She looked around, "Most of our clothes are in the bag that we're going to strap to the trunk, so I guess we are good to go there."

"Did you get your books to fit?"

"Yeah. And a couple of magazines. I had to leave the book on birds out though," she snuffled.

"That's okay. If we see an interesting species, we will kill it and identify the body later," I said, pulling her into a hug. I knew right then I would find a place for her bird book even if I had to staple it to my damn chaps.

Side note; staples stop hurting after about an hour and then itch like crazy. No, I'm not going to tell you how I know this.

She smiled. It was nice to see that smile. "It's going to be a good trip, isn't it?"

"Babe," I said and gave her a quick peck on the cheek, "it's going to be a wonderful trip. We are about to visit one of the most beautiful areas on the North American continent. We'll get some great riding on an incredible piece of modern technology, then we get to stay at an incredible Lodge and use that as base camp while we explore Banff. This little excursion," I said, meaning every word, "will be magical." She smiled again, and after all these years I felt my heart skip a beat. That smile of hers is still intoxicating. "Tell you what, I'll finish up packing the bike. Why don't you start taking some of this stuff back inside."

"Deal," she said and gave my arm a squeeze.

I won't go into the details, but I found room for *almost* everything. The bird book fit very snugly into the inside pocket of my mesh jacket, so thank Jeebus no staples. The last piece of the puzzle was to put the bag, and my collapsible cane, on the trunk and secure it with bungee cords.

Bungee cords. The bane of my existence. I don't know how much you've worked with bungee cords, but they should rename them, 'Hey! Look at what I put my eye out with!' cords. Although, that would probably be fairly difficult to market. The minutes ticked by, and after several failed attempts, plus a couple of very unattractive welts on my forehead, I managed to secure the 'whole kit-and-caboodle' to the rack on the Vision's trunk.

I stepped back to survey my work.

Well, I had seen worse, but not from anything other than first-graders making flower pots out of clay for Mother's Day. The sleek lines of the Vision were destroyed, and it looked like we were trying to use, and quite unsuccessfully, the nylon bag as an inverted rudder. The bag didn't so much rest on the trunk as it squatted there. The bungee cords sunk and bit viciously into the nylon, making it look like we weren't so much carrying a bag as trying to keep it from escaping. You think I'm kidding but I'm not. I swear, it looked as if a family of Gypsies were using the bike to caravan across the nation. Stealing babies. Tiny ones, to be sure because there was no room, but stealing babies none-the-less. I'm talking old 16th century Gypsies here, not the new modern Gypsies with shiny trucks and lawyers and small weapons. I cared not how the damned thing looked. The dead caterpillar was on there securely and that was my intent. Fashion be damned! For we were on vacation, and about to embark on a 7-day journey into paradise, and couldn't be troubled with petty things like style, and balance, and gas mileage, and visibility, and aerodynamics.

I climbed on the bike to test the load balance. I pulled her into an upright position and immediately noticed that the right side of the bike seemed to weigh approximately 6000 pounds more than the left side as I arced over and dropped the bike on the ground with a stomach-churning 'screeeeeeeeeeeeccchhhh'. Which, as any experienced biker will tell you, is - and this is a fairly technical term - really 'bad'. Luckily the engineers who dreamt and built the Vision suspected that the owners might be grossly incompetent and designed 'tip-over protection' into the body styling so that, heaven forbid, you ever DID drop the bike it would land on the front and rear tip-overs ensuring no damage to the machine itself. Not even a scratch. You have no idea how wonderful that is. I've seen some expensive bikes fall over in a parking lot and suffer thousands of dollars worth of damage.

That doesn't seem right, does it? I mean, you can drop a baby and do less damage than you would to most motorcycles. Not that I would know that. (If you're feeling your head for dents stop it right now!) Anyway, I righted the bike using the 'butt-lean-push' method and got her back on the kickstand without too much trouble. Amazing how a little bit of leverage will allow you to pick up something currently weighing more than a great Blue Whale. I stood back and considered my options. Unless I wanted to spend the entire trip leaning heavily to the left to compensate for the balance, I was going to have to do some rearranging.

It was then that I noticed that the nylon bag I had strapped down so well had slipped sideways and was now, to put it delicately, dribbling off the side of the trunk. It was a pathetic sight.

As you know, I am nothing if not tenacious, so after a couple of hours, some blood, some cursing, and a promise to the Elder Gods to finally complete my application to Miskatonic University, (Cthulhu makes a bitchin' mascot! Take that Jersey Devils!), I had managed to put everything in order. Mostly. Which was good, because I was exhausted and our departure tomorrow would dawn bright and early. It was time to get some rest.

In our attention to detail I thought we were prepared for any contingency. HA! The Fates, God, The Universe . . . whomever is pulling the strings on this sideshow we call life just loves that kind of crap. Gives them a target. Bastards. But I'm not bitter. Well . . . yes I am, but it has nothing to do with this trip.

Mostly.

*   *   *

After a good night's sleep and a hearty pot of coffee, Mom and I, chipper as a cheer-leading squad on ecstasy, stepped out to greet the day and embark on our grand adventure.

Oh the excitement! Is there anything more wonderful than starting out on a journey that you've been planning for months and months and months? There probably is, but I'm not going to ruin the moment by speculation. We were giddy, let's leave it at that.

Now as we stepped out the door the first thing we noticed was that it was cold. I mean really cold. Not just 'cold in relation to August', but cold as in . . . well, just cold. It was 51 degrees. Cloudy. Misting. Bone-chilling. Welcome to summer in the Pacific Northwest! As any true native Puget Sounder can tell you, summer begins on July 5th and ends the 18th of August. Then boom! Back again after Labor Day for 2 weeks. I think that those two weeks are strictly to mess with the minds of the kids who've had to go back to school. I remember, as a child, going to class on the first day of the fall semester, wearing my new coat and winter clothes because, "school starts in the fall', and immediately dieing because it was 80 flippin' degrees. Each year I vowed that next year I would do it differently. But, that first day of school would find me once again sporting a parka with sweat stains in the pits and suffering from heat exhaustion. Who needs kidneys anyway? Internal organs, in my opinion, are completely over-rated.

"Dang", I said, rubbing my hands together, "little chilly out here."

"That's an understatement. It's freezing!", Mom exclaimed, wrapping her arms about herself. "Well, I guess so much for the mesh jacket. I'm going to wear my heavier coat."

I don't think we had the mesh jackets the last time you were home, so you need to know that what I'm talking about is a full sized coat, with Kevlar armor in the elbows, shoulders, kidney area, and back that sports perforated holes on the sleeves and body. That way, when on the bike, the air flows through the holes keeping you cool. It's as comfortable as riding with a T-shirt, but wayyyyyyy safer. Well, relatively safer. If you like your skin it's definitely the way to go.

"I think you'll be sorry babe. Just layer up until we get over the mountains. It's supposed to be hot in Eastern Washington. Upper 90's in some places."

I have no idea why your mother had her doubts about my weather prognosticating abilities, but she gave me a look like our old dog Barkley used to give me when I was trying to hide a pill in his food.

"No, I'm going to stick with the heavier leather jacket."

"Tiger, I know it's cold, but this is a fluke. A local cold pocket. Let's at least try and bungee cord your mesh gear to the nylon bag. If you wear your leather I think you're going to be sorry."

"Well, I think *you're* going to be sorry for wearing your mesh."

I knew what this was. Your mom had caved one too many times in the last few days to my demands. She was drawing a line in the sand. She was holding her ground. This was her Masada. She was the Romans. I, logically, must be the hold-outs at the top of the mountain. And we all know how well that turned out for our Jewish friends.

I decided to try one more time, "Sweetie, with the heated seats you'll be fine. Please, let's at least try and take your mesh."

"I'll be fine," she said, quietly and evenly. "If I get too hot, I'll unzip the liner and take it out."

I could see that arguing would be pointless. Fun no doubt, but pointless. Possibly, given her mood, dangerous. No, we would find a way to deal with whatever came our way. If worse came to worse, I would buy her another damn mesh jacket, and mail her heavy coat home.

"Okay. Well, let's get this show on the road, shall we?"

And with a quick kiss before putting on our helmets, I started the engine, brought the bike up off the kickstand, (much more stable after yesterday's mishap), and gave your mom the signal that it would be alright to climb into the back seat. There are certain rules you follow when riding 2-up. Waiting for the driver, (or Pilot as we are referred to in the Victory Vision community), to tell you it's okay to climb on board is primary, You don't want your Pilot to be caught unawares. That's how broken arms happen. And yelling.

I hadn't told your mother, but I was a smidge nervous about putting a twist to the throttle and riding away. The Vision is hands-down the best bike I've ever owned, she has the comfort of a big touring machine coupled with the speed and agility of a sports bike. But we were seriously testing her load capabilities. So I eased off the clutch and slowly cruised down the driveway. The real test would be pulling out on the road. I would get a good feel, very quickly, for how this trip was going to proceed. With a bit of a catch in my throat I cruised down our driveway, eased out onto the arterial, and gave her a bit more throttle. She pulled straight and true. I was actually amazed to find that the bike handled very, very well. I'm more impressed each day with this machine. This blending of artistry and petrochemical explosions all rolled up into a ballerina of the blacktop. I couldn't tell a difference between loaded and unloaded as we hit the curves that led from our house to the main highway. Yay! This was going to be fun!

One more test to go. I eased up to the stop sign at the intersection and signaled right. Would the bike be top-heavy? Would it be hard to handle at stop lights and low speed maneuvers? The quick answer was no - once again I could tell little difference. Good! My last hesitation put to rest, I looked both ways, and with a gentle pull of torque put the tires on the path that we would follow for the next 120 miles or so. It felt good. Our trip was now properly underway.

Whereupon, as if on cue, a young girl on a cell phone and in a truck big enough to have Mini-Coopers stuck in its grill without noticing, materialized out of nowhere, roared up on us, and proceeded to tailgate. I mean really tailgate. Damn, that is not the way I wanted to start this trip. Young ladies on cellphones, or anyone on a cellphone for that matter, is a major hazard. Sight all the statistics you want, but 9 out of 10 times if we have a problem with a car, it will be someone yakking on a phone.

Mom immediately wanted to pull over and kill the nice young lady. I felt it was too early in the trip for assault, plenty of time for that later. So I hit the throttle. The truck behind us followed suit. We were now cruising a good 10 mph over the posted speed limit. (Shhhh. . .don't tell the boys in blue.)

Then it hit me; it was then I realized the girl behind us was an 'obstacle driver'. What is that you may ask? Why an 'obstacle driver' is a person that gets on the road, and drives until they encounter another car. That car then becomes an "obstacle" for them. You are in their way. If you pull over, or wave them around you, they will drive up and tailgate the next car in line. We are all just window dressing to their lives. We are all obstacles to their goals.

Which didn't matter to me - I couldn't care less about her day-to-day habits. Right now she was tailgating and putting our lives at risk. Mom was twisting in her seat, turning around and giving her the 'stink eye'. Your mother's 'stink-eye' normally causes strong men to crumble like greasy street-punks on the witness stand. There was a problem here though, the girl would have had to been paying attention to SEE the stink-eye. Mom leaned forward and shouted, "I'm going to throw pennies at her windshield in about 2 seconds!"

You know your mom. She would do it. I suppose I should have found some joy in that she wanted to throw pennies instead of spark plugs. Or a chair. But I didn't. It's a wonder I've kept her out of prison as long as I have.

"No you're not," I said, with what I hoped was an appropriate amount of authority in my voice.

"She's going to run into the back of us! She can't be more than 3 feet away!"

I looked for a place to pull over, but the Washington State Department of Transportation, in their far-sighted wisdom, had decided that the shoulders of the road were terribly, terribly passe', and replaced them with a bare six inches of tarmac and huge guard rails. Really huge. Really huge and really shiny guard rails that screamed 'Don't touch me our I will fudge you up!'. So I couldn't have pulled over had I wanted. And, as the hip-cats on the Netz say, do want! There was simply nowhere to go even if I found that we had spontaneously combusted and figured it was a fine time for a wienie roast. I was fast running out of options. Speeding up hadn't helped. There were no side roads on this stretch of highway, nothing but aforementioned wavy strips of aluminum death.

What to do? Well, I did the only thing I could do - I became drunk.

I've hinted at the maneuverability of the Vision, but you have no idea. You can swerve and swoop the beast like a fighter jet, and snap her back in a straight line before you can say . . . you can say. . . well, something very short and very witty. So that's what I did. I sped up, and began to weave my baby around in the lane, then slowed, sped up, weaved. Sort of like the directions on a bottle of shampoo. Weave. Speed. Repeat. It wasn't dangerous, but it LOOKED dangerous and that was the point. Oddly enough, the girl backed off. Way off. Mission accomplished. No doubt she was now dialing 911, reporting the 'dangerous maniac' on the bike. I hoped so. Those field tests on a cane are a hoot.

"Thank you," Mom said as she leaned forward with her face-shield raised.

"No problem sweetie," I replied craning my neck but keeping my eyes on the road.

Thankfully, that was the last incident before we pointed our metal steed over Chinook pass. Ah, Chinook. We are truly fortunate to reside at the base of the Cascades with their miles of great riding roads and spectacular views. Well, unless you count that whole "You're sitting at the bottom of an active volcano - an ACTIVE volcano for God's sakes!" thingee. Wimps and wusses one and all. Personally I believe thumbing your nose at nature adds to the excitement of living here. I mean, seriously - how many people have this conversation several times a week?

"Mt. Rainier sure is beautiful today."

"Why yes it is. Absolutely gorgeous. I never grow tired of the view. The sunlight on the glaciers - just stunning!"

"That it is. It's like an old friend that always there to greet you."

* Insert Long pause *

"Of course, you know that it could blow any second, and we would have no chance at escape. It would be certain death from the pyroclastic mud flows raging from the melting glaciers."

"Oh I know! We would be screwed! No chance to run."

"Yep screwed. Dead in minutes. So . . . you going to the Daniel's party this weekend?"

Plus, and you know this because you lived it, how many kids get to put together a 'Volcano Emergency Kit' for school every year? That was always a little creepy. Oh, not the peanut-butter crackers or the juice boxes, those are fine. No, it was the 'sealed note' that we, as parents had to write you every year to place in your bag in the unlikely event that you would, at some point, need comforting. I mean really, what can you say as a future dead person to your living child? We never let you peek, but I guess that now that you're all hoity-toity and Naval I can tell you now what we wrote in those letters. I can't remember exactly, so I'm paraphrasing here, but it was along the lines of, 'Hi! We're dead. Don't forget to brush your teeth', or something like that. Good thing you never had to use that, huh? Couldn't have been easy for you though. Remember that one special day in third-grade when they would sit you down and explain to you what a volcano was and what volcanoes did - chock full of useful charts and maps and pictures of Mt. St. Helens and Pompeii - and then walked you over to the window and pointed to this huge time-bomb ticking on our horizon? I always knew when they had reached that point in the academic year. It wasn't hard to discern. Watching a whole herd of eight-year-olds walk out of the class teary-eyed, shell-shocked, and trembling - well, it was obvious. Either they had just had the 'Volcano Talk' or Jimmy had finally choked to death eating the paste. And we all know how the class felt about Jimmy. Wanker.

Anyway, back to our trip.

As you'll remember, the road to Chinook Pass is no cake-walk. In less than an hour you climb from 500 feet above sea level, to 5400 feet, all the while winding through dense forest and up steep roads, literally clinging to the sides of the mountains. I remind you of this so that the next part of our story makes sense.

For you see I, the man who was adamant about this being summer, and now less than 10 minutes into our voyage, was beginning to get cold. The temperature dropped with every hill, every twist and turn of the road. I should have pulled over and put on some extra layers - and possibly set fire to my chest - but I thought the seat warmers and heated grips would be enough. Plus, there was that little pride thing I had going. No way I was going to admit I'd made a mistake in my choice of gear after the discussion your mom and I had earlier. I was able to fake it almost all the way to the top of the pass. I'm sure that your mom thought my shivering was nothing more than a bit of rough road. She may have had her suspicions, as evidenced by the following conversation that took place half-way up the mountain.

Mom leaned forward and said, "Sure glad I wore my heavy gear. Yep I'm warm and toasty back here. In fact, I was thinking about unzipping my jacket a little. Cool off a bit. How you doing?"

I would have replied, but my jaw was locked in a permanent clench. I think I may have bitten my tongue in half. It didn't matter. Hypothermia was setting in - hard. Less than an hour from home and I was about to die the death of the dinosaurs. Again, it didn't matter. It would all be over soon. Yet I'm a survivor. I'm scrappy. Somehow I managed to hold on the last few miles where we reached the final ascent to the top of the mountain. I don't know if you remember this, but the stretch of road from the intersection of Hwy 410 and Hwy 123, to the top of Chinook pass - while only 3.5 miles long - climbs almost 750 feet with some MAJOR switchbacks. I mean MAJOR switchbacks. No, even bigger than that! This is usually the 'fun' part of the trip. Usually. But the Universe was getting the game on early because as we rounded a corner it began to rain. Then the rain turned to snow. And the snow began to stick. In August.

Well, as I have said many times in my life - and never in a particularly positive tone - this should be interesting.

And it was. Interesting I mean. A little slippery. A little slidey. A little whoopsie-doo. Despite the odds, and I might mention that I was beyond cold at this point, we managed to make it to the top. I pulled into a little rest area just over the summit, cutting a black stripe through the slush to the blacktop below, and coasted into a parking space. I would have wept but my eyelids were frozen.

"Can you believe this?", Mom asked shaking her head in amazement. "It's August for crying out loud."

I tried to say something. I can't remember what. It was probably poignant, beautiful, profound. A statement worthy of being carved in stone. A summation of the human condition that would have birthed insight and peace between nations but was now lost because I couldn't move my lips. Such is the tragedy of man.

Oh wait, I remember! I said, "COLD!"

"Yeah," Mom said, and pulled off her helmet. "It is a little chilly. What does the thermometer on the bike say. Like 38, 39 degrees?"

I managed to tilt my head to look at the digital readout on the instrument cluster. Either I heard ice crack on the back of my helmet or I had shattered another vertebrae in my neck. I hardly noticed. The display was frosted over just a tad. "33", I said. Only it came out "Thhhhhh. . .thhhhhh. . .thhhhh. . ." Sounding much like I was trying to blow up a balloon with a lisp.

"Aw, are you cold babe?" she asked, cocking her head. "Guess you should have worn your heavier coat."

It wasn't so much what she said, although that stung, it was the particular way she giggled as she said it that nailed me. Were it not for my complete inability to speak, or let loose of the handlebars, there may have an altercation.

However, I knew the hard part was behind us. Soon we would descend down into Eastern Washington where the weather was warmer, the roads were less crowded, and granola was not on the menu. We waited at the top of the pass for awhile, watching the light snowfall, allowing the feeling to return to my limbs, and then with a mighty 'Hi Ho Silver! Away!' we set out on the twisty path that would eventually take us to Canada.

Of course, before we could get to our first stop at Galaway Bay, BC we would have to cover 350 miles. As I explained to your mother, "Piece of cake!"

Darn good thing it was early in the morning. Otherwise, we might have run into trouble.

September 14, 2008

Dear Amber,

I hope this note finds you healthy and happy. I don't know much about OCS, and to be honest I may not have been listening particularly closely when you were discussing it with Mom at various points in the last two years. I was busy.

I hope that you're getting plenty of rest and fresh air. Do you have some sort of physical exercise program there at OCS? Pilates? Some low-impact aerobics? If you're going to be a Navy Pirate, you have to be in good shape. It can't be all "Arrrggghhh" this and "Yo Ho" that. At some point you may have to actually run or something - you know, if the pillaging goes awry - so a quick escape might be a good skill-set to develop.

Oh! Have you got to road-test any parrots yet? So. Flippin'. Cool! I can't stress this enough - you and your parrot are going to be lifelong companions, so don't become infatuated with colorful plumage or a large vocabulary. There is much, much more to a parrot than flash and a well turned phrase. And dear lord, try to get one that's shoulder trained. The cleaning bills for striped shirts are outrageous.

How about your cutlass? Do you get to choose that, or is one assigned to you? And what about the dress code? Do you get to design your own Pirate outfit? If you do, go with red and black. It's a great color combination for your complexion. Although, you can't go wrong with basic black. Black just shouts 'I'm all evil and stuff, so hand over the Booty!'

Sorry for all the questions, but this Navy Pirate stuff is akin to a foreign land for me. Honestly, I didn't even know the Navy had Pirates! That reminds me, do you get to keep the treasure, or is it all turned over to Uncle Sam?

I'm so anxious to hear about the classes on profanity and drinking rum. Probably some plank walking thrown in there as well. Also, I imagine you're digging a lot of holes in the sand and drawing crude maps. What an adventure!

I hope you're enjoying these installment of Mom's and my big trip.

Love you,
Daddio

P.S. Had to evict the transients and while cleaning out your room we found 'the box'. If you survive OCS you are in big trouble Little Missy.

Chapter 2

The Great Brown

Frozen.

Twas a sad sight, watching your poor old father shiver and shake as I scooped slush off the windshield of the bike. Why the hell don't you ever see a motorcycle with wipers? That's what I'd like to know.

Oh yeah. Not supposed to ride a bike in the snow. That's why

We pushed on. Down. Down. Down. Away from the snow and the cold and the grey sullen skies of our homeland. I could go into great detail describing to you how I shredded the twisties as we descended the east side of the Cascades and navigated those rare and beautiful miles into the tiny burg of Naches. But I won't. I'll spare you the minutiae of each turn of the tire, each apex, each rise of the blacktop. I shall resist the urge to create a lyrical ballad - an ode to the pines and the rivers and the wondrous, wondrous curves. Let's just say if the road and I were both doing time in prison by the time we arrived at the bottom I could have traded it for smokes.

Oh stop cringing. I thought that image rather clever. You're a Navy girl. Suck it up.

The temperature inched steadily upward as the day progressed from early to mid-morning. Steadily but rapidly. Really rapidly. Climbing faster than a helium balloon escapes a toddler's sticky fist at the zoo. Not that it made much difference. My core was hovering somewhere between Minot, ND in January and the McMurdo Station in . . . well, pick a month. August will do. I had a ways to go before I would be warm again - if ever - and miles to go before I slept but that's a different story entirely. For a moment there I seriously considered setting myself on fire. I reasoned that it probably wouldn't be that bad, and I could more than likely put it out before I incurred too much damage. You know, finding the sweet-spot wherein the fire had warmed me enough that I could taste again, but right before I entered the burnt-marshmallow stage.

Just as I was contemplating whether to start the blessed fire on my arms or chest - not the face, I'm wayyy to pretty for that - I found sanctuary. We'd reached one of our favorite local haunts, a small cafe born of river-rock and grease and hard, hard waitresses. I pulled our two-wheeled motorcade of ice off the road and into the parking lot, then popsicle-hopped inside for a quick pot of coffee. Yes the entire pot. Then a quick trip to 'speak to a man about a horse' and back to our journey we went. Warmer, happier, and way less 'So cold . . . need a nap . . . WHOA that truck was close!'.

As we bounced along the outskirts of Yakima I watched the temperature gauge progress with tenacity to 60, 65, 70 . . . by the time we hit Interstate 90 in Ellensburg a half-hour later, the needle, (I know, I know. . . it's all digital so there is no 'needle' so to speak. Quit being so picky and let me get on with the story), hovered around 76 degrees.

Mom leaned forward and said, "Pull into the gas station. I can use the rest room and you can top off the tank."

"But we just stopped."

"It will only take a minute. And I need to take off one of these sweaters," she said, unzipping her jacket a little. "So stop whining. We'll have a full tank and be ready to knock down some miles on the freeway."

I would have argued with her - for the bike and her needs are my domain - were it not for a teensy, eensey, weensy little incident in Ellensburg a couple of years ago. This was with the Suzuki, back before we were cruisin' large with the Vision. We'd spent a pleasant weekend visiting your Aunt Vicky and Uncle Jahn in Spokane, (and by pleasant I mean no stitches were required and none of that 'if it pleases the court' crap. If there's one person on the face of the earth scrappier than your mom, it may be your Aunt Vicky), and were headed home. As we passed Moses Lake, about an hour-and-a-half out of Spokane, I said to myself, "Self, you really have no accurate way to measure how much gas you have left because the geniuses that designed this bike thought that a fuel gauge would just be added weight and clutter. You have a pretty good idea, based on past experience of how far you can go, and you should make Ellensburg with no problems. However, it might behoove you to take a moment, get off the freeway, and fill the bike. Much better to err on the side of caution."

That's what I said in my head. What I heard was, "I got plenty."

Stop laughing.

I blew past Moses Lake, past George, (and the now defunct "Martha's Inn - Home of the World's Best Cherry Pie! Say what you want, Martha's Inn in George, Washington - that is a fine sense of humor right there), and slid down I-90 into the basalt walls of the Columbia River Gorge. As I passed the town of Vantage, and my last exit and chance for gas for the next 30 miles, a curious thing happened - that little 'low fuel' light on the instrument cluster lit up like a trailer park at Christmas. After a sale at WalMart. On double coupon day. Refusing to believe what I was seeing, I told myself that I was registering low fuel simply because of the steep grade of the hill, and that as soon as we reached the top the gas in the tank would slosh back into place and the light would fade to naught but a fleeting memory. I held onto that hope until we had climbed the other side of the Gorge and leveled out onto the plains outside of Ellensburg.

Funny thing about that light fading - it didn't. I began to sweat. I watched my acceleration. I coasted as much as possible. 12 miles out and then something I had never seen before happened - that little 'low fuel' light on the speedo began to flash. It seemed to flicker in time to my heart, until the reality of our situation sunk in and my pulse raced to the tempo of an Aphex Twin song played at double-speed by a hummingbird on crack. Here is where I converted and began to pray - to any and all Deities that I could recall, and a few I made up on the spot. Demigods such as 'The God of Rusty Ford Trucks', or "The Supreme Being in the form of a Winnebago', and my favorite 'The God of Idiots Who Didn't Listen To Themselves And Were About To Run Out Of Gas With A Tiny Woman On The Back Of The Bike That Was Going To Be Majorly Pissed', who - believe it or not - happened to take the form of a shiny, nude goddess on the mud-flaps of a truck I was following.

At one point I tried flapping my arms to give us an extra boost but your mom failed to find the humor in this.

"Is everything OK?"

"Oh peachy", I said, much, much to cheerily through teeth clenched much, much too tightly.

I don't know how, and I don't know which God was looking out for us, but we made it to the Ellensburg exit and slipped down the ramp from the freeway. Slowing, but not stopping, I turned right onto the main thoroughfare, went up two blocks to the gas station. About this time the bike began to sputter and falter. It finally gave up the ghost and died as I pulled in the clutch and we literally coasted off the street into the the pump bay. I may, and I'm not ashamed to say this, have shouted 'hallelujah' a few times.

You know, it seems like I cry a lot on our trips. Wonder why that is? Allergies?

Mom climbed off the bike, took off her helmet, and said, "That was weird. The bike was kind of wobbling there at the end. Didn't it feel all wobbly to you? Was it something I did? I didn't think that I was shifting my weight around or anything was I?"

I was now offered a choice. One, I could lie to your mom and tell her that yes, it was indeed her fault and she should be more careful, or two, I could come clean and fess up.

Were I had it to do over again, I would have lied. Lied like a congressman caught in a public bathroom taking a way wider stance than was necessary.

It's funny, but even to this day your mom refuses to laugh about that particular escapade. No sense of humor whatsoever.

Anyway, the point of that little segue was that I now adhere to the biker's creed - 'Never give a gun to a duck'. Wait, I might be confusing that with a quote from B. Kliban. Oh, I know! 'Never pass a chance to top off the tank or use a bathroom.' That's the one I was looking for. Although, you should probably file away the tidbit about firearms and fowl for future reference. It's just sound advice any way you look at it.

So we took a short break before we entered, what I affectionately refer to as "The Great Brown". It's that vast area of Eastern Washington beyond the Cascade mountains stretching almost to the city limits of Spokane. Semi-arid. Basically flat, empty, rocky, and save for a brief period in spring - brown. Brown as an environmentalist's lawn in July. Brown as a eco-friendly naturally-died macrame hanger. Brown as a Charlie. Here the freeway is straight, and flat, and goes on forever and ever and ever and a bit further than that. Fortunately the traffic was light and everyone was behaving themselves.

That is to say that the next 100 miles was, no other way to put it, dead-on boring. Bang your head against the handlebars boring. Nothing to do but set the cruise control on the Vision and practice my mad skills of riding without hands. It's an amazing sight and one that never fails to get a reaction from the people on the road. I'm not sure your mom appreciates this particular talent. She doesn't say anything, but I can infer much from the screaming and the pounding of fists and the raking of the nails on my exposed neck as I stretch my arms out to the side like wings and make airplane noises.

"Rrrrrrooooooooommmmmmmm!!!! Zzzzroooooooooommmmm!!!!"

"Eeeeeeeiiiiieeeeeee!!!!", your mother would respond. Bam. Bam. Bambambambambambambambam!

"Whhooooossssssshhhhhh!!!" "VvvrrrrrrrrooooooommMMM!!!"

"Aaaiiieeeeeeeeeeeeee!!!!" Bambambambambambambam.

So as you can see, we found a way to entertain ourselves. Remember Amber, the secret to life is making your own joy no matter what the situation.

We finally reach the town of Ritzville, where we will leave our eastern heading and turn north towards Canada. Here we will pull off the "slab", as the freeway is referred to in the biking community, to give ourselves a much needed break and a bite to eat. For some reason, my upper back and neck was a little sore and Mom said her arms and fists were killing her. You just never know what muscles you use when you ride. We saw a sign that proclaimed - and quite succiently I thought - "EATS!" This was the place for us. I appreciate advertising that doesn't beat around the bush. There was no mystery here. No 'TJ McDoolde Hackers'. No 'Peach Tree', which, contrary to its name offers neither peaches NOR trees on its menu. Or 'Cannibal Jacks' which I won't even get into here but take my word was quite a disappointment. And despite what my lawyer said, I still think is open to a lawsuit for false advertising. Plus, the staff is quite testy and uncooperative.

After horking a delicious road burger we noticed something odd - the temperature, which if you'll remember started out in the low 50s, and had dropped to the low 30s at the top of the pass, had firmly planted itself around

100 degrees. I had warmed up long ago, and was feeling fine and fresh in my mesh. Your mom, bless her little heart, was not fairing so well. She had taken her lining out of the jacket, shed layer after layer like a snake in spring until she was down to a T-Shirt. She'd traded her heavy gloves for a lighter pair, and was still sweating. Quite profusely I might add.

"Go ahead. Say it," she said as she crammed her shed clothes into a zippered pocket on the nylon bag.

"Wouldn't think of it dear," I said and patted her on the arm.

Relief filled her eyes and I could see a little tension ease from her shoulders, "Thank you."

"Think nothing or it. These are the things we do for love."

That brought a smile to her face. "So, just for giggles, if you weren't so nice, what would you have said?"

"For giggles? Okay. I may have," I said, and busied myself with putting my gloves back on, "although it would be quite rude and unnecessary, pointed out the fact that, except for a brief time on the pass, you made the wrong choice of gear, and will now boil like a lobster for the remainder of the vacation, until you dehydrate into nothing more than a dried husk of your former self. And I certainly wouldn't point out the fact that I had told you so. Or, that if we had the UberBitchin' Tote 9000, I could have whipped you up an iced espresso at any given moment thereby saving you from death by thirst and at the same time searched on the Netz for how to remove sweat stains from chrome. But I, m'lady, am a gentleman above all else, so I shan't say a thing."

She shook her head and chuckled softly. "It's a good thing I love you so much."

For that she got a nice long hug. I would have held her longer but she was beginning to smell a bit. Plus she was a slightly slippery to the touch. One sweaty, sweaty little lady. Eww. No, double eww.

Now that the familiar part of the trip was behind us, the time had come for me to test out my newest toy. Our shiny, new, (RoXor - I told you I liked refurbs) GPS that we had mounted to the console of the bike a mere week before our trip. I had long lusted for this unit. If you do not understand the term 'techno lust' you are no daughter of mine. And I'm not speaking of the feeling that comes over you at a Rave from too much 'punch' and the pounding beat of 'The Crystal Method', I'm speaking of the romance of gadgetry. The seductive world of chips and processors and memory and astronomical pricing for first-adopters. God I love technology! I think I now understand, and I'm generalizing here, some women's insanity for shoes. Or maybe not. That's just weird. Anyway, back to the object of my current adoration. The GPS was a thing worthy of its own religion. Full color touch screen, its voice integrated with the speaker/sound system on the Vision - all the bells and whistles. The epitome of our technological civilization. The pinnacle of Homo Technus. A miracle really, think about it - I could have saved us so much time if I'd had a GPS when you were small. No more getting lost for hours. No more tears. No more frantic calls asking someone if they perchance knew where in the Hell we might possibly be. I was giddy as a lotto winner, (not a Megamillions winner - somewhere around a $5000 scratch-ticket winner), as I plugged our destination of Galaway Bay, British Columbia into the unit and watched, with fascination, as me lover-ly, lover-ly rudimentary autonamaton plotted our course.

My enthusiasm lasted about 30 minutes, whereupon, somewhere in the godforsaken badlands north of Ritzville, I had a minor breakdown and heated argument with the GPS. No kidding. I had set the GPS to a female Australian voice. She was hot. I named her Alice. Sweet, sweet Alice. As difficult as it to believe, my innate sense of direction was failing me that day, (I know!), and before you could say 'dust bowl' we took a wrong turn, then another. My precious was not amused. That little floozy got sarcastic in a hurry. I may love technology, but I hate uppity machines.

Our exchange went something like this:

Me: "Okay, well here we are, in the middle of a vast, flat nowhere. Flatter than a flapjack in winter. Flatter than a sod-buster's foot. I'll just clear everything out, and plug our destination into the ol' GPS again and we'll get out of this spot of trouble lickety-split. Shucks, this here ain't nuthin' but a little by-and-by no-how."

Mom: "Why are you talking like a pioneer crossing the prairie?"

Me: "Pardon Ma'am?"

Mom: "When was the last time you had a drink of water?"

Me: "Ummm . . . reckon I had me a taste of nature's nectar last time we stopped and shod the mule."

Alice: "Recalculating. . . ."

Mom: "How many fingers am I holding up?"

Alice: "Recalculating. . . "

Me: "Six."

Alice: "Drive 4.6 miles and take a right on Western Australia X-15."

Mom: "Did she just say 'Western Australia'?"

Me: "I think that Sweet Alice is a bit bamboozled with the abbreviation for Washington, (WA), and is recitin' our fair state as 'Western Australia.'"

Alice: "Turn right on Western Australia X-15, watch out for Roos."

Mom: "You named the GPS's voice 'Sweet Alice'?"

Me: "Seemed appropriate at the time."

Alice: "We don't have all day Mate! Get yer arse goin'."

To which I obediently did as she commanded. Alice is a harsh task-master, or task-mistress, but up to this point a fair one. So, I follow her directions. Surprise! The road she has taken us to is gravel. And 15 miles of it. I am not taking the Vision across 15 miles of gravel in the middle of nowhere. No how, no way. That will simply never, ever, never-ever-never happen. So instead of taking the suggested road, I ignore Alice and continue straight. I know this road will EVENTUALLY connect with another paved road that will take us where we want to go, I just don't know how far. With a plan in place we thundered into the hinterlands of wheat and dust and heat and lives long, long lost.

Alice: *"Recalculating. . ."*
Mom: "Well, that was less than helpful."
Me: "What in tarnation has gotten into that filly?"
Mom: "If you don't stop talking like that, I'll. . .I'll . . ."
Me: "You'll what there little Missy?"
Mom: "I'll poke you in the eye."

Now that takes me back a bit. She may be serious.

Alice: *"Recalculating. . ."*
Me: "Fine. But at the next stop as soon as you go to sleep I'm burning your mother's furniture for a campfire."
Alice: ***"Turn around and go back to Western Australia X-15. Proceed 17.2 miles to Us 86,*** (Which she pronounced as 'us', not YOU-ESS***), then take a right at the first junction."***
Me: "Um no." I keep the bike going straight down the road.
Alice: ***"Turn around."***
Me: "No."
Alice: ***"Turn around ya wanker."***
Me: "NO!"
Alice: *"Recalculating. . ."*
Mom: "We could just turn it off. . ."
Me: "No. We did not spend our hard-earned money for a dash ornament. Had I wanted that I would have bought one of them there little Jesus figures with the bobbly head. No, I have faith that Sweet Alice will chart us a course straight and true."
Alice: ***"Drive 87 miles back to Ritzville and try again."***
Me: "What the f ---?"
Alice: *"Recalculating. . ."*
Mom: "Please don't tell me we're going back to Ritzville."
Me: "No. No flippin' way."

Alice: *"Yer fucked mate. Yer off the map."*

Me: "Jumpin' Jehoshaphat! You're a dad-burned GPS for criminy sakes! You can't be lost!"

Alice: *"Oh, I'm not lost, you are. If you don't want to follow my directions it's not my problem."*

Mom: "Are you trying to strangle the GPS?"

Me: "Shut up and help me circle the wagons."

After some time we stumbled on a road that was paved and headed in a general northerly direction towards the golden land of Canada. I took it without hesitation. After a few miles we realized we were on the wrong side, (the SOUTH side), of I-90.

Mom: "I don't remember crossing I-90. How the heck did we get here?"

Me: "I have no idea, but there's the exit to Ritzville."

Alice: *"Ha Ha. Recalculating. . ."*

Eventually we found our way. I don't know how. It doesn't matter. If you have an explanation of how we headed north yet wound up on the south side of I-90 with no memory of crossing a 6-lane freeway I'm all ears. It may have been aliens, or the past hour could have been a joint hallucination in the parking lot of "EATS". I probably shouldn't have had the 'home grown' mushroom soup. The point is we persevered and pushed on, blindly cheerful as ever. Why this was nothing more than a minor setback. A blip in our schedule. Little things like this were bound to crop up every once in a while. Best just to take a deep breath and push on.

It was about this time that we began to hit the wind. Across the open, and at this time of year arid wheat fields, the wind was whipping something fierce. A constant 20 mph side wind, with gusts much, much higher than that. The Vision, packed as she was, became a sail. More precisely, a Mizzen topgallant staysail. (Ha! Navy talk!) A gust of wind would hit, and I would lean into the invisible force to keep ourselves upright and in our lane as much as possible, and then the gust would stop abruptly - while I was still leaning. Remember my 'drunk driver' trick from earlier? Yeah, a lot like that but without all the laughs and hilarity.

As we rode along, we could see mini-tornadoes racing across the landscape - giant twisting, pulsing, swirling columns of dust. It was here that I thought to myself, "Self, it wouldn't be a good thing to hit one of those." And I was right. I managed to dodge quite a few, but one colossal gyrating mass of liberated earth broke over a small hill and before I knew what was happening we were engulfed by the monster. I was a tad busy praying once again, but your mom was later able to describe what happened: She said that as the thing hit, the bike shuddered - hard, leaned WAY to the left, shuddered upright, then everything became still as we entered the eye. Then again the bike shuddered and growled leaned precariously to the right, and finally broke free of the hellish dark swirl back into the bake-oven of an August day.

That is what your mom says she remembers. Here is what I remember: "Shit,shit,shit,shit,shit,shit,shit." If I could have clicked the heels of my boots together chanting "There's no place like home." I would have. Unfortunately my eyes were full of grit and my mouth tasted like one of those mud pies you were so fond of baking for me as a child. Did you know that other dads didn't actually eat those things?

Having survived - barely - we trundled down the road. As we rode along, the lonely farms and empty wheat fields transitioned into miles of sparse trees, and then into dense pine forest as we approached Lake Roosevelt. All I can say about this particular section of the ride is that it was incredibly beautiful. We drove along close enough to the shore to catch the sparkles of reflected sunlight, tiny prisms dancing across our helmets and the body of the bike like nature's disco ball. Here there was hardly any traffic. This section of the trip verily defined great riding. Plus, there was nary a tornado to be seen. Although one may have been hiding in the bushes. Tornadoes are sneaky little bastards.

Yes, we were riding easy. The only problem was, if I were to believe the readout on the dash, and there was no reason not to, the temperature was now firmly planted around 12,000 degrees. No, it was really more like 106, but still flippin' hot. I was broiling in my mesh, and I became truly concerned for your mom in her heavy gear. So, we improvised. I stopped quite frequently, (schedule be damned!), and we would drink copius amounts of water, then pull an old biker trick - we would take a bottle or two of H2O and soak Mom's handkerchief and our shirts. As we drove along the wind would flow over our clothing evaporating the water and cooling us at the same time. Nature's air conditioning. This was critical. Especially for your mom. That kerchief rested against her cartoid artery, providing a direct link to her bloodflow. This would buy us some time, but when your mom would lean forward and say, "My, aren't the stars pretty tonight?" I'd know she was overheating. I would pull over, douse her with water as if she were a confused tourist at a WTO convention, and cruise back onto the road. I tried to enjoy the sights but your mom's imminent death distracted me from the natural splendor a tad. We sacrifice for love, no?

Somehow the hours slipped by - and I do mean hours, who the Hell knew Washington was this big? - and it was well past 5 PM by the time we reached the US - Canadian border. At this point I was MORE than ready to be at our hotel for the night, and your mom, who, thank goodness, had either stopped hallucinating or learned how to hide the fact, was ready as well.

We had one more gauntlet to run however. Canadian customs. (Cue dramatic dun-dun-DUN! music! Or, considering we were entering Canada, dun-dun-DUN-eh? music.)

Back in the day (What the hell does that mean anyway? Really. That's a weak descriptor of a point in time if ever I heard one. You don't hear "Back in the year", or "Back in the decade", now do you? No. And why? It sounds silly, that's why). Anyway, back in the dim past crossing the border was as easy as coming to a full stop and answering one question: "Where are you going, and how long are you going to stay?" I guess that's two questions, but it was usually slurred together - you had to pass the time in those booths as best you could, and alcohol is a quick cure - so you get my drift. Sometimes you didn't even have to stop, they would wave you right through. 911, as it changed so much in our society, changed everything at the border. Suddenly, Canada was actually a foreign country. Who knew? Now crossing is a bit of an ordeal, but we were prepared. Coming here was a great excuse for us to finally get passports. Mom was itching to use them for the first time. I was less enthusiastic. It had been quite a while since I had crossed over into Canada, and I'd never been to this particular border crossing - and never on a two-wheeled spaceship - so I had no idea of what to expect.

What we found was a small, two-lane road with a booth in the middle that could have been serving ice cream as easily as permission to cross into an alien land. How small? Our bathroom is larger than this entire station. Here was the thin blue - or red, or paisley - line separating 'Huh?' from 'Eh?'. Still, I felt some butterflies flit in my stomach as we rolled up to the window. Even though we had nothing to hide, it felt like we did. Know what I mean?

Yes I was guilty. Guilty of being an American.

The Canadian official, our gatekeeper to the splendor that is Canada, our ambassador to all things northy, motioned for me to turn off the bike. I gave him a quick glance to see what we were dealing with. He might have been 20, but I doubt it. His beard, if you could call it that, would inspire comments such as, "Aw, look! He's trying to grow a beard. Isn't that cute?". Or, "You know, shaving is 'in' right now." Or, "Dear god! Get a stick quick! That poor boy is being attacked by some varmint with mange! It might be a wolverine! Or a cat! Either way, that thing needs a good smackin'."

He was dressed in a crisp, khaki and forest green uniform and wore, what we in the USA call a 'Smokey The Bear' hat. He looked like the cutest boy scout ever. I thought it prudent not to mention this to him. It might spoil the moment.

After our initial greetings, and the typical, 'whereyoufrom-whereyougoing-howlongyoustaying?', the following conversation took place which, although you might not believe me, is reproduced verbatim:

Him: *"Do you have any guns?"*
Me: "No."
Him: *"Do you have any knives?"*
Me: "No."
Him: *"Any weapons of any kind?"*
Me: "Nope."
Him: *"How about Mace or other aerosol devices like Pepper Spray?"*
Me: "Umm . . . no. We don't have anything."
Him: *"You don't have any weapons of any kind on your person or on your motorcycle?"*
Me: "Noooo." (Although, at this point, I'm beginning to get a little nervous)
Him: *"Not even anything to protect yourself against animals?"*
Me: (Animals? WTF????) "No. Should I?"
Him: "Go on ahead and enjoy your stay in Canada," he said with a smirk and waved us through.

Mom immediately wants to pull over and buy guns. And knives. And brass-knuckles. Oh, and Mace. Possibly a Howitzer if we can find one. Poor dear, it's been a long day. It takes some talking, but I convince her that all she really needs is a rock that I picked up in the parking lot of a convenience store where we stopped to grab our umpteenth bottle of water. The fullness, the heft, the sharp edges all seemed to soothe her. Her eyes lost that wild saucer-shape that gives me the willies. She loved that rock. In the days to come, I believe she loved that rock more than me. I can't blame her. The rock never convinced her to go on a motorcycle trip to Banff.

Blinded by anticipation, and perhaps a touch of heat exhaustion, we journed on across the border to Galaway Bay. Beautiful country. The town of Galaway Bay isn't far across the border, which is a blessing because by this time we are bushed. It's nearing 6 o'clock. The heat has really taken the spunk out of us. And if you've ever been de-spunked, you know just how uncomfortable that can be. Luckily we've already booked a room at a motel that, while it isn't exactly 4 star quality, received very high-ratings on various websites for cleanliness, quiet rooms, and comfortable beds.

Galaway Bay proper is definitely a summer 'cabin on the lake' type place. No central core so to speak, just a collection of businesses and services lining both sides of the highway about a half-mile from the lake itself. As we drive through town we see several restaurants, most of them empty or closed, a good size grocery store, etc. We don't see any chain restaurants - no fast food except for what looks like a family-run drive-in - but that's okay. We try to avoid the chains when we are on the bike, preferring to spend our money locally. You know, like good little world-class consumers.

I decide to allow Sweet Alice the opportunity to redeem herself after her 'petite foible'. I plug the address for the motel into the little digital bugger, and her soothing voice purrs the turn-by-turn. We have forgiven each other our temper from earlier in the day. Friends again and full of trust, we follow the path she has chosen and soon enough we find ourselves at said Motel.

How best to describe this establishment? It is one of those old 50's strip-type motels. You know, single-story. Faded signs. Whitewashed cinder blocks. Neon that may or may not work. Psychotic maniacs peeking out from behind curtains and giggling. But, we have reservations, and it got good reviews, and we are exhausted and sweaty. Mostly sweaty. We have now been on the bike about 11 hours, 7 of it in 100+ heat. We just want off the bike for the night. Possibly forever. I'm sure you can sympathize.

I pull the Vision up to the front of the office, and we de-saddle. It takes us a couple of minutes to get the helmets off, and pry the sweat-laden jackets off our backs. I cast a cautious glance around the place. I don't know what I'm looking for, but the Border Guard's line of questioning keeps running through my head. Just possibly there are roving bands of agitated Canadians about - mayhap a family of vicious baboons skulking about the trees, or, more than likely considering how our day has gone so far, an ovulating T-Rex with a failed relationship and a knife. Throwing caution to the wind I open the door and step inside the small office.

Oh goody. This should be fun.

Firstly, there is a man. The thing that catches my eye is his lack of upper garments. The gentleman is in his early 70's, balding, but with tufts of unruly hair on either side of his head that looked as if it were trying to escape. Or coalesce into wings for an escape. Very gray. Not the tufts, they are pure black, which is odd because it is his chest-hair that is gray. I don't let my eyes drift if-you-know-what-I-mean. Please God, let him be wearing pants.

The front 'desk' itself, and I use the term loosely, looks as if it possibly doubled as a Formica lunch counter at some point in the not too distant past. The heat is heavy in this place. Somewhere buried deep in the rooms behind him I hear the rasping, dying gasps of an air-conditioner. Oddly, the whole office smells of bologna. Bologna, beer, and failed, failed dreams.

I try not to judge. It is very, very hot. I shudder to think of what your mother and I look like. I don't know about myself, but your mom is a sweaty, sweaty, sweaty little lady. She wears a bright yellow bandanna around her neck, and her shirt looks damp. (It is.) Her head looks like it may have been improperly cured during the formative process. Primarily because of her hair, but I'm not ruling out that her skull may have become squishy in the furnace of her helmet.

Her 'doo' is sort of clumped all over to one side, giving her the appearance that she had just stepped off the fore-deck of a ridiculously fast boat. Then applied a liberal coating of shellack.

I smile, and she smiles back but it looks odd, out of place, and forced.

"Hot enough for you?" He asks, and breaks into the kind of grin that causes people to get hit in the head with bricks.

"Yeah," I smile, "it's been a warm one."

"Oh yeah. Been near 40 degrees here all week!"

Now I know this next part sounds cliche' but I swear it's true. He casually swats a fly on the counter with a vicious 'WHACK", then scrapes the remains onto the floor all the while maintaining eye contact. I suspect the fly has more than likely been contemplating suicide for several days, but couldn't muster the energy nor the enthusiasm until this moment.

Something he says wedges in my brain. 40 degrees? What crazy-talk is this? If it were 40 degrees I could see my breath, and all I can see is a faint stream of steam wafting lazily from your mother. I look at the man blankly, then I remember - Canada! Different measurement system! My brain hums and vibrates, trying desperately to convert Celsius to Fahrenheit. All that I can remember is 0 degrees Celsius is 32 degrees Fahrenheit. I madly do mental gymnastics. I carry a two. I divide by Pi. Finally I give up. 40 doesn't sound that hot to me, but what do I know? So I do what I do whenever someone is trying to impress me with a bit of knowledge that they assume I will appreciate. I whistle softly, then say "Wow".

"Yeah," he says, and starts to move around the counter. God, please let him be wearing pants! Please let him be wearing pants!

We have a good turn of fortune and he IS wearing pants. Not very attractive ones, but that's beside the point and I don't want to start criticizing his fashion. I have no idea of the local culture. This could be semi-formal dinner wear for all I know. For this is Canada - land of mystery.

"Been a scorcher all right. A real heat-wave," he adds with a slight bob of his head.

Mom and I smile and nod vacantly. I don't know about your mom, but I'm having trouble focusing. I think - and this is just some crazy speculation on my part - that I may be a little low on the moisture content.

"So, where you folks from again?"

Now here is a dilema. What do I say? Do I tell him we live in Enumclaw, and spend the next 10 minutes discussing what an odd name that is and where it came from and all the other peculiar Native American names from our neck of the woods? Or, do we offer a generality, like "Oh, the Seattle area, little town 40 miles to the south." That's my preference. It gives enough information to satisfy their curiosity, but not enough to invite further inquiry. Due to my impending loss of consciousness, I opt for the latter.

"Oh," he says as if he's just confirmed a long-held suspicion, "you're from THE STATES!" Then he gives us a look that I have no idea what it means, but I would come to see often over the next few days. I think that somehow in his mind, this explained everything.

I cursed silently under my breath. I'd dealt with Canadians before. I'd sat at various conferences with them. I had studied them online for months. Oh, I've done my homework. I'd watched my share of 'Anne of Green Gables' and 'The Red Green Show' and tons of stuff with David Suzuki and Alanis Morisette who, as we all know, is actually God in disguise, but that's best left for another day. There is one common thread that runs like a polluted river amongst our comrades to the north, be they white collar or blue collar, man or woman or some combination thereof, conservative or rabidly liberal. That thread is this: More than likely it is the United State's fault.

And really, in the late summer of 2008 who in their right mind could disagree? All that Bushy-ness, you know? It didn't matter for I had no energy for debate. I absolutely could not rally any enthusiasm for apologies. I prayed that 'shirtless old dude' as I now tagged him in my head was apolitical. Or, barring that, at least polite as he pointed out our list of deficiencies and crimes.

Turns out the gentleman was very nice, and our room which we previewed - while small - is spotless. As we conduct our business, we inquire as to the local cuisine. "Dave", (yes, that's his real name although he shall always be 'shirtless old dude' to me), ponders for a bit, scratching his chin.

"Well, there is a pub down the road. You MIGHT give that a try. Or there is this Greek place . . . " He continues to rattle off a few more happenin' spots around town. None of them were what I would call strong recommendations. "It's kind of hard on a weekday. The places stay open later on the weekend. I think most of them close pretty early." He gave us a slight shrug of his shoulders as if to say in a semi-apologetic way, "What ya gonna do, eh?"

Close early? It's 6 flippin' o'clock! In the middle of summer! How early do they eat around here? I mean, we aren't on "Moore Time", you know?

What's 'Moore Time'? You're mom, in what I assume is rehearsal for old-age, prefers dinner at 4:00 to 4:30 in the afternoon. For me, that's lunch. Over the years, like so many tiny conflicts in our marriage we've managed to find a compromise, a middle-ground if you prefer that is mutually acceptable to us both. When possible we usually eat dinner at 4:00 to 4:30 in the afternoon.

Stop laughing. You know it's true.

We fill out the proper paperwork, get our key, and thankfully the next few minutes are uneventful as we unload the bike and settle into the room. The bed is very comfortable, and to my surprise we have a wireless internet connection. We have an air-conditioner. A toilet that doesn't smell of port-o-potty chemicals. Plus, the room isn't moving and weaving. After the day we've had this is the Ritz. Life is good.

We collapse on the bed for awhile, each of us lost in our thoughts. It felt great to be still and better to enjoy the quiet. It takes a while to shake the ride, much like a sailor getting his sea legs back. I begin to drift off to sleep when your mom utters the fateful words: "Hey sweetie, you want to go grab something to eat? I'm getting hungry."

So we saddle up.

Gah! There's one problem to traveling by motorcycle, when the day is done the LAST thing you want to do is climb back on the bike. It's like an evil, evil carnival where you've spent a fantastic day riding the Tilt-O-Whirl and you're ready to go home but the Carny-folk won't let you because you were pitching the ride-operator crap due to the fact that you may have consumed enough tequila to anesthetize Connecticut and the semi-insulted dude at the button was now going to make you suffer by not letting you off the ride until you spin in the Tilt-O-Whirl for another three straight hours.

No, you may not ask how I know this. Grrrrrrr. Don't get me started on Carny-folk. They cost our family the Presidency back in 1916.

We cruise down the road. Lots of people out and about. I notice that they are all unusually tall and blond. For some reason this unnerves me. I detect something sinister afoot. They all look related somehow – sharing the same facial features. I make a mental note to study on this matter further. Anyway, we see the Pub. It's close to the Motel, and that for now is one of my main criteria.

"Want to try there?", I ask innocently.

"Sure," Mom replies.

We pull into the access road that parallels the highway, and cautiously roll into the parking area of the gray, blockish building. I'm confused immediately. It seems that one side is a family restaurant, with a parking lot that is nearly empty, and the other side is the Pub with a few more vehicles in the parking lot but not what I would call crowded by any stretch of the imagination. So I wheel the bike around, pull in next to a car and a couple of motorcycles, and proceed to back into a space next to the other bikes by the front door.

Before we can get our gear off, two guys come running up to us. Literally running. They want to talk about the Vision. That's fine, we are used to the bike attracting attention, but we're very weary. We spend the next 15 minutes discussing the Vision, and motorcycling in general, with the "boys". At last, the conversation begins to wind down. They may have gotten the hint when I started to claw my own eyes out of their sockets and your mother began to weep softly. We wrap up the conversation, say our good-bye's and venture inside the Pub for a hearty meal and some tasty, tasty cool drinks. As you know, no alcohol on the road, but an iced tea would certainly hit the spot.

The first thing that strikes us as we sort of lunge through the door is - it's dark. Really dark. Like bat cave dark. As our eyes adjust we see that the room is fairly full. All kind of bunched together towards the front of the room oddly enough. What made this weirder was there were a good number of tables spread through a deceptively large room. I mean this thing was huge!

Another weird thing - there are not enough cars in the parking lot to accommodate the number of people in the Pub. From the looks of the crowd I assume that most of customers have given up and simply live in the bar. And the whole creepy, clumping thing they had going on - I mean they were really bunched up. Eerily bunched up. Like a swarm of Canadians. Possibly we were witnessing some innate flocking instinct. If this were a raft, it would have capsized and everyone would have been eaten by sharks. Or squids. Or, by the most terrible horror of the deep - Shark-Squids! But I digress, back to the Pub. The next thing we notice is that the conversation stops. I mean dead. Eyes turn to us. Hushed and whispered comments are exchanged. I look down to make sure we remembered to put on our pants. As you know, it's happened before.

What to do? I mean do we sit and wait for the staff to bring us menus? Do we order at the bar? After a bit we take a seat at one of the tables near the rear of the group and wait.

And wait.

And wait.

Conversation in the Pub picked up a bit. I assume they realize we are not there to eat their young. Fatal mistake on your part silly Canadians! Bring out the babies!

And still we wait.

I leaned over and sniffed your mom.

Mom leaned back and whispered, "What the hell are you doing? Did you just sniff me?"

"I did. I thought perhaps, in light of our day, you were a bit on the odiferous side and that's why we weren't getting served."

Mom stared at me, never breaking eye contact.

"You aren't. Odiferous I mean. Gamey maybe, but not truly odiferous."

Still nothing.

"Just a little," I said, and held out my thumb and forefinger to show her the universal sign for 'teeny-weiney'.

Mom leaned close to me because - well because we were beginning to get truly creeped out at this point and didn't want to call undue attention to ourselves, and said, "You know, I wouldn't call you 'daisy fresh' either."

I would have argued but that would have taken more energy than I could rally. Plus, every time our voices rose above a hushed tone, the entire population of the bar twittered like a flock of starlings on a three-day espresso binge

With the patience of Job we waited, but even in our degraded state we soon realized that we could sit here until the Stanley Cup turned to rust and we were never going to be acknowledged.

"I guess we should go order at the bar," I whisper to Mom.

We get up, and sort of tip-toe to the bar. Once again the place falls silent. It must be a predator-prey thing. I can imagine the group as a herd of gazelles on the Serengeti, ready to bolt at one threatening gesture, ever on the alert for teeth.

Behind the bar is a man. At least, I think he was a man. But he seemed like an empty shell of a man. Zombie like. He wouldn't look at us. He just stood there pouring pints as Mom and I cleared our throats and looked at the menu. Not even a "*Y hallo thar.*" I don't know for whom he was pouring the beer, for there was no one picking them up once they were tall and frosty. I believe it may have been a rote action. The minutes ticked by. Curiously, and pointedly, he would busy himself at the counter, then wander away. Then come back. Nary a word escaped his mouth. When he did cast a glance at us it was less than friendly. Blankness tinged with contempt is more like it.

Come to think of it, I didn't look for strings. He may have been a life-sized puppet. This whole experience could have been grand performance art, and we were just too stupid to get the joke. That would explain the bunching. Everyone wanted a good seat to the show.

After a while, (and it seemed like an eternity), Mom tugged my arm and said "This is just weird. Let's get out of here."

I believe she hit the nail on the head. Time to get the Hell out of Dodge before there was trouble.

As we began to make our way to the door, a man walked over to us and said, "The food is actually pretty good here."

Too late silly Canadian. The whole place had taken on a sinister 'Invasion Of The Body Snatchers' vibe. The crowd may have, I fear, on some unspoken alien-commander type cue, silently, and in unison, stood up and stabbed us in our red-blooded USA lovin' hearts with sporks. Then later served us on toast to other unsuspecting tourists. If, that is, they ever got around to taking their order.

In case you didn't know, sporks are the national utensil of Canada. It's true. Sporks are also referred to regionally as "foons" or 'runcible spoon'. See, this is why I can't remember my address half the time - my brain is chock-full of useless, yet somehow mildly amusing knowledge.

Anyway, we left post-haste.

Safely back on the bike now, we cruised up and down the highway looking for someplace to eat. People began to point as we rumbled by them for the fourth, fifth, even sixth time. We didn't want burgers, so we passed by the drive-in. Mom didn't want Greek food as it doesn't sit well with her when we are motorcycling. Hmmm . . .

We finally spotted a Pizza place off the main drag, spent five precious minutes navigating and doing u-turns on the bike only to discover it was take-and-bake. We became more frustrated by the minute. Although, had it been three hours earlier, we could have bought a double-cheese and thrown that sucker on the blacktop. About 10 minutes and the crust would have been crispy.

We traveled the length of the strip again. Finally, we decided to just go to the grocery store, (it has a big sign that says 'Deli' prominently displayed out front), and just pick up something to take back to the room. At this point, Mom is tired and I'm getting cranky. And when I say tired, I mean really, really tired. And when Mom is that tired . . . well . . . I'm Atilla The Hun with hemorrhoids. Or so she tells me.

So we wander into the grocery store. I use the term 'grocery' in the broadest terms possible. There are a bunch of tourists picking over the shelves, all in a hurry - frantic even. Maybe the animals the border guard was talking about come and attack after dark. That would explain it, for the sun was setting. Or, and this is much more likely, the town was lousy with Vampires.

There is a large, and I do mean large - no, even larger than that! - section of beer, wine, and hard liquor. Mom doesn't say it out loud, but I can clearly see she's contemplating taking to the hooch. Who could blame her?

I manage to pull her over to the 'deli section', (Yes, the quotes belong there. If I were talking to you in person, I would have made air-quotes around that bit of descriptor), and we survey the bounty of the Galaway Bay deli.

There isn't a lot from which to choose. There is a ragged and dog-eared sandwich wrapped in plastic. I can only imagine how many times this particular combination of bread and 'other' has been picked up, examined, and rejected. How can a sandwich be mushy and hard all at the same time? There's a spot on it that looks like someone pushed their thumb through the wrapping. Would I eat that? Not even on a dare.

Next shelf, wrapped in cellophane, is a lone dill pickle, slowly leaking it's life-force into the bottom of the cooler. There are a couple of packages of cheese. I have no idea how old they are. They could have been there since the Carter administration. They seem chock-full of malaise crusted with good intentions. I'm impressed. That's a pretty deep piece of cheese.

I point to two pieces of what I assume are pizza - and I'm taking a leap of faith here - and say to Mom, "Hey, you feeling adventurous? We could try that."

You know that dead-pan look mom gets right before she knees you in the groin? Perhaps you don't. Unfortunately I've seen it on a few occasions. Sometimes, I'll see that look in my minds eye just as I'm about to drift off to sleep. That's why I scream when I nap. That was the look I saw on her face.

The weirdness of the day, the heat, the fatigue, the Twilight-Zone ambiance that is Galaway Bay beats us down like two drunk frat-boys at a Slipknot concert. At any moment, the whole scene may begin to drip and run and melt like a Jackson Pollock painting. I would not be surprised.

Suddenly the entire experience comes into clear and sharp focus. We have no choice but to flee for our lives. Our very souls are in danger. For as the seconds tick by it becomes readily apparent that this place is cursed. Cursed with the demons of Canada. We make a quick escape to the bike and scream like bats out of Hell back to the strip.

Mom communicates all that needs to be said in one word: "Burgers."

I'm relieved, the Drive-in looked a tad old, but not that bad. As we drove closer we noticed. . . AT LEAST 75 FRICKIN' PEOPLE LINED THREE ROWS DEEP AT THE WINDOWS. We drove down - the place was empty. We come back ten minutes later - it's the cast of 'High School Musical' with grips and drivers and demanding stage-mothers all vying for grease and cheese. It's a sign. We give up. Well played Galaway Bay. You've defeated two weary, slightly crazed travelers from THE STATES. I hope you're happy.

Back in our room, with the door shut, curtains pulled, and air-conditioner blasting, we regain a bit of composure. By this time it's late. It may even be next week for all we know. Time has ceased to exist. I can't let the day end like this. I won't let the day end like this. It is up to me to salvage this vacation.

I struggle to my feet and journey the 10 steps to the motel office. As I walked I remembered our suicidal fly friend from earlier. I now understand. Perhaps Dave would take pity on me and smack me with a rolled up paper as well. No matter, all I need is something to sustain us. I think I saw a pop machine in there somewhere. Or it may have been a heat induced hallucination. I didn't care. Shirtless-old-dude may be my only hope.

I pull open the door to the office and a blast of slightly cooler air rolls over me. There is a woman behind the Formica now. Dave is nowhere to be seen. I don't know where he's gone . . . possibly back to the parallel universe from whence he came. I am ecstatic to spot an upright glass-door cooler, like you would find in any grocery store, stocked full of muffins and bagels and fruit. Saved! I smile, go to the cooler and start loading my arms with all things fruity and carby.

"Excuse me," the woman says, none too kindly as I ogle an apple, "that's not for sale," and sucks a bit of food from her front tooth. (Yes, tooth. Singular.) It's for the continental breakfast in the morning."

WTF? CONTINENTAL breakfast? In a one-story cinder-block motel in Galaway Bay, BC? Really? CONTINENTAL? I'm not ashamed to say that a small "Eeeep!" escaped through my clenched teeth and slid past my lips all Nancy Drew like.

"Okay" I sigh, heavily. "How about the bagels and muffins?"

"Same deal."

It is then that I realize I may have to commit a crime. I wonder what the prisons in Canada are like? Probably much like the US, only they're polite when they rape you. I try a different tack.

"You know, we're staying here tonight, and leaving very early in the morning. It wouldn't be a stretch to think that if we were staying later we would certainly be attending your continental breakfast. So . . . could we have our bagel and a muffin now please?"

The woman looks puzzled. "But they're for the breakfast in the morning," she repeats, as if this explains everything.

In my imagination, I'm pounding my fists on the side of my head. Or her head. Whatever. Yet I remain the very epitome of patience and international good will.

"Okay. Look. If we were here in the morning, we could have all the bagels and muffins we wanted, is that right?"

"Well, within reason," she says.

I nod in agreement. "We certainly could have ONE bagel and ONE muffin, right? So, can't we pretend," I look at the clock on the wall, "that I'm just really, really early?"

I have hope. That's some sound, sound reasoning right there. I mean seriously, I'm not asking her to empty the till.

She narrows her eyes and says, slowly, as if talking to a complete idiot, "But those are for the continental breakfast in the morning for the motel guests."

Inside I scream and commit a crime of which I'm not proud. Suffice it to say that the Coroner would be quite surprised at what you could fit up a Canadian's wazoo. Yet I could see no matter how persuasive I was there were no bagels or muffins on the dinner menu.

Fine. Forget the food. I try once again.

"You know, all we really want is something cold to drink. How about the sodas?"

"That," she says with a smile, "I can sell you."

This makes no sense to me, but in order not to kill the positive momentum I've got going I say, "Great!", and pull out my wallet. "Umm . . . All I have is American money, is that okay?"

I can't quite describe the look that passed over her face, but it was much like she had just experienced an ill smell in an elevator and heavily suspected it had originated with me. I'm a proud man, but this was not time for hubris or ego. I beg her to take my useless American money in exchange for three ice-cold cans of pop. (Yes I said pop. Screw soda. I'm from the Northwest. Deal with it.) I'm fixated on those drinks. That's really all I want. Something cold and familiar. After some hesitation, and a fair amount of disgust, she caves to my pleadings and accepts my pathetic American currency.

You ever tried to carry three cans of pop, sans bag, with a cane? I shall leave it up to your imagination.

Triumphant, like the mighty hunter returning to his clan, I bring the cold nectar-of-the-Gods back to your mother. I approach her cautiously, warily. She has that wild look in her eye again, and her head still hasn't sprung back to it's proper shape. I drop to my knees and raise the mighty can of Noza-La Cola over my head. The provider returnith. Victorius. A kill of carbonated beverages as a supplication.

The offering appeases her.

"Okay," I sigh. "What do you want to do about dinner?"

"Well, I noticed some crackers in the bike. But not very many." She takes a long pull from her drink. "You know, usually I have all kinds of snacks. Beef Jerky. Peanut Butter. Candy. Cheese. More candy. Trail Mix. Nuts. A rasher of bacon. But you were the one that insisted on packing light."

I detect a hint of sarcasm and reproach in her voice. I know, hard to believe but it's true. I wonder just how long she's been waiting to make this particular point. Probably since we left the house.

She swirls vindication mixed with cold cola in her mouth and smiles.

The day is lost. I'm defeated.

We get the crackers and each of us take one - just one - for our evening repast. We chew slowly, in silence, and contemplate the day.

At least the bed is comfortable, and I has my Nets.

Tomorrow, I vow, will be different.

I mean really, could this trip get weirder?

September 20, 2008

Dear Amber,

Well, I guess I need to apologize. After talking with your mom I found out you're not going to be a Navy Pirate, but a Navy PILOT.

That's cool and all but damn . . . I was really looking forward to visiting you and scuttling a few of Her Majesty's schooners. Well, whatever. I shall get over my disappointment. Eventually.

Dammit! Could you still get a Navy issued parrot?

So, I've been looking into this whole Navy Pilot thingee - wow. Double wow. The more I read, the more I'm thinking this might even be COOLER than being a Pirate! Pirate's don't get to fly. Well, not unless they're unruly and get launched out of a cannon.

So now I have a few questions for you:

Do they let you check out the aircraft on weekends? You know, for pleasure trips?

Mom says that if you graduate Officer Candidate School, then you go to ground school. Really? I would think you would go to air school. I mean, don't you want to avoid the ground?

Do you get to pick your own call sign? If so, might I suggest 'Bubbles', or 'Perky', or possibly 'Smiles'? Those are some bad-ass pilot names right there and I believe they would fit your personality quite well.

Is it too late to apply to Pirate School?

Love ,
Daddio

P.S. Your cat came back. It took him a few days to dig himself out of the ground. I guess he wasn't dead. Just really, really tired. My bad.

Chapter 3

Of Ferries and Frogs and Vegans - Oh My!

When last we met our daring duo, sleep had descended on the famished pair as they hunkered, like suspicious lab-rats, in a small Canadian tourist town populated by high-strangeness and low expectations. And this, with the first Michelangelo-esque stirrings of the dawn-clad world, is where we pick up their story.

After a sweet night in the arms of Morpheus, (No, not the guy from the 'Matrix', that's just weird. The Greek God Morpheus. You know, the one that. . . aw forget it. I've bored myself), Mom and I awoke simultaneously at 5:00 in the AM. Remember, we'd collapsed about 9 PM the night before - did I mention we were tired? - so this was no surprise. Exhaustion will do that to you - give you the sleep-of-the-dead as a consolation prize for pushing your body far, far beyond its limits. Or, if the nocturnal sojourn is a little lighter, the nap-of-the-quite-seriously-ill. Possibly the doze-of-the-I-think-I'm-coming-down-with-a-bug. Whatever. We were rested, refreshed, wondrously hungry, and blessedly suffering almost total amnesia concerning most of the unpleasantness of the previous day. You know, much like the Bush Administration.

However, as charming as things appeared in dawn's early light, we were ready to beat a hasty retreat from "Casa de Whacked", and get back on the road. We, (I need another word for 'blind optimism'. Maybe 'foolhardy cheer'. 'Idiotic hope'. Hmmm . . . I'll figure something out.), anyway, we, in our blithering stupidity, convinced ourselves that what lie up the road had to be better than what lay behind us. So, time to throw our crap back on the bike, shake the mud off our boots, and get the hell out of Dodge.

Here was some fun: Our extra bag, our 'absolutely 100% guaranteed waterproof' bag, was a pain. No matter how I tied it down, I would turn my back and find the cursed thing escaping off the luggage rack of the motorcycle's trunk. It was the Houdini of soft-side luggage. Oh, what could the answer be? More bungee cords to the rescue!

I know I've asked it before but I will ask it again - whomever thought putting a metal hook on the end of a huge rubber band was a good idea? Probably the same people that invented lawn-darts back in the 1970's. That's back before people tried to protect the young and were still allowing various mass-produced consumer products to thin the genetic herd. *"Here Timmy, go long and I'll hurl this large, winged projectile with a sharp, 3 inch metal-tipped spike at your head. Extra cookies if you catch it in your mouth!"*

True to form, I almost put out my eye with a bungee cord. It's God's and my little joke. The scratched cornea went surprisingly well with the welts on my forehead from the day before.

Somehow I managed to lash "Mr. Drippy" securely, and with our luggage attended to, our belongings stowed, and our protective gear zipped, buckled, and sometimes stapled, we climbed on the bike and prepared to bid farewell to our new found friends in Galaway Bay, vowing never to return. At least for a year or so when the memory of our night spent here would lose its sharp edges and become simply, "That lovely little town just over the border."

In all honesty, it might take more than a year. It might be the next life. Those thoughts could wait until later. For now all we knew is that we were really, really hungry. Surely we would find a appealing restaurant just up the road.

But first, we had to make our escape. Like Ninjas. Sneaky Canadian Ninjas. Lest we forget ourselves and wake in a week or two sitting in the Pub with 'Zombie-Dude' pouring drinks for those only he can see. Quiet was the order of the day. Eager to avoid a scene, we decided that we would PUSH the Vision far, far from the Motel so as not to wake nor rouse the Local Pitchfork Mob with the rumblings of our mighty exhaust. You know us, deep down beneath the leather and the helmets and the tattoos on our foreheads that say 'KILLER', we try to be considerate people.

Mostly. The operative word being 'try'.

Now, I don't know if you're aware of exactly how much the Vision weighs. The dry weight --- and what the hell does that mean? What if you live somewhere it's raining all the time? Dry weight will do you no good. What you need is wet weight for a really informed decision. Or, at the very least, slightly moist weight --- anyway, the dry weight of the Victory Vision is 849 pounds, give or take an ounce. The saddlebags were stuffed with easily another 45 pounds or so, the trunk was crammed with another 40 pounds and then you had that diabolical "100% FRICKIN' GUARANTEED WATERPROOF" bag and you can tack on another 25 pounds. I go 200. Your mom is 101. The gear we were wearing, combined between us was at least 20 pounds with the armored mesh and helmets and Mom's security rock. A full tank of gas, (6 gallons), adds another 50 pounds rounded up. As you can see, if you've been doing the math, I was going to attempt to push well over 9000 pounds around with no reverse gear, no motor to help, and every inch uphill - and backwards. And why in God's name someone had coated the driveway with butter I'll never know. Perhaps it is some quaint Canadian custom of which I am unawares. Much like the Canadian propensity for human sacrifice around harvest time. Oh, those silly Canadian farmers and their festivals hearkening back to simpler days. I envy their simplicity.

Any-who, I pop a hernia just thinking about it. Sherpa-ing an epileptic baby elephant - on crack - up the side of Mt. Everest wearing roller blades would be easier than rolling our beast backwards and uphill.

I pull up the kickstand and we promptly fall over.

HA! Gotcha! No, I pull up the kickstand, take a deep breath and push backwards with my legs.

And . . . nothing. Not even a budge. I try several more times without success.

"What are we going to do?" Mom asked.

"Hmmmm . . . " I pondered, "set fire to the bike and claim the insurance?"

"That would be fine, but we would be stuck in Galaway Bay," she said and cast a nervous glance about, "possibly forever."

I saw her point. So through super-human strength, and a promise to the Elder Gods, (Cthulu, are you listening?), to give them my first-born son, (Jokes on them! I done been all fixapated! No more genetic wealth from this guy!), I finally got the bike rolling and managed to wrestle it far enough away from the motel that we believed we could make our escape without alerting the authorities. Which, thankfully, we did and trundled off down the highway with flowers and puppies in our hearts, and me a slight headache from exertion. Oh, and a major leg cramp. I was pushing over 9000 pounds after all.

Now that we were putting Galaway Bay in our mirrors we both relaxed a little. I can't tell you how gorgeous the day broke. There are no words. It was the magic moment - the first light seeping into the landscape bathing every mountain, every tree and rock and transient sprawled in a ditch with the hyper-reality of razor sharp detail.

We floated along incredibly wide roads engineered to perfection with nary a pothole nor frost-heave in sight. Our spirits soared as the Vision carried us along, effortlessly climbing up rugged valleys, through dense cotton mist hanging from the sides of granite peaks, only to descend to lake country where the road would meander through hamlets along emerald shores, skittering through dark forest and deep meadows as the black-ribbon propelled, no --- commanded us along its path. Lulled us Siren-like with the rhythmic twist and turns and sweeps and climbs of a road hungry for travelers and adoration. I swear that a couple of times I heard the musical notes of divine communication, (You know, BAA - DAA!!!) as we would glide around a corner to be surprised by a view even more stunning, more incredible than the last. The bike hummed beneath us. The sun shone upon us. The road was our partner, and begged us to rush without care along its snaking length.

We didn't even mind that we were starving.

I should have realized that we were being charmed into a false sense of security. But oh no, ever the 'I'm-shoveling-through-all-of-this-crap-because-I-know-there-must-be-a-pony-in-here-somewhere' kind of guy, I cried, "It's good. it's good.", and offered silent gratitude behind my helmet's shield.

After a couple of hours in this land of dreams and "Tim Hortons" (although, none that we could find), we rolled off one of the mountain passes into the small town of Stonekeep.

Stonekeep! God I love those Canadian names! We have Federal Way. They have Revelstoke. We have Ritzville. (Which, does NOT live up to its name in any way.) They have Castlegar and Calgary, Dead Man's Flats and Crowsnest Pass. The Great White North must fuel the imagination. Either that or they've been reading way too many fantasy novels and dime-store westerns.

We pull into Stonekeep, find a gas station, and pause for a much needed fill-up and a leg stretch.

After we have satisfied the needs of the bike, we cruise up the street looking for a place to eat. That cracker had done its best, but it was no match for the raw beauty of Canada. We were famished at 5:30, we were now bordering on insanely hungry. If we didn't find food soon I might have to consider eating your mother. I'm sure you wouldn't be surprised to find that it wasn't the first time I'd thought of this.

I should explain that all of Stonekeep is spread along one road that nestles against the base of a mountain, crosses a bridge over the Columbia River, and picks up its journey on the distant side of the valley. What I'm trying to say is - it ain't that big. But it is sprinkled over about 3 miles in a long, U-shaped strip. Still, by Canadian standards this is Gotham.

We spot fast food - closed at 8 AM in the morning. There are pizza places, Greek restaurants, pubs galore. There are Delis. There are Steak Houses, Italian restaurants, and a couple of seafood joints. But - and this is a big one - nary a chain restaurant nor breakfast cafe to be seen.

Thus begins, what Mom and I lovingly call the new vacation game of "Where in the Hell is somewhere to eat?" We never spoke of it, but visions of the night before sprang into our heads like ill-trained Golden Retrievers that had just horked down a bottle of Ritalin from frazzled little Jimmy's backpack.

After scooting up the road, then crossing the river, it became apparent that we had run out of town. There were scattered houses, and at one point we thought of just pulling up in a random driveway and knocking on the door. We were fairly sure that the residents of said house would be too polite to deny us a poptart. Or, Eggs Benedict. Maybe Prime Rib, we wouldn't be choosy. By now we'd wasted about 30 minutes on this little hunt, this early morning exercise in futility. Agitation spread over us like a spilled glass of whiskey at the dinner table. I tried not to think of our schedule, but I couldn't help it. Today was THE long day. No time for lolly-gagging.

Right about then I spot a sign for "Krakland's Tomb". (I don't think that was the real surname, but it will suffice for our story.) Just a small blue sign with an arrow pointing up a tiny road that spiraled up the mountain.

Finally, something interesting! Who can pass up something like that? I mean, it's a TOMB! I could have ignored a sign alerting me to "Krakland's Grave", or "Krakland's Final Resting Place", or "Krakland's Remains", but a TOMB? I would have sooner passed up a road-side stand giving out free money. Plus -and I can't emphasize this enough - your mother had begun to nervously tap her rock against the back of my head. I knew a little diversion would do us both good. So, I turn up my least favorite surface - a gravel road - (I KNOW what I said, so hush) and carefully wind our way up the side of said majestic mountain. After a bit the roadway widened into a packed-dirt parking lot and sure enough there's a sign pointing to "Whose-his-head's Tomb".

So. Flippin'. Bizarre. Especially at 8:00 in the morning and malnourished to boot.

Here, on the side of the mountain, nestled with boulders, and dirt, and scrub vegetation, and the primal stink of the wild - with absolutely nothing else around - is a beautiful garden ringed by a high, wrought iron fence. A garden full of flowers and benches and presumably a Tomb, but the gate is locked. Evidently you can't visit the dead until 9 AM on weekdays.

We could peer through the fence and speculate on what we weren't able to see. It looked fascinating and very zombie-ish at the same time. I mean who hasn't seen countless movies wherein a nice couple on a huge, futuristic motorcycle accidentally wanders up the side of a mountain to an elaborate tomb only to be eaten in the next scene? Amiright? It was just so utterly cliché it made my fillings hurt.

This is possibly the very definition of the phrase " high-strangeness". My Dr. Hunter S Thomps-o-meter pegged off the scale.

Then there is this; the icing on the cake. Or Tomb. Whatever. Outside of the gates, there is a flat granite wall that is at least 25 feet high. When I say flat I mean flat - it must have been shaped with chisels and hammers. A massive wall of solid stone speckled gray with flecks of quartz. Not unusual in and of itself, but here two long columns of words had been painstakingly hand-painted the length of the slab.

On the right side is a passage in Greek. Or Russian. Or Slovakian. Or Martian. Or something. I am no linguist, although I occasionally claim that as my profession to people who don't know me, so you'll have to go with my best guess. On the right side of the stone is a translation of the previously noted words. A translation that apparently had been transcribed into English by a gang of drunk monkeys on a dare. It's true. We have pictures. Not of the monkeys for they were long gone. Or perhaps hiding in the bushes to ambush us and take the bike.

I can only imagine how many monkeys and how many typewriters, or possibly laptops, needed to be assembled for a proper translation. I'm also thinking hard liquor rather than beer. The text rambles something about God and powerful acorns and tree trunks and heaven and the value of Vodka, and I think, but I'm not certain, a garden of golden bananas. This must have been where alcohol really kicked in, hence the banana and Vodka reference. Now, these curious simian ramblings are on the wall for eternity. Or until the paint fades. Or the monkeys sober up and come back for a re-write.

I can only imagine the consternation the translation must have caused the deceased's family. But, as my old Grandfather used to say - and possibly the best advice I could ever pass to you --- "You don't fuck with a gang of drunk monkeys. Well, not twice anyway."

Words to live by my dear.

Balancing this strangeness are the views. The views were beautiful. We snapped a couple of pictures. Long river valley, spectacular hills, the town spread out before us, the air so clean and crisp that it burned our pollution laden lungs, yada yada yada. Suddenly, out of nowhere, the hair on the back of my neck began to rise.

Mom shifted about nervously. "You get the feeling we're being watched?"

Gah! She felt it too? "Ah, yeah. Strongly."

Mom looked about. "Animal?" she asked, scouring the tree-line opposite the entrance to the tomb.

And then it all became crystal clear. The hair raising could only mean one thing - a true "Zombie Vibe". It was evident to me now that this was nothing more than a trap. A place where they lured unsuspecting tourists to feed their irritatingly polite Canadian zombie hordes. No sense using up all the town folk when there is a steady supply of idiots from THE STATES to appease their undead hunger. How typical.

I explained the situation to your mom in pantomime, fearing that to make a sound would be to seal our fate. I had no weapons with which to defend us against the nightmare. Nary a chainsaw or a shotgun or a Bruce Campbell to be found, so if we were attacked it was obvious we were pretty much screwed. No, pantomime was the way to communicate for sure.

"Why are you chewing on my head?"

"Brainssssss. . . ." I whispered.

"You're getting my hair all wet and stinky. Stop it."

"Brainssssss . . . "I hissed, and shuffled about a bit but I think the effect was lost due to my cane. You ever notice that you don't see a lot of handicapped zombies? What's up with that? When I get home, I'm writing a strongly-worded letter to the management. Come to think of it you could probably count being dead a handicap. And the rotting flesh. And the defaulting on loans. Aw fudge. Just forget it.

"You're telling me we're being watched by zombies."

It's funny how so many of Mom's questions really aren't questions at all. You ever noticed that?

"Brainssss . . . ," I whispered, and nodded my head up and down in the affirmative.

It was interesting to watch your mom at this point. I saw her rally herself for an argument, then right before she launched into some bit of logic a wave of doubt played over her face. She looked from the Tomb to the trees then back to me. She concentrated hard for a minute, and then concern stepped out of the way for a touch of fear to take its place on the canvas of her soul.

"You know, I'm not going so far as to validate your zombie theory, but it is creepy and I think it's time to go."

Whereupon your brave mother, the woman that gave birth to you and your sister sans any kind of pain killer or anesthesia, ran like a scaredy cat over to the bike.

For some reason watching her kind of spooked me. As if her willies were contagious. I ran in a modified-panic to our baby, my skin a patchwork of goose bumps. Before you could say "Screw you zombie du Canada!" we beat a hasty retreat back down the hill.

Protip: Never ignore a zombie vibe. It very well my save your life someday.

Although, Canadian zombies would make an excellent Cirque Du Soleil show, don't you think? I'm not positive that the high trapeze act would work, what with the limbs falling off and all, but I'm sure they could put a twist on the show that would knock our socks off. Maybe name it "Zomballa". Yeah, I'd pay money to see that.

In hindsight, it probably wasn't zombies. I don't think they handle the cold very well. Most likely an animal of some type was watching us. I suppose it could have been a Zombie-Beaver, or a Zombie-chipmunk, neither of which would frighten me terribly. I mean think about it - it would take quite a bit of effort for a zombie-chipmunk to eat your brain. Unless there were like 3000 of them and . . . Lord . . . that's a scary thought! You can't see me but I'm standing in front of my desk doing a major ookey dance. Just like when I see a spider. Or Dick Cheney.

Anyway, we were tail lights. I navigated down the steep gravel road. Carefully. Painstakingly. At the bottom of the lane, ever hopeful that maybe they've built a IHOP while we were at the Tomb of the Alcoholic Primates, I stop the bike and ask Mom, "Hey, forgot to ask but did you see any place to get breakfast? I mean, before we went to Zombie-ville. Am I missing something?"

"No. Not really," she replies, somewhat cryptically.

"Yeah, me either."

As I search the clutter that is my mind for a solution to our current dilemma something tickles the recesses of my brain. I ponder Mom's phrasing. "What do you mean 'not really'?"

"Well, there was one place back where we filled up with gas. It was a seafood place I think, but the sign said 'Seafood and Pancakes".

Sure that I misheard her, I asked, a tad more abruptly than I had intended, "What the hell? Seafood AND Pancakes?"

She squeezed her new friend, Mr. Rock, a little too hard for my comfort. "It was that fast-food looking place across from the gas station."

My stare must have said it all. Somewhat, although not fully apologetic she said, "There was a motorcycle out front."

As if this solved everything. As if since there was another person on a bike willing to gamble on what I could only imagine were shrimp-flavored pancakes, then since we were on a bike, it should be good enough for us as well.

My eyes narrowed. I believe that my stare is a laser, piercing, cutting. I catch a glimpse of myself reflected in her helmet. I look like I've had a minor stroke.

"Seafood and Pancakes?", I snort, "I'm not that hungry." I eyed her suspiciously. What was her game? Had an empty stomach and a long trip put her in a place where SHE was willing to try a 'Seafood and Pancake' place? Where was my wife? Oh Canada, what have you wrought? What madness have you visited upon my bride?

"Well, we always have crackers." She shrugged. A calculated pause and then, "We would have had more, but you had to pack light."

Touché, good lady. Touché. I am suspect that we are seeing the birth of a recurring theme. A marriage Meme if you will.

Trying to nip this in the bud I say, "I understand that I may have cut back on the food items a bit too much. My apologies."

"Maybe a little. Too late now though."

I was plunged into the depths of despair, sure that I was about to experience the 'French Toast Calamari', or 'Cold Oyster Cereal' or the horror of 'Scrambled Fish Eggs'. Then - inspiration!!!

"Hey! Sweet Alice will show us where we can find a restaurant! I completely forgot that she'll list all the local amenities!" I was giddy. Mom was relieved. Technology was once again our savior!

"Oh, so you and Sweet Alice have made up?"

I pause. "We've come to an agreement. An understanding if you will."

"Well, I'm happy for you both. Send me a card when you announce your engagement."

Deciding that this is a conversation best left for a time when my blood sugar was not in the basement, I pulled up the menu on the GPS, punched some info onto the touch-screen and sure enough, Sweet Alice spit out a list of places to eat.

There are pizza places, Greek restaurants, Pubs galore. There are Delis. There are Steak Houses, Italian restaurants, and a couple of Seafood Joints. GAH! What is it with the Canadian gustatorial scene? Oh Canukistan, you are nothing but a restaurant tease, you hussy! Sliding quickly back to despair, a lump grows in my throat when I notice a listing for a hotel with a restaurant! Eureka! Breakfast! I pull up the address, look at the directions. Mom peers over my shoulder, "Hey, that's right next to the gas station where we filled up!"

Well of course. Of course it was. Why would it not be?

"Hey," Mom says, "Everything for a reason."

I can't argue with this logic. If it were not for the detour, we would have never found the 'Tomb of the Drunken-Monkey Translators'.

"Let's just get something to eat," I say and fire the bike. "I could use a rest and I could eat almost anything. Except beer-battered scrambled fish eggs," I add with a side-long glance.

We meander back through deserted streets that is Stonekeep. This is so bizarre. Where the HELL are the people? We've passed like 4 cars all morning. I suspect the zombie infestation has crossed the river. As soon as it gets dark, the streets will be filled with Canadian zombies, wandering and feasting in a very orderly and polite manner. Hopefully we will be long gone by then but I'm not taking any bets.

We needed food of our own. So, we retrace our steps and sure enough, right next to the gas station that we had stopped at 40 MINUTES AGO was a hotel. Akin to a slightly upscale chain hotel. You know, nice, familiar, generic, and most importantly serving breakfast.

Without any trouble at all we find the hotel, park the bike and de-gear. We dash into the restaurant, and the wonderful aroma of real food wafts gently over the tables to smack into our nostrils like the push at Normandy. Minus all the death and carnage. And Nazis. I hear your mom's stomach growl with anticipation.

Well said dear lady, well said.

The hostess - I assume she's the hostess but could be a very aggressive prep-cook - comes over and gives us a smile. After we establish that it is just the two of us, she guides us over to a large booth that looks out into the hotel's central atrium. This was a bit of a surprise because you couldn't see this architectural marvel from the outside. Ah the wonders of this modern life. I'm in Canada, wayyyyy up north, gazing into a tropical oasis. The atrium was the core of the hotel, stretching six stories high to a green-glass domed ceiling. It was lovely with the morning sun lighting the flora, outlining the leaves and fronds of a tropic paradise.

Our waitress is young, probably mid-20's and wearing, what I can only describe as a black and white striped frock. The outfit, although I am no fashion critic, is not flattering. She looks like a prison waitress. Once again, I lay no claim to expertise in this area but I don't think they have waitresses in prison. Oh sure, there are a few fellas that would be happy to fill the role, but no females. Unless it's a women's prison. Come to think of it, I may have seen an after-school special concerning that very topic. No matter. This goddess of the feast hands us a menu, then takes our drink order, and disappears.

There are a few other couples in the restaurant, some small groups of businessmen and women hunched over tables, conferring quietly. No doubt planning some revolutionary activity for they are very much 'on task' if you know what I mean. I deduce that there must be a convention taking place at the hotel. I wonder what type? Real Estate? Dentistry? Used Moose dealers? People cast curious glances at us. Not unfriendly mind you, just curious. I smile when we make eye contact. I hope I don't look demented from hunger.

"What are you going to get babe?", I say, and turn the page of the menu to the 'specials' section.

"One of everything.", Mom says from behind her menu.

"Get two of everything - we'll share."

That made her smile. I love watching your mom smile. Her blue eyes twinkle and her entire face brightens. After all these years the sight still catches my heart.

"Look here," I point to the "Good Morning!" special. "They have a breakfast buffet!"

Your mother, as a general rule, hates buffets. She's lacking the 'glutton gene'. It's a huge drawback in our relationship, but one I'm willing to overlook primarily because I get to finish her steaks.

"You know, that actually sounds good this morning. If they have waffles I think I'll give that a try. I've been craving waffles," she says, with an evil little grin blossoming. "You know, we could have had hot, toasty waffles earlier this morning, but you'll remember - we had to pack light."

I let the remark go, but for some reason this made a lump grow in my throat. Why would this make me so emotional? As I began to black out I realized that in a hunger-induced stupor I had eaten my napkin. Again. A nice glass of water fixed that.

Our waitress floated over to our table with coffee for me and steaming hot tea for your mother.

"Are you folks ready to order?" she asked, setting our drinks on the table from the tray she carried.

"How is your breakfast buffet?"

"Oh," she said refilling our water glasses, "very popular and very good. All of the usual breakfast stuff, a wide array of breakfast meats plus some very nice freshly baked cinnamon rolls, danish, and some wonderfully ripe locally grown fruit."

"By any chance do you have waffles?" I ask on behalf of your mother. As for me I'd already decided. She had me at "meats".

"We do! We have a waffle maker, and some delicious strawberries and whipped cream if you want."

I think I actually saw your mother drool.

"We'll both have the buffet," Mom added quickly, as if the waffles were going to evaporate before she could get the sentence out of her mouth.

"Okay," Denise - for that was the name stitched on her prison uniform - said, taking our menus. "Plates are out there," she pointed to the atrium, "help yourself when you're ready."

I swear, we sprinted to the long table of food faster than a pack of feral German Shephards chasing a pair of late-spring Mormons.

Mom dove for the waffle maker, but not before saying with that same evil grin, "but what if we DO want waffles?" Your mother can be quite funny. This wasn't one of those times.

As for myself, I was in meat Nirvana. There were chafing dishes overflowing with ham, maple smoked ham, thick-sliced bacon, thin-sliced bacon, pepper bacon, sausage patties, sausage links, venison sausage, drifter sausage (WTF? Well that would explain the lack of hobos and transients in this neck of the woods.), scrapple (sausage mixed with cornmeal then fried - I KNOW! It made my knees go weak.), polish sausage, and finally turkey bacon. Considering the meaty spread, I thought the turkey bacon an interloper and refused to give it any real estate on my plate. In the end it didn't matter. I promised myself that I wasn't going to go overboard, but wound up with a plateful of meat that would have gagged an emaciated hyena.

Mom had long since returned to our booth. With a cane in one hand, and the contents of a well stocked butcher shop carefully balanced in the other, I weaved my way through the stares and slack-jaws and took my place across from your mother.

"So," she said, looking over my plate, "should I get the defibrillator, or do you think you'll be able to navigate to the hospital on your own?"

"Funny woman. Such a funny, funny woman."

I glanced at her plate. I suppose that there might be a waffle under there but it was hard to imagine through the strawberries and - I mean this in all sincerity - a Matterhorn sized pile of whipped cream.

"Just sweets for you this morning babe?"

"Oh hush and eat your cardiac arrest," she grinned.

Nary a word passed between us for the next 15 minutes. I hadn't realized just HOW hungry we were. If anyone had tried to take our plates, they would have come away with a reduction of phalanges.

Ummm . . . phalanges. Those would have been delicious.

While I appreciated all of these fine Canadian meats, the one that I fell in love with was the sage pork sausage. Yum. No, double yum. I polished off the remaining bits of ham, the lone survivor if you will, the General Custer of my breakfast, and stood to brave another round. I knew that I would be sorry yet I cared not. I was an animal. An animal bulking up for a long winter to come.

Mom glanced up from the remains of her Belgian waffle and her eyes said 'Really?'

"Can I get you something while I'm up tiger?"

"No," she said, wiping a glossy strawberry glaze from her lips, "I'm stuffed." She leaned back in the booth with a contented sigh. "Are you really going back?"

"Watch me," I said as I walked back to what I now referred to as 'meat heaven'. It's just like regular heaven, only a tad greasier, and much more delicious.

I walked through the double-doors into the atrium and spotted trouble immediately. There were three men there, probably mid-fifties. What struck me is that all of them were unnaturally tall. One lanky and the other two a bit on the rotund side, all wearing cowboy hats and bolo ties and boots.

Ah, so that's the subject of this convention! It obviously was one big dress-up party. I only wish I'd been here on 'Dorothy Gale' day instead of 'Cowboy Bob' day. The skinny dude would have looked stunning in pigtails.

No matter. As much as I would have enjoyed seeing a herd of Canadian cross-dressers, these men were now nothing but an obstacle to my goal of clogged veins. There they stood chatting, blocking access to the delicious, delicious meats. Pattering on about cattle and fences and veterinarian bills and how much they disliked sheep farmers, but agreeing they were preferable to hippies. I was astounded by their attention to detail. These guys took their 'dress up' days quite seriously. Kudos to them. You have to commit to something like that to really carry it off.

I was more than happy to wait patiently as they laughed and joked their way down the table, taking a little here, a little there. Perfectly happy that is, until I realized that there were only eight sage sausages left. Eight lonely little sausages. But still, that was okay. Plenty for all.

The small guy passed by these tubes of deliciousness completely. The second guy - oh oh - took two. Panic began to swirl about my carnivorous soul. I had to act quickly lest disaster strike. I maneuvered, quite deftly I thought, to a spot near the sausage. Think man! Think! Time was precious. The guys gave me a cursory glance, but went on with their conversation. I could see the last man eying the sausage. This may call for drastic measures.

Drastic measures indeed.

I did the only thing I could. I'm not terribly proud of what I am going to tell you, but it was sausage after all. You understand.

I began bobbing my head, ducking and weaving my body. "Bat!" I screamed. "Dear God it's a bat!"

Ha! That brought them up short. Their eyes widened as they scanned the hall and the vegetation therein, half ducking in anticipation of death from a dive-bombing, disease ridden tiny winged rodent.

"There!" I shouted, and pointed at an imaginary spot across the atrium, and fairly high in the air. "Oh Lord, here he comes! It's HUGE!!!"

I put a hand to my mouth and made a series of "thwup-thwup-thwup" noises in a very realistic impression of bat wings.

Whereupon the guys scattered like chickens in a thunderstorm, running behind the table for cover.

"Watch out for your hair!" I screamed. "For the love of God, don't let it get in your hair!"

This seemed to be the universal signal for complete panic. As they ran, hither and yon, ducking, bobbing and weaving, I took the opportunity to shove the remaining six sausages in my mouth. So delicious. For added measure I took the two off the guy's plate as well.

Don't get that look on your face - I'd earned them.

Adding a final, 'Here it comes again!' garbled through my mouth of greasy sausage, I beat a hasty retreat back to the safety of your mom where she sat in the booth, half wondering, half dreading, whatever, or whomever it was causing all the commotion.

I grabbed my coffee, and gulped it dry, washing the spicy, wondrous evidence down my throat. An unexpected and hearty burp passed over my teeth. "Excuse me dear." I patted my bulging stomach. "Ummm . . . Not to alarm you, but it might be a good time to take our leave."

"Oh no David . . . what did you do?"

"You know," I said with a touch of reproach, "some wives don't automatically assume their husbands guilty. Why would you think I had something to do with the ba. . .", I caught myself, "with whatever was going on in there?"

"Stop it. I heard you fake-screaming like a little girl. Plus, you had a sausage sticking out of your mouth when you ran inside."

Curse you delicious meats, you have undone me again.

"There may be a small, flying-rodent problem in the atrium. Doesn't matter," I said, slapping enough cash on the table to cover our bill plus a hefty tip. "Come on come on come on! Time to hit the old road!" I tapped my cane on the floor. "Daylight's burning." I glanced at my wrist to an imaginary watch, "Tad behind schedule here."

Mom followed me as I hobble-sprinted (Damn you cane! I should have brought my crutches. I am on Olympic runner with crutches), but there wasn't much enthusiasm in her effort.

"I need to use the restroom on the way out," she said.

"Oh, no time dear. We'll stop at the first rest area we come across. We really need to leave." She looked at me blankly. "Trust me," I added. I had no interest in exploring the local jail, branded as a 'sausage thief'. Too many misunderstandings packed into that moniker to be doing time - Canada or not."

As we power-walked through the lobby to the parking lot, I note the staff arming themselves with fishing nets and brooms and what I think might have been a can of insecticide, running full-tilt towards the restaurant. They didn't give us a first glance, let alone a second. HA! Once again my carefully calculated ruses had saved us.

We opened the double glass doors to walk outside, and I noticed a printed white piece of paper hastily taped to the door that brought me up short. In fact, not one but 3 pieces of paper. I was sure the flyers were advertising some local festival or event, but upon closer inspection the paper read:

"**WARNING. You are in Bear Country!! Be Bear Aware!**" Above the text they had printed a large, clip-art bear paw.

As we passed I point the signs out to Mom. "Well, that's a little odd, isn't it?"

"Yeah. I saw those on the way in. Do you think it's a Bear Festival of some sort? Or a Band?"

"Either that," I say, holding the door open for her, "or something to give the tourists a thrill."

We laughed it off and made our escape. Yet as we drove back to the highway I pondered if the zombie vibe I felt earlier was really a bear vibe. Or, worse than that - bear zombies. You can keep your Bear Calvary, bear zombies would rule the earth. I decide not to share this tidbit with your mother as she spooks quite easily and I didn't need her to be sitting on the back contemplating death by bear zombies for the next few hours.

Back on the highway with full stomachs, full petrol tanks (oh no . . . I had been infected with kanuckadoodle slang), and our head full of dreams of the ride to come, we journeyed henceforth into the complex tapestry that is Canada. A bit greasier to be sure, but anxious for the marvels to come.

Out of the corner of my eye, I catch a few clouds drifting over the peaks surrounding the town, but don't give them another thought. Nothing is going to spoil this day. Nothing. I smile, drop the hammer, and we rocket into the mountains.

Literally.

*   *   *

You ever notice how things look closer on a map?

Again we are sailing along a chain of lakes, drinking in the scenery like, like . . . like someone thirsty for scenery. No traffic, just miles of winding roads, forests and mountains. Picture perfect. It is a repeat of our early morning minus the primal hunger. The bike is running like a dream, Mom is relaxed on the back, and I'm shredding the corners. Life is good. This is the vacation we sought. True, I'm a tad sleepy as my stomach tries to decide whether to digest my breakfast, or to shoot it straight out of my mouth, but all is well. I vowed to keep my ill-gotten sausage down. Not to brag, but I can handle my meats.

I notice a sign for a rest stop - thank you Ceiling Cat! - just as I had promised your mom. Did I tell you Canada is lousy with rest stops? All very nice, and very clean, and usually centered around some geographic or historic curiosity. Although I wonder if this is less a community service than an attempt to mask the notoriously weak Canadian bladder.

It might also be a government mandate. Are Canadians, by law, forced to urinate every 50 miles? Is there a compulsory hydration program of which we are unaware? Will I be questioned about my bathroom habits when I cross back into the US? ("Okay Mr. Moore, says here that you consumed 50 liters of beverages on your vacation, but we were only able to account for 42 liters. You'll have to park over there until Canada gets all of her moisture back.") How did they manage to make everything so convenient? Did someone get a grant? Was there an elected official with a potty obsession? Just what are the oversights of these bureaucrats?

See? These things keep me up at night.

Where was I? I'm old and my mind tends to wander. And suddenly I have to pee.

Oh! The rest stop! Okay, so we come to the rest stop beside this absolutely GORGEOUS blue-sparkled lake nestled at the base of a particularly spectacular mountain. The sun is shining, the birds are singing, at least I think they are. Canadians like to drive fast. I mean FAST. No, even faster than that! So I can't really hear too much other than an occasional sonic-boom as yet another SUV blows by. There are two driving speeds in Canada: One; so slow you want to tear *your* face off, and two; so fast you want to tear *their* face off.

It's like the 'Fast and the Furious' without the 'Furious'. More like the 'Fast and Extremely Cordial'. But I'm from "THE STATES", so, I'm a rebel - an 'Merican. I go any damn speed I want. I shift out of Warp 3, slow, make the turn, and glide down the gently sloping parking lot to the edge of the lake, do a quick "swoosh" of a u-turn, and then point the bike uphill for an easy egress.

There is one other car here, with a young woman that casts furtive and concerned glances in our direction, but relaxes as we de-gear and she hears us talk to each other in loving tones. It would have been great fun if Mom would have jumped off the bike, ripped off her helmet, and back-handed me as she screamed, "Why you stop the bike bitch? Did I TELL you to stop the bike?". But alas, she does not, so we are immediately cast as 'the-cute-older-couple-on-the-motorcycle-that-are-obviously-in-love-and-having-a-great-time-and-will-probably-not-stab-me-in-the-heart'.

I know, it's a curse, but someone has to bear the burden of giving the world hope - might as well be us. The point being, I watched her visibly relax. A little. Although, somehow I had a feeling this girl was in a constant state of flummox.

We scamper to the building housing the facilities, and after a much needed break we walk together back towards the bike. The young woman is still there and still nervous.

She is in her twenties. Are all women in Canada in a perpetual state of mid-20s? Probably. Although, on second glance this young lady might have been a bit older. Not more than 35 anyway. Slender, but not with the 'I-just-ate-a-sandwich-and-I'll-be-full-for-a-week-unless-I-throw up' kind of look, but rather a 'I'm-very-active-and-I-like-to-hike-and-listen-to-Dave   Mathews-on-my-Ipod-and-I've-had-lattes-named-after-me-in-the-coffee-shop-where-I-play-my-guitar-on-Saturday-afternoons-so-I'm-more-hip-than-you-are' look. More than likely a Vegan. She doesn't have the look of meat about her, if you know what I mean.

Mom and I walk down to the edge of the lake and the girl, with some alarm in her voice, yells, "Watch out for the toads!"

Mom and I look at each other, scan the parking area, and then look at each other again. I see no toads. Mom sees no toads. There ain't no stinkin' toads around here.

"They're all over the place!", the girl remarks with more than a bit of agitation as she makes a broad sweeping gesture of the parking area, the lake, and the grass beyond, "I don't want any more to die."

Now that's a curious statement, I think to myself. I look again for toads. I even look in the trees. Maybe this is the nesting place of the elusive Canadian Hawk-Toad that I have read so much about in journals of lesser credibility. But no, nary a Hawk-Toad to be seen. However, I have my wits about me, and decide that a gentle approach to this delusional female is the correct response rather than, *'What the fuck are you talking about?'*.

"Well of course not," I answer gently, ever so gently, and begin to back away slowly, ever so slowly. "Who would?"

Still, I see nothing. Nary a toad, nor toad-like creature anywhere. Mom looks at me questioningly. I shrug my shoulders, and nod towards the bike intimating it may be time to depart, stage left.

"I don't know what to do, it just makes me so sad.", the girl says.

"And who can blame you?", I say, in what I hope are non-judgmental tones as I tug at Mom's arm, smiling but careful not to show too many teeth in case she interpreters my smile as an act of aggression and strangles me right there in front of God and everybody with her Ipod cord while the last words I hear on this earth are some Indie band singing, *'Everybody says they love me but I know better, 'cause I'm alone. So utterly alone.'* And as we both know, that just ain't right. That's not a warrior's death.

Now believe me, and all kidding aside, (I KNOW there are no Hawk-Toads. That's just a slogan to sell T-Shirts to the tourists), I'm still looking for the toads. I *want* to believe her. This girl is VERY concerned - very genuine in her dismay, but despite my best efforts I'm seeing nothing. With all my heart and soul I hope to see a toad, just so I can put her at ease. Validate her reality, if you know what I mean. But nada. Zip. The big EL Zero on the toad front.

Yet obviously, the girl is sensing something. In a rush of mental activity I ponder many things: Are invisible Canadian Toads poisonous? Is this what the border guard was trying to warn us about? Is the girl insane? On some really, really good drugs?

Or is she the victim of some enchantment. Maybe she and her boyfriend were just sitting there, enjoying the view of the lake and the mountains, when an evil Witch pulled up in an old beat-up Chevy Nova with rust spots and a "Kill the Vegans" bumper sticker, flipped them off (presumably because they looked like they might be Vegans, or know Vegans, or just have a fondness for vegetables), and turned said boyfriend into a swarm of invisible Toads. It happens you know. Random curses like this occur far more frequently than anyone cares to mention. The Gummit just doesn't like to admit it because really, what are you gonna do to protect yourself against something like that?

Maybe the girl is simply mistaken. Maybe later her boyfriend will show up, after a leisurely stroll around the lake and she will beat him within an inch of his life for making her worry. It's the feminine way.

"They're so tiny," the girl says to Mom, and kneels down on the pavement to point at what I think is a piece of gravel, but turns out to be a hopping piece of gravel that motates quite quickly towards the water several feet away. Funny behavior for gravel, I think, but hell - this IS Canada. Stranger things have happened. As evidenced by the girl having her boyfriend turned into an invisible swarm of toads by an evil, vegan-hating witch not more than an hour before our arrival.

Mom kneels down next to the girl and motions me over with a frantic wave of her hand. "Hey! David! Look at this!"

I look to where the two kneeling women are pointing, and realize that it's not magical hopping gravel at all, but a tiny, tiny little frog. Or Toad. Whatever. These things at their biggest are about the size of a dime, and literally ALL OVER THE FRICKIN' PLACE! Really! How could I have not seen them before? There must be thousands and thousands of these little buggers! They are all over the road, all over the grass, all over the shore of the lake.

It gives me the willies. I mean, just how fat was her boyfriend?

This is not a good development. I would have to tread carefully here. You know how your mom feels about amphibians. It's a close race between frogs and squirrels and birds and raccoons and stray cats in Mom's bestiary of love. She was enthralled. Nay, smitten even, and began to take numerous pictures and copious amounts of video of this miracle of nature. I feared, now that Mom was held in a toady-spell, that we may never leave this parking lot.

Regrettably, another car pulls into the rest stop at this time. I can hear the 'crunch crunch' of tiny lives coming to an abrupt end underneath tires. Now, fully engaged in the National Geographic moment, all I want to do is save the frogs. Or toads. Whatever. Your mother has infected me with the spirit of nature. I want to wave the car off, but really - there is nothing I can do. It is the balance of natural world. If by balance you mean tiny dime-sized frogs in fierce battle with car tires for their niche in nature. Or toads. Whatever.

The girl, enthusiastically friendly now that Mom and her share a love of all things croaky, explain to us that this is an annual migration. That the frogs, (or Toads - although they look like frogs to me - and I've seen many frogs in my day. I can tell by the color and the eyes and the hoppity-hop-hop motions), come down the hillside across the road, make their way to the lake, and then party like it's 1999 in Toadville. She recounts, in graphic detail, how they had to install a 'Toad Bypass' underneath the road, and into the parking lot because in years past, and I quote, "After a few hours, the road would become very, very slick with dead toads and it was causing many, many horrible accidents."

Yeah. Hitting, what I can only visualize as a 'smear' of toads at speeds just below the sound barrier on a slight corner would be a bit tricky. In fact, it would probably be like hitting an ice-sheet in the middle of a Tokyo Drift. (See, I'm hip...I'm with it.) Oh sure, it would be all laughs for a split second, then WHAM. Who wants that in their Obit? "Henry was driving like a typical Canadian maniac and bought it on Toad Smear Curve."

Wait a minute. On second thought . . . that would be an AWESOME Obit!

Mom is now wandering around the grounds, lost in a euphoric trance celebrating the natural splendor of thousands of tiny frogs. There is a twinkle in her eye. A faraway look that comes from deep concentration. I know that look, and it scares the Bee-Jeebus out of me. She's thinking that we need to find someplace to buy a couple of tons of bugs to feed these little darlings. I must get her out of here. Time is short. I've lost her to the squirrels. I've become second banana to the birds. I'll be damned if these froggy-toads are going to replace me in her heart. I turn to talk to her and she's gone. She's all over the place. How can she move so fast? One minute she's down by the lake's edge. Next I see her over by a concrete curb that separates the parking area from the grass, squealing with delight.

It's become quite obvious. She's been possessed by Amphibiana - Goddess of the Frog. Or toad. Whatever.

"Aren't these the cutest things you've ever seen?"

I must admit, although not aloud, and not to her, that while not the cutest thing I've ever seen, they are certainly right up there on the scale of adorablility.

"They are amazing", I agree. But you know sweetie, it's getting late. We've got about 300 miles to go. Probably should be heading back on the road."

Thoroughly enchanted, Mom feigns deafness.

Another car comes into the rest area. Vegan folk-singer-latte-sipper girl makes a run to get the car to stop but too late - another hippity of toads has met its fate.

Don't look at me that way, a 'hippity of toads' is an actual term describing a grouping of toads. Or frogs. Whatever. It's like a 'herd of elephants', or a 'murder of crows', or a 'retch of Republicans'.

What . . . you doubt me? Look it up on Wikipedia. Wait . . . give me a minute . . . . just a sec . . . . and done. It's on Wikipedia now so you know it's real.

Schedule or no schedule, the hand writing was on the wall. I'm no genius, but I can see that if we don't leave soon, this has the potential to cast a pall over the vacation. I don't want this to be remembered in my later years as "Frog Kill Trip", (Or toads . . whatever). I put an arm around Mom, share a toad moment with her, then casually pull her towards the bike.

A couple of other cars have pulled into the rest stop as I steered Mom towards the Vision. Latte-slurpin' hippie-girl is now cornering other travelers, going over the same story with each visitor. Some feign interest. Others are truly disturbed. One group of tall blond men, possibly a gaggle of quintuplets, ignored her completely.

In a flash that sears my brain I realize that this girl is not a hippie. No, she is something far worse . . . she's an Emo-toadie. I can hear the plaintive wails of her song as she strums her guitar, bringing her gut-wrenching experiences to the dozen or so people that are either near death and unable to escape the coffee-shop couch, or, and this is a worst-case scenario, supportive of her art.

"I'm so sad for my toadie friends. Nobody loves them. Nobobdy loves them. Just like meeeeeeeeee....oh just like meeeeeeeeee. We all wind up as paste on the road of lifeeeeeee."

I swear to all that is holy, I'd hurl a day-old cruller at her head if I were to hear that song then burst my eardrums with a pencil for good measure.

Anyway, I manage to get Mom back on the bike, and with a wave and a hearty roll of the throttle I weave our way through Frog Fest 2008, (or Toad Fest . . . whatever!!!), and manage to make it to the highway with nary a crunch neath our tires.

It takes us a few minutes to find our rhythm. But eventually, I clear my head of toads. I can feel Mom behind me, cocooned in warty-green thoughts, relaxed and smiling. The air is clear, the sky is blue - although, it seems to be clouding up a bit to the north. Nothing to worry about I assure myself. Relaxed, refreshed, and rejuvenated the road rolls out before us like the tongue of a giant dog on a hot, hot day. But without the terrible smell. Or the spit. So maybe not exactly like a giant, hot, dog tongue but you get the picture.

I glance down at my new compadre, Sweet Alice, cradled on the dashboard of the Vision. Never tell your mom - but my love for her grew by leaps and bounds as the miles ticked away. I love her. I love her so hard. Even if we have our little spats now and then, she fulfills my needs like no map ever could. Techno-lust pure and simple. What? Again with the 'I've never heard of 'techno-lust'? There's a complete page with references and annotations on Wikipedia. You can look it up. Wait . . . . . wait a second . . . . okay. There's one there now. Go educate yourself for goodness sakes.

Ah . . . good times . . . good times.

Funny thing about what Sweet Alice is showing me. It looks like this road, a very major road by Canadian standards, it's about to end. Abruptly. In about 5 miles. (Or about 9 kilometers in Can-speak.) Ending directly into a huge lake. I blink, thinking I've seen wrong. No, there is no mistake, the road just ends.

I lean back in the seat, and motion for Mom to raise her visor. "Hey, get a load of this. The road just ends. It runs into a lake."

"Really?" Mom says. "Well, is there another road we can take?"

"Funny thing, that," I answer, trying to mask the panic in my voice, "No. According to the GPS, this is the only road. For like . . . miles."

"Oh," Mom says, with no surprise in her voice. "Is there a bridge?"

I consult the oracle of Sweet Alice. "Ummm . . . no."

I zoom out on the map. There is a dotted line across the lake labeled "Ferry".

"It says we have to take a ferry," I tell her, just as we pass a sign that says "Shelter Bay - Galena Bay Ferry 10 km."

"Cool!" Mom replies and settles back in her seat. She loves Ferries.

"Yeah," I agree, and pull down my face-shield.

I'm thinking that a ferry ride is going to be a nice little break. And how pretty is this going to be? I mean we are in the middle of INCREDIBLE scenery. There's no wind. The sun is. . . hey . . . where did the sun go? I hadn't noticed that. Ah well, it is still warm.

So there are a few clouds. Big deal. We may get a sprinkle or two. Just a passing summer storm. I'm a Seattle boy. I can take it.

I mean. . . how bad can it get?

Right?

September 23, 2008

Dear Amber,

I hope you enjoyed these installments on what has turned out to be quite a trip. Buckle up - we haven't even reached the good stuff yet.

Oh! I watched "An Officer and a Gentleman" last night, and "Top Gun". If they try and give you the call sign 'Goose', run and don't look back.

Love you,
Daddio

P.S. Your car was stolen and set afire last night. It was the coolest thing I've ever seen.

Chapter 4

Ferry of the Damned

A few more minutes and we see the sign for the ferry. We follow the only path available to us which I now notice is wet. It looks like it may have sprinkled a bit in the last hour. Down we go and start a rather steep descent towards the lake.

We had been gently climbing for the last mile or two, but I hadn't realized just how much. We came around a bend in the road, and saw a line of cars parked on the incline, waiting to board the boat. I cruised behind the last car in the queue, turned off the bike and set her gently on the kick-stand. I stayed on the bike while Mom climbed off the back. I didn't want to leave the bike unattended. Did I mention how steep the hill was? Think of one of the hills heading to the waterfront from downtown Seattle. But without the bums. Or the smell of urine. Actually, replace the vagrants with tourists, and the smell of urine with the smell of trees, and the saltwater with fresh water, and the . . . well, this is just getting silly now. It was steep. Let's leave it at that.

Anyway, we are sitting there with nary a boat in sight. Now what?

"I wonder how much this will cost? Not that I really care, and not that we have a choice, but I'm curious."

Mom pulls off her helmet, and attempts to smooth her hair. It is a lost cause. I don't tell her that though, because I like my teeth.

"I don't know," Mom says, "I don't even see any signs listing the charges."

By this time a few other cars have pulled in line behind us. People are getting out of their vehicles, stretching their legs, walking their dogs, and generally doing what people do when they wait for a ferry. Two teenage girls, carrying a bag of chips, explode from the car behind us and run down the ramp bursting with giggles and squeals to see if they can spot the boat. The woman driving the car climbs out, yells after the girls to be careful, then sort of loiters by the driver's side door.

Mom and I give her a quick smile and nod of our heads in a "Look at us, we are friendly American types from THE STATES and will not harm you. Probably. Mostly.", which seems to put her at ease. I hate to generalize like this, but these Canadians are way too trusting. I smell an opportunity.

Anyway, she strolls over, gives the bike a good once over and says, "Wow. That is a really nice bike."

I love her immediately. The way to a man's heart may be through his stomach, but the way to a biker's heart starts with "Wow. Nice bike."

Of course, as is normal, she then proceeds to tell us every horror story in her repertoire associated with a motorcycle. It's mandatory you know. When people do this, all I hear is the line from 'Christmas Story', *"You'll put your eye out with that!"* Evidently, she had known many a good man that had, through no fault of their own, spontaneously combusted while riding a motorcycle. But not before their legs were ripped off by vicious moles. And their arms, well, they simply fell off. Fell like over-ripe plums in a summer breeze. Not really a reason for the arm thing other than they were on a bike. She never came out and said it, but strongly implied that what else could one expect from such a lifestyle?

Once she finishes with her itemization of accidents, deaths, severed limbs, halitosis and chronic constipation, we strike up a proper conversation. She's Native American. Although in Canada, "Indians", as they are sometimes referred to by the less educated, are called "Carl". No wait . . . that's not right. They are referred to as "First Nation People". Although she calls herself an Indian. And maybe Carl. The sociological structure of Canada is highly confusing to me.

She looks at our license plates. "Oh, you're from THE STATES!"

Yes. Yes we are. And we are not armed. Probably. Mostly.

We continue talking. We learn that she and her granddaughters, who are now running back up the hill at a pace that makes me want to sweat or puke, I can't decide, have been camping for the last week with their extended family at an annual reunion. I think she said there were 60 or 70 people at this particular gathering. I'm impressed. I could barely manage the 11 of us in Winthrop. For three days. I give her a silent, 'Well done good lady, well done'.

The girls have now joined us. Sweeties. Probably 10 and 12 or 13, but not in that stage of what I fondly refer to as the "Pffffftttttttt" years. As in, whenever you ask a question of a child in this stage of development, you get the same answer. "How was school today?" Answer: "Pffffffftttttttttt." "Would you like some toast?" "Pffffffffftttttttttttt." "Shall I kill you with a brick, or would you prefer to be dumped by the side of the road to be ravaged by a homicidal postal driver with a speech impediment?" "Pffffffftttttttt."

We chatter away. Time passes. Seasons change.

I ask Carl how often the boat runs, and how much it costs.

"Oh, it doesn't cost anything. There's no roads up here you see. No way to get across the lake. So the government has to provide some way across, and there's no way they could charge for that," she chuckles.

I don't say anything out loud, but I beg to differ. In THE STATES they would have found a way to charge you, tax you, and made you feel guilty for even driving up here in God-knows-where in the first place.

"The boat runs every half-hour. Or every hour." She pauses. "Or maybe hour-and-a-half." She shrugs. "It'll get here when it gets here."

She looks at the long line of cars in front of us, and looks at the trucks backing up behind us. "Hope we all fit. It isn't a very big boat."

In my mind's eye I picture a smallish canoe with a Canadian Mountie in the bow, decked to the nines in his traditional uniform. The canoe powered by tame beavers. Now there's a thought: can you tame a beaver? That would ROCK! I would lash like six tame beavers to a rowboat and have them pull me around. Ah someday . . . the good life. What would you call a group of beavers? I think a bevy. A bevy of beavers. A bevy of beavers at my beck and call.

Damn I crack me up.

Mom and I prepare ourselves for a long, long delay. I hadn't figured this little escapade into our schedule, and although it is still early in the day I'm beginning to get a bit concerned about exactly what time we are going to arrive in Carnack, Alberta. We have Glacier and part of Banff National Parks to drive through, and although we will be on the Trans-Canada highway most of the time, I really, REALLY, want to get there before nightfall. For various reasons. Not the least of which is I promised your mom.

Suddenly the girls let out a squeal. "Oh . . . there's the ferry Grandma! It's coming!"

I look out into the brilliant blue water and am greeted with a pleasant surprise: There, skimming across the lake, gliding like a back-handed pimp-slap on a sweaty thug's face, is a ferry that looks like it will hold about 50 cars. Plenty of room. It's a one-deck, flat-bottomed craft with an elevated wheel-house off to the right side. Very old school, yet it looks fairly new. I notice it's hauling some serious ass in the water. It is, after all, staffed by the same speed-crazed maniacs that drive the roads around in these parts.

The ferry is moving faster than even I had realized, and before you know it everyone has bid adieu to their "line friends", crawled back into their vehicle, and started their engines. Mom and I hurriedly gear up, climb on the bike, and wait for the next phase of our adventure. But you know that odd feeling you get when you've been in line with someone and the conversation has run its course and then you realize that YOU'RE GOING TO THE SAME PLACE SO YOU ARE GOING TO BE WITH THEM FOR A WHILE YET ONLY NOW IT'S AWKWARD BECAUSE YOU DON'T HAVE ANYTHING ELSE TO SAY?

Yeah. That's how people were looking at us. Like they might just sit in their cars, pretending to be engrossed in what has become the most fascinating steering wheel they have ever seen, in order not to have to notice us standing outside their window. The ferry, in all its glory, has no seating - no room at all really except for the open deck.

It takes a bit for the ferry to unload. There are 18-wheelers. Campers. SUVs. Cars and delivery vans and trucks galore. We even get to see a small rear-end accident between a camper/trailer and a rental car as they exit the boat, so that's a bit of a spectacle. Really - you can't buy entertainment like that. We all slow and gawk as we board. In retrospect, I probably shouldn't have giggled like a maniac at the people exchanging insurance information, but what's done is done. You can't put the cat back in the box. It does no good to close the barn door after the horse has run away. Well, unless you want to spite the horse in case it wanders back. But if you do that, you also need to reinforce that you are spiting the horse, because as you well know, subtlety is usually lost on an equine. It would probably be best to tape a sign to the barn door that reads "I'M LOCKING THE BARN DOOR SO YOU CAN'T GET BACK IN. SO --- FUCK OFF HORSE!".

Seriously, you can't be too blunt with a horse.

Finally the line to board the boat begins to move. Slowly. Very slowly. So slow in fact that it made me contemplate if driving a 900,000 pound bike down an incredibly steep slope with Canadians fore and aft was really such a good idea. The brakes on the Vision are great . . . but man, did my legs wear out. I had to paddle that puppy most of the way. Of course, the insanely steep hill bottoms out and then climbs up an INSANELY steep ramp up to the level of the deck. For a moment I want traffic ahead of me to clear so I can gun this baby. Catch some air. I think if I did it right, hit the angle of the ramp at just the right speed I could probably not kill us.

Probably.

We wait our turn and the Ferry-folk point us to where we should park the bike. The space they have allotted us is maddeningly small, and they want me to pull so far ahead that the tire is almost touching the bulkhead. It is then that I notice something is amiss. Something is very, very wrong here. The staff manning the ferry are . . . well . . . there's no other way to put it - they're smiling. Smiling and friendly. Instantly my spidey-sense tingles. I hear General Akbar's immortal words echo in my head. It's a trap of some sort, of that I'm sure. I've ridden enough ferries in my day to come to understand how ferry staff should behave. They do not smile. They do not make eye contact. They sigh a lot. They're armed. They have all the personality of a pit-bull PMSing. I tense - just exactly what is your game, Canada? What diabolical schemes do you have for the people from THE STATES? Will they eat us? Are we the 'afternoon tea' for this boatload of maple-leaf worshiping hockey sacks?

Turns out my fears were unfounded. They were just nice. I'm not used to that kind of crap. I find it unsettling.

So we park and Mom debikes. Or disbikes. Or crawls off the frickin' thing. Take your pick. Another motorcycle pulls up behind us. It's a Suzuki S-50. They used to call them 'Marauders', I think. It's quite a bit smaller than the 800cc Suzuki C-50 that you ride - a bullet-proof cruiser if ever there was one - but it is still a good, solid bike none-the-less.

The person riding it is a young woman, and we find that she is very sweet and very shy. We strike up a friendly conversation, and I can't stop thinking of how much she reminds me of you and how much I wish your sister and you were here with us.

Peripherally I notice that the sky has taken on a bit of a dark tone, but about that time we are DELUGED with people wanting to talk about the Vision. I kid you not. We were surrounded. So much for my fear of awkward silence. You know those jungle movies - like Tarzan, or his lesser known cousin Mark - where the cameraman walks out of the bush and the natives appear, "plop, plop, plop", like they are being squeezed out of some unseen dimension? Yeah, like that. Only less bushier. Anyway, the point being that the deck is just jam-packed with these friendly northerners, and the cries of "aboot" and "eh?" and "shed-you-ell' are deafening. I begin to feel queasy. Too many smiles, too many "that there is an interesting bike, eh?". I contemplate throwing myself overboard, or faking a 30-minute coma, but I can't leave your mother to deal with this alone. Mom has problems of her own. She has her own group of admirers that includes the girl on the bike, the Pilot of the boat, (so who the F is steering?), and various passengers. I have a throng of guys around me, all talking about bikes. The various merits, or delinquencies, of every brand and model imaginable.

As you are aware, my knowledge of the history and lore of motorcycling is, like my knowledge of most other subjects, thin. Broad - yes. But thin and transparent and not much in the way of support. Thin like the ice of an October pond - and by that I mean - umm - really thin. Yet I manage to nod my head, smile and laugh at the appropriate times so after about 5 minutes I'm regarded as a genius with an encyclopedic knowledge of all things two-wheeled with a motor.

There's a guy who used to own a scooter and motorcycle shop in Kamloops, BC. This man is a living database of all things bikey. I have no idea what he's talking about nine-tenths of the time. We chatter away about the specs of the Vision and what I like about the ride. I always end one of the spiels with "Of course, there are a couple of things I don't like." Then I make something up. "The tires have too much air capacity," I'll say. "The headlight gets too hot." I pat the seat of the bike, "and the seat, well, I don't know about you, but I like to FEEL the road. With this thing, it's like I'm carried along on the wings of Angels." People love it when you do that. It gives you instant cred. Instead of a Brand Lemming, you are now a serious connoisseur of the riding experience.

He says, "So, do you prefer a Garbin-Frankle delimeter, or a straight beckner with the over-sized spootner?"

Gah!

I panic. I'm afraid that were I to falter in my authority the assembled group may pounce on me like a gang of wayward and drunken Weeblos at a Girl

Scout Convention. Some of these guys look like they wrestle moose. And win.

Think David. Think!!

"Well, there's much to be said for both. You're going to hear guys try and defend each one, but I think it comes down to a matter of personal choice. And really, isn't that what this whole crazy world is all about?"

Only, I say 'aboot', and it feels just fine.

He eyes me. The crowd goes silent. I feel my heart beating in my chest, the sound of blood rushing in my ears. I don't want to check, because it may be regarded as a faux-paux by my hosts, but I might have tinkled a bit in my chaps. It will dry when we are back on the road, I tell myself . . . it will dry.

His eyes grow wide. "That's just what I was telling my friend the other night!!! How can you say one is any better than the other?"

"Oh you can't," I quickly reply. "Anyone who argues that point, well . . . Pffffffttttttttt . . . that's just crazy-talk."

He turns to the man standing beside him, and points to me with a hitch of his thumb. "This guy knows bikes." To which the crowd nods in agreement.

I would like to look at the scenery as we cross the lake, but my adoring fans will have none of that. I am now THE NICE BIKER FROM THE STATES. I sneak a quick glance here, a look over my shoulder at the far shore there. As the ride progresses there are two things that I DO notice however, and they are:

1. Your mom is a now a celebrity.

2. Suddenly, it's getting dark. Very, very dark. And the water, which a few minutes before was as flat as a North Dakota ski resort, is now white-capped and slapping the sides of the boat.

Well isn't that curious, I think to myself before I'm dragged back into conversation.

"So tell me," one of my new-found friends asks, "after buying a bike like that, you must have ridden a Molokoi B-30. Right?"

You would think so," I say without missing a beat having yet not a clue as to what a Molokoi B-30 is, "but regrettably, I never had the chance."

"Really?" he asks, somewhat shocked. "They were all over the place in the late 70s and early 80s. Everybody rode one."

"Well, there you go."

Hardly noticing, I brush a few raindrops off of my bald pate' with the sweep of a fingerless glove. "That would have been about the time I was with the crew in El Salvado - - -" I feign a look of utter shock, with an exaggerated motion, I bite my lip. I bow my head, and bang on my brow with my fist. "Whoopsie. Let's pretend I didn't say that, shall we?"

They all nod in agreement. HA! I could have gone all Pirate on their asses and taken over the boat had I wanted, they were mine. You dodged one there, Canadian Maritime Fleet! But alas . . . as you have no doubt noticed, my quick wits and the ability to lie on the fly has painted me, yet again, into a bit of a corner.

I smile. All teeth and charm. I can't wait to hear what I'm going to say next.

Luckily, right at this particular moment, God intervenes. And as God is wont to do, takes a righteous whiz over the whole of creation.

And the rains . . . the rains they came a pouring down.

*　　*　　*

As a native North-westerner, you know that 'rain' comes in many flavors. There is the gentle 'mist' that creeps into every crack and crevice and soaks you to the bone in seconds. There is the 'light rain' that trickles down gently from the skies, and soaks you to the bone in seconds. There is the typical 'rain', as in "Hey, it's raining!", that pelts your skin and soaks you to the bone in seconds. There is the 'cloudburst rain', that comes from nowhere, and soaks you to the bone in seconds. Then we have the 'deluge', the big splattering drops that . . . well, soaks you to the bone in seconds.

These are the rains you know. Throw those conceptions right out the window. But first check to make sure there is no one walking on the sidewalk below. You don't need a lawsuit.

Oh, the first few drops were innocent enough. Sort of a "Hello, I'm rain. Pleased to meet you. Just passin' through. Just makin' the grass and the trees grow. Don't worry about me, I'll be on my way soon enough. You enjoy your day now."

Stupid rain. Once rain starts on a train of thought, much like a Pokemon aficionado or a model train enthusiast, it's hard to get it to shut up. So I became aware of this wet little bastard before anyone else on the boat. There are few advantages to being bald, but being the first to know when it's raining is right up there, second only to the ego stroke one receives from the never-ending stream of, "Hey! You have a really nicely shaped head." Every time someone says that to me, I think, "What the hell? Is it because they feel bad about me being bald? That's the only compliment they can think to say? Really? Would you tell a one-armed person, "Hey, the remainder of your arm is very cylindrical?

Or is it something else? Is the shape of my head so important that they feel the need to comment? I mean, it's not like I did anything. There are no special exercises to produce a 'nicely shaped head'. No creams, lotions, or injections. And what, I wonder , do my brothers with the less symmetrically shaped noggins hear? If human nature and past experience is any guide, it probably isn't pleasant. "Oh dear. Well, that's unfortunate, isn't it?" Or, "My, were you left on your back in your crib a lot as a baby?" Possibly, "Jesus! Did anyone live in the accident?" Why comment at all? How many times has someone come up to you and said, "Wow. That is a really attractive elbow you got going there." Or, "May I just say that is one round eyeball. Very nice." No. You never hear, "I don't want to be forward, but your knuckles are particularly attractive today." And why? Because . . . it starts . . . it's probably just . . . well I have no idea, but as your Great Uncle Jonathon the Priest used to say when referring to the Church's position on celibacy, "that shit's just gotta change".

Odd duck that Jonathon.

Within seconds a few pitter-pats of God-juice turned into something much darker, much uglier and definitely much wetter. Think of a drop of regular rain. Now give it steroids. Make it do dual workouts at the gym. Give it a subscription to "Bodybuilder's Monthly". Got a picture? Good. Now put seven of those together, squeeze them into a ridiculously small space like a Japanese commuter on an afternoon train, and you begin to see what I'm talking about.

When rain's big brother started falling, it actually stung my head - I kid you not. The drops were easily the size of quarters. And not wimpy Canadian quarters either, big burly 'real money 'Merican quarters' from THE STATES.

Ordinarily this would be no big deal. But I believe I have come to understand how a rock star feels: Groggy, confused, and unsure of their gender. No wait, that's not right. Unable to get away from people even when death is imminent, that's what I meant to say. I could not get my crowd of Canadians to shut the hell up long enough to put on some rain gear. Srsly. Each time I tried to make my way to the saddlebags, someone would come up with another question about the Vision. Or query my views on the nature of being, and whether we live in a self-constructed reality built from a mathematically provable 'fuzzy-cloud' of possibility spawning alternate dimensions that break from our own universe at every juncture of choice, or, are we simply existing in an illusionary prison of pre-determined fate. No lie. I thought that was a pretty insightful question for a third-grader. But apparently, other countries actually educate their young in the public schools, unlike in THE STATES where we are happy if they don't shoot each other. At least during social studies. And, since I was trying to maintain my new-found image as, "the-guy-you-think-is-living-the-life-you-dream-about-and-is-having-more-fun-than-you'll-ever-have-because-he-has-a-really-cool-bike-and-a-nicely-shaped-head-while-I-have-to-work-pushing-paper-for-people-I-hate-and-am-horribly-worried-about-that-lump-I-found-under-my-arm-when-I-took-my-shower-this-morning-oh-God-it's-cancer-IT'S-CANCER-I-just-know-it!!!!!", I just stood there like a moron and got wet.

Here is the really funny part: The people in my particular group would wander away, one at a time, AND PUT ON FRICKIN' SHIRTS AND JACKETS AND

HOODIES, then come back to tag-team each other, so the under-dressed could go put on some more appropriate clothes while the idiot from THE STATES gets soaked. Bastards. And you know why they acted so unconcerned? THEY HATE AMERICANS!

No, that's not true. They had things like . . . oh, I don't know . . . maybe HEATERS, AND ROOFS, AND DEFROSTERS, AND CUPS OF COFFEE IN LITTLE DOOR HOLDERS, and NICE SMELLING AIR FRESHENERS so that the rain was nothing more than a small bother.

Then, as if the cake were not sweet enough - thunder and lightning!

"Whoa," my scooter-selling friend remarked, "dats a bit of weather dere, eh?"

I wanted to shout "Ya think?" but I wasn't ready to alienate an ally just yet. Water was now dripping from my nose. Cascading. A nasal waterfall to rival Niagara. (Niagara. . . Viagra. What the hell?) My glasses were covered in streaks, and the parts that weren't dripping were foggier than Keith Richard's childhood memories. I could feel water running through my mesh, soaking my shirt, and beginning to drip into my 'nether regions'. I looked up at the sky. Bad mistake. Water poured into my nostrils, making me choke.

"Is it raining?", I gasped." Another flash of lightning, this one too close for comfort. "I hadn't really noticed," I added nonchalantly, as parts of me that are never supposed to be wet unless I'm swimming, bathing, or suffering a mild seizure, became saturated.

Saturated, cold, and shriveling by the minute.

"Oh yeah, we get some heavy weather here in dese 'ere mountains. Weather report said it was gonna rain this afternoon. In fact, they said it was gonna rain all week." He looked at me as I began to shiver. "Bummer dat, you being on the bike and all."

Show no fear . . . show no fear, I chant in my head.

"Pfffffttttt. We never let a little bad weather stop us," I managed to say through chattering teeth. "You know the saying."

He looked puzzled for a minute, glancing around at his fellow Canucks to see if anyone would volunteer the answer. None did. Crap. Now I was going to have to make something up.

"Well, they say. . . ."

Everyone leaned a bit closer.

"They say. . . ."

I falter. I need an ending - something dynamite. Several things go through my head. What do they say? 'Take your vitamins.' But I don't really see how that applies. 'Wear a condom.' Sage advice, but not appropriate for the circumstances. 'If life gives you lemons, take the frickin' things back and demand a refund, or at least an in-store credit.' That one is a possibility. 'There are two things in this world you should never trust - Carney Folk and mobile Dentists.' Solid wisdom right there, but again lacking that certain spark. 'If it's too good to be true you're probably hallucinating." Well, you can't argue with that. But. . . but. . . suddenly, inspiration strikes!

"It's NEVER Lupus," I say with a satisfied smile.

Ha Ha! Hoisted on your own petard! Refute that logic silly Canadians!

I would like to take a moment and ask you if you have ever experienced a blank stare? A truly 'cogs-turning-in-the-machinery-but-nobody-to-push-the-start-button' stare? Time slowed. Sound and motion stopped. I could feel the mood turning.

Did I really just say that? What the hell? Lupus? I realize that I may be suffering from hypothermia. Curse you Gregory House! Be gone demon doctor of the airwaves!

"I mean," I stumble, "that if you don't ride in the rain, it's not Lupus."

Well this is going nowhere. "No wait, I may have gotten my metaphors crossed. OH! I remember! If you don't ride in the rain, you're a *&$#@ pussy."

Protip: Profanity is always a proper choice and a good way to garner respect. It makes any situation more fun for everyone involved. But you knew that. You're in the Navy for God's sakes.

Had my ploy been successful? I look around at the faces staring at me for reassurance. The theme from "Jeopardy" is suddenly pumped over the boats PA system. My suspicions have been confirmed. The captain is an ass-hat.

"Oh," says scooter-boy, and offers a hearty laugh, "boy that there is the truth. You can tell the bar-hoppers from the real riders. You never see the bar-hoppers in the rain!"

The group agrees and we all share a good chuckle. Yet I see the signs, I know what will happen next. I've reached that certain plateau in my social skills where I go from absolutely amusing and entertaining to - and this is the absolute truth - dead on annoying. It's a short trip. I'm cold, wet, shivering, slightly confused and out of ammo. In other words, I got nuthin'.

Luckily the rain is now coming down so viciously that even the die-hards have no choice but to return to their vehicles.

After the mandatory, "Well, good luck with all that, eh?", I can finally turn my attention to your mother. Her group has scattered like a bag of dropped marbles, and all that is left of her entourage is her and motorcycle girl.

The time has not been kind. She - how can I put this gently - no matter how you slice it, she's not a pretty sight. Her hair is wet and matted and clumped to the side of her head like day-old oatmeal. Her mascara is running down her face giving the appearance that her eye may be leaking ink. Or dark, dark tears. I vote for the tears. We make eye-contact, and a silent thought passes between us. A shared observation between long-term companions that is understood immediately - there is no need to give it voice.

Although, had we chosen to speak, our communication would have been a simple "FUCKIN' A!!!".

I feel bad for the poor girl on the bike. With the enthusiasm of youth beaten out of her, she looks like the family dog that's been caught chewing on the baby one too many times.

I approach your mom cautiously. Tentatively. Careful not to make any sudden movements. "Hey babe, how you doing? Have I told you today how beautiful you look?"

To your mother's credit, she didn't punch me in the throat. I love vacations!

"Little wet, little wet," she says, in a voice that is the einsiest, tiniest, itsy-bittiest four or five octaves too high.

"Yep," I reply. It seems like I should add something else, but, as I said before, I got nuthin'.

The ferry picks this moment to blast its horn. I look around, dumbstruck, forgetting where I am for the moment. Then it comes back to me in a flash. I'm in Hell. And not a regular Hell, but a maple syrup swilling north-of-the-border-down-the-rabbit-hole Canadian Hell. I expect Gordon Lightfoot songs over the ferry's speakers system at any moment.

"Looks like we've made it to the other side," Mom says. "Do you want to dig out our rain gear, or should we wait to get off the boat and then pull over?"

I notice that we are HAULING ASS into the dock. It looks like we are quite a distance away, but everyone on board has started their engines. I trust they know what they are doing. But it may be that they just want to turn on their heaters. The temperature has dropped from a pleasant 77 degrees, (that's Fahrenheit - in Celsius it would be like 10 kilometers), to a chilly 60. Sometimes I really regret having a thermometer on the Vision's instrument panel. I KNOW I'm cold, I don't need it quantified. And lucky us, the skies are looking angrier and more foreboding with each passing minute.

"Guess we should put on the rain gear but I don't think we have time. Looks like we will be at shore in a couple of minutes. I'll pull over once we get off, and we can put the Frogg Toggs on then."

Mom nods approval.

It's now apparent that the skipper is winding the engines out to ramming speed. We may skip the dock altogether and just run this baby right up on shore Omaha Beach style. To no one's surprise but ours, he throws the engines in reverse at the last minute and we cruise at a civilized speed to the dock.

Now, I don't know if you've ever had this experience, but once in a while in life you will stumble across a situation where, earlier in the day you admired someone, then, through no fault of their own the situation changes and you pity them. That was us in a nutshell. As we disembarked none of our previous friends would look at us. If they did, it was to sneak a quick glance in our direction. But I knew what they were thinking. It was the same thing I would have been thinking had the situation been reversed. "Sucks to be you Chester!"

Yes. Yes it does. Thank you for noticing.

We wait our turn and I roll on the throttle and pull up the now rain-soaked steel ramp. Ever experienced the delight of a half-blind, (my glasses and visor were still fogged up), fish-tailing ride on a motorcycle up a steel ramp in the rain with maniac Canadians inches from the back of your bike? Trust me, not as much fun as it sounds. Then, just as our tires kiss the tarmac, it quits raining! Oh benevolent God in heaven, why must your sense of humor be so cruel?

At the top of the hill leading to the ferry is a small parking lot and a squat building that may be a smoke-house or a rest-room. I slow the bike, take a sharp curve and cruise into the lot. This looks like a good place to re-group, catch our breath, put on our rain gear, and attempt to think through the rest of our day.

"Well," I say, as I pull off my helmet with a definitive sucking sound, (Think of pulling a suction cup off of a sheet of glass, or Robert Downey Jr. circa 1995 from a post Oscar party with an open bar and a group of Colombian "fans".), "that was something, eh?"

Mom cocks her head slightly. "Did you just say 'eh?'

The woman I love looks at me with the eyes of a fish. Dead, terrible eyes.

"If you start talking like a Canadian I will be forced to kill you. Kill you dead. Right here. Right now. Do you understand? Get your rain gear on while I visit the rest-room and try to dry out a bit."

I think that this deserves a calculated reply but then my brain starts working and I decide to smile and pursue the path that has kept our marriage on the right track for almost 30 years - I keep my mouth shut.

Doing as I am told I get the gear out of the saddlebags and begin to put on the Frogg Toggs. These are great. Best investment in rain gear we've ever made. Light weight, breathable, and completely dry. It is a simple two-piece suit, with an extra long coat that fits over the high-rise pants so nothing gets where it shouldn't. The jacket even has a built in hoodie to go under your helmet should you so desire. They are fantastic. Except for one small, tiny little problem: I'm soaked to the bone already. I believe that may defeat their purpose. Like counting the calories in a Triple Burger with Cheese and an Insanely Large Fries after you've scarfed it in your car ducked behind, and slightly below, the steering wheel so no one will see what a horker your are.

When your mom gets back from the bathroom I have managed to put on my rain gear. Now, usually, this wouldn't be a huge accomplishment. In my defense it was the first time I had actually put on the Frogg Toggs. And it had been raining. And I was cold. And we were in a foreign land, with foreign customs, and everything was all "kilometer this", and "liter that", and "no it's not play money just because it's a different color and no that's not Bob Dylan's head it's the Queen for Christ's sake so stop giggling and fork it over." So when I tell you that I struggled for a bit, and through sheer determination and perseverance, managed to put the jacket on my legs, over my boots, and had a hoodie hanging from my crotch, (I thought it was just to make it easier to pee with the chaps), you'll understand and not think less of me as a rider. To my credit I discovered my blunder rather quickly. It may have been the howls of laughter coming from the cars passing me on the road. It may have been that when I tried to put the pants on my upper torso, I looked like a giant "V" and lunged hither-and-yon for a few minutes until I hit a light pole and realized something was amiss. But what it came down to was I just didn't feel comfortable with no hole for my head or slot to peek out through and the whole hoodie-in-the-crotch thing, the more I thought, was a dead giveaway. Typical 'Merican technology. You'd think something as complicated as this would have come with instructions.

It took your mom like 2 seconds to get the things on. She is such a show off.

By now the traffic from the boat is long gone, blasting at a break-neck speed to God knows where. I couldn't worry about them. We had our own place to go, and we were WAY behind schedule.

Nothing to do but get back on the road.

For the next two hundred miles, (or 8000 km in Canadianeese), we wind our way through some of the most beautiful scenery in the world. Nothing compares to the Canadian Rockies. They are unimaginably beautiful. The size, the sheer granite cliffs, the peaks reaching into the clouds lend an aura of antiquity that is rarely experienced elsewhere.

I would have probably enjoyed the scenic grandeur much more had the deluge from the Sky God not returned with a vengeance. But it gets better because what party would be complete without rain's other two friends? Fog and mist. Certainly not this one. Rain, fog, mist, and horribly, horribly wet roads. Oh! Did I mention through all of this splendor of nature that we were on the Trans Canadian highway which evidently is THE ONLY FRICKING ROAD IN CANADA???

So, if by enjoying the scenery you mean traveling at 80 miles an hour through mountain passes with heavy traffic tail-gating you at every turn while riding through a lake, then yeah - this was a stroll in the park.

You have to understand that I was concentrating so hard on keeping the bike upright and on the road that much of this portion of the trip is a blur. So, if I'm a tad scant on details you'll have to forgive me. At some point in the future I may be able to access the memories through hypnosis, but I seriously doubt it.

To give you the flavor of this leg of the journey you only need three words, a mantra so to speak. Learn them and repeat them for the next 4 hours. Rain. Mountain. Maniacs.

Yet, as I've come to learn, every dark cloud may have a silver lining, but it also has a much darker - and definitely evil - core. In fact, I've come to understand that the 'silver lining' much ballyhooed in lyrics and prose is actually a tin-foil hat for the cumuli-nimbus bunch. Dark clouds are, straight off their rocker, toys in the attic, monkeys in the fridge, bees in the glove box, fundamentalist Christian women with eyes open WAY to wide banging on your front door because you just happened to leave your 8 foot 'Christ on a Stick' neon "WWJD? He'd pick up some harlots and PARTY LIKE HELL" sign turned on and it's causing a row at Easter Services - bat-shit crazy. These Canadian clouds would just not stop hammering home their point. Whatever that was.

Oh yeah. . .it was "LET'S KILL THE GUYS FROM THE STATES. LOL".

Frickin' clouds typing in all caps and using leet. I hates 'em.

I thought of home. It was nothing but a distant memory.

Right then I knew one thing for certain: if we survived this vacation Mom was going to kill me.

And honestly, I couldn't blame her.

September 27, 2008

Dear Amber,

*I'm really having a hard time letting go of you being a Pirate.
Is it too late to change your course of study?*

*Love,
Daddio*

PS. You may want to ignore any notes posted to you by your friends on Facebook or in email. I couldn't sleep last night, and with a little sleuthing I found your password and login, so I posed as you for a bit.

Ever notice how sometimes things that seem hilarious at 3 AM, seem a little crude the next day? Ah well. Water under the bridge and all that.

P.P.S. Um . . . I may have taken a bit out of your bank account as well. It's ok. You owe me.

Chapter 5

The Road to Hell is Paved with Canadians

Did I mention it was raining?

As I said before, most of the trip was a blur. Literally. Riding in the dense mist of a rain-soaked road with spray kicked up by thousands of tires. Did you ever see the freeway during rush hour with a good rain pounding the pavement? If you're not driving through the thick of the storm it really is an amazing sight. A gray tunnel of dirty spray. But we WERE driving through it, and it took A LOT of concentration just to keep the bike going down the road. We were wet, tired, cold, and, as Mom pointed out numerous times, for some reason when she gets tired I get cranky. Luckily our communication was kept to a minimum, for each time I raised the shield to try to say something - surprise! A mouth full of oily Canadian road juice. Yum.

So we droned on and on and on. Through mountain passes. Through small towns. Through the heart of the Canadian Rockies. I don't remember much other than the recurring thought of 'Hey! We're going to die!', yet there were a couple of interesting moments worth mentioning.

At some point in the trip, I can't tell you exactly when, or exactly where, because I may have had an out of body experience where I was having warm tea and crumpets with the Queen, or Bob Dylan - it doesn't matter really except if it was Bob Dylan I should probably get some therapy because roving hands from the Queen is one thing, but from Bob . . . but I digress. The fact is at some point Mom had to pee.

Fine. I'll just whip this baby across three lanes of certain death and find her a bathroom because that's just the kind of guy I am. Far be it from me to point out that she has a bladder the size of a grain of rice. Did I mention I may have been a tad cranky by this point? Did I mention how hard it was raining? Take that and double it. Visibility was only a few hundred feet at best and often much less.

Finally, through the haze I spotted a sign for a 'Tourist Centre'. My hackles were up immediately. Which, with the cold, was quite painful. What abomination was this? What diabolical mind changed the spelling of 'Center' to 'Centre'?

Eff'n French Canadians, that's who.

Protip: Never trust a person that lives in one country, but believes they are in another. Aw screw that, I'm just trying to be politically correct here.

Protip: Never trust the French. Canadian or otherwise.

In my defense, I may have been slightly paranoid after all the excitement of the day.

As we fish-tailed down the road I explained to your mother that this place was most certainly a trap where tourists went in - but they never came out. Much like a Roach Motel. A horrible place of death and exported Canadian pot-pies, (New and improved flavor from THE STATES!"), to which your mom argued - quite successfully - that it was NOT some cannibalistic house of horrors, merely a bathroom and some brochures. Possibly a Mountie. Certainly a stuffed Beaver or two.

I resisted stopping, but in the end I capitulated to ensure domestic harmony. Oh, it took some convincing on her part, but the phrase that sealed the deal, and made me pull into the 'Tourist Centre Du Death' was, "I want you to stop now. You should know I've fashioned a 'prison shank', and I will stick it hard and quick between your fourth and fifth rib. . . straight into your liver."

I have no idea how, or when, she had the time to fashion a 'prison shank', but that's not really the point. I thought it over for a minute and was going to call her bluff but two things prevented me from taking that action:

1. Your mom had A LOT of time to sit on the back of the bike and think while enduring the rain.

2. I felt a sharp object, pressing hard against my Frogg-Toggs in the region of my kidneys. I calculated the risk. She may, or may not know exactly where my liver was located, but the point was moot. She was prepared to do damage, and in the end quibbling about whether I was hemorrhaging out of a liver or a kidney didn't seem all that important.

So I closed my eyes and change lanes at 649 LPH. LPH. That's Liters Per Hour. Finally, I'm getting the hang of this Satanic measurement system. My eyes are closed because I'm not stupid - I don't want to see death coming. After a few seconds of leaning the bike I figure I'm either in the right lane or on the shoulder about to plummet into a ditch. Either way we are coming to a stop, the question is how fast? You know how much I like surprises.

The gods were favoring us and I maneuvered safely to the right turn lane and gently braked to take the exit to the Centre. I breathed a sigh of relief. I hadn't realized how tired I was, or how much I needed to use the Loo until we were circling the building, looking for a parking spot.

This wasn't a rest area - no small port-o-potty for this place - it was a huge building with a parking lot that could accommodate more than a few large buses. However, only a few cars populated the stalls nearest the building and we had our choice of where to put the bike. I pulled into a slot a bit away from the other steaming vehicles. Mom hopped off the back the second the bike stopped moving. Evidently she wasn't kidding when she said her need was urgent.

"Sorry. Come and meet me inside," she said, and sprinted in the direction of the door. Although 'sprinted' may be too strong of a word. She hadn't even stopped to take off her helmet.

Which was probably a good thing, for now there was no rain - we were simply living in a lake with tiny air spaces between the water. How can I convey how she looked as she semi-bolted towards the rest room? Words fail me but I shall try my best. She looked large, bulbous, and sported a cherry-red helmet-shaped head. Layers of over-sized outerwear. Frogg Toggs that look like a haz-mat suit, and a strange, strange waddle to her walk that I can't erase from my mind to this day.

I turn away. I can't look anymore. What have I done to the woman I love?

It's about this time that I come to my senses, and realize I'm wet. Wet and cold. Wet and cold and confused and not entirely convinced that we are not about to encounter cannibals. Don't let anyone ever tell you that hypothermia can't be fun. I wanted to curl up next to the bike, on the black tarmac of that wet parking lot, and take a nice long nap. Slip sweetly into the river of sleep to ride forever on dream currents of fancy. The only thing that stopped me was that nagging urge to pee. The human body is an amazing thing. All kinds of checks and balances.

So rather than drift into oblivion, I busied myself locking up the bike, getting my collapsible cane from the trunk, and making my own way towards the Centre which, although it is less than 200 yards away (or 7892 grams) I can barely see through the rain and the fog and the mist. But I steel myself for I am from 'THE STATES' and will never give in, never give up, and never... ummm never . . . ummm . . . never go to bed without brushing my teeth.

Did I mention this place is big? Huge. As I approach the massive, wood framed double-glass doors I see a family milling about the entry way. Milling is like loitering only with more hand gestures. The family consists of three kids and two adults. Or maybe two adults, two kids and an evil troll - I didn't get a good look. Concern is written on their face like talentless graffiti on a police car window. Have you ever watched a dog trying to cross a busy highway? That was them, trying to make a break for their vehicle between cloud-bursts and sprint for the car.

As I do the three-prong shuffle to the door they held each other close, the adults clutching their children's shoulder with the grip of a paranoid hawk. Evidently I was the deciding factor in their little dilemma. Right before I stepped up on the sidewalk they made a dash, flying past me with brochures touting "See Canada's Unspoiled Wilderness", and "Visit Lake Louise in Banff National Park", and "STDs The Canadian Way!" positioned over their heads like cub scout pup-tents.

Before you ask, I have no idea what's the difference between Canadian

STDs and regular, good ol' USA STDs. I don't think the family picked them for their content as the publication was large enough to shelter at least two of the trolls.

As I reach to open the doors, I catch a glimpse of myself reflected in the glass. I look like an alien astronaut that might have pulled a ham-string. Or is suffering from a really bad crotch fungus.

Now, as I peer inside, and before I pull the door open, I notice that the place is just chock full of older Canadians. Packed. There is a scattering of younger people, some families, (oddly enough, all fighting for the last of the STD pamphlets), and a few people that looked shell-shocked. This brings me up short, I mean . . . where the hell did they come from? I look to the parking lot, then back inside. Unless everyone of those Volvos and Subarus parked out there doubled as clown cars then something is amiss. It's like a doorway to another dimension. A dimension with a much higher population than ours, and with a penchant for Helen Reddy songs.

Oh Canada! Land of mysteries, why must you taunt me so?

I debated turning around and heading back to the bike, or stepping through the door to meet my fate, whatever that may be. In the end, I stepped through the door. I had to pee, and parallel Canadian Dimension or not I was willing to take the chance.

As I pulled open the glass a wave of welcoming heat blasted my face and hands, reinforcing how cold I really was. The heady aroma of tea and wood burning in a huge fireplace tickled my nose, and the cacophony of a hundred conversations assaulted my ears. At least until I stepped through the door. Then, like a record player winding down, the place went silent. Dead silent. Much like when the gunslinger pushes his way into the bar room of a spaghetti Western – if that happens you just know the shit is going down! Somewhere in the recesses of the Centre the dying notes of a honky-tonk piano plucks its last discordant notes, and the echo of the tuneis-interruptus hangs as heavy in the air as smoke in a Junior High bathroom.

I swear that for a brief instant, as I hovered in the threshold, a bolt of lightning struck behind me, outlining me in blazing glory. Hundreds of beady Canadian eyes fall on me. I spy a couple of stuffed Mounties on a table and a couple of beavers manning an information counter. I shake my head. Those aren't beavers, just some sort of Canadian Ranger with an abundance of facial hair. On the guy it was okay, but the woman . . . well not so much. And the Mounties on the table turned out to be --- stuffed Mounties on the table. No doubt road-kill victims brought to the taxidermist so they could be put on display in their native habitat as an educational attraction. You don't want to waste a dead Mountie. I thought to myself that I'll bet your mother felt vindicated. There were Mounties. There were Beavers. There was nary a cannibal in sight.

I stood there dripping, cold, and wet. I eyed them. They eyed me. I heard soft whimpers and hushed whispers from the corners of the room.

From behind the desk a deep and raspy voice says, "There's a fireplace in the corner where you can warm yourself."

The guy standing next to her shakes his head in agreement and points over to the far wall where a group of elderly women are jockeying for position, pushing each other to the front of the group trying, unsuccessfully, to use their friends as a human shield.

My head swiveled, scanning the room looking for your mother. Eye contact was made with several of the other tourists. Much like submissive Chimps, they avert my gaze and shield their eyes with their hands making soft "oh-oh aw och" noises. Someone flung a banana, or it may have been monkey poo, I didn't look. The point is your mother is nowhere to be seen. I hope they have not, in Kubrickian glee, clubbed her to death but I'll have to deal with that later. Right now I have more pressing issues as my bladder begins to rupture.

Besides, she's pretty scrappy and I believe she still has her shank and her rock.

In the friendliest tone I can muster, under the circumstances, I say, "Thank you. You're all so very kind and I appreciate your hospitality. You certainly have created a warm and inviting environment for a weary traveler on this awful, wet, horrendous day. I believe I will skip the fire for now, but if you could, perchance, direct me to your facilities I would be forever grateful." I smile, showing my teeth in what I hope will be interpreted as a charming gesture but I'm not making any guarantees.

Unfortunately, what came out, rather loudly and in a screeching tone, was "I GOTTA PEE!", and instead of smiling I just kind of drooled a little out of the corner of my mouth.

The room, in unison and as if on cue, much like the flocking behavior of geese, or fish, or Rotarians, pointed me to a tile lined hallway that led off the main room.

I turn my back on these frightened Albertans, against my better judgment - for we had left the sanity of British Columbia sometime during the day — and head off down the hallway, my cane making squeaky noises on the wet flooring.

On reaching the bathroom the pressure of having to pee increased ten-fold because - well because I was near a toilet. See my bladder, in anticipation, was about 6 steps ahead of my body. I tried to explain that I had 57 frickin' layers of clothing on, and that it would take me a few minutes to disrobe, but my bladder was having none of it. So I hurriedly, and I do mean hurriedly, stripped off as many layers as possible while crossing my legs and bouncing up and down in the stall.

I will not go into details, but you can ask any man and he will agree, that one of the greatest pleasures in life is taking a much needed pee. I know it's not the same for women. But for men? If you could bottle that feeling or put it in pill you could make millions.

Success! Having accomplished my mission, I struggled for the next 10 minutes trying to re-layer. I may have once again put the top of my Frogg-Toggs on my legs but I don't know. The euphoria of warmth, and dryness, and an empty bladder all blended into one magical blur and before I knew it I was back out in the great hall looking for your mom.

I finally found her standing outside like the trooper she is, ready to get back on the bike. I was relieved to see that she hadn't been eaten.

"Where," I asked her, "did all those frickin' people come from?"

"Well, I overheard some of the women talking. Evidently there was a tour bus, or maybe three, that dropped them off here and they were waiting for another one to pick them up."

I wondered, was this a habit of the Canadian Tourism Industry to randomly abandon the elderly at Tourist Centers? You couldn't blame them. Old people can be a real pain in the keester with all the "I'm tired" and "I'm hungry" and "Dear God George isn't breathing!" It just never stops.

"Come on," Mom said, "time to hit the trail."

Against all common sense we saddled up and hit the wet, cold, misty road. Again. We were now so far behind schedule that it wasn't even funny. But the lodge beckoned. A non-refundable deposit is a harsh mistress.

The afternoon progressed much as it had since we left the ferry. A wet, sodden hell.

There is only one more remarkable thing that happened between the Tourist Center and reaching Carnack, Alberta.

Some town we went through, (and believe me they all began to run together at this point), had a fast-food restaurant that may, or may not, have had yellow arches and a clown - that provided easy access from the highway. It had been a couple of hours since our last stop at the Centre, and we were both in dire need of warmth, food, and some time off the bike.

Now fast food chains in Canada are like fast food in the US, only more northerly. Booths are the same, layout of the restaurant is the same, menu (mostly) is the same. That sweet, sweet generic goodness that reinforces the realization that we, as a species, are really not so different from each other pours out of every napkin holder. It is strangely reassuring that we all have the need for a cheeseburger and fries every now and then, and if the ' Quarter Mega Cheese' is called a 'Half-Liter with Curds', well it's not so far out of your comfort level to be disarming. In fact, it's just safe enough to be charming.

So, what made this stop unique?

We went to the rear of the restaurant to order, and I realized that the staff were all Circus Midgets. No kidding. They could barely see over the counter. I wondered if this was some government program to help the Little People, or if perhaps their Caravan had suffered a breakdown, and they were making some extra cash to get a new distributor for the elephant truck.

The thought crossed my mind that I may be, once again, hallucinating. Strangely everyone else seemed normal size.

I tugged at your mom's arm, "Are those Circus Midgets?"

She leaned close and whispered "I don't know, and I don't care. I just want a burger and for this day to be over."

We waited our turn in line and I got a good look at the person tending the cash register. Why, these weren't Circus folk at all! These were children!

The boy, in a pre-pubescent octave only audible to dogs and squirrels said, "Welcome! Can I take your order?"

Now I'm not kidding when I say this kid is young. What kind of a country uses forced child labor to serve hamburgers? What kind of monstrous society put's its youth into corporate slavery? This is the dark belly of Canada that they don't tell you about. This is the ugly flip-side to all the politeness and beauty and well maintained roads and health care for all.

He took our order and tried to make change. After fumbling at the till for a minute he said, "Um . . . can you help me? We don't learn subtraction until next week."

Your mother began to weep softly.

"Just keep the change son, just keep the change," I said.

His face lit up like a carelessly tossed match at the gas station. "Thanks mister! Woo Hoo!" he shouted and held two quarters above his head in triumph.

I didn't have the heart to tell him that I had given him a $20 for a $12.28 purchase.

Later we would discover that due to the boom in the oil and natural gas industries in Alberta, the minimum wage, service-oriented jobs were impossible to fill. So Canada had lowered the minimum working age to 14. They are seriously discussing lowering it to 12. No joke. Soon, I imagine, your fries will be served by toddlers. Oh, you'll get your order, but you'll have to change their diapers first.

So began our last stretch to the Holy Grail of the day – Hidden Valley Lodge in Carnack Alberta. Here we were to take a 3 day rest, explore the area, and enjoy the ambiance and soak up some nature. It looked like a fabulous place when I booked our reservations, and we were more than ready to get there. But we still had a bit of traveling to do, so we wolfed our burgers and with a heavy sigh once again hit the road, but a little less stressed now that we could see the end in sight.

After traveling for a few miles, Mom leaned forward and tapped me on the shoulder, "When will we get to Carnack?" Which really meant "When will be done with the Godforsaken day?"

I shouted into the wind, "Shouldn't be more than a couple of hours at the most. Maybe quicker if this rain would let up."

Yes, our day was almost done.

Or so we thought.

September 28, 2008

Dear Amber,

Okay, I'll let up on the Pirate stuff. Mom says it's making you feel bad.

Mom, always with the feelings.

Mom also says that the Marine Drill Sergeants are being awfully hard on you. Maybe Daddy should write them a note? Get them to back off a bit?

On a brighter note, I ran into that boy you liked so much in high school. I gave him your number. Crazy how we met – it just happened that I was crossing the street in front of the half-way house when I noticed him in a fetal position on the sidewalk. I didn't even know he was out! Stroke of luck there, eh?

Love you,
Daddio

Chapter 6

Dah Bears!

So we weaved and hummed our way through the afternoon gloom down a freeway that alternated between blinding sun and a very thin, partially suspended flash-flood. I don't mind admitting that, perhaps in retrospect, a marathon day through the Canadian Rockies was - well, let's just say optimistic at best. The words 'foolish', 'stupid', 'ninny-brained', and 'completely off yer flippin' rocker' could also apply, and your mother, in the days to come, would remind me of this fact. Quite frequently. And with emphasis on the 'stupid'.

Yet, low and behold, we survived, and we were finally on the outskirts of Carnack. Hidden Valley Lodge was close enough to taste. In my head I could feel the softness of the bed and the warm inviting clutch of a hot shower. Inside my damp and pungent helmet my nostrils flared in anticipation of the divine aroma of something other than wet Canadians and muddy roads. Yes, we were close, oh so joyfully close, that for a moment I thought we were already at our destination and this was nothing more than a nightmare, a fever dream of insanity and maple leaves.

Before I go on, I should probably tell you a bit about our destination. As you'll remember from earlier, I had scoured the internet for lodging that was both unique and wonderful. Remember, our plans were to spend three days using Hidden Valley Lodge as our base to explore all the wonders that encapsulate the adventure that is Banff. I wanted this to be an EXPERIENCE. You know? After all, isn't that what life is about? A collection of experiences? I felt it my duty to create a memory so powerful that I would visit it for years to come, and draw pleasure from each detail etched in my mind. You only get so many chances in life for something truly exceptional, and I wasn't about to let this one slip away. So, with that in mind I had spent days looking for 'just the right place to stay'. Luckily, I found Hidden Valley Lodge.

I suppose that some people would conclude that my enthusiasm and lack of attention to detail could be perceived as a negative. Your mother is often in that group. I, on the other hand, like to think of myself as a free-spirit, a generalist that lets the details work themselves out. It's only life, you know? And as long as no one is dead or seriously injured, or in prison, then what really is the problem? Ha Ha! Take that you conventional thinkers! I am an explorer, a Pirate of life sailing on the outer bounds of human experience.

You know, as long as that experience involves a comfy bed and a working bathroom. Oh! And lights. . . I like lights. And heat. And something to eat. And maybe a little drinky-poo. But other than that I'm zipping along the edge every day, unfettered and free.

OH! And TV and a wireless internet connection.

This is rather a long walk to set the tone for the rest of the story, and, as you shall soon see, I offer this not so much as an explanation but rather as a defense.

So . . . where was I? Oh yes . . . Hidden Valley Lodge. This place looked fantastic. A lodge in Carnack, AB, (please note the "in Carnack"), where the wildlife came right up and knocked on your door. Where your balcony hung over a 'wallow' and the deer and moose would make a daily pilgrimage to slurp the salts that lined the banks of the muddy pit below. An enchanted abode where every room had a fantastic view of a gorgeous mountain valley, full of meadows and creeks and butterflies and rainbows and possibly - yes, just possibly - Unicorns and Gnomes. Although they didn't say that in their advertising, it was **strongly** implied.

I had booked an all-inclusive package. Everything was covered; meals, snacks, 'high tea'. The only additional charges were for beer, wine, and spirits. The Lodge garnered the highest ratings on various websites, and was written about, quite elegantly, as a 'gem', and a 'hidden treasure', and 'an experience not to be missed'. A place where the food was "indescribable, delicious and a rare gourmet treat not often found outside of Europe". I was sold. I was the target market.

There was one caveat however; the place was not, by any stretch of the imagination, cheap. Gripped by the fever of adventure, I had hovered my quivering hands over the mouse and throwing caution to the wind clicked the button and committed ourselves to three non-refundable days at this alpine paradise.

You might want to remember the words 'non-refundable'. Those two words lead to insanity. Which brings us back to the outskirts of Carnack.

Now, as you recall if you've been paying attention, your mother was not in the best of moods. Who can blame her? It had been a weird, weird day. From the night before in Galaway's Bay to the ferry and Toads and Rain and Cannibals and Beavers and a guy named 'Ted' that I don't have the energy to write about. So, the day is winding down, the sun is slipping away, and it's frickin' raining buckets. Again. Or Still. Doesn't matter. But at least we are near the Holy Grail – Hidden Valley Lodge.

We rolled through the city limits of Carnack, (motto: Hey! You just drove through Banff at insane speeds! Well done! Enjoy your stay! Bye!"), and Mom, in her ever inquisitive, and I must admit that at this point in the day, somewhat annoying voice, leans forward on the bike and asks, "Thank God. I'm beat. So, where exactly is this place?"

Hmmmmm . . . that's a really good question. As a man is want to do, I supply an answer, even if it is less than helpful. "It's in Carnack."

She doesn't hesitate, she just pulls back and thumps the back of my helmet. Hard.

"Oh," I say, trying to inject some levity into the situation. "You mean the address. Well tell you what, we will find a parking lot, I'll consult Sweet Alice, (how I long to hear her sultry Aussie voice!), and I'll have you warm, dry, and dozing peacefully in half an hour. Hour tops."

"Okay," she says, but I can hear the suspicion thick in her voice as she answers, much like the subtext in the voice of a film-noire' gumshoe grilling his prime suspect. And not the hot girlfriend suspect. The ugly thug suspect.

With all haste I find an empty parking lot, shut down the bike, and pray that the oracle of the GPS will deliver us.

I bring up the map on the touch screen. Sure enough, my suspicions are confirmed. We are in Canada. More importantly, we are in Carnack. I punch the button for "Local Attractions", then "Amenities", then the sub-menu for "Hotels". An alphabetical list of all the wonderful places to stay in this paradise are displayed crisply and precisely on the screen. "Here we go," I say with confidence, "I'll just scroll down and find. . ."

Well that's curious. There is no "Hidden Valley Lodge" on the list.

I don't panic, because I know it will be listed under "Lodge, Hidden Valley". I chuckle at my mistake and Mom returns a hopeful, yet weary smile. The rain is dripping down the side of her helmet, resembling - although I would never tell her this - a garden fountain gone horribly bad.

I continue to scroll through the listings. It goes directly from "Lola's Mountain Manor Motor Lodge" to "My Converted Garage That Still Smells a Bit of Wet Cat and Mustard But Looks Kind Of Victorian if You Squint Your Eyes and Tilt Your Head To The Right Bed And Breakfast."

Uh oh.

Ever so quietly, barely audible, I hear the sultry Aussie voice of the GPS whisper "You're not gonna find it Mate. Take my advice, turn around."

"Shut up," I mutter, now frantically pressing the scroll buttons hoping beyond hope that I had somehow missed the listing.

"Game oveh. Yer screwed. I suggest suicide," purrs my digital Sweet Alice.

I lean close to the screen, "Shut the hell up before I rip you out by your wires and chuck you into the ditch."

"Who are you talking to?", Mom asks.

"Nobody," I reply, a bit more harshly than I intended.

Like syrup being poured from a bottle, the GPS whispers, "Tell you what Mate. How 'bout if'n I direct you to the nearest Hospital 'cause yer gonna need one inna minute."

Mom leans forward. "Are you strangling the GPS again?"

I look to my hands. Unconsciously, they've gravitated towards the GPS and are now engaged in some serious squeezing.

"Umm . . . no. I think there's a loose wire, I was just trying to fix it."

Even through the rain and the helmets I can hear your mom sigh.

"Strangling a helpless piece of technology. You've gone round the bend, eh? Toys in the attic and all that? You f'ed it up right good now, ain't ya?", whispers my sweet Aussie princess.

I may have started to weep. I don't know. Suddenly inspiration strikes!

"Suz! We have the confirmation email in the saddle bag. The address and phone number are on there. I'll just plug the address directly into the GPS and whoopsie-doodles, we will be there in a flash!"

Ha Ha! Take that you commie-pinko GPS! Your taunts mean nothing now! I've beaten you at your game for I am an AMERICAN! I am from THE STATES! Our kind created you, and our kind will destroy you at will! Well, until the eventual takeover by our Robotic Overloads. Which we all know is a given. All hail Gigantitron369!

Mom climbs off the bike and instantly her seat is wet. I don't think she cares anymore. She rummages around in the various articles that we've stowed and, after what seems like an eternity, finds the confirmation paper. It starts to get soaked immediately, so she folds it in half and hands it to me, trying to keep the printing dry. We don't need any more mishaps on this fine and beautiful day.

Triumphantly, and with a wag of my tongue in the general direction of the GPS, I unfold the note. HA! There is the confirmation. There are the dates. There is how we paid. Salvation!

There is, quite quizzically, no phone number. Perhaps I should have noticed that before. No matter, there is an address. Oh yes . . . there is an address. Hope flushes through my system like Mentos in a Diet Coke. Rain had peppered my glasses and I squint to read the print in the dimming gray light. The address is . . . PO Box AB804, Carnack AB.

I swear I heard the GPS snicker.

"What's the matter?" Mom asks but her tone says she really doesn't want to know.

"Well. Well, well, well." I brace myself, "Seems like the only address we have is a PO Box."

I can feel something building in your mom. Something dark and disquieting. Something powerful and ominous and thoroughly unpleasant.

"Oh for God's sake. This is ridiculous." She punched me on the shoulder but there was little enthusiasm in the act. "I saw a sign a bit down the highway for an 'Information and Tourist Centre'. Let's just head over there, I'll go inside and I'll get directions."

This was the best idea that I'd heard all day. "Suz," I say, "you my dear are absolutely brilliant! No wonder I love you so much!"

She looks at me. Or maybe through me.

"Sure. Whatever." She casts a weary eye about our surroundings, "Let's just get to the Lodge."

With the optimism that can only be mustered by the seriously mentally ill, we wheel the bike around and in a few minutes are pulling into the parking lot of the Information Centre to get the low-down on all things touristy. I don't even mind that the place is spelled all Frenchy.

"Tell you what," Mom says as she pulls off her helmet, "you stay here with the bike and I'll just pop in. I'll be back in a jiffy."

I think this has less to do with saving time, and more about having a short break from me, but I'm smart enough not to press the issue.

"That would be grand sweetie. Thank you."

She heads off towards the building. Slightly shuffling, shoulders hunched. The day has certainly taken its toll. But I'm positive this will soon be just a memory that we can laugh about later.

I'm sure I make a sight, sitting in the parking lot alone in the pouring rain on a weird shaped bike, arguing with a GPS, but I could not care less. Any modesty had been beaten out of me long, long ago. Just for giggles I plug the PO Box into Sweet Alice. To my surprise, it actually registers on the screen! Although it is obviously wrong, because it shows the location up in the mountains where there are no roads. Yet, I'm encouraged that the Lodge is around here somewhere and not an internet scam as I was beginning to suspect.

The minutes tick by. And tick. Then tock. And eventually they drag on and there is no sign of your mother. I'm actually beginning to get worried. What if my premonitions were right, but I had the wrong Tourist Centre? What, if at the very moment, my loving wife of 28 years was being all molested by cannibals? Canadian cannibals at that?

Right then and there I began to hate Canada.

As I was preparing to take one for the team and go in to rescue her, she emerged from the building holding a piece of paper in her hand. Victory! Sweet, sweet accommodations here we come!

However, I can see that your mother isn't exactly exuding joy. I can tell from her body language. It's those subtle motions that are visible only to someone you've spent your life with. No one else would be able to pick up on these clues, and if they did, they would have no frame of reference from which to decipher their meaning. In this case, your mom was banging her fists on the side of her helmet and jumping up and down. I studied her as she approached. Ah. . . I recognize this - it's her universal signal for "I have great news! I love you and I'm sorry if we've been short with each other for the past few hours but all is well now, all is well."

Mom steps to the side of the bike and says, "We're fucked."

Oh. Well dang.

"Okay, how fucked? Fucked as in 'I forgot my wallet', or as in 'Hey, look! The right wing just fell off?'"

"Fucked - fucked."

"Well alrighty then. So, was this some internet scam? Is there a Hidden Valley Lodge? Wait . . . don't tell me, did it burn down this morning?"

"Oh," Mom says, a tad sarcastically I thought, "there's a Hidden Valley Lodge alright."

"Okay," now my patience was running thin, "so what's the problem?"

"Did you," she asks as she pokes a finger into my arm, "think to actually look where this place was before you booked it?"

"Well if I had, then we wouldn't be asking for directions, would we?" I say through clenched teeth.

She stares at me long and hard, and for a moment I think she's reaching for her shank. Or her rock. Or any number of other things she could use as a weapon.

"When I asked directions they looked at me horrified. It was obvious I was on a motorcycle. This place isn't IN Carnack. It's OUTSIDE of Carnack. Actually OUTSIDE and ABOVE Carnack and still another 40 kilometers away!"

I do a bit of mathematical calculation on the fly. That means that we have another 157 gallons to go. Damn you Canada.

"Alright, so we still have a bit of traveling to do."

"Forty kilometers away," she says and pokes my arm again for emphasis, "up the side of a mountain. On a narrow, one-lane gravel road. While it's getting dark."

I feel my stomach knot. The Vision is a wonderful bike, but it is definitely a street bike. Not a dual sport. With all of the water she weighs as much as a binging hippo. Or, in the metric system, 6000 stone.

My mind frantically turns, I'm trying to salvage this day somehow. Eventually I give up. I got nuthin'.

"What are we going to do?" she asks, but it's not really a question. What she REALLY said was, *I can't believe you didn't check this out and now here we are exhausted, wet, cold, and with no place to stay and we've forfeited a bunch of money because you're an idiot and IT'S ALL YOUR FAULT!*

I panic. The ball is squarely in my court. I am, as our illustrious President Bush had said, the decider. I got us into this mess, and it's up to me to get us out. Silly woman trusting me. She should know better than that. I thought that I could use this line of logic to put the blame on her, and then realized there were other things in life I wanted to experience. A Canadian Hospital was not one of them. I was in the pit of despair, then - BOOM - another flash of inspiration!

"Okay, here's what we will do. We've come this far, let's give it a shot." And then, because I haven't made enough mistakes, I add, quite casually the most damning statement that I've ever uttered in my life. "Worse comes to worse, we will just turn around, find a motel, and try to get our money back tomorrow. I'm sure they'll understand if we cannot physically get to the Lodge."

I can see Mom weigh the options in her mind. On one hand, she could go along with this scheme. On the other hand, she could trick me into taking my helmet off and hit me in the head with her friend, the rock, and try to claim that I'd run away.

I can see in her eyes that at this point it's a coin toss.

"Fine. You want to try it, we'll try it. The lady inside gave me directions. She said about 5 miles out of town, beyond the Nordic Centre, is where the gravel starts. I asked her if the road was good, and she said "Well, good for a car. It's hard-packed. I don't know how it would be on a motorcycle and honestly I haven't been up there in years." Her eyes pierce me like an ice-pick in peanut butter. "That was a direct quote."

I become distracted by the 'Nordic Centre', but shake the thought out of my head. I have more important matters to contemplate.

Now I know what I wrote earlier about driving on gravel. I had driven the Vision on gravel in the past, and while it is tricky, it can be done if the gravel is packed hard and there aren't too many pot-holes or soft spots. You don't want to hit a soft patch with the front tire of a bike. It has a tendency to dig in and not want to move. Yet our friend inertia, and the back of the bike, will have none of that. So best to avoid the situation entirely. But if all was well you could put the baby at a constant speed of 15 to 40 miles an hour - depending on conditions, easy on the brakes and easy on the throttle, with a very light touch for steering and you should be fine. 'Should be' being the operative words. But it's edging towards dark, it's been raining for days, and your mother, bless her soul, is delusional. Possibly – although I have no proof - possessed.

"What's a Nordic Centre," I ask.

"I have no idea, but it really doesn't matter."

"You think that's where they herd Scandinavians to keep an eye on them?"

"No. I think it probably has something to do with the 1988 Winter Olympics."

I stroke my chin in contemplation. Which is ridiculous, because I'm wearing a helmet so it looks as though I'm trying to get bugs off my face-plate in a slow, drunken motion. Suddenly an image of countless tall, blonde people that we've encountered since crossing the border fills my mind and it all comes together in a flash.

"Could be, could be. But these Canadians are a wily bunch. Remember all those tall, blond, semi-identical people we keep seeing? It's all too plain now. Evidently, they're trying to clone Vikings. How would you like that? Herds of Vikings pouring south across the border, downloading music illegally. Sharing files. Littering."

Mom pounded her gloved fist on the side of her helmet. "They are not cloning Vikings!"

"You can't prove that. But," I add, "at least they would be polite Vikings. I don't know about you, but if I'm going to be pillaged and raped, I want to be treated with a little respect."

It's then that I notice that your mother had developed a nasty - and by no means attractive - eye tic. Perhaps I should leave this line of speculation for another time.

"Come on babe," I say, "let's have a look at that map she drew for you."

Mom held the sheet of paper out to me, and before I could grasp it and take a gander, the ratio of water to paper became too much. It disintegrated like a ball of toilet paper in the tree of a cranky old fart that one day pushed the neighborhood kids too far.

I heard God laugh. I kid you not.

Turns out, it wasn't God. It was just your mother sobbing.

"Whoopsie!", I say, with a melodic lilt that manages to annoy even myself.

"Well great," Mom sighs.

It is now that my masculinity kicks into high gear. I need to take control. I will not stand idly by and let this cursed day get the best of me. I will solve this problem, like so many men before me have solved problems of their own creation.

I will lie.

"Look, standing here is doing us no good. Get on the back of the bike and we will push on. I know how to get to the Nordic Centre." (Lie #1)

"I'm sure Sweet Alice can get us that far, and probably a bit beyond." (Lie #2)

Really, it can't be that bad. (Lie #3)

"I told them in the note when I booked the place that we were coming in on motorcycle. (This is true.) If they thought we couldn't make it, they would have told me." (I believed this to be true.) It's going to be fine. (Lie #4)

Your mother - my wife, my companion, my friend, co-conspirator, cheer-leader and all around pal these last 30 years - knew right away I was spewing total bullshit.

"Fine," she said and without another word climbed on the back of the bike.

Though silent, I could read her body language under the layers of clothing. She had not so much capitulated as she had decided, as if she were on a dare, to see how this would play out. And of course, then hold me accountable later. It's a little game married people play.

I took a deep breath, fired the engine, and without further ado set off to find this Canadian / Scandinavian Cloning Facility masquerading as some sort of ski operation. I had turned the volume down on the GPS, but I could see our rough path laid out on the map to where Sweet Alice thought the PO Box might be. It was just a big arrow pointing towards the mountains on the other side of town. It did nothing to calm my nerves when the screen started flashing red and the word DANGER in all caps popped on and off the screen like a demonic jack-in-the-box. F' you Sweet Alice! I've had enough of your silliness for one day! I clicked into first and hit the gas. Right or wrong, I was at least moving and that felt good.

We wandered through the streets of Carnack for what seemed an eternity. Missing turns, pulling u-turns in parking lots, changing lanes abruptly - you know, all the stuff that makes taking a HUGE FLIPPIN' MOTORCYCLE THROUGH UNFAMILIAR TERRITORY DURING RUSH HOUR IN A MONSOON so exciting. But my perseverance paid off. At last, I spotted a sign for the Nordic Centre.

I patted your mom's leg in what I hoped was a reassuring manner, and we took the turn into the mountains. It was probably gorgeous and breathtaking. I have no idea.

Now, it was about this time that we started seeing the warnings for Bears tacked to sign-posts every . . . oh, I don't know . . . every ten feet or so. I didn't want your mother to worry, so I tried to distract her whenever one drew near. "Hey," I would say and point in the opposite direction, "is that a squirrel?" Or, "Quick! Look over there! What kind of bird is that?" Or, "Look! Carnival rides!" Much to my chagrin I don't believe it worked.

We passed the Nordic Centre, (Motto: "Nothing Sinister Going On Here. Certainly No Cloning. Please Move Along."), and happened on our first bit of good news in what was proving to be one of the longest days of our lives. A sign. Literally.

"Look!", Mom shouted in the first true enthusiasm I'd heard from her since leaving home, "The sign says, 'Hidden Valley Lodge - 40 Kilometers', we're going the right way!"

I thought about adding, 'You had any doubts?', but decided that silence and a smile were more apropos.

As we passed the Nordic Centre's entrance, the wide, flat tarmac began to narrow. While the surface was fine, the width closed in on itself going from a very wide two-lane, to a narrow two-lane with no markings, to a wide one-lane road. Not a problem. Others had traveled this path. In addition to guests at the Lodge, I reasoned that there had to be delivery trucks, carriers, etc. that supplied the Lodge and whatever else was up there. I relaxed. I felt as though our 'day from Hell' was at last coming to a close.

Then, the road began to climb. Ha. Not a problem. Then the road REALLY began to climb. Still no problem. Then the road . . . well it just kind of ended into a ridiculously steep one-lane gravel path with washboards deeper than speed bumps.

This might be a problem.

Let me pause and give you a bit of advice that will serve you well in the years to come. When you hear yourself saying, "Oh, well I'll just go a bit further, I'm sure there will be someplace to turn around." --- just turn around. NOW. No good will ever come of this situation. The road never gets wider, or better, or flatter. The only thing you can expect to encounter taking this route is madness. Madness and death. I know this now, and I knew this then. So why, in the name of all that is holy, did I push on?

It's simple really. I'm an idiot.

As the tires hit the gravel, and the nose of the bike pointed toward the Orion cluster, I hear your mom utter one hushed word that summarized the situation precisely.

"Shit!" she said.

Yes. Shit. Shit indeed.

I was now in a situation where the burden of choice had been removed. Even if we were not at a ridiculous angle on gravel, the road was too narrow to turn this beast around.

I leaned back and whispered to your mom the only thing I could, "Hold on."

I don't know if you've ridden the equivalent of a GoldWing up the side of a steep mountain, on marbles, and a cheese-grater surface, but it's really not as much fun as the brochures make it out to be. The dynamics of the ride change dramatically. Imagine riding a jack-hammer - pogo-stick style - up the steep side of an icy glacier. Now add a rhinoceros strapped to your back. Make that rhinoceros an epileptic. Just for kicks, tell the rhino that he isn't getting into medical school because there is a 'quota' on rhino doctors and you know that it's unfair but he can always go home and take over the family business which happens to be eating grass and dodging poachers.

I leaned over the handlebars of the bike, bringing my feet behind and underneath my body. This gave me a bit of an advantage, allowing me to counter act the fish-tailing motion of the rear of the motorcycle as it skidded over the gravel washboard. I didn't look too far ahead - it made my stomach turn. Because - and this is where it gets funny - the road was not a straight path as I had hoped, but turned into a series of switchbacks. Hairpin switchbacks. Gravely, certain death, hairpin switchbacks that became progressively steeper and steeper.

Mom leaned forward, "Are we doing okay?"

I would have liked to have said something witty, but I was concentrating too hard. "We are okay. We are upright and that's good. Just try to relax back there and keep your weight steady."

"Okay," she breathed and sat back.

I'm sure I've been in worse situations on a bike, but honestly, I couldn't remember when. I've been in places where the path was no more than a goat track, and walked the bike as best I could until I fell off the trail and had bike land on top of me. That was fun. Also while riding trail, I've hit slimy, moss covered logs at the wrong angle and been shot off the road into the brush and trees faster than you could say 'howdy-doody'. I've hit patches of oil and diesel in a blind curve at 60 mph. I've been caught in freak storms and played 'run for your life' with a funnel cloud east of Yakima one notable spring day, and with a queasy stomach prayed that we would make it to shelter before the cyclonic demon caught up with us. I've blasted around corners on Chinook, making our way down from Paradise on Mt. Rainier and had to thread my way between a herd of Roosevelt Elk — close enough I could have reached out and touched their hindquarters - hoping beyond hope that they wouldn't spook and crush us while we were in the middle of the herd. One time, in a moment of sheer stupidity in my youth, I took a turn WAY to fast on a motorcycle, and with shorts and a tank top, (but I was wearing a helmet!), rode the bugger straight into a patch of nettles and blackberry vines with enough time to contemplate how much it was going to hurt. I've crashed, wrecked, ate the asphalt, and sported lovely, lovely road-rash more times than I care to remember.

I will not hesitate to admit that I was never more nervous . . . oh hell . . . I was never more scared than I was right then. It wasn't just me this time. I had your mom to think about.

And I will admit something else. I say this next part with all sincerity because I know you'll understand completely. It was a most excellent rush!

So there we were with no place to go but up. Pardon my language, but I worked that bitch. Slipping and sliding, keeping a fast enough speed that I could corner but not so fast as to shake us off the bike. Watching out for the big rocks, the ruts, and whatever else came my way. I completely lost track of time. All that existed for me was the 30 feet in front of the bike, and the bike itself. We had melded into one. I felt every change in balance, every bump, every twist, and growl, and groan from the engine. I fought to keep the bars from being wrenched from my hands. I worried about your mom. I worried about wrecking in a place like this. Visions of a helicopter rescue tried to invade my thoughts but then the rear of the bike would slip sideways, and I was brought back to the here and now. And the rain. . . the rain would not let up. At times I couldn't see through the fog. I finally flipped my shield up and let the water hit me full in the face.

Then . . . Joy! For what did I see? Three Jeeps headed DOWN the mountain. I had time for one thought to cross my mind; Well, this was going to get interesting. In a hurry.

To this day I don't know how we made it. Passing those Jeeps with inches to spare, so close I could see the slack-jawed purity of astonishment on each of the driver's faces as their brakes locked and their over-sized tires slid on the gravel. But make it we did. We must have been quite a spectacle to them. A HUGE retro space-bike with two clowns riding tandem in a place where no bike like this should be. Even on the best of days. We must have looked like a crippled UFO. But I knew what those guys were really thinking. They were thinking "Got more balls than me."

Ha! How many times is complete idiocy taken as courage? Probably more times than anyone would care to admit. If you make it - hero. If you don't - wanker.

The road went on and on and on and then finally a PARTICULARLY steep patch that when we broke over the top leveled out. I felt Mom relax. The knots in my stomach untwisted, and I breathed deeply for the first time since we started our ascent however long ago that had been. There was just enough of a wide spot to pull the bike over lest another Jeep came up behind, broke over the ridge, and smacked squarely into our rear.

I put the Vision in neutral, and slumped over the console.

"Wow," Mom said. "Did we really just do that?"

"Yeah," I said, and laughed half-heartedly, "we just did that. Sorry."

"Wow," she said again.

I thought her remark an understatement.

I took a deep breath and sat up, stretching the cramps that had set into my arms and hands. I surveyed my surroundings. Well, we definitely were at the top. There were some rolling hills in front of us, but nothing to compare to what we had just navigated. Later, I would discover that we had climbed about 1700 feet in 12 Kilometers. Or, in devil-speak Canadian measurements, about 4.5 liters a minute. Not too shabby. After I restored my heart rate to a manageable level, and decided that I hadn't wet myself, (okay, who am I kidding - hadn't wet myself TOO severely), I took stock of our situation .

While we were level, the road surface had not improved. The rain had not improved. Your mother's mood had not improved by any appreciable degree. Our hypothermia situation had not improved - in fact, it was worse. The temperature had plummeted as we climbed into the Rockies. And, like a big, moldering mutant strawberry cradled in the congealed whipped cream of a day-old Belgian Waffle, twilight was descending - rapidly.

But, on the positive side, we could be hit by lightening at any moment, so there was always hope.

"What do we do now?", Mom asked in a dazed voice. "Do we turn around?"

I thought, however briefly, of turning the bike around and riding down the mountain, and my boys - and you know what I mean by 'the boys' - don't feign ignorance - shot straight up into my throat, through my head, and were dancing somewhere above the tree tops trying to escape. The only thing worse than coming UP that road in this weather, was going DOWN that road in this weather. Miles of braking down the side of a gravel mountain didn't appeal to me. Somewhere, in the recesses of my brain a tiny voice reminded me that I would, at some point, need to take the bike down this very same road. I hate that voice. It's annoying. All high-pitched and squeaky. And preachy to boot. And usually right. Damn you internal monologue!

"I think I would rather feed marshmallows to alligators with my lips than try and ride back down that road," I said and wiped rainwater from my glasses. It was an exercise in futility. "Hopefully the worst is behind us. Let's just push on and get to the Lodge."

"Does the GPS say we are close?"

"I don't know. When we met those jeeps Sweet Alice let out a tiny scream then passed out."

Mom pondered this for a moment. "Was passing out an option? I wish I'd known that. I would have blanked out as soon as we hit the gravel."

Let me say this again: Your mother is a wise, wise woman.

I collected myself enough to take a further assessment of the situation. The road had leveled out - and thank the Gods for that - but the path that lie ahead looked like . . . well, like we were going to be driving possibly THROUGH or INTO a lake. Seriously.

The tiny voice inside said, "Sure. Why not?"

STFU internal voice or I swear to God that I will lobotomize myself here and now. Where's that screwdriver?

"Let's get going," Mom said, and settled back into her seat. "I really, really, really, really need to be off the bike."

Wuss. We had only been riding for . . . okay, we'd been riding for about 13 hours. Still, that's no reason to get testy. I made a mental note to have a talk with your mom about her attitude. But not right now. Probably not this week.

Sometime after Halloween seemed safe. And then I would put it in a letter and make sure I was out of town when she read it.

With another sigh I pulled back onto the gravel. An old sound clip from MSTK 3000 popped into my head, (Yeah, it was getting crowded in there.), and said, "Off to meet my doom Mom. See you after school!"

So we putted along the gravel towards the lake. It was definitely easier going now that the road was not at an insane angle, but it was getting very soft between the washboards. 15 mph was about the max speed. Any faster and I felt like my fillings were going to rattle out of my teeth.

As we approached the water the view grew more and more disconcerting. Ahead was a lake. Big lake. Deep lake. On the right side was a sheer rock cliff that rose, from what appeared to be directly from the water, to a height of maybe 150 feet. Or 7000 grams in hell-measure. Naught but water on the left. The road looked like it simply ended.

I wanted to cry, but no one would have heard me and I don' know about you, but that just seems a waste.

As we progressed the road curved to the right, and I thought for a moment that we were going to skirt the back side of the cliff and escape the water all together but . . . no. It swung back on itself and headed straight for where the water met the rock wall. Fine. Drowning seemed like a fairly quick death of which I was sure your mother would agree, so I pushed on.

Fortunately, the road didn't end! HA! Our luck was improving! I hadn't been able to see, but the road actually skirted between the cliff and the lake! Now here is what made it so weird - the level of the lake was possibly an inch below the road level. Lake on one side, cliff on the other, it looked like we were driving on water. It may have been exhaustion or hypothermia, but it was one of the most bizarre optical illusions I've ever encountered. It actually made my stomach flutter.

Mom leaned forward and said, "Well, this is just unreal. It feels like we're driving on the lake."

Yes. Yes it does.

We drove on and on around the lake for what seemed like an eternity, but was probably more like 4 minutes. Or 17.6 Kiloseconds. Whatever. The point being it was long enough. Up ahead I saw that the lake ended, as well as the cliff, and the road, (Yay!), continued on through an extraordinarily beautiful meadow. I breathed a sigh of relief. Which immediately fogged my glasses and I didn't tell your mom but for the last quarter mile or so I was driving purely on instinct. I don't think she would have appreciated, nor been amused, by my mad riding skills.

As we traveled further from the lake the road improved a bit. Now there were brief sections where there were no washboards and the gravel was packed down firmly. I bumped the speed up a few notches. The Lodge couldn't be far now.

We began to climb, and the road deteriorated once again. The path became narrower, and instead of lush meadow we were heading into a stand of forest. Big trees on each side with the road cutting a swath between them.

I leaned back, "You doing okay Babe?"

"Yeah. Fine. Funny, 2 hours ago riding on this part of the road would have scared me to death. After coming through what we just did, it seems like a well maintained freeway."

I nodded in agreement. "I'm exhausted, but the place can't be too far now."

Yes. The place can't be far now. That became my mantra.

We settled back, each in our own silence, the bike humming beneath us. The drone of the engine was rhythmic - melodic. A soft purring lullaby that, were I not running on adrenaline, would have made me sleepy.

We continued on for about 10 minutes, both of us relaxing by the yard, and finally able to appreciate the beauty that surrounded us as we broke from trees to meadow and back to forest again. There was a small creek running through the valley, and a series of postcard like lakes nestled in the low spots. I had hope. So did your mom, I could feel it in the way she held onto my sides.

We came around a particularly tight corner, the bike slipping sideways a bit as we rounded the apex, and something caught my eye. The stands of trees on my left were sparse with lots of brush and grass in between. The stand on my right was much thicker and denser, almost shutting out what little light was left. I noticed something on my left, and about 20 feet, (Yes FEET! Screw metrics!), off the road.

"Hmmmmm. . . .", I said to myself, "Why would someone park a rusted '57 Buick up here? That seems odd."

I got a little closer and chuckled to myself. Oh my silly, tired, eyes were playing tricks on me. That wasn't a '57 Buick, it was a van abandoned in the woods.

A little closer and I realized that it wasn't an auto at all, but a large, reddish-brown boulder. Which made much more sense except for one thing - the boulder was moving. Rather quickly. And towards us.

And another odd thing . . . this boulder had legs.

Now, I know that things are a tad different up in Canada, but not so different that rocks walk about all by themselves. The only time I saw that was once in the '70s. And I may have been - well, let's just leave that story for another day. So what fresh madness was this?

The boulder approached the road. We approached the boulder. I slowed down so as to not run into said boulder.

The boulder stepped off the slight bank onto the gravel in front of us and promptly resolved itself into a bear. A huge bear. And by huge bear I mean a HUGE HUGE HUGE FRICKIN' BEAR.

I have seen a few bears in my time, mostly through the mesh of a zoo enclosure or painted comically on a coffee mug. Plus, I've watched many, many programs on the nature channels, so I'm pretty much an expert on all things Ursal. Despite my encyclopedic knowledge, and possibly due to the stress of the moment, there are only two things I could remember off hand that pertained to our present situation.

One, this is a species known as 'Grizzly'.

Two, we are going to be eaten.

THE BEAR started to saunter - yes . . . saunter. There was no rush - or if you prefer, 'lumber' across the road in front of us. Did I mention this thing was HUGE. Not like the smaller black bears we will on occasion spot in the Cascades. This was a proper bear. A mighty bear. A top-of-the-food-chain, rip-your-head-off-for-fun bear. And it was female. Probably, if the journey so far was any indicator, PMSing. And more than likely just broke up with her boyfriend that used to ride a motorcycle and was bald and breathed oxygen.

Just - like - me.

Time, which anyone that deals with intense situations will confirm, is not a constant. The flow of time varies with the situation. Here the seconds slowed to a crawl. I stared through the drizzle and realized that the haunches of this beast towered over the height of the Vision by a good degree. If we were sitting side-by-side, and we almost were, I would have had to look up to see her jaws of death.

Lord but this bundle of muscle and ill temper was HUGE.

And I was on a ridiculous motorcycle on a ridiculous day on a ridiculous collision path with this behemoth. She hadn't begun putting on weight for the winter yet, so I could see the muscles ripple beneath her fur with every step. I could see the size of her paws, larger than my head, slap on the wet gravel. I stared, slack-jawed, as her rear haunches rolled and shuddered, slightly swaying from side to side. You should know that in times of extreme stress the mind will grasp at any straw to comfort itself. I am not ashamed to admit, that for the briefest of moments the lilting strains of a song rushed through my head. Sir-Mix-A-Lot streamed like a beacon into my skull, crooning his epic regarding the size and likability of a healthy-sized posterior.

I have just enough time to ponder that I may look into all of those kind suggestions for therapy should I make it out of this alive.

THE BEAR swings her massive head to look at us. It's not a particularly friendly gesture. She is obviously not frightened - curious would be a more apt description. Annoyed would be another. I jump on the brakes as hard as I can without skidding. The only thing worse than running INTO the bear, would be to tip over and SLIDE INTO the bear. I've seen enough cartoons in my day to understand this would be, according to animated mythology, 'bad'.

It was then that I realize that I should probably inform your mother, for the umpteenth time on this journey, of our impending death.

I reach back and pat her on the leg to get her attention. "Suz, I don't know how to tell you this, but after all we've been through today it looks like we are going to be eaten by a bear. A Grizzly Bear. And a huge one at that. With a big butt. But that's beside the point. I'm so sorry sweetie, I didn't want it to end like this. I will offer myself first. I'm twice your size, and perhaps she will fill up on me, giving you at least a fighting chance for an escape. I love you."

But what came out was a high-pitched girly-girl EEEeeeiiiiiieeeee!!!"

Frantically, I fumble for the horn button. It's somewhere on the handle bars, but damned if I can find it. I do manage to change the headlight from bright to dim to bright again. I think THE BEAR may have interpreted this as an attention getting device for she slowed a bit and turned her massive shoulders towards us with a calculating eye. I'm hoping that the bike is enough to distract her. That she will appreciate the flowing lines that are the Vision. Marvel at its unique design, the subtle engineering, and the beau coup enhancements that escape the casual glance.

No luck, THE BEAR could care less. Evidently, she's more into sport bikes.

I attempt, once again, to warn your mother.

"Bear. Bear! BEAR!!!", I shout, with each word spoken more distinctly, louder, and in a slightly higher pitch than the one preceding.

The 'boys' - and once again, don't feign ignorance - have not only left the building, but taken a cab back to Seattle forgetting to close the door and turn off the lights. A part of me, the detached observing bastard inside, marvels as the words escape my mouth. Evidently certain death adheres to the rule of three. As in, the Three Musketeers, the Three Stooges, and the three things you shout right before you die. Usually, and this is documented on Wikipedia, (Wait just a second . . . okay . . . it's documented now), the three things most often said right before you die an untimely death is, "Shit. Shit! SHITTTTT!!!" Or, if it is really untimely, just "Shi-. . . "

THE BEAR kind of sways her head back and forth, as if she may be singing to Sir-Mix-A-Lot as well. Or possibly the Foo Fighters. I make no judgment as to her musical taste. The important thing is that I've seen this behavior on the Discovery Channel. To put it politely, we are screwed. This is what's commonly referred to in the animal kingdom as 'Le Dance d'appetite'. Or, in the vulgar, 'I'm gonna boogie me up a hunger'.

Somewhere deep inside a memory bubbles to the surface. I hear Jacques Cousteau intone. . .

"But de intrepid motorscooterists are no match for de bare. We shed ze zmall teer as nate-chur, in all her splendor, keeps da balance. Eef it were not for de bares, the landscape wood be over run with motorscooterists. Once again we are reminded dat de miracle dat ez life ez harsh as well as bee-yootefull. Now, let's sit back and watch as she mak ze keel."

Frickin' Jacques Cousteau. Go back to the ocean where you belong!

Your mom leans forward, "What? I was wiping the fog from the inside of my shield."

"Bear."

"What?"

I want to point out the massive reddish-brown mountain that is now two thirds of the way across the road, but taking my hands off of the steering seems like a bad idea. I try to motion in the direction of THE BEAR with my helmet, but it's useless. It just looks like I've developed a tic of my own. Mom is leaning forward on my left side, and THE BEAR is on the right. I'm effectively blocking her view with my head. It's probably for the best.

For whatever reason, and I assume it is pure pity, THE BEAR steps off the road and ambles to the edge of the trees. Here she stops, and turns to watch us roll by. I hit the throttle and Mom is rocked back into her seat. I pick up speed, trying to put as much distance between us and THE BEAR as possible.

Mom grabs my shoulder and leans forward again. "What's going on?"

I try to unclench my jaw. "Bear."

"Really? You think this is the time for a beer?" she asks with disgust.

I shake my head in the negative.

Mom pauses for a second. "Did you say 'Bear'?"

I shake my head, a bit too vigorously, in the affirmative. Stars explode inside my skull.

"Yes. Bear. BIG Bear. REALLY BIG BEAR."

I keep looking in the mirrors to see if we are being followed and then decide that I would rather an attack from behind be a 'surprise'. There's nothing I can do. I can't go any faster, so anticipating massive jaws wrapping around my head is an exercise in futility. Although, I must admit thinking that if that were to happen, at least this cursed day would be at an end.

I feel your mom tense. "Where?"

"Just walked across the road in front of us."

"How close?", she asks in a whisper.

Despite my best efforts, I giggle. "Close. Really close."

"Close as in 'Boy, that mountain looks close', or 'The store is only a couple of blocks away, so it's close'?"

"Close as in, 'Hey. Don't sit so close to the TV or you'll go blind."

She contemplates this for a minute. I know what she's doing. She's trying to get enough information to decide what level of panic is appropriate. "25 yards?"

"No. More like 15 feet. 10 right before we passed. Maybe. I saw puffs of steam coming out of her nose. The hair on her rump was flattened and wet on one spot. She may have been wearing blue eye-shadow."

Mom makes a slight 'Urk' sound in her throat.

"A black bear?"

I giggle again. The hysterical tone and quality of the laugh frightens even me. "Nope. Big Bear. HUGE bear. Grizzly."

"You sure?"

"Oh, pretty sure!"

I can feel her shift her weight as she swivels her head from side to side, scanning the brush around us.

"Grizzly?"

"Yep."

"Crap."

"Yes. Crap. That about says it all."

"But it's gone?", she asks, looking for reassurance.

"Um," I say, stalling. "umm . . . . Sure."

I feel both of her hands tighten their grip on my sides. Were her hands to get a good hold I would have several cracked ribs with which to contend.

Now that the initial rush is over, my mind shifts into high-gear 'what if?' mode. I search the corners of my memory, dragging up every piece of information I have about bears. What concrete knowledge do I possess?

Well, bears like picnic baskets, and are pretty friendly with Park Rangers. That eases my apprehension a tad. They also like honey, and have a wide array of animal friends such as donkeys and rabbits and tiggers, (which we all know are wonderful things). They like porridge. Okay. This isn't so bad. I'm calming down and feeling better by the moment. Plus, there's only one day a year when you have to be especially careful. That would be the infamous Teddy Bear Picnic. It's sort of like Burning Man. Only in the woods not the desert. And there are far fewer hippies. And generally it smells better.

But the more I ponder, the more I'm unsure of my intel. Curse you public school education!! Curse you Saturday morning cartoons!

Okay. What do I really know about bears. And especially, Grizzlies? Well, I remember that a Grizzly can run. Fast. They can run up to 35 miles per hour for short distances. Oh fudge. I glance down at the speedometer, and see that we are currently cruising at about 20 mph, and I can't safely move the bike any faster.

I remember that female Grizzlies, are called 'Sows' - although you wouldn't want to call her that to her face - unless you were looking to get your lips chewed off - and they give birth to their young in the spring. By late summer, the cubs are old enough to follow their mom on hunting trips. During this phase, the Sows are EXTREMELY protective, and aggressive, especially when they think their cubs are threatened. Damn. Maybe that's why she kept looking back. A big honkin' ultramodern looking motorcycle between a Grizzly and her cubs.

Or, to put it another way - snacks!

So, to summarize: Cranky and fast. Really fast. Large teeth. Large claws. Guess that's all I really need to know.

We traveled about a half mile up the road and I am not ashamed to tell you that I was a smidgen paranoid. I'm scanning for bears. I'm looking in my mirror. The Pucker Factor came on full. Once again, don't play me like you don't know that a tightening sphincter is rated on a sliding scale. Dear God, you're in Naval Officer Candidate School. I would think your eyes would pop open every morning at about a 5. 'The Factor' is usually graded on a scale of 1 to 10, with 1 being a pleasant cup of tea with Aunt Marge, and a 10 narrowly missing being incinerated by a falling comet. Our scale was pushing upwards and establishing new territory around 15 or so.

It's difficult to balance looking back and keeping my mind on the road ahead. I think for a moment of asking your mother to monitor the situation behind us. 'Say sweetie, if you feel hot breath, a soft grunting, and spittle on the back of your neck, would you be a dear and tell me?' I decided against it. Your mom, champ that she is, was near the breaking point. So, I pushed the throttle when I could and hoped for the best.

Fortunately, the road began to level and smooth. It had also become a bit wider, and the wash-boards were less severe. I could actually pick a hard-packed line and get the bike up to a good cruising speed of 30 mph or so. I dared to think, just briefly, that we may get out of this yet. I began to offer supplication, deals, and bargains to whatever higher power may be glancing our way.

Here. Write this down. The problem with most higher powers is that, (now brace yourself for this is the truth), most are ass-hats. Complete knee-biters. Snickering into eternity, comparing stories. Picking out a pair of middle-aged mortals trying to enjoy themselves on a motorcycle, poking each other in the ribs and saying, "Here, hold my beer. Watch this!"

Remember that for the rest of your life. It will serve you well when you get too cocky.

This is where the story takes a funny turn. As we climbed a small hill, and curved round a small bend, I looked ahead to a straight stretch to see --- a moose. Yep, a frickin' moose.

And this was no friendly looking Bullwinkley animal. This moose, which was standing full in the road, looked about 38 feet tall. Seriously. I've never seen taller legs on an animal in my life. It looked like one of the pictures that a child would draw where they get the legs all out of proportion. ("Ah, that is a marvelous drawing sweetie. Nice giraffe. Wha . . .? Not a giraffe? A dog? Well . . . a fine dog it is sweetie. A fine, skinny and extremely tall dog with a loooooong neck.") As with the bear this moose was huge. What the hell, I thought, are there ANY small animals in Canada? Is Alberta the Costco of fauna? Couldn't I encounter an animal with a glandular disorder, so that, you know. . . I could feel superior for even a second?

The moose was completely blocking the road. Crosswise. Just standing there doing moosey things. Possibly calculating next year's taxes. I have no idea. I am not learned in the ways of moose. I know they like squirrels, have their own University, (Whatsamata U), and can, when plied with applause do simple magic tricks with hats but that's as far as my knowledge extends.

Oh! One more thing. Sometimes if you say the right word ping-pong balls will drop from the ceiling.

I hit the brakes on the bike and immediately your mother leans forward. At first I'm alarmed because I can smell the fear coming off her in waves. Then I realize it's just the smell of damp, musty, sweaty, human. And it's coming from me.

Mom chooses to conserve her energy lest she have to shiv someone, or something, and speaks one word. "BEAR????"

"No." Although In my mind I can see the bear closing the gap behind us, and after the kill, slipping a couple of bucks to the moose for the assist.

"No, this would be a moose. Big moose. Really big moose. Standing - well, make that blocking, the road ahead. See?" I say, and quickly take a hand off of the handlebars to point at what now looks like a tank on stilts a few yards ahead.

"Oh," your mom says, as if this were the most rational thing in the world. I could have probably told her that we were approaching a band of Mongols playing chess in pajamas and she would have just shrugged.

"Hopefully," I say, "it will not like the bike and move."

"Hopefully," Mom agrees.

I think you can see where this is going. As we crawled closer, but keeping a safe distance, the moose didn't so much as raise its head nor glance in our direction. It just stood there, licking the road. I am not kidding. Licking the fricking road. As if wet gravel and mud were the Cherry Garcia of the wilderness. It may be for all I know. Next rainstorm, I'm going to find a country lane and give it a try. You never know. Someone has to be the first to try something new. Think of the idiot that ate oysters for the first time. "Hey Thag . . . how oyster?" "Not bad. Like snot. Only fishy. Here. You try." "Screw you Thag. Me still recovering from licking live mountain lion you tell me taste like cotton-candy."

I stopped the bike. Moose in front. Bear in back. Cranky, wet woman sitting behind me. Full on dusk. Happy vacation!

Mom raised her shield. "What do we do now?"

"Cry?"

"Too late," Mom says.

Where in the hell were seven identical Svens and a Hagar when you needed them?

"I'll rev the engine a bit. That should get her moving."

You know that I'm not a fan of loud exhaust. The whole "loud pipes save lives" argument never held water with me. Supposedly, a loud exhaust will make drivers in their cars hear you better, and, the reasoning goes, will help them to be alerted to your presence. Which is good because people in cars don't pay much attention to anything smaller than they are. What the loud pipe crowd fails to acknowledge is that the sound coming out of the exhaust is directed BEHIND you. Sure, you have a bit of a rumble zone, but the blast goes out the back, alerting THOSE YOU'VE ALREADY PASSED that you're there. I know guys that aren't happy until they can rap the throttle and set off a car alarm. And it may piss off those that might ever read this, but I'm calling you out - the reason you have loud pipes is to be cool and scare the straights. To each their own. That's what America is all about. Me? Well I never saw a reason. I'm confident in the size of my . . . um . . . maleness. However, should one of the many fine manufacturers of after-market exhaust advertise that their products would scare the hell out of a moose or a bear, I'd have my money on the counter so quick you'd think I was a congressman on a fact-finding tour of a house of ill repute five minutes before closing.

So, I give the throttle a good crack. Nothing. The exhaust on the Vision isn't nearly as quiet as a lot of bikes I've ridden, but I might as well be miming my actions for all the response I'm getting from the moose.

I rev again and again. Nada.

"She's not going to move, is she?", Mom says with utter despair.

"It's okay. I'll honk the horn, that will get her moving."

All the while I expect THE BEAR to pounce on us at any moment. I honk the horn. I honk the horn again. I honk the horn one more time, and I can't be sure, but I believe the moose raised her front hoof and flipped us off.

"Umm . . . ", Mom says, "did the moose just flip us off?"

"I believe it did sweetie. I believe it did."

"What are we going to do?"

Good question that. Amazing question. I vote for hysteria.

"Well, let's give it a minute. Maybe the nice moosey will move on her own."

So we sit there, two idiots on a touring bike in the middle of the Canadian Rockies, with the day dying around us, bookended by an insane killing machine dressed in a bear costume and a moose with a bad attitude. Prisoners awaiting execution have been less nervous. The moments tick by. The gloom deepens. It becomes readily apparent that Mrs. Moose, (It could be a Mr., but for the sake of the story let's assume it's a female.), is in no particular hurry. Visions of us sitting in the dark, awaiting our death, come to mind.

"Hey, do you have cell phone reception here?", I ask, clinging to some futile hope.

"And just how is that going to help? You want to call the kids and say our last good-byes?"

"Good point."

Mom sighs, "We can't just sit here. This isn't good."

I honk the horn. I rev the engine. I hurl moosey-taunts into the evening air. "Moose's scientific name is an echo! Alces alces? I've heard better names for Naked Mole Rats!" I squeal. "Moose is so stupid she thinks the interwebs are a series of tubes!" Zip reaction. "Moose is so stupid, they think . . . umm . . .", my mind draws a blank. I need a dynamite ending, and I'm reaching for air. "Umm . . . so stupid they can't use 'self-check' at the grocery store!"

Ha! Recover from that one, oh tall, brown, and lanky one!

"Do you really think that's going to help?"

"I have no idea."

Mom looks up the road, "Well it didn't. So, I ask again, what are we going to do?"

My mind races. "Okay, cross your arms, take my hands, and on the count of 3 throw them up in the air and clap against my palms while we shout, and this has to be in unison, we shout, 'Wonder Twins power activate! Form of a giant sloth!'"

Mom took a long time to answer.

"Did you ever go outside as a child, read a book, play a game, or did you live in front of the TV eating a steady diet of mental drek?"

"Drek? Drek? The Super Friends were, and are, not drek. As to my emotional and mental growth, and general well-being . . . well, that's a debate for another day, my dear. Right now, in case you haven't noticed, we are in, what the professionals like to call, 'a bit of a tight spot'."

"What 'professionals'?", Mom asks with what I thought was more than a bit of sarcasm.

"What?" I reply.

"You said 'professionals'. What kind of professionals would call this 'a bit of a tight spot'?"

Oh . . . now it made sense. It was clear your mother, bless her little pea-pickin' heart, had been driven to insanity and I knew I had only myself to blame. I slumped over the console, head to the side, revving the engine, honking the horn, flashing the lights. It was not my finest moment. Perhaps this display of patheticism would prompt the moose to find pity in its big, moosey heart and move on.

The moose looked at us and yawned.

Don't ever tell anyone this, but I nearly panicked right then and there. I looked at that moose, and how tall she was. How long those legs were, how high her belly was off the ground and for a split-second I considered just popping the clutch and seeing if we could zip underneath her. Really. I figured we may have to duck a bit, and the luggage strapped on the trunk may scrape her belly, but I was fairly certain we could make it.

"Don't even frickin' think that you could drive underneath her," Mom warned.

Spooky, spooky woman. Fine. I didn't want to anyway. But I know I could have made it. That aside, it was clear that I had to do something. Hopelessness seemed appropriate.

I literally ground my molars together and said, "Much as I hate to say it, we are going to have to turn around and go back down the mountain. I have no idea what else to do. I know there is a bear back there, but there could be a bear right here, any minute. I would rather be a moving target than a sitting target."

I feel the hope drain from your mother like air from a pin-pricked balloon. "Go back down?"

"I know, sweetie, but we have two options. Stay here, for I don't know how long. How long does it take a moose to get bored? For all we know this one could be 'Regina Moose - Ritalin Queen of the Rockies'. We can't go in front of her, we can't go behind her . . . you've completely ruled out going UNDER her - but we know I could have made it - so we either sit here until God knows when, or we turn around."

Mom doesn't say anything, but I know she doesn't want to stay sitting any longer than I do. I turn the bars on the bike, brace my feet, and with all of my might push backwards. The gravel slips under my boots and I lose traction but I quickly recover and the bike, the giant that she is, begins to slowly roll backwards an inch at a time. Or a deca-mile. Whatever. Mom usually offers to get off the bike when I'm trying to wheel this baby backwards, but she doesn't offer this time. She knows that no matter what, she's safer on the back seat than standing alone. I strain and grunt, begging the bike to turn far enough that I can straighten the front tire to ease the push. All I have to do is get it backed crossways in the road, then I can ease on the clutch and finish pulling the bike around, pointing it in the opposite direction, and head down the mountain. It all sounded so easy in my head.

Unfortunately, pushing a hella-big bike, loaded with gear, backwards with the front wheel turned on soft gravel during a rainstorm while you are sure that you will be eaten at any moment is not as easy-peesy as it sounds. Before I got the forks straightened out, my thigh muscles were cramping into what looked like lumpy oatmeal. I kept looking at the moose, but she wasn't moving. So, finally I get the bike back far enough that I can give it a little gas and before you know it we are pointed in the direction of Bear Mountain death.

As I sit there, the full realization of what we have to do - to drive back down that treacherous slope in what will be in a few minutes pitch darkness - hits me like a blue-haired lady backing a 1980 Lincoln Continental out of a parking stall at the Mall. We are screwed.

I stop the bike, grip the brake and the clutch, trying to get my nerve up to move when your mother says - - -

"Hey! The moose is gone!"

Well of course. Of course it is.

"Now we can go!" She says with a voice full of hope that somehow hit me wrong.

"'Okay. Good. Go we shall. Well, I'll just whip this baby right around and we will continue on our way because it's SO FRICKIN' EASY TO MANEUVER THIS THING!"

Damn you Victory engineers! What the hell about skipping a reverse gear on the Vision sounded like a good idea?

"WHAT A JOY! I WOULDN'T MIND DOING THIS ALL DAY. IT'S A PIECE OF CAKE, IT IS! ISN'T THAT RIGHT MISTER LEGS? YOU DON'T MIND TEARING THE REST OF THE TENDONS FROM THE BONE, DO YOU?"

Mom lets a few beats pass and says, "Are you finished?"

I grind my teeth. "Maybe I am and maybe I'm not. Let's take a wait and see attitude."

"Okay," she says, "well let me help. You're finished."

And then, and I swear this is true, I heard the soft snuffle and grunt of something in the trees.

I turned that bike back around like it was a hovercraft on ice. Lickety-split. Easy as pie. Quick as the impending collapse of the US economy. By the time I was finished, and we were headed back in the right direction, I was panting, aching, steaming, and experiencing tunnel vision. I forgot my name for a few minutes. I had a nice little interlude in my head where the days were warm and sunny and the roads were dry and clear. Then - BOOM - I'm back on the bike in the Rockies being a moron.

I turn half-around to your mother. "Let me ask you something . . . if we had stayed there too long, and I know you only packed a few crackers because you tell me every 10 minutes or so . . . you'd have eaten me, wouldn't you? A little Donner Party of one. Amiright?"

Mom sighs. "Just get the bike moving."

Sage advice that. So, without further ado I put the bike in gear and we are once again hurtling down a rainy, dusky, gravel road towards oblivion.

Things do begin to look up though. The track in the road gets better. I can get the bike up to about 35 mph now. The stretches are long and straight with plenty of visibility ahead. I suppose the area is gorgeous, but at this point I could not care less. I'm dead. Beat. Nearly defeated. But I would never admit that to anyone. Umm . . . until now I guess.

Dang.

The rest of the journey, thank the Gods, was fairly uneventful. Except one particular part where your mother leaned forward and said, "Bear. Bear! BEAR!!!"

"GAH", I reply. "GURK", I say, trying to form a word.

"BEAR!", your mother reiterates, as if this concept needs reinforcement.

"Where? For the love of all that is Holy, WHERE?", I shout, swiveling my head like a possessed Linda Blair. I had no idea it would turn all the way around like an owl. This trip is just one surprise after another. I'm pushing boundaries. I'm testing my limits. When all is said and done, I may need extended care, but for now I'm on a journey of self-discovery.

She pats my shoulder, "Back there on the side of the bank, next to the tree line. It's okay, it just kind of followed us for a while but it's gone now."

"Followed us?"

"Yeah . . . just kind of popped in and out of the trees . . . following us."

Well, isn't that . . . dandy? I have no words left. I just shake my head that I understood.

Five more minutes up the road and I see a sign. A lovely sign. A wonderful sign. It was bathed in a ray of light. Bunnies scampered at its base and there was a blue bird perched on its rim. I may have glimpsed the tall red hat of a Gnome peeking out from behind its wooden supports. (Ha! I knew the brochures wouldn't lie!) It read. . .

"Hidden Valley Lodge. Welcome!"

Mom gives a small squeal and pounds my back excitedly. "We're saved!"

Pfffftttttt. . . . as if there was ever any doubt.

September 30, 2008

Dear Amber,

Well, the Pirate uniform I ordered came in the mail today. Lot of good it does me now. Although I do look stunning. Even the mailman said so before he ran away.

I only hope I can return the ruby-encrusted saber.

And the ship.

Love,
Daddio

Chapter 7

Home Sweet Lodge

Not a hundred yards past the sign was the turn-off to the Lodge itself. Here the road was extremely muddy - just mud, no gravel - so we had to take special precautions as we bounced up the small hill into the parking area opposite the building.

The place looked gorgeous - the part we could see in the dusk anyway - and now that safety was but a few steps away, the day caught up to us - in a hurry. Every muscle, every square inch of my skin was tender and achy. All I wanted was a hot shower, something to eat, and a clean bed. Your mother wanted the same thing, but also to be more than 6 inches away from me for an extended period of time. She didn't tell me this, but later when I tried to hug her she hit me with her rock. Not hard enough to do damage, but more than enough to get her message across. Oh your mother - ever so coy and demure.

There were 7 or 8 cars in the parking lot. Well, not cars really, but SUVs and trucks. All 4-wheel drive. No other motorcycles. Fancy that.

I collapsed into a quivering heap over the front console of the bike.

"No giving up now. Let's get someplace warm, shall we?" Mom said with false cheer, framing her sentence not so much as a question but a demand.

"Good idea," I replied from my prone position between the handlebars, "do you want to unpack now?"

"No," Mom said as she pried off her helmet, "let's go check-in first."

"Capital idea, my dear."

I straightened up, and small firecrackers went off up and down my spine. I steadied the bike, and allowed your mom to climb out of the saddle. The ground was very soft. I had Mom look for a large, flattish rock to place under the kick-stand so that the bike wouldn't sink in the mud and tip-over during the night. That would put, what we professionals call, a 'damper on the party'. We carry a flattened aluminum can for just such a reason (HA! You thought I packed it for nothing!), but it was currently residing at the bottom of the saddlebag and it seemed way too much of an effort to dig it out when we were surrounded by rocks that would suffice just as well.

Mom walked a few feet away, and bent to pick up just such a rock. Then I saw a hulking shadow glide through the trees behind her, but thought it best given the day and the current situation not to scream. I decided, and convinced myself, that this was naught but fatigue and a trick of light. Later, we would discover that it was more than likely one of the many moose that visited the lodge throughout the day. Mostly more than likely. Hopefully more than likely. Yet in my heart I knew it was a bear.

Really - it was probably best that we were clueless.

You know, that could easily be the title of this entire trip - "It Was Probably Best That We Were Clueless."

Yep. That sums it all up. Sums a bunch of things. In fact, I've decided that's what I want as my epitaph. 'It was probably best that I was clueless'.

You should write that down. That is some deep shit right there.

Where was I? Oh yeah, Mom returned with a suitable rock, and once in place I grabbed my collapsible cane off of the trunk. Whereupon, the spring-loaded demon that it is, once free of its constraining tie, quickly expanded and straightened with a loud *'shooook-CLANK'* - - - and promptly thwapped me in the only place on my body that wasn't protected by leather or Kevlar or multiple layers of clothes.

Yes sir, smack-dab right in the boy-zone.

Mom watched me squirm and contort for a minute. "See, every time that happens, it just makes me a bit more thankful that I'm a woman."

That's nice," I squeaked in a gnome-on-helium voice.

"Looks like it hurts."

"Mmmmmmmmmhummmmm," I manage.

"Yep, definitely looks very painful." She shakes her head and gives a little click of her tongue for emphasis as she folded her arms across her chest.

I was able to suck in a partial breath. "Enjoying this, are we?"

Mom looks me up and down. Apparently she has a bit of buried resentment and is blaming me for this day. I have no idea why. It's obvious that she's irrational from fatigue.

"Why no", she says, "No, not at all."

I narrow my eyes and point my finger at her in a grand accusation. "LIAR!" I shout.

Only the 'boys' are still fox-holed and deeply entrenched, so in my exuberance it comes out much like the sound a squeaky-toy makes while being ravaged by a spiteful dog.

"Come on," she sighs, and gently tugs my arm, "let's get inside where it's warm and dry." I start to protest - just for kicks - but then I fold and follow obediently. I have a small, resilient nugget of attitude deep inside, but that is all. No strength. I have no resistance left in me. I am all wiggly gelatin. I believe myself petulant, but in reality I'm just sad. You see where this is going of course. Yes, I - through the trials and tribulations of the day - have become French.

Before I describe what happened after we entered the Lodge, it would be best to step back and take an objective examination of how we must have appeared to the outside world.

They say that people's opinions are formed in the first 2 seconds of meeting. If so, we were screwed. Mom was a soggy, muddy, bulbous, pale version of her regular self with the added attraction of dark circles and eyes that were open wayyyyyyy too wide.

I looked way better than she did. I was a soggy, muddy, bald-headed and goateed man on a cane, wearing leather chaps and bulky upper garments.

Protip: A guy that is fairly large and muscular, in his late forties, bald, wearing leather, riding a motorcycle, and walking with a cane garners mad props. Mad props I say! I highly recommend the look. It might be tough for you to pull off, being 22, blond, and a girl, but I think you could manage. No one ever comes up to me and asks what happened, but you can tell they assume it to be a motorcycle-related injury. As I walk past, or pogo-cane-hobble to be more accurate, they cast furtive glances, and try not to make eye contact. I can read their faces. Their expressions say, "How hard-core do you have to be to crawl back on one of those murder-machines once it's crippled you?" Ha! Works for me. Think they would have the same attitude were they to discover that whomever writes the sorry scripts for this thing we call life had decided I didn't need cartilage in my spine? Arthritis is not a party story. Well, not a fun one at least. Fleeing police at crazy speeds on your bike with a bottle of Rum in one hand, a saber clamped twixt your teeth and a one-eyed mangy meth-addled monkey riding on the sissy-bar flinging poo and flipping off everyone we pass - that is a party story. Discussing the nuances of arthritis is - well, just so damn pedestrian.

Anyway I hope we don't frighten the staff too badly, but I have my doubts. Mom's giving me the willies and I live with her.

Back to our story. The front of the Lodge is exactly what you would expect the front of a Lodge in the Canadian Rockies to look like. Very woodsy. Very outdoorsy. Very Canadian.

We make our way to the front and open the massively planked and wrought-iron hinged door with a rumbling squeak. Soft yellow light spills across us. Your mother sneaks a glance at me in this new light and draws in her breath with a quick sucking sound, for apparently I'm not as dashing as I had assumed. From the interior of the building a wave of warmth rolls over us mixed with the odors of something wonderful cooking. It sucks out what little energy I have left like a junior Congressmen sucks up donations at a PAC luncheon. I am a leather-clad, three-legged, quivering mound of goo. I have hit the wall and pushed through to the other wall that is bigger and thicker and painted an unsightly color. I am all in.

We stumble into the foyer with our clothes dripping and forming puddles on the slate floor around our boots.

Now that we are inside, I see that the building is much bigger than I'd inferred from the parking lot. I believe this to be true of all Canadian architecture. Somewhere, somehow, these tricky - and extremely affable people have managed to break the space-time continuum and are keeping it a closely guarded secret from their brothers to the south. Fine. See if we bail your asses out next time Hitler decides to annex Quebec!

As I look around the interior I realize this may be a hologram. Beyond the slate-tiled entry is a small room doubling as registration / gift shop. Beyond that another room with comfy chairs and bookshelves. The rest of the Lodge is hidden from our view. From what we can see, however, the exterior motif continues to the interior. Very woodsy. Very outdoorsy. Very parallel-universey. Very Canadian.

Before you can say "The Right Honourable Stephan Harper", a small woman with short, dark hair and a semi-hippy casual look about her springs forth from the woodwork - for I have no idea where else she could have been hiding, possibly another dimension entirely - and rushes to our side.

"Oh, my God!" she exclaims, takes a good look at us, and adds a troublesome, "Urk!", to the end of her sentence. "You made it!"

That's curious . . . she seems overjoyed that we are alive. Mom and I exchange blank looks. This is not the greeting we were expecting. It carried so much more concern than we are accustomed to from the hospitality industry in our country of origin. I immediately became suspicious. What's your game Innkeeper?

"Yes," Mom agrees, but casts a slightly scornful glance my way. "We made it."

"We were all so worried! We were getting ready to send a couple of cars out to look for you!"

"Really?" I ask, with true surprise.

"Oh yes . . . we've been waiting for you all day. On your reservation you said you would be arriving in the early afternoon. And then it got later and later and darker and darker and we didn't know which direction you had come in. Although since you're riding a motorcycle I assume you came up from Highway 40 . . . well, let's just say that this isn't the area you want to be riding a motorcycle in after dark!"

Concern shone in her eyes and relief poured from her body. And this wasn't fake 'how is your day going?' concern. This concern was genuine. Real.

This emotion, coming from someone we had just met, was disquieting to say the least. What fresh insanity was this? My mind worked like a jack-hammer. It was a trap. No human was this friendly. It had finally happened. They were going to kill us. Or quite possibly they were on drugs. In which case I hoped they would share. And was I imagining it or . . . did I detect a slight Nordic accent? I cast a sly eye about for Viking paraphernalia.

Through the addled oatmeal that was my brain, the phrase 'which direction you came in' stuck in my mind like a stubborn raisin on a spoon fourth time through the dishwasher. What craziness was she on about? There was more than one way into this fourth circle of Hell? And more importantly if this was true how could I keep this knowledge from your mother?

"Did you get lost?", she asked, as she ushered us into a large and well appointed dining room.

Other staff floated in from . . . well I have no idea. Possibly the ether. They gathered round and studied us, much like I would imagine the caretakers at a zoo would study new arrivals. If those new arrivals rode motorcycles. And were muddy. And wet. And from THE STATES!

"Lost?", I queried, "No . . . not us. Just delayed a bit. It was raining, and . . ."

I looked to your mother for confirmation. She sold me out quicker than tickets to a Cher concert in San Francisco.

"Yes, we got lost."

"Only for a bit," I retorted, trying to salvage some shred of my manhood. Mom gave me the death-stare. "Well, quite a little bit. But that's beside the point. We're here now. I have to tell you, I wasn't sure we were going to make it there for a little while."

I smiled. Or snarled. My lips were tired. And numb. And chewed to bits.

"Oh you poor things. Stacy, show these folks to their room." She motioned one of the young women floating on the periphery over to our little party. "I'm sure you guys want . . . ," and here she paused for a moment, trying to triage our needs, ". . . some dry clothes and a hot shower. We missed you for dinner, but the cook has kept a couple of plates warm for you. Take your time and when you're ready come back to the dining room. You guys look bushed!"

Mom smiled, for what I realized was the first time in hours. Possibly days. "That sounds great."

A middle-aged man, a bit on the chunky side with a heavy Boston accent, approached us with the confidence only found on the East Coast of the USA, and thrust his hand into mine. "I'm Donny. Anything ya need while you're at the Lodge yah just let me know. My wife's the cook and I'm her lackey," he grinned, pumping my hand up and down vigorously.

"Pleased to meet you Donny," I replied. "I'm David, and this is my wife Suzanne."

"Pleased to make your acquaintance," Donny said, finally releasing my hand in order to greet your mother.

Introductions with the rest of the staff followed, and once all the *hello*'s and *pleased to meet you*'s and *oh so you're from THE STATES!*' had been bandied about, Donny gave us one final look up and down, and said, "So, what kind ah bike ah ya ridin'?"

No. Please God, I can't talk about the bike one more time today. Shoot me or sedate me, but don't ask me about the Vision.

"Ummm . . .," I stammer, trying to figure a way to make this as short a conversation as possible, "we are riding a Victory Vision." I looked to the group surrounding us for a flicker of recognition. Nothing but friendly smiles and blank stares and an implied "And . . . ?" "It's a new model from Victory. Kind of a space-agey looking design."

"Oh," Donny said. Silently the group had appointed him the point-man for all inquiries regarding motorcycles, "dual-sport?"

"No," I say, and shake my head. "No, it's more along the lines of a Honda Goldwing. Only more Jetson-like. And we've learned already," I give a quick wink to your mom, "that it doesn't impress the moose around here." I grin like a loon. If that loon were bald, and horribly, horribly chafed.

"You saw one of our moose, huh?", Stacy said, and began walking / herding us towards the door.

"Yeah," I smiled. "One of the reasons we're so late. Darn moose was blocking the road and we couldn't get around."

"They do that sometimes," Stacy agreed with a gentle smile.

"Wait a second," Donny said, shaking his head, "ya rode a big-ass touring bike up here?" He glanced around at the ladies. "Pah-don my French girls."

I nod in the affirmative and turn back to Stacy. "It would have been cool any other time, but as you know it was getting dark and the darn thing just wouldn't move, and I don't think it would have been so nerve-wracking, but we'd just had the encounter with the bear . . ."

"You rode a touring bike up here in this weather from Highway 40?", Donny asked, with a bit on incredulity in his voice. "Where did ya stat out this morning?" Calgary?"

I turned back to him, and answered, "Highway 40, is that the one that comes from Carnack? Oh, and we had a pretty long day. We left this morning from Galaway's Bay."

"What bear?" asked the woman that had greeted us originally, whose name we would later discover to be Leeza - not 'Lisa', but 'Leeeeeezzaaa'.

"Well, we were coming up the hill and all of a sudden this huge, and I don't mean to exaggerate, but I do mean HUGE bear came out of the woods onto the road --- "

"Let me get this straight," Donny interrupted, "ya rode a Goldwing sized bike up the Carnack side?" As he said this his voice crept several octaves above the normal register. I took a quick glance to see if perhaps Donny had a 'boy-zone' incident of his own. He hadn't, but he was clearly impressed with our mad riding skills.

"Well . . . Yeah.", I answered.

"And you ran into one of the grizzlies?", asked Stacy, fear tinging her voice.

"Yes," Mom added, beginning to pick up on the vibe that had suddenly taken hold of our small welcoming party, "and another one that . . . kind of followed us along the tree-line for a while." Mom smiled, looking for reassurance that this was a normal daily event in the cavalcade of fun that was Hidden Valley.

Mom's description of the 2nd bear brought silence and quickly exchanged looks of panic from the staff.

One of the other people, I have no idea who, piped in. "You rode up from Carnack? In the dark?"

"Where the hell is Galaway's Bay?", Donny asked Stacy.

"It's in BC," I answered, "just across the US border. Above the northwest corner of Washington." I smiled reassuringly at the crowd. "Long day. I guess we did about 600 KM."

Other people, some guests, some staff, wandered in to hear what all the excitement was about. Now the small foyer was bursting with Canadians, and we were in the middle. If this were a Tootsie-Pop, we were the chewy-chocolatey center. There were hushed whispers as people brought the new arrivals up to speed on what all the fuss was about.

"And a moose blocked the road?" Leeza added, as if she were trying to make sense of our story.

"Yeah. For a bit. Which, wouldn't have been too bad, but like I said, it hadn't been that long since we'd seen the bear so I wasn't sure how far behind us . . .", I let my voice trail off. There was really nothing more to add.

Fear bathed the room like cheap perfume at the penny-slots in a failing Casino. Hasty looks were exchanged, but without a history with these people I had no idea of the subtext. I couldn't tell if they were afraid FOR us or OF us.

"Jesus," Donny said and excused himself, "I gotta take a look at this bike," and bolted out of the door into the night.

Silence. Curtains rustled on a night breeze. Somewhere in the distance a wolf howled. I could hear the steady patter of water as it dripped off our clothes onto the slate floor.

I had to break the silence, for it was beginning to creep me out. "You guys have a lot of bear up here I take it. Lot of moose. So, this is like normal. Right?"

They stared at us. We stared at them. An old man coughed.

Leeza shook her head as if coming out of a dream. "Well you have had quite a day. Quite a day indeed and as anxious as I am to hear the details I think we'd better get you out of those wet clothes before you freeze completely. Stacy, please show David and Suzanne to their room."

Stacy wore two brilliant, neon pink pig-tails on top of her head, exactly like 'Red' from Fraggle Rock. She was pierced in the lips, nose, and eyebrow. I could see tats on her arms and stomach. Heavy blue and black eye shadow completed the look. She was adorable!

Stacy smiled, and took your mom by the elbow, steering her back towards the front door. "Come on guys, let's get you warm and dry."

Mom followed Stacy, and with a brief goodbye to our new hosts, I followed your mother. As soon as we cleared the door, I could hear the buzz of conversation erupt behind us.

"We've got you booked into the 'Moose-Snot Roost' for three nights, is that right?", she asked as we stepped into the darkness. Out of the corner of my eye I could see a flashlight playing over the Vision in the parking lot. Evidently Donny was making a thorough inspection.

"Ummmmm . . .", I stammered. Moose-Snot Roost? What the hell? I'm all one for adventure, but that seldom requires moose mucus.

"Don't be put off by the name," Stacy giggled. "It's one of the best rooms in the place. The balcony sits right over the Moose-wallow. You'll be able to watch the moose come and go all day. So close that you could reach out and touch them." She giggled a bit, then stopped in dead her tracks, so quickly Mom almost ran into her, and in the dim light of the porch lamps I could see a severely concerned look flit across brow. "But don't - okay? I mean, don't try to touch a moose. Although they look all cuddly they're wild animals. And sometimes, you'll run into one that's aggressive. Some of them have quite bad attitudes."

"Oh," I said. "We know. The one that was standing in the road blocking our path flipped us off."

Stacy studied us then, trying to decide if she should call for reinforcements when her face brightened. "Oh! You're joking!" She giggled. "Good one eh?"

I wanted to explain that in our Universe, the moose really had flipped us off, but thought better of it. You can only expose so much of yourself at the beginning of a relationship. Otherwise people tend to avoid you. Or run. Or possibly call the authorities. But that's just been my experience, your mileage may vary.

We walked about 10 feet to another smaller door on the front of the building that I had assumed was some kind of a service entrance, but turned out to be the door to our suite.

Stacy stepped onto the small, wooden deck, and opened the door. "We don't lock things around here, so there's no key to give you. But there is a lock on the inside of the door so you can secure it at night."

Stacy flipped on the light-switch, and we stepped through the door into a wonderful, warm, dry, and surprisingly large room. Although, with the state of physics north of the border I shouldn't have been surprised. Pale olive-green walls matched perfectly with the natural wood of the vaulted ceilings. The bed was king-sized, and continuing with the motif the frame was constructed entirely out of logs. The rest of the room contained two high-back library style chairs, a small couch, all arranged in a semi-circle around a gas fireplace. We could see a huge walk-out deck, and a bay-window overflowing with cushy pillows on the built-in seat. Right then I knew that spot would become your mom's favorite place to curl up with a book for the next few days. The room was immaculate. Freshly painted, and all of the furniture looked quite new. Off to the side of the bed was a small, yet fully updated and functional bathroom with a walk-in shower.

Stacy walked around, showing us the light switches, thermostats, towels, etc. It was all fairly self-explanatory. Evidently, toilets and electricity work much the same this far north. Not like Europe or Asia. Bastards.

After concluding her tour of the room, Stacy said, "So, don't hesitate to call with anything you need." She smiled, and with her punkish-pixie looks was simply chock-full of awesome. She reminded me more than a bit of you and your sister. Well, until you got all Navy-a-pated on us.

"Oh, just so you know since this is your first time here, all of our meals are served in the main dining room. Breakfast is at 7, and then we offer a make-your-own box lunch after breakfast. Most people do a lot of hiking while they're here, and we find that letting them pack their own bag works out best for everyone."

She looked at us in our gear and me on my cane, and added, "Of course, not everyone hikes. There's plenty to do here in the Lodge, or you can just 'relax'."

She teased out the word 'relax' until it actually sounded quite naughty, and gave us a wink. I was too tired to blush.

"We have high-tea at 2 to 3:30, then dinner at 6:30. Wine, beer, and spirits are offered at our bar anytime, or we would be happy to bring you a fine bottle of one of our local Okanagan wines on request."

See? There is that frickin' Canadian spelling again! As you know, I was born in the Okanogan Valley of Washington. Do you see it? The US side, it's 'Okanogan'. Canadian side, it's 'Okanagan', and they are pronounced the same. For being so nice and polite to your face, Canadians, as a people, really get a kick out of screwing with spelling. I can't help but think that what they're saying in reality is: "See? We don't have to follow you silly Americans and your silly American words! We shall assert our independence and distinguish ourselves as a separate nation by these mystical spellings! So 'F' you, all you from THE

STATES! Bugger off! Unless, you know . . . someone invades or attacks us. Then you better get your sorry asses up here pronto. Until then, it's naught but Celene Dion, Rush, and Cirque' de Soli for the lot of you!

"Thank you," Mom said. "Everything looks great."

Stacy smiled again, "So, when you get cleaned up come back to the dining room. You two must be starving!"

She flashed us a quick wave, and then she was out the door and into the night.

I looked at Mom. Mom looked at me.

"Well," I said, "we made it."

"Thank God," Mom replied. "I had my doubts."

I decided, in the interest of domestic harmony, to ignore her little jab. "You want to shower first, or do you want me to?"

"I think," she said, "that we should go unload the bike. Otherwise, we have nothing to change into."

"Ah . . . yes. That would help, wouldn't it. Unless you'd like to give them a shock by showing up nude, then feigning ignorance?"

Crickets. I kid you not. The sound of flippin' crickets. Evidently your mom was in serious need of finding her sense of humor. I decided to let it slide - just this once - and would attempt to get her back on track in the morning.

So, despite it being dark, and us exhausted, and raining again, and having nothing but a tiny little pen-light, and the woods being full of lions, and moose, and bear, (Oh my!), we scampered back to the bike, crammed our arms full of bags and bundles and satchels and cases, then dashed back to the room trying our best not to smell like prey.

I didn't tell your mom this at the time, but as we unloaded the bike I saw another huge, dark mass move through the trees to our right. I believe that it was a hippopotamus. I mean, what else could it have been? A hippo in the Rockies would have been the cherry on top of the sundae. The icing on the cake. The chocolate sauce on the asparagus so to speak. So yes - hippopotamus it was. A large, hairy, toothy, snuffling, sharp-clawed hippopotamus. And that's the story I will tell myself until the day I die.

It was then that we made another discovery. A wonderful marvelous discovery. We found that the absolutely, positively, money-back guaranteed water-proof bag - the Fort Knox of luggage - and in which we had stored our clothes and then lashed to the outside of the trunk without a care in the world - because we are from THE STATES and are consumer lemmings that believe every piece of advertising known to man - wasn't so water-proof after all. Or, it would seem, even water resistant. Point of fact, it was rather water-attractable. Water laden would an accurate description. A more appropriate marketing slogan might have been, "The Big Blue Waterproof Bag! Now 50% More Spongelike!".

As we unpacked, I tried to cheer up your mom. "Let's look on the bright side. The clothes in the middle are hardly damp at all!"

Your mother turned to me slowly. So slowly, that the deliberateness of the gesture made my stomach turn. She grabbed both of my hands in hers, brought them close and kissed them gently. She looked me deeply in the eyes with a soul-penetrating gaze and said, "I love you. You know that. But if you open your mouth one more time before I'm warm and dry, I will punch you right in the throat."

Now here's the deal, and you know exactly what I'm talking about because you struggle with the same thing - a million inappropriate thoughts raced through my mind, begging to be given voice. I couldn't help it. You know the Moore's motto: "There is absolutely no situation that can't be made more awkward, more uncomfortable, or more hostile by a well placed smart-assed remark." Seriously, I'm absolutely pathological. However, in this situation - and you would have been so proud - I actually edited myself. I know! It's amazing! Cigars all around!

As gently as I could, I say, "Go take a nice warm shower babe. I'll hang these clothes up to dry." I was going to give her a hug, but that would leave various body parts vulnerable. A business-like pat on the shoulder seemed safer.

Your mom's eyes narrowed. Having spent over 30 years with me, she had a right to be suspicious. "What, no pithy comment?"

"The pith has been leeched out of my bones. I am pith-less. Pith-less in the Northern Rockies," I said, then caught myself before I went on a riff and woke up dead with my larynx crushed by a little tiny wet woman in leather and boots.

Your mother glared, but held her tongue. She slipped into the bathroom and shut the door. I busied myself with draping various pieces of wet clothing about the room. When I finished, it looked like a washing machine had spontaneously exploded and disgorged its contents helter-skelter. I tried to make it a bit tidier, but it was no use. I didn't have the energy.

I heard the water run in the shower, and, when I was sure it was safe, stripped off my wet gear and clothes. Several hours being damp had - in NO sense of the word - been kind. I disgusted even myself. I collapsed on the bed in a damp, wrinkly heap.

Mom finished in the shower and said with a refreshed sigh, "Okay. Your turn." She walked back into the bedroom, and I was glad to see some color in her face. She glanced around our quarters at first quizzically, then with a bit of disgust. Finally with a shrug she gave up. It made me sad to see the spunk gone out of her. There were pants hanging from curtain rods, socks adorning the arms of chairs and the sofa, and underwear draped over lampshades. You know, much like a dorm room on a Sunday morning.

She shook her head, massaging her temples.

"Go take a shower. I'm starving."

Without further ado, or comment, I did as I was told.

I have had many a shower in my life, but none ever felt as grand as this one. I could have just stood there all night, letting the hot water cascade over me, washing away the past 14 hours, emerging in the morning as refreshed as a converted Catholic after confession. But I knew your mom was waiting, and it was wayyyyyyyy past her dinner time, and I wanted to put this all behind us and make a fresh start. So I hurriedly washed, dried, and put on some (semi) dry clothes, and sprang from the bathroom fresh as a daisy. If that daisy had been sitting in a flea market flower stall for the last week slowly fossilizing.

Had we really only been gone from home two days? Felt more like two months.

"I have a question for you," Mom said and I wanted to bang my head against the wall because have you ever noticed that when someone says "I have a question" they say that for one of two reasons: One, they are preparing you for some kind of bombshell, as in "I have a question for you. Has the baby always been on fire?" Or two, they are not really asking you a question. What they are doing is establishing a logic framework in order to make an accusation, as in "I have a question for you. Where were you on the night of February 4th between the hours of 7 PM and 9 PM, and were you aware that not only were you being tracked by LoJack, but we have sequential security camera footage of you on your little adventure with the Camel and the Nuns and the AK-47 badly disguised as a doll?

Guess which line of questioning your mother was pursuing.

"Oh good. Had a bit of time to ponder the day whilst I was showering, have we?"

She ignored my question, but narrowed her eyes all snake-like. If she were John Wayne I would have been staring down the barrel of a peace-maker and the lead would have been about to fly. She smiled, ever so slightly. There was not a hint of love nor kindness nor femininity in that smile.

"Did you pick up on the fact that this is more of a 'Bed and Breakfast' type place rather than a 'What would you like from the menu?' type place?" And of course she knew the answer to that, but as I said, that's not what this particular conversation was about.

My blood ran cold. For some reason, I had hoped that the powers-that-be would have taken pity on me after the gauntlet of our day and let this one rest. Just for tonight. Silly me and my silly expectations. As you know, your mother has many, many, many, many, (is she still reading over my shoulder?), many, MANY wonderful qualities and attributes. Being thrust into social situations with large groups of strangers is not among that pantheon. I can clearly recall having a discussion on this exact subject some . . . oh, I don't know .

. . 7 or 8 thousand times in our life. Phrases like 'I never want to stay in a Bed and Breakfast.", and "I can think of nothing more unpleasant than trying to make idle conversation with strangers first thing in the morning." and "If you ever book us in something like that there will be Hell to pay." sprang to mind.

I have one hope. I will play dumb.

"Really?" I say, and open my eyes all puppy like. "I didn't know that. Hmmmmm . . . Well, I guess we will just have to make the best of it."

I prepared myself for a lecture. I would have welcomed a harsh word, possibly some cursing. Slight physical punishment was not out of the question. But it was worse. Mom just shook her head and sighed.

"Let's get this over with," she said, and slipped damp tennis shoes on her pruney little feet. "If this is like the rest of our day, they'll probably douse us with acid before dessert."

Great. Not only have I almost killed my love countless times on this trip, now I have disappointed her as well. This day just keeps getting better and better and better. Well played, Good Sir. Well played. I had been successful in inflicting the maximum emotional damage possible in the shortest amount of time while expending the least amount of energy. That, my young daughter, is what marriage is all about.

I slipped my boots on over my sore feet - my other shoes were very, very wet - and we made the short journey out the door, through the dark, and into the Lodge.

Leeza was waiting for us in the foyer, and with a smile reserved for idiots that have no idea how close they've just came to death, ushered us into the dining room.

I had paid little attention to the dining room on our previous visit to the lodge owning to the fact that I was in the first stages of shock. Or maybe the 4th stage. Which one is death? 3? Then it was definitely stage 4. Now I had a chance to look around, and what I saw was lovely. The room could accommodate probably 50 to 75 people. There were four large tables with 4 chairs on each side, (you doing the math here?). Floor to ceiling windows on two sides of the dining room opened onto a wrap-around deck just visible in the light spilling outside. I could spot the entrance to the kitchen on the back wall, (near where we had walked in), and on the opposite side I could see a doorway that led into what looked like a small sitting room, complete with a massive river rock fireplace. I had noticed this room on our arrival but not the fireplace, which was gorgeous, and I made a mental note to spend some time by that fire with a good book.

In addition to the tables and chairs, there were a few other pieces of furniture in the dining room. A hutch here, a sideboard there. A statue, remarkably life-like, of an elderly gentleman looking as if he had just stepped off the Alps. He may or may not have been wearing lederhosen. The tables and chairs were all of natural wood, but varnished to a high sheen. The ceiling was low here, and it made the space seem cozy. The warmth of the earth-tones complimented each other, and the room was neither sparse nor cluttered but balanced just right. The tables all had fresh flowers in simple vases. At the table nearest us, and looking out into the darkness, were two place settings. We were alone in the dining room, but I could hear soft laughter and the lilt of conversation drift from other parts of the Lodge.

Leeza motioned us to the table, "Come, come. Sit down. You two have to be starving!"

Mom and I obediently took our seats. The bike has great seats, but the cushions on the chairs felt like heaven. As you know, I suffer from TAS. That's right I said it. I have 'Tiny Ass Syndrome' wherein - well to be blunt - I have no ass. So as I'm sure you'll understand the cushions were nirvana to my tush.

Leeza poured water into the tumblers on the table. "Cook has your plates warming. Can I start you off with a drink?"

As you know, your mom doesn't drink. I believe it to be a character flaw, but that's beside the point. However, for the briefest of moments I saw her contemplating takin' to the bottle. This would be bad. You have no idea how hard it is to try and ride with a drunk on the back of your bike. Don't ask me how I know this, just trust me when I say they have a tendency to fall off at the worst times, and if they survive they get all lippy.

"Water will be fine for me," Mom says, saving her journey into alcoholism for another day.

Leeza looks at me and raises her eyebrows. What I want is a keg of Guinness. Make that 2 kegs of Guinness with a fifth of Glenlivet as a chaser. What I settle for is a cup of coffee. Alcohol, for me anymore, is much more enjoyable as a concept rather than an actual consumable. Much like when you're sitting around with your friends and you say, "Hey, you know what would be fun? We should all just take off for the mountains this weekend. We could rent a cabin, each one of us could be responsible for a meal, we could play board games and strum guitars and talk about the meaning of life. What say you?" And everyone agrees that is EXACTLY what you should all do but each one of you is thinking "But first, I'll need a bullet to the brain".

Without further ado Leeza disappears back into the kitchen.

Mom and I sit in silence. Reflecting.

Protip: That's never good.

I'm sure in the light of day the view from the dining room is wonderful. Everything in Canada is wonderful. Every-Frackin'-Thing. But in the darkness, all we could see was our own reflections. How's that for symbolism?

We sat there, in silence, and the statue in the corner coughed, then walked into the library. I nearly jumped out of my skin. What would animate a statue like that? There was dark, dark magic afloat here, no doubt about it. I would need to be wary.

After a few minutes Leeza returns with my coffee, two salads that look like they've stepped off the staging table at the Food Network's 'Let's-Compete-For-The-Most-Ostentatious-Salad-EVER-And-Be-Sure-To-Use-A-Live-Badger!' competition, and a generous portion of what we discover is freshly-baked honey-wheat bread.

As Leeza puts the plates in front of us, she says, "The Honey-Raspberry Vinaigrette is one of our trademarks. The honey is collected in the wild, where IOUs and apologies are issued to the bees. We also set them up with a Health Care Plan. The greens are supplemented with native foliage gathered daily from our forests and meadows. Mostly native grasses and root shavings. We harvest our own apples from a Heritage Orchard in Carnack, and process them into the vinegar you are about to taste, as well as some delicious apple cider. The wheat for the bread, unbleached of course, comes from eco-friendly ranching cooperatives on the plains of Alberta."

Leeza nods her head as she speaks, plainly proud of their food, and rightfully so. "The hazelnuts," and here she pauses, clearly bracing for an admission that will blow our socks off, "are from . . . the Costco in Calgary." She dips her head slightly as if embarrassed. I want to tell her that like her hazelnuts, my underwear and socks are 'Kirkland branded' as well, but in a moment of clarity I realize she may not care to hear about my skivvies.

"Enjoy!", she says with a smile. "I'll be back in a few minutes with your main course."

I feel slightly saddened that in my state I am unable to appreciate the nuances of the food set before us. You could have popped a can of cat food, (and not the good kind either - the cheap stuff from China that may or may not be made with political dissidents and a dash of cyanide), and I would have devoured the pasty goo without pausing to taste. However, as anyone knows the ultimate insult to a cook - well, non-verbal anyway - is to scarf your food like a hyena, never giving it a chance to register on your taste buds. I was sure we were being watched by the cooks, and as I wanted a mucus-free dining experience, I fought my nature and ate at a respectful pace.

I doubt that I've had a better salad in my entire life. The bread was akin to Manna. Warm, but not too hot. Sweet, yet not overpowering. I look over at your mom. She has devoured half a loaf already and I'm prepared to protect my portion should the need arise. Rock and shank be damned! This was some fine, fine bread we are talking about here.

We ate slowly and steadily in silence. The soft noises that did reach our ears were soothing, like an aural massage after the assault of a droning motor, wind, whimpering and screams that comprised the background music of our day. As soon as we neared the end of this soul-smart salad, Leeza appeared with two covered plates that she promptly sat before us. She removed the covers with a flourish and the scent of heaven wafted towards me.

"You both look so tired, I won't go into the details, but here we have stuffed pork tenderloin with wild mushrooms and a red wine reduction, wild rice pilaf, and a variety of steamed in-season vegetables from our gardens and our own hand-churned butter." Here she paused, clearly fighting the urge to inform us as to the lineage of the cow that produced the cream, and how each night before bed they read said bovine selected passages from 'Animal Farm', skipping the parts that she would find objectionable or disturbing. It leaves rather slim-pickings, but they manage.

Both of us offer appreciative comments, and satisfied that we are pleased Leeza returns to the kitchen.

The meal surpassed the salad. It was, in a word, bliss.

Nary a squeak passed between us for the next 15 minutes. I know! That may very well be a record for me! Well, at least without sedation. We each scraped our plates clean, which may have been a first for your mother. I was a tad distraught that I had not been required to help her finish her plate.

"That was incredible. I'm not fond of wild rice," your mom said, and dabbed a napkin to the corner of her mouth, "but that was tasty."

"Oh Man! That was one fine meal. I can't believe how much I ate."

Mom shook her head in agreement. "I know. That's the most I've eaten at a single sitting in years."

Stuffed, exhausted, and getting drowsy, we relaxed a bit leaning back in our chairs and exchanging smiles. If all went well, I may yet get out of this day alive.

"Oh my God," Mom exclaimed and my heart jumped into my throat. BEAR? MOOSE? UFO with probes at the ready? What? What manner of death was approaching us now? But then I realized she was watching as Leeza returned with two huge - and I do mean huge - plates of cake.

"Our special Rocky Mountain Mud Cake with double Swiss chocolate sauce and hand-turned vanilla ice cream. I hope you left room."

Silly, silly Leeza. It was chocolate. Your mother would slice open her own stomach to make room for chocolate, especially after a day like today.

"Oh my. Leeza, if this is anything like the rest of our meal, you are the Devil." I said with a smile.

Leeza gave a small laugh and leaned down to whisper, "This is my absolute favorite. I make sure that the cook bakes an extra cake just so the staff can have a treat."

"I am so stuffed . . . but this looks so good . . . " Mom said as she picked up a fork.

We all knew that it was a display of etiquette for social interaction, and what she really wanted to do was face-plant directly into the icing. She pulled the cake close to her, and took a tentative bite making sure to get equal portions of cake and frosting and chocolate sauce. She gently placed the bite in her mouth, letting it rest on her tongue. I saw her eyes close, and her upper body wilt into ecstasy. She swallowed.

"Oh . . . oh yeah. That's good." She took a larger bite. "I mean REALLY good."

Leeza smiled and patted her arm. "Glad you like it. Stay here as long as you like, there is no need to rush off when you finish."

"Give the cook our compliments. Simply wonderful."

"I will," she said over her shoulder. And with that Leeza disappeared into the depths of the Lodge. Probably to churn more butter. Or prepare a pep-talk for the bees.

For the first time in what seemed like forever all was right with the world.

Much to both our surprise we managed to finish our cake. We then scampered back to the room where, warm, dry and with the lights off we were asleep in seconds.

Take that Canada. We, the people from THE STATES, had survived your worst and come through in one piece.

Mostly.

October 1, 2008

Dear Amber,

It was good to hear your voice on the phone the other day. I could have done without all the whimpering.

I apologize. Mom was twisting my arm really hard to keep me in check.

I had no idea they were working you that hard. SOYA? Sand up your what again?

Still all quiet on the western front. Nothing to report around here. Well, nothing that our lawyer will let us discuss anyway.

Oh! Good news! We got the woodchucks out of your room! Not the smell, but we're working on that.

Love you,
Daddio

Chapter 8

Breakfast With Canadians. What...no bacon?

As I've said before, sleep comes in a variety of flavors, textures, and colors. Notice that I didn't use 'colour', Canada has not drilled so deep into my soul that I'm throwing extra vowels hither and yon simply for the lulz.   To wit: there is the fitful slumber of the damned - it is as bitter and dark as a cup of fast-food coffee. There is the troubled dreaming sleep - it has the flavor and color of an old apple, mostly it's good, but every once in a while you hit a spot that makes you want to scream. There is the evil sleep where you dream that you are awake and can't *GET* to sleep, and is the color of copper leaving a foul, foul tang on the tongue.

My personal favorite sleep is the sleep of the dead. It has no flavor or color. You know, much like supermarket sushi. This was the sleep of our first night at Hidden Valley and it was, to put it mildly, glorious.

We awoke early - very early - to the first glow of dawn peeking from behind the mountains, their hulk blocking the sun, punching perfect silhouettes in the brightening sky.

I assume that is what we would have seen had it not been foggy and gray and raining. Again or still. I didn't care. I was dry! Let the heavens descend! The point being we were refreshed, rested, and ready to take on whatever adventures the day would bring, as long as those adventures took place indoors and included a lot of napping.

Mom was the first to spring out of bed. Well, spring might be too strong a word. Slithered is more like it. You can't imagine how many muscles you use riding a motorcycle. Then add several hours of intense panic on top of that and it tends to tax the tendons a bit. Think of a rubber band that's been twisted along its length, oh . . . several thousand times.

I pried my eyes open and managed a garbled, "Morning tiger."

Mom looked at me through the fog of sleep. Her eyes squinty and puffy, and with a slight hint of drool around the corners of her mouth. "Morning," she mumbled.

"Sleep well last night?"

"Oh yeah. I don't think I moved once my head hit the pillow. Completely exhausted. How about you?"

"Like a baby. Or like someone that's been sedated. And none of the dentist office, 'we're going to give you something to help you relax' sedation. I'm talking the good stuff. The major surgery sedation. The black hole sedation. The

'Okay, the procedure will take about 7 hours so we're giving you . . . time to wake up! It's all over!' sedation."

She looked at me, blinking. "Well. I guess that's good. I'm going to go take a shower. We have about 45 minutes until breakfast."

She gave me a quizzical look, trying to decide if she was going to bring up the fact that we were going to be eating 'family style' with a group of people that may, or may not, be hostile. I saw her calculate, saw the wheels spin, and finally - thank Jeebus - she decided that this particular battle could wait until she'd washed the cobwebs from her brain.

"Okey doke. I'll be here," I said with what I hoped was a friendly grin. I very much wanted the day to start out right.

She looked at me hard. As if she hadn't decided whether my still being here was a positive or a negative. Oh cruel woman, must you carry a grudge? I hadn't had her close to death in what . . . 9 hours? Some people just can't let go. Sad really. Anyway, with a shrug she stepped into the bathroom and closed the door. I had survived one of the most dangerous times of the day - pre-shower. Whatever followed should be a piece of cake.

Or so I told myself.

While Mom enjoyed a good scrubbing, I busied myself the way I do most mornings and promptly fell back asleep. This time not the sleep of the dead, but more like 'Hey it's really cold because it's December and the electricity is out so let's bring that big honkin' BBQ into the house, fill 'er to the brim with briquettes, and fire that baby up! That'll warm us all toasty and put a healthy glow into the kid's cheeks' kind of sleep.

Wait a sec. . . . ummm . . . I guess that's the sleep of the dead as well.

I don't know if you're aware, but another of Mom's and my favorite games is: If-David-Falls-Back-Asleep-Don't-Wake-Him-Until-It's-Five-Minutes-Before-The-Time-We-Have-To-Leave.

It's not my favorite game, as waking up in a modified panic does funny things to my heart and can cast a pall over my morning, but your mother has grown quite fond of it over the years. I don't share her enthusiasm, but she puts up with quite a bit from me so I allow her these simple pleasures. I've asked her many, many, many times why she does this to me, to which she replies, "I woke you once. Be an adult and get your keester out of bed."

Silly, silly Mom. I've tried to explain to her that obviously, after all these years she KNOWS I'm going to fall back asleep, so why play this silly charade? Why not just wake me again? To which she replies that I KNOW she won't wake me again, and I KNOW that I have to get up, so why do *I* insist on playing this silly charade and just get the hell out of bed?

Oh . . . now I get it! Gah! Well played good woman. I've done been bamboozled with me own logic.

Luckily, nature intervened on my behalf so unpleasantness was avoided. Mom woke me again, only this time with a "David! David! Get the camera and come here!"

I cracked open one eye, dreams still flitting across my synapses light as butterflies, and I couldn't figure out why Mom wanted a picture of me running down a hallway being chased by a grizzly in a pink tutu while an elk played goalie at the other end. Then, the world swam into solidity and I saw that she was standing by the glass door to the balcony, towel wrapped around her head, pointing excitedly at something down below.

"Grrrrk", I said, quite plainly. My vocal dexterity of moments before gone.. Stupid tongue paralysis. I opened my mouth and tried again. "Whatizit?"

"Just get the camera and come here!"

I bounced out of bed and promptly smacked my knee on a log. Really, who the hell builds a bed out of logs anyway? Poor lumberjacks? Beavers forced into labor camps? Carpenters with a raw timber fetish? I managed to teeter over and grabbed the camera off of the end table closest to the bed, then hobble-gimped over to where your mom was fairly bouncing by the window.

"Look!"

Remember that we hadn't seen the view from 'Moose Snot' in the daylight, so you can excuse my sleep-addled brain as it struggled to interpret what I saw.

A postcard. That's the only way to describe the scene spread out before me . . . a flippin' postcard. In the daylight we saw that our room sat perched on a small bank 25 feet, (or 7.93 NLM - that's nano-liter-meters to you plebeians), above the valley floor, and overlooked that same gorgeous meadow that we had traveled by in the twilight. Iridescent green grasses, lush bush, and a small stream that looked close enough to touch lay before us. The meadow widened close to the Lodge, playing over hollows and slight slopes for a half a mile. (Oh I said mile, yes I did. So SNAPS!) Then the green blanket gave way to a gentle hill and the grasses transitioned to scattered trees. After a short distance the trees gave way to the dense forest of the foothills, that then climbed rapidly into some of the most stunning mountains I've ever had the privilege to view.

Yet, spectacular as the view was, this wasn't what had, for lack of a better term, put your mom all in a bunch. There, right below us, and I do mean right below - I could have spit and hit them - not that I would, that's disgusting - was the much touted 'wallow', and a Moose and her calf frolicking about in the mud.

"Oh my god! How cute is that?"

Mom jerked the camera out of my hands, and proceeded to take well over 9000 pictures of mother and child in various poses. It was the equivalent of a Canadian Sports Illustrated Swimsuit Edition. Minus the beautiful girls. And the warmth. And the beach was replaced by mud. Other than that - spot on!

As a side note, what is it with baby animals? Somewhere, in our genetic makeup is the trigger that transforms anything under a year old into cutest frackin' thing on the face of the earth. Really. Think about what I just said. Name me one totally ugly, disgusting baby animal. No, even Naked Mole Rats are adorable, so don't go there. Snakes are precious. Baby opossums make me weep. Okay, I've seen baby pictures of Rush Limbaugh at 9 months - that may be the exception. If we could isolate and harness the power of that infantile essence, there would be no lonely, ugly people in bars. What a gift to humanity that would be.

I stood there, slack jawed, my head about to explode in a cavalcade of candy-canes and daffodils from the damned cuteness of this tiny, adorable, and long-legged wee beastie.

"Oh look! The mother is nudging it out of the mud!"

That was it. I now needed insulin. We spent the next few minutes in a chorus of 'ooooohhhhsss and awwwwws', punctuated by the occasional gasp of delight.

Another quick side note: maybe it's just me, but I've noticed that cuteness has its limits. About 5 minutes and the miracle becomes mundane. 'Yes, yes. . .the baby is doing a jig to the soundtrack of 'Oklahoma'. Yes, the top hat and cane are adorable. I told you that 3 minutes ago. Definitely cute. Yep. So . . . what's for lunch?'

As we stood there, we saw other moose make their way through the meadow to the wallow. It's possible that they had to punch a time clock hidden amongst the trees. There were deer as well. And what I now believe to be a lost hiker, but at the time thought to be a hobo seeking a therapeutic mud bath. Man, that guy could hold his breath for a long, long time. I think now that we probably should have reported that, but hindsight is 20 - 20, no?

As much as I would have liked, I could delay the inevitable no longer. With a sigh and a smile, I broached the subject that I had been dreading. Please, if there is a God, let this go smoothly. Let her be cheered by the miracle of life, and decide to give me a pass on this one. I braced myself, took a deep breath and said, "So honey," I put an arm around her waist drawing her into a hug, "shall we go have breakfast?"

Have you ever had a cat nestled in your arms, relaxed and purring, when startled by some noise transform in the blink of an eye from an animal with no bones into a piece of steel? Steel with claws and fangs and a penchant for assigning blame? It's a joy, really. You should try it sometime.

Protip: Wear gloves, a heavy coat, and a goalie mask. A baseball bat is not out of the question.

"You mean the wonderful group breakfast with 30 people I don't know that by now consider us idiots at best and insane at worst?"

Damn. God has failed me again. I swear, as soon as I'm back in THE STATES I'm gonna go all Pagan. That'll learn ya God. Learn ya good. Or maybe polytheistic. I think you get more paid holidays with polytheism.

"Well, if you put a spin like that on the situation, anything can sound bad."

"Really," she said raising an eyebrow, "let's see. . . .how could you spin this? Mr. Moore, the limo is here to take you to your awards ceremony."

Crap. She was in test mode. No worries, I'm fast on my feet when the need arises. I cleared my throat and in a crisp voice said, "Yeah, your awards ceremony. . . IN HELL!"

Ha. I've beat her at her own game. Two points!

She started to say something, then shook her head in defeat and said, "Go brush your teeth and shave. Let's get this over with. But I swear by all that is holy, if this goes the way I think it will, I'm going to stab you with a fork under the table."

"In the knee?"

"You wish," she said.

"Fair enough good lady. But don't jump to any conclusions. This may be an exciting new experience! Let's go with an open mind, shall we?"

Mom looked me in the eye for what seemed like an hour, but was probably only a few seconds at most. With a dead-pan voice and a slight shrug she said, "Sure."

Ah, my little dove. Her exuberance overwhelmed me.

After a cursory check on the bike, (Yep! Still a motorcycle!), we made our way into the Lodge. The place was alive and bustling. Voices and laughter poured from the interior. Yet your mother was as tense as an OCD sufferer in a light-switch factory. We took a deep breath, casting caution and judgment to the wind, and stepped through the alcove into the dining room.

The first thing I noticed was that in the daylight, the bank of windows had one of the most staggering views I've ever witnessed. I know I keep hammering this home, but it really was indescribable. And yet I blather on anyway. Jagged granite mountain peaks, the lush meadow, the creek . . . this must be what heaven looks like. Well, if heaven were in Canada. And all metric-y. I stood mesmerized, drinking in the scenery like a parched CEO with the first Mai-tai of the day brought to my office by the new, (nod nod wink wink) secretary.

Really, I couldn't turn away until I realized that there were 30 pairs of eyes on us, and from their perspective it didn't look so much like I was soaking up the natural beauty spread outside the windows behind them but rather staring directly at them with a slack-jawed expression.

Great.

Fortunately, Leeza skip-danced over to us and ushered us to a seat at a nearby table. "Good morning David and Suzanne. I trust you slept well last night?"

"We sure did," Mom replied. "The bed is very comfortable, and the room is great. Although after yesterday I probably could have slept on a freeway."

Leeza smiled, "Oh you poor things. Well, you're here now and we're going to take good care of you. Here," she pulled out the chair for your mom, "have a seat and I'll get you started."

Mom and I took our places at an already occupied table. My suspicions from the night before were confirmed: It was large, square, and could fit four on each side. We sat alone on our side, two empty chairs bookending us.

This was no regular table. It was a square of Canuckian humanity. Possibly a tribunal. From the moment we sat down, it felt like we were at a job interview that had gone terribly, terribly wrong.

"Thank you," Mom said, "Is it possible for me to get a cup of tea?"

"Of course. David? Coffee?"

"Yes please, black."

"Be right back," Leeza said, and whisked herself into the kitchen. This woman never walked, never bounced. She floated around like a Fairy-Tale Princess on ecstasy. Minus the cat-in-the-hat striped stovepipe, and the propensity to disrobe with each new song.

I squeezed your mom's hand, which meant, "See? This isn't so bad." Mom didn't return the squeeze, and I looked at her questioningly. She moved her eyes in a darting fashion to indicate our breakfast companions.

Crap. You know I'm not the most observant person in the world. Unless you have an extra arm growing out of your forehead I'm pretty likely not to notice. And even then, the arm would have to be unusually large. Or waving. Or have some of those huge rings on the fingers. On further inspection it appeared that we had been seated with the only unfriendly Canadians in the entire world. There were over 300 of them with knives, and daggers, and what could have been - although I'm not positive about this - an attack army of trained weasels hidden in their shirts.

No, I'm exaggerating. Here is what we were facing: One large, suspicious, and slightly nervous family. There were two men, in their mid-forties, two women about the same age, an elderly woman in her 70's, and various children that seemed to expand, then contract in number every time I glanced at them. None of this northerly entourage smiled. The two men sat with crossed arms. It was a symphony of flannel and denim and boots. My mind reeled at the sight. Sweet Mary and Joseph, what have we gotten ourselves into?

For you see, these were the most dangerous of Canadians. These were the out-doorsy flavor of Canadians. No mistake, and no other way to put it gently - these were authentic Canadian hikers.

A table of Canadian hikers all related to each other and two frazzled bikers from THE STATES. Woot woot! All aboard the fun train!

As you know the motorcycling community is generally treated as lepers by the likes of hikers and bicyclists. This is completely understandable. We are a loud, noisy, and sometimes quite unruly bunch. I always give the courtesy of a wide berth on the road but I don't think that helps. Basically, internal combustion is anathema to these groups. If you run across a 'herd' – that's the proper term for a group of bicyclists, no. . . you don't need to look it up – anyway, if you encounter a herd on a bike, derision will pour forth upon you like syrup from a pitcher. Unless you yourself are part of a larger motorcycle group. Then, all of a sudden people get all friendly in a hurry. But when we are riding alone, and happen to stumble onto a feral herd, if confronted I will take a moment to point out that they didn't walk to the mountains. And if they are so eco-friendly why do they have cycle racks on their cars? Yet you must be careful. Logic like that only leads to madness. Madness and bent bicycle frames and hiking sticks stored where no hiking stick should be. Oh that's right! I'm one mean cripple when pressed. I am Hell incarnate. At least within a six-foot radius. Beyond that? Not so much.

Not that anything like that has ever happened. In reality I just give them room, wave and smile. Oh, but the 'Hell incarnate within a six-foot radius' is completely true.

Back to breakfast. I decided to take the proverbial bull by the horns, for this was your mother's worst nightmare. I could intuit this from the fact that she was kicking my ankle quite viciously under the table. I grimaced and ever so gently moved the forks out of reach.

Casting caution to the wind, I cleared my throat and took the plunge.

"Hi, I'm David and this is my wife Suzanne." I smiled, projecting confidence and warmth and mostly no insanity at all.

Mostly.

Now usually, when you introduce yourself to a group, unless you're holding a gun in a dark alley while the introductions take place, everyone speaks in turn and introduces themselves. This is what happens in what I've come to call 'normal society'. Apparently, from the land where milk really does come in bags, this was not the custom.

The gentleman sitting closest to me leaned forward. He wore wire-rimmed glasses, and a scruff of beard that complimented his flannel shirt quite well. His hair was mid-length, and parted on the side with just a shock of a black bang draping his forehead. He was of medium build, and on the skinny side of that. But not the 'I have some horrible medical condition' skinny, more of a 'I am an outdoor enthusiast, lean, mean, and packing my own crap out of the forest so as not to disturb the delicate balance of nature' skinny. His facial features were sharp. He fairly glowered behind his glasses, his eyebrows knotting and twisting like a flag in the wind.

Evidently this was the alpha Canuck for all members of the family, (Or is there a different nomenclature for familial groupings in Canada? Clans? Covey? Covens? Hockey Teams?), for all other eyes at the table turned to him.

"I'm Mark," he said with a nod of his head. "This," he said, indicating the elderly woman on his right, "is my mother Martha. Next to her is my wife Cathleen, my brother Carl, and our children, Amanda, Stacey, Jeff and that's", he said pointing, "Carl's wife Camila, and their kids, Jennifer and Brandon, and Brandon's friends Kevin, and Alex.

I sat mesmerized. Like music his voice was. His was a thick Canadian accent. A proper Canadian accent. A 'screw you to the STATES' Canadian accent.

I pushed on, "Please to meet you," I said, pivoting my head, nodding, and making eye contact with each member of the group. Your mother did the same, but I noticed a slight catch of nerves in her voice. The family returned the nod, reluctantly I thought, and after a couple of minutes we realized this was the most we were going to get out of them. There they sat, studying us, casting sidelong glances at each other.

Well, what a fine morning this was shaping into. Hostile Canadians surrounding me on three sides. Hostile tiny woman to my right. Nature's glory over my shoulder. Flop sweat forming on my shiny, shiny bald head, and I hadn't even had my first cup of coffee.

Mark cast a quick glance to his family. Evidently there was some bizarre telepathic connection between the lot of them. Children of the Corn comes to mind. Or the Albertan equivalent. What would the Albertan equivalent be? I would have to ponder that at a later time. Something cold and flat no doubt.

"So," Mark said, but it came out as an accusation which I actually had to admire. It's hard to pack so much emotion into two letters without the aid of weaponry. "You're the ones with the motorcycle. And from THE STATES!"

He then rocked back in his chair, folding his arms once again across his chest. Not a question, just a statement. A statement tinged with contempt and accusations and devilry.

Ah . . . now I get it. We were evil! I actually felt your mom scoot her chair out from the table, preparing to bolt. I put a hand on her knee, and held her in her seat. She wasn't going anywhere. If the ship was going to sink, we were going down together. My mind raced. Was there any possibility of salvaging this moment? More importantly, did I *want* to salvage the moment? Hmmmm . . . it might be fun to adopt a scorched-earth approach. I could insult the Queen. I could declare my complete contempt for all things cheesy. I could tell them that, as a profession, I raped babies but had a side job as a litterbug. So many options . . .

In the end - and this had nothing to do with the fact that your mom was chewing on her lower lip so hard that blood was squirting willy-nilly about the room - I choose the path that will, in most situations, deflect animosity. SDH. Self Deprecating Humor. It's the magic wand of social interaction. It's the salve of awkward situations. The 'special sauce' on the burger of cringe that smothers everything and makes you forget that what you're eating is 90% cardboard.

"*Idiots* on the motorcycle is more like it," I said, bobbing my head. I looked from one Canadastanie to the other giving each of them the grin of the dangerously stupid.

No response. Alpha Canuck narrowed his eyes. I could see the wheels turning. 'What is your game, stupid American? How dare you challenge my expectations?'

Martha, much to the consternation of the rest of the table, giggled. I immediately felt a twinge of fondness for this lady.

Leeza chose that moment, bless her free-spirited soul, to arrive with our coffee and tea. "Here you go folks. I hope you like the tea. It's one of our special blends."

"Thank you," Mom said for the both of us. I was afraid to break eye contact with the alpha male lest he take advantage of the situation and go for my throat with his foon. Or spork. Or runcible spoon. Whatever.

"Be right back with some wonderful oatmeal. And I do mean wonderful! It's handpicked pesticide-free organic oats lightly soaked in spring water gathered from the local mountain peaks above the 3 kilometer mark by imported Sherpas using thatch-baskets woven by First Nation people. It is grand cereal if I do say so." Leeza turned to walk away then stopped abruptly, turned to us with a narrowed brow and added, "Free-range Sherpas, of course."

Well of course they were. I would expect nothing less. I hadn't tasted it yet, but somehow I felt intimidated by a mound of steaming, gummy lumps. Oat anxiety. Although, if you were to look that up in the DSM, (Diagnostic and Statistical Manual of Mental Disorders - no, you don't need to know how I know that.), my apprehension may have more to do with white-haired men in buckle shoes, lace, and 17th century hats.

Gah! I just gave myself the creeps! Curse you Quaker Oats!

Despite my feelings of inadequacy concerning hot cereal, I knew if Leeza left we would be lost. Two souls from THE STATES ripped to shreds and devoured by this eco-outdoorsey-anti-American minded family. I wanted to say something - anything to engage her in conversations but alas . . . I had nuthin'. Panic and fatigue had drained my creative juices. Were I a lemon I would be all crushed and lumpy with the pulp naught but a disorganized mess in the rind. Still, I had to try and convert these northerly heathens into friends, and quickly. A stolen glance at your mom confirmed that she was about 2 seconds away from a full blown case of the social willies.

I opened my mouth to address the group and prayed that something coherent would pop out. It was a 50-50 gamble. "Come here often?" I asked.

Great. I've just used the lamest bar pick-up line ever on an entire family. That may be a new low for me.

Mark cleared his throat. "Yeah. We come every summer. Carl here," he said, jerking a thumb towards his brother, "lives in Peru. He doesn't get home much. So, it's a nice way to get the family to reconnect."

Carl, who was a smaller, younger version of Mark, even down to the hair and glasses, nodded his head.

"Oh," I said, "that's pretty cool. What a great place for you guys to gather. Not a ton of distractions up here." I made sure to keep my tone light and breezy.

The brothers, in complete unison, nodded their heads three times. Not two. Not four. Three. I felt my stomach turn. This was some scary, scary stuff right here. It really was 'Children of the Corn', only much farther north. 'Children of. . .' what the hell does Alberta grow this far north? Oh yeah. 'Children of the Flax Seed'.

Now that I see it on paper, it doesn't sound that scary.

"So," Mark said, glancing at his demon-twin, "where are you guys from in THE STATES?"

Ah. Social pleasantries. There just may be hope yet! I look at your mom to see if she's picked up on the subtle change in the tone of the conversation. It was hard to tell. I noticed that during the last few minutes she'd started to twitch slightly.

"We're from the Seattle area. Well, actually a small town about 40 miles southeast of Seattle next to the Cascade foothills."

I find that adding 'small town' usually will put people at ease. I have no idea why. Maniacs and psychopaths are abundant in small towns. Why, visit any Rotary Club meeting and you're sure to see at least three serial killers at any given time. Don't even get me started on local Chambers of Commerce. Let's just say that most of the Boards of Director's for Chambers are full-blown, unrepentant, closet Satan worshipers. Anyway, back to the small town thingee. I look to the group to see if this bit of info has had a calming effect.

More simple nodding, but this time I detect a slightly positive vibe.

Carl spoke for the first time. His voice was exactly like his brother's, but a tad higher. "I've been through Seattle a few times."

Pause. Silence. I waited for the follow up. The 'and it's a really nice place', or 'incredible scenery', or 'not as bad as I expected'. But no . . . nothing followed. Just a blank stare.

"Oh," I remarked, "well . . . good!" I mean really, what else could I say?

"Yeah," he said, "too many people for my taste."

Martha, his mother, cleared her throat and rolled her eyes. Admiration for this beautiful lady had now blossomed into full blown love.

I study Carl. How dare he not acknowledge the awesomeness that is the Pacific Northwest? And I'm not fond of your nose there chuckles, but I'm not going to point it out. Well, at least not yet. The day is young. I sized up the brothers as a unit. Even though they could outrun me, I was pretty sure that in a street fight I could handle myself. Or at least bean them with my cane into some form of submission. Mom could have kicked their asses straight up, but I was hoping it wouldn't have to come to that.

However, I was beginning to get annoyed - I mean WTF? You would be proud to know that I pushed on, for I was still in the 'Hey I'm all friendly-like' mode.

"There certainly are quite a few of us in the Puget Sound region these days. The area has grown quite significantly over the last decade or so. Big influx from California a few years back. Shoot, even out little burg has grown so much that I hardly recognize it."

I look to your mom for some kind of confirmation, but she is staring at the napkin in her lap.

Leeza was once again our savior. I should just have started calling her 'Jesus Leeza', but you know how picky some people get about things like that. Panties all in a wad and the next thing you know you're standing on a pile of brush, tied to a post, flames licking your ankles. Let me tell you, that can ruin a Monday fast. Anyway, Leeza pushed a cart to our table brimming with steaming bowls of oatmeal and pitchers of milk. Each of the other tables had a similar cart, with a similar attendant.

"Okay folks, here's round one. We'll let you work on that for a bit before we start on the main course."

She worked her way around the table, passing out bowls. She also set out three large dishes of mixed fruit. The smell of strawberries rushed around the room, giving off a lovely delicate perfume that screamed of spring and hope and happier times.

"Can I get you anything else while I'm here?"

Everyone glanced at each other and shook their heads in the negative.

Isn't that odd the way people will do that? What are we looking for - confirmation? As if we might be forgetting something and are waiting for a member of the group to remind us? Like the whole situation could change if only one of us spoke up? "Okay, her iz zee deal. We meet zee English dogs at zee

Waterloo. Everyone agree? Anybody not zink dis iz zee good idea? No? H'okay zen. . . Wait. Did someone in za back zay zomething? No? Oh, screaming from zee battle wound. My mistake. H'okay. I thought maybee you had zumzing to say. Nuting? H'okay. Zen peek up your rifles and off we go to zee victory!"

Leeza waited for someone to say something, and when they didn't she said, "Good! I'll bring some carafes of coffee next trip. Until then . . . enjoy!"

I silently begged Leeza not to leave us. I felt our tenuous hold on civility could cross over to unpleasantness at any moment. Much like every family reunion we've ever attended. Except for that one in the park where your Uncle Jahn baked all those plates of brownies and we spent the day laughing and laughing and laughing and then 27 of us hid under the picnic table for an hour because we thought the people at the next shelter were FBI agents.

That reminds me, I need to write Uncle Jahn and get that brownie recipe.

Luckily, the oatmeal was so indescribably delicious that no one spoke for quite some time. I know! Oatmeal! Come to think, it might have used some of the same ingredients as the brownies. The fruit was ripe and firm and. . . umm. . . sweet. What else can you say about fruit?

With food in our stomachs the mood around the table lightened a bit. The family began to talk quietly amongst themselves, and your mom and I held hands under the table offering each other support. True, your mom held a little too tightly, and I had to pry her fingernails from the palm of my hand with a spoon, but it really wasn't so bad. Hardly any blood at all. If anyone were to notice my wounds I would swoon in a religious fervor, claiming stigmata.

As we finished the last bites of our cereal, Donny came bounding out of the kitchen and made a beeline for our table. "Boy, I gotta tell ya, that is some bike you got there."

Hmmm . . . was this a positive or a negative remark? He was smiling, kind of, so I decided to take it as a positive.

"Umm . . . thanks!" I said.

"Oh yeah, no problem. Dat things a wicked honker. I can't believe you rode it up here last night in that storm."

I smiled. "It was a challenge to say the least."

Out of the corner of my eye I could see Mark and Carl exchange a look and a smirk. That was it. As soon as I got my bacon - for this was Canada, how could we NOT have bacon? Plus, I was jonesin' for some meat – anyway, as soon as I got my bacon, it was a fork into the eyeballs for the lot of them. See how well you can hike all blind and weepy you snotty Albertistanies!

"Not fond of a gravel road, eh?" Carl asked with the corners of his mouth upturned so slightly that it would have made me less angry had he just made a silly face and spit at me.

Donny jumped to our defense. "Well you should see this thing. I don't know whether it's a bike or a spaceship." He shook his head and chuckled. "It's big. I mean really big. Wicked big, ya know? And to think it was almost dark," he shook his head again, "then the bear and the moose? Boy, I don't know if I'd have the guts to do that."

"Well Donny," I said, leaning back in my chair, "sometimes through sheer stupidity you get yourself in so deep, you have no choice but to push through to the other side."

"Boy, ain't that the truth." He clapped me lightly on the shoulder, and with a wave of his hand, and a "Enjoy your breakfast," walked back into the main part of the lodge presumably to continue his business.

All eyes of the family turned to me. I had their undivided attention. Had I known all it would take to win them to our side was the mention of wildlife it would have made the last 20 minutes much, much simpler. As a typical child of the 1970's, I'd watched many hours of "Mutual of Omaha's Wild Kingdom". If I had known this simple fact I would have lied through my teeth and reveled them with stories of my wilderness adventures based on my memory of the TV shows. True, my recollection was a bit spotty, a tad fuzzy, but I'm sure I could manage. I watched that damn show every Sunday night for years. Why? Because it was something that you had to endure to get to the "Wonderful World of Disney". Which was as close as we got in those days to kiddie-crack. Wild Kingdom was like penance. Anyway, if pressed I would have regaled them with the tale of hunting the Great White Whale on the open seas, and how I had lost my leg to the demon-beast of the depths.

On second thought, that may have not been "Wild Kingdom". I think that was one of the Brady Bunch vacations. I'm old. I get confused sometimes. Deal with it.

Mark was the first to speak, "Saw a bear in the valley as you came up, did ya?"

His tone was a bit softer, a tad less confrontational. It was obvious that he had seen well over 2 million grizzlies in his life, and had hand-fed most of them so our encounter was - for lack of a better word - 'cute'.

"Yep," I said. "It was quite a trip. Especially the bears. Well and the moose. But the bear was a heck of a lot closer than the moose."

Carl, ever the life of the party, said "You know a bike hit a grizzly last week down on Highway 40. That was a mess."

Oh joy. We were now at the 'maiming and death on a motorcycle' part of the conversation. I decided to play it cool. Besides, there was that 'Highway 40' thingee again.

"Highway 40 ," I said, "that's quite a ride up from Carnack. I don't know if I'd call it a 'highway' though."

Carl looked at me quizzically. "Carnack? No, that's on the other side."

What the hell?

"The other side?"

"Well yeah," he said, "it comes up from the south. Still gravel though."

I'd have to take a look at that. I wondered if this mythical road was an option for our departure. If it was less than the sheer cliff back to Carnack I wouldn't hesitate - grizzlies or not. I was dreading that steep, slippery, twisty trip back to civilization already. I'd half decided that it might be better just to feed ourselves to the bears and be done with it.

Or at least feed myself to a bear if it turned out there really was a different, and probably easier way up here. Just to escape the wrath of your mother.

"Any who," Carl said, not 'how' but 'who', "yeah. That biker got messed up pretty good. And they had to wind up putting her down. Real shame."

Again, what the hell? They shoot the wounded up here? That seemed a tad harsh. Even for people on a motorcycle. What if I got a splinter or something?

"Yeah. Shame." Mark added, "I hope she didn't have cubs."

Oh good. They put the bear down, not the biker. I filed away several taunts and insults that sprang to my tongue for future reference. Not that the death of a bear is a good thing by any means. You know I love all wildlife. Well, as long as said wildlife isn't chewing on my head. Even then, it has to be chewing pretty hard. Remember how our big ol' Newfoundland Barkley chewed on my head all the time? But it was a chew full of love. And slobber. And a really atrocious odor. But mostly love. Mostly.

The table, minus your mother and I, went on to discuss every motorcycle accident they had ever seen, heard, read about, dreamt, or fantasized. I shall spare you the details, but most of it ended with decapitation. Even if the biker simply fell over in the parking lot while sitting still. Evidently, and this was a good thing to know, in Canada a rider could trip on their own shoelace and their head would spontaneously eject from their body like cork from a bottle of dropped Champagne. I blame it on the metric system and their architecture. It's just not natural. You don't dally about with the laws of time and space like that without serious, serious consequences.

The staff arrived with the main part of the meal, carefully placing the plates of piping hot food in front of us and clearing the remains of the oatmeal at the same time. We listened to Leeza describe each item in excruciating detail. Here is the short version - biscuits, scrambled eggs, country potatoes (four different varieties of potatoes, green and red peppers, onions), eleventy-million types of humane and eco-friendly jams and preserves, and sausage. Beautiful sausage. Lovely sausage. 'Take me home and love me' sausage. No bacon, which was a disappointment, but it would have probably been that fake Canadian Bacon, which, as any connoisseur of the flesh will tell you, is just frackin' ham. Sausage would do fine. I know everyone likes meat, but for me it goes a little deeper than that. I also knew that your mom was probably full from the oatmeal, so the sausages on her plate were as good as mine. Ha! This day was looking up already. My arteries would be clogged faster than you could say 'Canada's monopsonistic health-care system'.

Somewhere around my second helping of 'Dew-kissed Wild Heritage Raspberry and Hydroponically Grown Dwarf Orange Preserves' Leeza made an announcement to the room.

"Okay folks, we've put all the makings of a wonderful box-lunch on the sideboard in the library. Help yourself when you're ready and if there is anything we can do for you don't hesitate to ask."

I couldn't help but notice that the clutch of Albertans at our table were light eaters. Which is to say, they hadn't finished their sausage. I was rustling up a diversion whereby I could snag those tasty links from the plates nearest me when your mom, ever vigilant when I'm around breakfast meats, leaned over and placed her hand on top of mine.

"Don't even think about it."

Gah. Busted. I think Carl may have noticed me ogling his sausage. Now that I put that to paper that sentence sounds so very, very wrong but you know what I mean. I didn't care about the chain of ownership. Meat is meat.

While the rest of his family busied themselves making box lunches for the troupe, Mark leaned back in his chair sipping coffee. "So," he looked at my cane propped against the table by my chair, "I don't suppose you hike a lot."

"Naw," I said, "not too much anymore. How about you guys? What's on your agenda for the day?"

"Probably a hike up to Bowman Lake. The kids have never been up there and it's a pretty easy hike from here." He turned in his chair and looked out the window over the mist-laden meadow. "Of course, if it doesn't quit raining I'll have to listen to whining all the way up and back."

I smiled and shook my head. "I know what you mean. Our kids got to a point where they whined anytime we took them anywhere."

"Oh," Mark said, "I wasn't talking about the kids. Carl is a major wuss."

Whoa Nelly! Was this humor? I had to tread carefully here. As you know, I have a tendency to laugh first and ask questions later. Well, more like laugh first and apologize later.

Mark broke into a wide grin. It was a nice change of pace from the scowling. Carl overheard his brother, and shouted "Hey! Who was it that wanted to call it quits on day 3 of our week-long backpacking trip? Huh? Who was that eh? Wasn't me now was it?"

Mark waved his hand at his brother as if he were swatting at a gnat. He turned to your mother and me, "I had been wet, cold, and hungry for three days. There comes a point where it's just best to pack it in. That's not being a wuss. That's using common sense eh?"

Carl went back to making his sandwich. "Gorby."

What was this word? It sounded like an insult, but for the life of me I couldn't figure out how calling your brother a nickname for Michael Gorbachev was insulting. Unless Carl at some point had presided over the fall of the Eastern Bloc. It was possible I suppose. He had that Ruskie-scowl about him. Sort of a grimace tinged with Vodka.

Wait . . . I just looked up 'Gorby' on the interwebs. It is a term for a tourist in Banff. Very derogatory. I'll file that one away for future use.

Mark shook his head and went back to his coffee. "So what are you gonna do today?"

Hmmm . . . good question. If the looks coming from your mother were any indication, I may be defending myself. With a switchblade and club.

"I don't know," I said, turning to your mom. Probably just hang around the Lodge catching up on some reading. We were going to go out and explore the area on the bike, but I've had all the riding in the rain I care to do for a bit."

Mark kind of chuckled at this, but I couldn't tell if it was sympathetic commiseration or a thinly veiled insult. "Well, whatever you do," he said, pushing himself away from the table, "have a good one, eh?"

"We will. Enjoy the trail."

And with that he and his troupe were out the door, off to do all things hikey.

Finally we were alone at the table. I patted your mom on the leg. "See? We made it! That wasn't so bad now was it?"

Mom just stared at me.

Ah good. I was right. What a fine, fine morning this was turning into. I wondered, should I lobotomize myself now, or save it for the afternoon? I hate to peak too early.

"Okay, point taken." I shrugged. "But it got better towards the end. Right? Well, a little better anyway. What say we just move on? Put it behind us. Now, shall we go make ourselves a sandwich for later?"

"Yes, but let's wait for the crowd to clear. Let's just sit here, take in the scenery, and sip our tea and coffee."

Which was your mother's polite way of saying, 'I would like you to shut the hell up for a little bit.'

So that's exactly what we did. We sat watching the wildlife in the meadow, the mist swirling, rushing over the mountain peaks, and a steady stream of bundled hikers spread across the valley like a hatch of new spiders on a warm spring day.

After a long period of silence, Mom said, "Okay, I'm not really hungry, but let's go pack a lunch. I'm sure I'll want something to snack on later."

Now that the initial rush had cleared, we had the box-lunch buffet all to ourselves. This beauty was enough to bring me to my knees. Four kinds of breads. 6 different cheeses. Meats - oh glorious MEATS - in abundance. There were onion slices and lettuce and tomatoes, and all the fine fixin's you could imagine. And, to your mom's delight, 4 different kinds of cookies! I made two sandwiches that would choke a malnourished Pit Bull. Mom busied herself with the cookie paradise. It was around this time I began, sight unseen, to fall in love with the cook.

We were about to return to our room when Leeza walked past and said, "Don't forget high-tea at 2. I think you'll enjoy it. And remember we have books and games a plenty if you get bored." Only, she winked again as she said this, and it made me feel . . . prudish. That's quite an accomplishment.

*   *   *

We wandered back to our room and did a little redecorating. By that I mean we pulled the clothes that were dry from the shelves and light fixtures. I was perfectly fine living in the 'launderette d'explode-o', but I think Mom was tired of moving socks out of the way to get to the balcony. Luckily most of the smaller items were dry, or if not dry, well on their way, but the big stuff like jeans and sweaters would take a bit longer. No rush, we were here for three days. Three wonderful days. 6 more meals. Yum.

As I busied myself with America's favorite game, 'Find The Missing Sock', I was silently designing a litany of excuses, pleadings, and bribes for the 'discussion', and yes . . . I mean 'discussion' with the quotes, that I knew was coming regarding our stellar first meal at Hidden Valley. Mom was just as quiet as I, which made me jumpy. You don't want that woman thinking too long about something without the safety valve of conversation. Have you ever seen a pressure cooker? Yeah. Like that. Only a pressure cooker that could hold a grudge. It would be best for all concerned - and by all concerned I mean me - to deal with this situation as quickly as possible.

I took a deep breath, ready to plead my case but before I could form a word with my slightly chapped lips, your mom said, "So. That was some breakfast," beating me to the point and punching a hole in my tactics.

Oh, how I wish I had never given her Sun Tzu's "The Art of War" as a Mother's Day gift. What the hell was I thinking? At the time I thought it would come in handy for family gatherings. Never once did I imagine that she would turn her studies upon me. However that did settle one thing. There was no way in Hell I was giving her the copy of "Attila's Guide To Winning Friends And Influencing Enemies" that I'd bought as a birthday gift. You know how Attila died don't you? That great warrior, the fierce and ruthless leader, conqueror of eastern and central Europe, survivor of battles untold? Stabbed by his wife, that's how. Stabby-stabby right in the gizzard. Oddly enough after a family-style breakfast in the Canadian Rockies.

My mind raced, the gears spinning and calculating, the neurons firing faster than bunnies with a cotton candy addiction. I decided to play dumb.

"Wasn't it though? I thought that the oatmeal was probably some of the best I've ever tasted. That's saying a lot. You know I'm not a huge fan of oatmeal ---"

"Oh, you're not getting off that easy," she said, grabbing a pair of my underwear from a lamp shade and tossing it directly at my head.

"Hey, you didn't stab me with a fork like you said you were going to, so I assumed that you had a good time."

As soon as I added 'good time' I wanted to smack myself upside my own head with a hammer. Couldn't I have just left it at 'you didn't stab me with a fork?', must I add 'good time' in conjunction?

"Define 'good time'," she said, chucking clothing at my head. "If by 'good time' you mean sitting with a bunch of hostile people first thing in the morning, counting down the seconds until I could get back to the room, then yes. I had a 'good time'. If that's the way you define it, I also had a 'good time' at my last IRS audit and root canal."

"Well," I said, picking up the mound of clothing growing at my feet, "I will admit that there were a few tense moments."

"Tense? Tense?" She said, ripping shirts from the curtain rods. "I've seen Israeli - Palestinian negotiations that were friendlier."

She had me there.

"I will admit that it wasn't exactly the warmest reception we've received."

She turned to look at me, "Ya think?"

"A fluke my dear. We have to cut them some slack. After all, we are a bit out of our element here, not being the outdoorsy-hikey type and all. And we're from THE STATES, so you know. . . that detracts some points from our overall score as well. But you have to admit, they relaxed and loosened up a bit towards the end."

Now your mother is many things, rational being foremost among her numerous winning qualities. Usually. Mostly.

She sighed. "That's true. It went better towards the end."

Oh thank GOD! I had her agreeing with me! There may be hope yet!

I walked over and put my arms around her. "Sweetie, we'll all be lifelong friends by the time our stay is over. You'll see. We just have to show them the 'real' us."

She lay her head on my shoulder. "Do you really think that's wise?"

Good point.

"Probably not. How about an edited, toned-down version of us?"

She moved over to the bed, stretched out, and patted the blanket motioning me to join her which I did. "That would be a good idea. No sense traumatizing them."

"Agreed."

We lay there in silence for a few minutes. I turned to your mom to say something but there was no point. She was fast asleep.

Within two minutes I'd joined her on the sweet dream highway. In my dreams the road was dry and bright and there was nary a Canadian to be seen.

*   *   *

Somewhere around 10-ish, I awoke. I didn't open my eyes right away, but lay there in a glorious state of semi-consciousness, drifting with my thoughts. Most of them involved being at home far, far from all things Canadesque. When I did manage to pry my eyes open the first thing I did was scream. Scream like a 10 year-old girl at a Hannah Montana concert. For you see, I was not greeted with the pastoral splendor that was the Hidden Valley. I was not greeted with the twitter of birds and the scamper of woodland creatures. I wasn't even greeted by a run of the mill peeping Tom. (Although in Canada, I believe they are referred to as 'Peeping Liams, eh?') No, I was greeted with the full-on view of moose ass backed up against our bay window.

Fully conscious I could have handled the exhibition, but in my semi-stupor of exhaustion I thought that we were being attacked by a hairy giant with a stupid looking nose. Then a new terror struck deep in the marrow of my bones – this was probably a genetically altered Norseman. The thought sent shivers down my spine.

Mom, who as you know, is used to me waking from a dead sleep screaming, yawned and said, "What. Dreaming about rats again?" She rolled over putting her back to me. "You and your stupid rat dreams."

"No," I mumbled in a hushed tone and pointed to the window.

Mom followed with her eyes the length of my arm, down to my finger, and over to the window where she studied the situation for a moment, chewed it around, offering the only comment one could offer under such circumstances.

"Ewwwww . . . . Moose butt."

"Yes," I said, and hoped that said butt wouldn't push through the window. For, as I'm sure you'll agree, the only thing worse than moose butt against your window is moose butt sticking into your room.

"And a fine example of moose butt it is, yet it is not the first thing to which I wish to be greeted upon awakening from a nice nap."

Having given us a 'free show', as it is referred to in these northerly climes, the moose, no doubt late for some foresty appointment, twitched her tail and ambled back into the woods. Your mom was too quick for her though, and we now have around 700 pictures of a gently receding moose ass. I don't want to spoil the surprise, but this may be the Christmas-card picture for which we had been searching. Nothing says the holidays are here like a well-framed moose heiney.

After 'mooses-tushes-exitus', I realized that despite having consumed enough at breakfast to kill me, I was once again famished. Evidently Canada burns the calories. I blame it on the latitude and elevation. Both of those numbers are larger than they are at home, as you know, so it would make sense that the caloric intake required for existence up here would be greater than what is required in the lower 40.

Or, and this is a distinct possibility, Canadian food simply has less calories. Much like broken cookies, which any connoisseur of the sweet biscuit will tell you, has a fraction of the calories of a whole cookie. This is straight from the expert on all things sweet, your mom. Evidently most of the calories escape from the cookie when it's broken. Like a geyser erupting in a shower from the built up pressure of super-heated water, the calories are ejected from the cookie break into the ether where they roam freely until they attach themselves to unsuspecting middle-aged men all across our fine land as they relax on couches watching sports.

The point being I was hungry. Thank goodness for my glorious meat-feast box lunch. I tore into that thing like a crazed shop-a-holic with a new, no limit credit-card on Black Friday. To my surprise, and a bit to my dismay because I'd been sure I would get at least half, your mom devoured her lunch as well. Whereupon, after a bit of light reading, we promptly fell asleep again.

Apparently, (and who knew?), our little adventure of the day before had left us exhausted. Or, and this is a distinct possibility, they were putting something in the food to subdue people from THE STATES.

We spent the remainder of the afternoon dozing and talking. Watching the moose, the birds, one very, very curious chipmunk, and generally enjoying the heck out of the day. By the time 'High Tea' arrived, we were ready to get out of our room and enter back into the world of the living for a bit. As we readied ourselves I asked your mom what exactly was 'High Tea', and how did it differ from 'Low-Tea', or 'Middle-Tea'.

Mom paused putting on her semi-dry socks. "I have no idea. I'm not even sure what 'High Tea' is exactly." She pulled damp cotton up her ankle and winced. "I guess we'll just have to find out."

I walked to the mirror and looked at myself in my jeans, T-Shirt, and riding boots. "What if we're under dressed? I mean, what if we are supposed to be in formal wear? I didn't bring my tux you know."

"I'm pretty sure," Mom said, "that a Lodge catering to hikers in the Canadian Rockies would not require formal wear for High Tea."

"Sweetie. This is Canada, land of myth and legend. It's entirely possible that all men are required to hike in full formal wear."

"And the women?" Mom asked.

"Floor-length gowns, high-heels and tiaras."

"I'm no expert," Mom said, "But I'm pretty sure that's not the case."

"Hmmm. . . ." I looked about the room. "You don't have any scissors, do you?"

"I'm not going to even ask. But the answer is 'no'. I don't have any scissors."

"Bummer. I could have made a stunning leather sport coat from the couch."

"You're dressed fine. Let's go," she said and walked to the door.

Guess what? Yep. Still raining. And as an added treat I was now paranoid about walking the 20 feet to the Lodge door lest I be accosted, and molest-a-pated, by rogue moose fanny. I opened the door and peeked through the crack, (Ha! Pun intended!) looking right and left. Once I assured myself the coast was clear, I pushed your mom through the opening and used her as a shield against anything that might be skulking about.

It was then that I noticed something for the first time. Your mom sighs a lot and rolls her eyes more than a normal person. I believe I shall schedule her an appointment with a neurologist when we get home. That just ain't right.

We walked into the golden hues of the Lodge and made our way to the dining room. There were couples scattered around the room - some laughing softly and others engaged in deep conversation. The valley was flowing with a river of mist, and we could see small dots in the distance, moose or deer - possibly poshly dressed hikers, the jury was still out - meandering about the far side.

We took a seat at a table next to the windows, and settled into our chairs. The floating rhythm of the conversation, the warmth of the stone fireplace, the vastness of the misty mountains and the gleaming green of the meadow was exactly what I had in mind when I had booked this place lo those many weeks ago.

I reached over and squeezed your mom's hand. "Now how cool is this?"

Your mom returned the squeeze. "Pretty darned cool."

"Damn straight woman. See, this is going to be great. Soon the rain shall depart, we will be able to go for a short ride on the bike, and all will be well with the world."

"Um hmm . . .", Mom said, "or not."

"What?"

"Or not go for a ride. I think I'm finally beginning to unwind. For some strange reason sitting here in the lodge has a much stronger appeal than gearing up and climbing back on the bike for another fun-filled day in the rain."

I shook my head. "Wuss. And it will stop raining. Eventually."

"You can call me a 'wuss' all you want. As long as I'm dry."

Even though she had given me permission, and it was mighty tempting, I decided not to call her a wuss again. She was near cutlery. I'm not a complete idiot. A partial idiot, I'll grant you that, but not a complete one.

Stacy, today wearing pink tights to accompany her pigtails and an adorable summer dress, came over and patted your mom on the shoulder.

"Well you guys look a little more rested today. How are you doing?"

"Much better, thank you," Mom said.

I nodded my head in agreement.

"What can I get you folks to drink? Tea? Coffee? A nice glass of Okanagan Merlot?"

"I think some tea would be wonderful." Mom reached over and patted my arm. "What about you sweetie?"

"Coffee for me please, Stacy."

"You got it folks."

She pointed over to the same side-board where the box-lunch spread, or, as I now refer to it, "Meat-a-palooza", was earlier this morning.

"Help yourself. Our Teas are quite good. People coordinate their hikes so that they reach us by early afternoon simply for our Teas. And be sure to try the pastries." She opened her eyes wide, "Yum!"

"Thank you," Mom said, "I think I will."

"I'll be right back. In the meantime there's a good selection of games in the library. You're more than welcome to grab one and bring it in here, or one of our books." She turned to walk to the kitchen, and with a glance over her shoulder added, "Glad you guys got some 'rest'." Then she winked again.

Dammit! I hope no one else saw me blushing. In my fluster I knocked my cane to the ground with a mighty BANG! causing a dead-stop in the room's chatter and heads to snap in our direction.

"Sorry," I said to the room, and held my cane up so they could see I had simply dropped it and was not, as some suspected, shootin' the place up.

See, here is the damned thing about walking apparatus - canes, crutches, whatever - it's all good and fine when you're up walking about, but the minute you sit down you realize, 'What the hell am I going to do with this stick?' I know it sounds trivial, but you have no idea how complicated of a matter this really is. Do you put it on the floor and risk someone tripping? Hold it and there by render one of your appendages useless? Lean it against the table and risk, as I had just done, a noisy clang to the floor? I once asked your mom to affix Velcro to the shaft, so that I could wear the corresponding piece of Velcro on my head in a band, thereby sticking the damn thing to the side of my face where it would be out of the way. Your mother, ever the party pooper, spent quite a while explaining to me why this would be ridiculous. I was buying none of her reasoning until she said, "Would you like to be called old cane-head?" I think you'll agree that, while I've been called many things in my life, 'Old cane head' is not one to which I aspire.

"You know, I've got to figure out something to do with this thing. It's always in the way."

"Why don't you bring your strap and fold it up? You could hold it on your lap?"

Immediately a sequence of images flooded my brain like the backed-up toilet at your prom date's house. A series where the cane, demon possessed - for this foldable metal stick is really the bastard cousin of the bungee cord, (and you know how well I get along with those) - would break free its minimal bindings, and do bodily injury to myself in a thousand and one ways. 800 of them involving my nether regions. 150 or so resulting in permanent blindness. 25 with a broken nose or shattered teeth. 15 concerning a crushed or heavily bruised larynx. 8 resulting in decapitation. 2 in spontaneous combustion. And 1 wherein I won the lottery and bought a large yacht where I cruised the world taunting indigenous wildlife with native fruit and pithy insults from the safety of my boat. (To be fair I may have drifted off towards the end of this fantasy for as you know my attention span is. . . .oh look! Shiny!)

"Probably not a good idea. I'll figure something out. Maybe I could make a bitchin' holster and strap it to my leg? Whatcha think?"

"You do that sweetie."

"You say that like maybe you think this is not a good idea?"

"Well one," Mom said, "I'm not sure that a giant holster, even if it is empty, would inspire much confidence if you wore it in public. If I saw something like that my first thought would be 'where's the rifle'? My next thought would be, 'Where's the Police?' Is that really the first impression you want to make? And let's be honest, you'll never get around to really doing it so rather than get into a lengthy conversation - like right now, I offered my support like the good wife that I am."

She had a point. Well, maybe multiple points. As you know I have been known to engage in many a brain-stormed creation, many a dream-fueled project that about 3/4 of the way through became . . . boring. And yes I'm talking specifically about that huge pond in the backyard that was going to be filled with Koi and have dragon shaped fountains and gas flames and a huge backdrop made of inlaid wood that rotated, not only to the phases of the moon and sun, but also predicted crop failures, that's now just a muddy hole in the ground and - and I'm making no admissions here - may be the reason we haven't seen the paper boy in a few months.

"Come on," Mom said standing, "I'm not really hungry but let's go see what they have at the buffet. I wouldn't mind a cookie."

We walked into the small side room and . . . OMG! No. Not OMG! ZOMG!!11 I thought to myself, 'Self, you're going to weigh the same as a walrus if you're not careful.' It didn't matter. My brain is second banana to my appetite. There, spread before us were numerous varieties of salami and 6 different cheeses - hard and semi-soft - and crackers and smoked oysters and caviar and toast points and 5 different breads and jams and jellies and creams and veggies and torts and pastries and cake and pie and cookies galore! There were things that I had not a clue as to their contents, but looked so yummy that I had to taste them.

"Oh my. . . ." Mom said, and steadied herself on my arm. "Oh my. . ."

So this was High Tea. Did you know that High Tea is also referred to as 'Meat Tea' in some parts of the colonies? Now there is an idea I could lend my full support. I might be jumping the gun, but your mom and I might be compelled to move to a more civilized region of the world. One where 'Meat Tea' is an actual event and not a garage band formed by 14 year olds with mimicked ennui and braces.

"There's no way," Mom said as an answer to a question no one had asked.

"I know. But it would be rude not to at least sample these tasty offerings. We don't want to be rude, do we?"

"It hasn't stopped us before."

I shook my head. "This is true, but we are turning over a new leaf. A maple leaf, to be exact. It's time to embrace our considerate side, our 'inner Canadian', if you will."

Mom was still staring at the vast array of goodies splayed before us like offerings at the Temple. "And if that involves meat and pastries?"

"It's a sacrifice I'm willing to make."

"Me too," Mom said, whereupon we dove into the feast like bulimic cheerleaders at a chocolate factory.

We returned to the dining room, and to our seats, where we spent the next hour playing cribbage, nibbling and noshing our way to that time-honored American tradition - obesity. It was a grand voyage punctuated by shouts of 'fifteen-two' and 'fifteen-four' and 'stop cheating ya bastard!'. After an hour or so of this delightful diversion, I looked to your mom and said, "I have to stop eating. It's only 3 hours 'til dinner."

"I know," Mom said, cramming the last few bites of a tort into her mouth.

"I mean seriously. I feel like a beached whale." I patted my expanding girth. "I wonder if I could sue for obesity?"

"Not in Canada." Mom managed, around the remainder of a chocolate-chip cookie. "Now if we were back home, in the US, then sure. I'd say sue away. But I don't think they have the same level of love for frilly lawsuits up here."

She could be right. Here is another thing about Canada: In THE STATES if you stop at some natural wonder, in a state or national park, the view is usually obscured by 27 signs telling you what not to do followed by a chain-link fence with barbed wire. In Canada, you can drive to a designated overlook, hundreds of feet of sheer cliff, and there will be a small fence. And that's it. No 'DON'T CROSS THE FENCE', or 'KEEP AWAY FROM EDGE, or 'DO NOT THROW STUFF OFF THE LEDGE - THERE ARE PEOPLE BELOW' or 'DON'T FEED THE BEARS CARAMELS FROM YOUR LIPS". In Canada, they treat you like an adult. You want to walk to the edge of what, by any standards is an unsafe cliff? Then be their guest. You want to dive off the ledge into the spillway of a Dam? S'okay with them. I have a feeling that the Darwinian concept is fully embraced up here. Little gene pool cleaning isn't necessarily a bad thing in the great white north.

"Are you telling me that I may have to actually bear the consequences of my actions?"

"Fraid so," she said, patting my arm.

I stared at her long and hard. "That's crazy talk."

"I know sweetie, and you can go back to your blame-less ways as soon as we cross the border."

I found this vaguely comforting.

We finished our third, or fourth, or possibly fifth plate of deliciousness, put away the cribbage board, (I, once again, had managed to lose the game by saving a 'pegging hand' - stop laughing), and took a walk out on the huge deck that was literally the front of the Lodge. The clouds had thinned, and the sun was playing peek-a-boo with the mountains and the meadow. It was amazing seeing the valley in sunlight, then in mist, then back to fully lit sun. About 20 feet away on the deck was an older man leaning against the railing smoking a cigar, watching the spectacle with us.

"What an amazing sight," I said to him.

He took a big puff off of his cigar, knocked the ashes into a can that the Lodge had supplied for just such occasions, and nodded his head. "It's a sight I never get tired of." He took another puff and as he exhaled the smoke billowed in the air and immediately dissipated on the breeze. He looked us over slowly, deliberately. "This your first time here?"

Mom and I shook our heads in the positive.

"You should see it in the fall, or early spring. It takes a while for the snow to completely leave, and it does come back pretty early, but even that's a sight to behold."

I pictured the meadow in winter. The even layers of snow blanketing the floor of the valley, the stream cutting a meandering ribbon through the stark whiteness. Although, in reality it probably froze over, but I wouldn't let little things like reality spoil this moment.

"I'll bet it's breathtaking."

"That it is," he said and shifted his weight to his right leg.

"Do you come here often?" Mom asked.

"Oh, not as often as I used to." He took another puff from the stogie. "My wife and I would come here a couple of times a year. We'd hike the valley. We never were much for the all out 'scale the mountain' type of hike. We liked to walk through the meadows admiring the wildflowers."

He paused here, and butted his cigar against the railing of the deck.

"She's been gone for five years now, but I still come up here once a year. Although," he grabbed his left leg at the thigh. "No more hiking for this old bird. Shrugging his shoulders he said, " But that's alright." He looked over at me leaning against the railing with my cane. "I don't suppose you hike much anymore, do you?"

"Not too much," I smiled.

"Eh," he said, and waved his hand. "Leave it for the granola bunch. Me? I'll sit and sip a nice Scotch, smoke a Cuban, and read a good book."

"Sounds perfect," I said.

He smiled, but it was wistful and somehow heart wrenching. He placed his cigar stump in a nook at the end of the railing. "For later," he said with a wink. Turning to leave he added, "You folks enjoy your day."

"You too," I said, and with that he disappeared into the Lodge.

Mom inched closer to me and I put my arm around her shoulder bringing her tight into a hug.

"We're pretty lucky, aren't we?", she asked. Her eyes were glassy and wet. She didn't have to say anything else for we both knew what the other was thinking.

"Damn fortunate sweetie. Damn fortunate."

We stood there holding each other close, looking over the meadow and mountains for a long, long time.

*   *   *

We spent the rest of the afternoon reading, dozing, and watching the never ending stream of wildlife parade in front of our window and in the wallow down below. Mom was curled in the bay window seat, (told you!), and I was futzing with the computer, stumbling around da netz. For future reference here is a solid piece of advice: Some things on the interwebs can't be unseen. You'll thank me later.

Sitting there I was struck by how bizarre our world has become. Here I was, for all intents and purposes in the middle of nowhere, a moose freeway not 5 yards from my window, yet I was still able to make a call on my cell phone, and with the click of a URL catch up on my LOLcats. (Will that poor walrus EVER find his bucket? I hope so. The theft of his most treasured possession breaks my heart. At least they didn't get his cellular.) I purposely gave a wide birth to any and all news. This was vacation. If the Apocalypse happened while we were away I'm sure someone would fill us in on the details.

I believe I told you before of my 'cuteness' threshold - about 5 minutes on a good day. You know that your mother, tragically, has no such inhibitor in her brain chemistry. Therefore each new addition to the 'ol waterhole demanded an intense scrutinization and comparison of colorings, head shape, dewlap, height, solidity and speculated political persuasion.

Protip: All moose are rabid liberals. Although the bulls have a natural tendency to be fiscally conservative.

I didn't mind this litany of beastie specifications the first . . . oh, I don't know, seven million times, but I had trouble mustering enthusiasm as the day wore on. Not so for your mother, who was becoming enamored - nay, smitten I say, smitten! - with all things moosey. I politely reminded her of the devil-moose that had us trapped on the roadway not 24 hours previous, but in a textbook case of 'Stockholm Syndrome' your mom was now a moose apologist, defending the beasts actions as 'natural' - whatever in the Hell that means. I didn't mind. She could give her heart to the *Alces Alces* while we were at Hidden Valley. The thing that I was afraid of - and you know this was a distinct possibility - was that once I got home I would be required to build a HUGE litter box, and a garden shed to house the moose chow. Quit laughing. You know I'm right.

So, that's the way the afternoon went. Examining moose as they traipsed hither and yon around the Lodge and the wallow.

"Oh . . . come look! Another baby moose! This one's even smaller than the last, and it has a lighter hue to its coat."

"Adorable," I said, from the bed where I had stretched out with the computer.

Mom put the binoculars down. "You're not even looking."

"I'm sorry sweetie, it's just that - and don't take this wrong - I've seen close to a dozen of the little guys this morning. Is this one really so different?"

Mom raised the binoculars back to her eyes. "Well, this one has a patch of hair missing from its leg."

I failed to see how this was justification for excitement. "Tell you what, if you see one tap dancing or riding a unicycle let me know."

Mom, for some reason, ignored me. She's been doing that a lot lately. Like the last twenty-five years or so.

"What do they call baby moose?" Mom asked. "Are they calves?"

"I believe," I said, peering over the computer screen, "that it depends on the gender."

"What, like colts or fillies?"

"Something like that, although I believe that female baby moose are called 'Brenda', while the males are known as 'Hank'."

"Hmmm . . . I'm going to buy a book on moose when we get home."

To most people this would seem like an innocuous statement. A simple deceleration of an appallingly innocent action to be taken at a later date, and one, depending on the person, that may or may not happen. With your mom there was no doubt. Within three days of returning home your mother would have the Amazon truck backing up to the door, unloading every book pertaining to moose that had ever been written. She would devour these books within a few short weeks. Most people would be spewing information like a lawn sprinkler whilst they read on the subject - but not your mother. She would never, ever mention the topic while she was reading, or thereafter. That's just creepy. However, her arcane and detailed knowledge of the moose, if the past was any indicator, would pop up from time to time taking me completely by surprise. She did the same thing with women's gymnastics, NASCAR, mountain climbing, a small South American tribe that the name escapes me, and men's ice skating.

I don't think skating was so much an issue of studying the subject as I believe it to be a kind of 'channeling'. For example, when the topic of Olympic skating would worm its way into our conversation, oddly enough every four years, your mom's eyes would glaze over and she would stare into the distance as she repeated each contestants given and 'Christian' names, their skating history, their home life, religion, social practices, pet's names, favorite foods, childhood friends, lineage, and blood type. I TOLD you it was creepy! As you can see, the handwriting was on the wall. Your mom was well down the path to that darkest corner of the natural sciences - Moose-a-thology. Tragic, I know. There was naught to do but stay out of her way until the fever ran its course in ten years or so.

How many moose are we talking about frolicking below? As the day wore on even your mom got bored watching them. Let's just say there were a lot. Then add four to that total. All I could think was 'Damn. That's going to be a lot of shaggy beasties to dodge when we ride back to civilization'.

Which triggered another thought that had been playing on the periphery of my mind, but one I thought too soon to mention to your mother. Don't think bad of me for what I'm about to tell you. The thought was this: 'I wouldn't mind seeing another bear'.

Yeah, probably way too soon to bring that up to your mom.

No, definitely too soon.

October 3 , 2008

Dear Amber,

Having a bit of trouble here. Seems that I'm coming down with a bad case of laryngitis. My words are all scratchy and screetchy.

I may not write for a bit. I fear that would be futile. You wouldn't be able to understand what I was saying anyway. Damn you laryngitis!

On another note, let me apologize. I did not realize that Marine Drill Sergeants suffered from no sense of humor. No sense of humor at all. I would have never written that letter.

On the plus side, I hear push-ups are good for you.

Love,
Daddio

P.S. I decided to keep the ship, saber, and costume. It should be a good Christmas this year!

Chapter 9

Dinnertime or 'Political Potluck', take your pick.

Dinnertime.

I was hoping that the moose would have softened your mom's stance regarding another 'family style' meal, but no such luck. That woman can carry a grudge. Not unlike China and that whole Great Wall thingee to keep out the Mongol hordes. Talk about taking something too far. I mean really, after a couple hundred years it just becomes silly. Well, until your village is sacked and pillaged. Then suddenly a well fortified border makes perfect sense. Which is to say, that as dinnertime rolled around your mom became increasingly agitated as the minutes ticked by. This probably wasn't evident to the outside world, but after living and loving this woman for so many years I can pick up on the subtle clues such as a slight narrowing of the eye, a sigh, a softly spoken "Great. Another damn group dinner."

Someday, when the time is right, possibly while she's under a heavy dose of drugs, I shall query your mom as to the origins of the particular phobia. I suspect some childhood trauma. I'm thinking a tragic first day at Kindergarten. A buried memory of a disastrous preschool snack time. Or, and this is more likely, a murky recollection of our first date.

"Suz," I say, because that's her name and calling her 'Carol', or 'Cindy', or 'Dude' doesn't go over well - not well at all - "Suz this is going to be great. Remember sweetie, it's all a matter of perspective. Instead of looking at this as a potential negative experience, let's turn the tables on these Canadians. Let's have fun no matter what. Let's MAKE them love us!"

Mom paused brushing her hair and looked at me through the reflection in the mirror. "You think that's possible?"

"I think it's entirely possible. Not only possible, but probable! I shall dazzle them with witty repartee! I will spin yarns and tales so engaging that you can steal their desserts right from under their noses without them noticing. If necessary, I will jump on the table, grab my cane, and do my awesomely wicked Fred Astaire impersonation."

"Hmmm . . . I seem to remember you doing that at the Collin's wedding. It wasn't exactly a show stopper. They asked us to leave remember."

See? There it is again. Does this woman let go of nothing?

"That's because I forgot the words to 'Singing In The Rain'. Remember? It came out 'I'm singin' in the rain, just singin' in the rain! What a glorious feeling mmmph mmmph da da dee dee something . . . "

I don't think that was it," she said, and returned to brushing her hair. "I think it had something to do with all the broken China, and when you fell you landed on top of the bride's Grandfather."

"Pfffftttt. . . he was fine." I reached down to zip my boots. "Besides, little incidents like that that build character."

"How much more 'character' does an eighty year old need?"

"Honey," I said, and pulled my pant legs over the top of my boot, "I don't know. I just have to trust in the Universe that it was the proper thing at the proper time."

Mom breathed deeply. "I don't want to get into this again. Let's just finish getting dressed and get this over with."

"That's the spirit!", I cried, and swept her into my arms. "See? It's that type of 'can-do' attitude that makes me love you more each day."

Mom pushed me away to arm's length. "But no dancing on the table. Okay?"

"Alright, but I think you're limiting my social tool-box here."

"I know."

"So, let me get this straight. It's just dancing on the table right? Not dancing in general."

She reached up, surprisingly fast for such a small woman, and tweaked my nose. "Very funny."

"But I do a mad Mamba. I think that the hikers would appreciate the rhythm, the grace, and the spectacle of a bald man on a cane dancing by himself to music only he can hear. Really, would you deny them that?"

"It's a loss they'll just have to suffer. Now come on and let's go find a table."

Back we trudge to the main Lodge, but I'm looking over my shoulder the entire 20 feet. I mean come on! I've been watching Buicks on toothpick-legs wander, stumble, run, bounce, jump, and meander mere feet away from my present unprotected location all day long. I'm taking no chances. They could have used the wallow as a distraction, and were now sitting in the trees. With sniper rifles. Call it species-ism if you want, but I just don't trust moose. Shifty eyes. Fancy dewlap. Who do they think they are anyway?

Mom stops abruptly and I nearly run into the back of her. "Why do you insist on hiding behind me every time we step out the door?"

"No reason. Keep moving. And walk a serpentine path - you walk straight to the door they're going to zero in on you, then 'ffffffffffttt' SPLAT! There goes your chance of ever getting a hat to fit properly again."

Mom grabs my hand and pulls me alongside her. "I'm taking away your Call Of Duty 4 when we get home."

Ha! Idle threats and she knows it! Besides, COD5 is due out in the fall.

"Just trying to add a little distraction and lighten the mood sweetie."

"My mood is light. Don't push it."

Perhaps now is not the time to point out the inconsistencies in that sentence.

The moment we step in the door our noses are accosted - yet again - by wave after wave of delightful aromas. Even though I haven't yet digested breakfast, let alone lunch or High Tea, my stomach answers this olfactic symphony with a grand and mighty gurgle. Stacy is there, and with a broad sweep of her hand lets us know that we can take any seat we wish. The room is fairly full, but not overly so. All but one of the tables has at least a few people scattered around the perimeter sipping wine and drinks.

Now here is the dilemma: Do we sit at a table that is already occupied or do we grab the empty one? If we do sit at the empty table will we be seen as 'snobs', or as considerate visitors sparing this collection of landed gentry the coarseness of our pedestrian Americanism, sheltering them from two dolts from THE STATES? Before I could contemplate the ramifications of such a decision, and I want you to realize that wars have started over less complicated social interaction, your mom dragged me to the empty table. Oddly no one seemed to mind. Your mom breathed a sigh of relief as we took our seats.

"Good. Maybe we'll get lucky tonight and have the table to ourselves."

I opened my mouth to chastise her for her audacity. A statement like that can't go unchallenged. You should never ever taunt the Universe in such a manner. Remember my previous advice; the Universe, as I'm sure you've discovered in your 22 year stretch on this planet, will reach right up and bitch-slap you proper the moment you make such a bold declaration. Cases in point: Remember these innocuous bits of verbiage? "This ship is unsinkable!" Or, "There's no way we will elect him a second time." Or, and burn this one into your memory, "It's just a minor territorial expansion to retake historical homelands. They'll stop at the border." Yeah. That one left a mark. Anyway, next thing you know an ominous shadow fell across the room and our "Breakfast Family" was taking their seats at our table.

I swear, I heard the dirge-like "Dun Dun DUN!". Those few simple notes foreshadowing disaster. Only in my head it was played slap-base style by Les Claypool, some of that Primus hometown-heavy, which made it a tad less creepy.

Carl, Mark, (Oh my GAWD they're commies!) their wives and children, and their wonderful mother Martha, took their places around the other three sides of the table. The energy that had bubbled so profusely from the group was gone, replaced by a quiet look that can only be obtained by walking miles and miles and miles in the wet and cold with whining children. And wives. And brothers. Except Martha, who we would later discover was in our camp when it came to hiking, if by hiking you meant sitting on your butt and reading a good book and occasionally getting up for a bite to eat.

I turned to your mother to say something, something no doubt witty and soothing and terribly, terribly apropos, but her eye-tic was back. I slowly slid the cutlery out of her reach and smiled the smile of a physician trying to act cheerful for his patient while all the time he has horrible test results in hand. ("Hello Mr. Johnson, having a good day? You are? Well, you might want to back off of that a bit.")

Taking a page from your mother's copy of "The Art of War" I plastered a smile on my face and said, "Hello everyone. How was your hike?"

Carl fell back into his chair rather harshly. Evidently his hike had played a bit of havoc with his knees for they weren't bending well. Not well at all.

"Wet. Wet and cold," he said opening his napkin with a flick of his wrist and deftly dropping it into his lap.

How should I respond? My mind raced. I calculated a hundred responses, seventy-five of them completely inappropriate. I pushed them away and said the most neutral thing that came to mind.

"Oh. That sucks."

He shrugged his shoulders and one corner of his mouth contracted. "It was okay. The kids enjoyed it."

"Well, as long as the kids enjoyed it." I nodded my head and smiled.

As long as the kids enjoyed it. Oh, a dollar for each time I said that line as you girls were growing up! Let me translate for you - 'It was absolute Hell! Hell I tell you! But it kept the children occupied for a few hours and reduced the whining to a minimum resulting in an afternoon where, for a brief moment, I didn't have to contemplate putting them up for adoption. So, it was fine and hopefully, I will heal.'

Anyway, now that the two alpha males of this particular table had established a somewhat tentative detente we turned our attentions away from the posturing, chest-thumping and possibly, although I admit to nothing, making Orangutan noises, back to our respective families.

Mom leaned close and whispered "That was some stupid male-dominance thing, wasn't it?"

If by 'stupid male-dominance' you mean the establishment of boundaries and physical superiority through verbal greetings and gestures then yes. That's what that was."

Your mother, clearly impressed, shook her head and rubbed her temples in slow circular motions. "I will never understand you."

Now this seemed like a rather grand generalization, but I knew from whence it arose. See, your mom hadn't a clue as to the true nature of male interaction. I had been trying to explain this relatively easily deciphered subtext for many, many years but your mother was simply incapable of grasping the importance, the grace, the nuance of manly interaction. Although, to her credit she had tried. I blame an abundance of estrogen or that cursed extra chromosome. Poor thing, it's a foreign language with nary a Rosetta Stone in sight. I can't count the times that we will be walking somewhere, and I'll pass a guy and say "How's it going?" To which, if he's a man at all, will replay with the carefully crafted "Not bad. How about you?" Which demands the proper, "Not bad at all." We then smile and go about our way.

Mom will usually say, "Did you know him?"

"Who?" I will reply, genuinely befuddled.

"That guy you just talked to."

"Him? No. No clue."

"Well then why did you talk to him like that?"

"Oh," I'll say, "completely necessary. That was a fight for superiority."

"What are you talking about?" She'll say, acting all confused.

"Honey, honey, honey. How many times must we go over this? Let me break it down for you. As we walked down the sidewalk I noticed this guy walking towards us. I didn't like the looks of him for a number of reasons."

"You knew you didn't like him when you saw him walking down the sidewalk? Why would you think that?"

"Well for one he was walking way to close to our side. Did you see how his shoulders were pulled back? That guy was looking for trouble. His head was held at a cocky angle and I didn't much care for the color of his shirt. I won't even get into his choice of footwear. So, as he approached I had to take the initiative and establish my dominance, showing him that his stance was neither frightening nor threatening in any way, and letting him know that I was not one to be trifled with.

So, the 'how's it going' was really 'Hey chump. I see you. I see your posing and far from feeling threatened, I'm going to become the aggressor and call you out. This will, in no uncertain terms, show you that while you may be able to play this game with others it's not working on me. I am potentially more trouble than you need at the moment, so just keep walking.'

He then responds with any number of replies, each carrying their own meaning yet he chose 'Not bad'. Now this tells me that he has carefully considered the consequences and decided that perhaps he will back away slowly, never exposing a weak spot, while still maintaining the illusion of his alpha status but we both know that I'm allowing him that position for the time being. He then defers further with the 'How about you?' showing that he's concerned that he put me at ease and suggesting that he is no threat. I recognize his backing down and acknowledge it with my 'Not bad at all', letting him know that I have no further business with him, at which point our interaction is complete, both of us secure of our place in the pecking order."

"And what would have happened had he replied differently?"

"Well," I say, "there are a million permutations of this little ritual, but most of them end with drawn weapons."

To which your mom says, "Men are insane."

"That's a distinct possibility. But let me ask you this; when we went to the clothing store the other day, and at the check-out you smiled at the girl behind the register and said 'hello' and she did the same, there was a slight edge to both of your voices. Are you telling me there was no subtext to that?"

"Oh sure there was. But that's different."

"So, indulge me. What does "Hello" and the reply "Hello" translate to in regular speech?"

Mom will pause for a moment. "Hello Bitch."

I rest my case.

Back to our story. Leeza and Stacey, and a few staff members that I hadn't met yet, walked amongst the tables taking drink orders and making small talk with the guests. Leeza came to our table and said, "So, I hear you two play a wicked game of Cribbage."

"It's true," I replied. "We are the Cribbage Masters."

"So who won?", she asked as she filled our water glasses from an ice-filled pitcher.

"Well, Suzanne may tell you different, but I believe were it not for her cheating I would have taken every game."

"Oh," Leeza grinned, "so how did she cheat?"

I looked at your mother. "I have no idea. Possibly mirrors, or a second deck cleverly concealed behind her back. Some of the staff may have been in cahoots with her. But it was obvious there was something amiss, something not quite kosher about the whole affair."

Mom patted my arm. "He's saying that because I beat him seven out of eight games. He won the eighth because I took pity and let him."

While this was true it also stung.

"Wait until tomorrow. I was simply lulling you into a false sense of security. Tomorrow. . . no quarter!"

Leeza giggled. "Well I'm glad you folks found a way to occupy yourselves." She put the pitcher on the table and rubbed her hands together. "Now, as for tonight's menu. . ." Whereupon she launched into a glorious description of the gustatory delights awaiting our palettes. Salads and breads. Duck. Crusted Salmon. Both of which had received extensive counseling before their demise from old age. My eyes glazed over during the description. I was in paradise and Leeza was the heavenly chorus. She went on and on until, and I'm not proud of this, I may have drooled. "And for dessert we have white-chocolate brownies drizzled with a wild Raspberry-chocolate sauce and a dab of fresh whipped cream with a bare hint of mint."

"Oh, that sounds good," Mom said.

Leeza picked up her pitcher. "You have no idea. It's like the best of all possible worlds on your tongue". Addressing the group she said, "If you folks are set I'll be back in a minute with fresh bread and salad." Then she swayed ever so gently back to the kitchen.

So far this was shaping into a very pleasant evening. We talked amongst ourselves for a bit enjoying the gentle pulse of words and laughter that filled the room. I recognized a few faces here and there from breakfast or Tea, but owing to the nature of the Lodge the clientele was in constant rotation. Mom, for maybe the first time since we had left home, was relaxing minute by minute. Life was good.

I should have smelled a trap.

Carl leaned back in his chair, placing both hands behind his head. He did that a lot. "So. You guys have quite an election coming up."

Aw shit.

Really? Was he going to go and ruin a perfectly good evening with talk of politics? It's not that I mind, you know I love a spirited discussion as much as the next guy, but this was Canada and these were Canadians. In my experience what was about to take place wasn't so much a discussion as a prolonged series of accusations and indictments against all things from THE STATES. Too late now, we had left the calm water and were heading head-long into the vortex with the Kracken waiting below for the killing blow. I glance at your mom, who, as you know, hates political discussions even when both parties agree. She was trying desperately to self-induce a coma, but so far was having little success. She just looked sleepy.

"Why yes. Yes we do."

If Carl wanted to 'hike' down this particular path I was going to make him work for it.

He looked at me. I looked at him. The conversation amongst his family dwindled to silence, much like the final gasps of a car running out of gas which, owing to your childhood, you should be intimately acquainted with. Or, like any holiday dinner conversation we've ever hosted at the house. Especially those attended by Uncle Bob. Bastard. But I digress. There we sat, eyeball to eyeball, two minds locked in a silent battle.

Finally Carl said, "So. I guess the good thing is they can't re-elect Bush, eh?"

Now as you know I've never been a Bush supporter - father or son. I'm socially liberal, fiscally conservative, and a moderate regarding foreign policy. You can put a check mark next to my name in the 'other' column. It seems that a radical political ideology, either right or left wing, was all the rage in August of

2008. There wasn't much middle ground. You were either red or blue, and that's all anyone needed to know to either think you were the most brilliant person ever born on the earth or full-fledged maniac hell-bent on ruining our country. I detested Bush. Thought John McCain had traded his soul for political clout, and sat firmly in the Obama camp. Yet there was something about this semi-snotty Canadian espousing his views regarding MY country that prompted a visceral response deep in this American heart. As I believe I've told you before, I've never met a Canadian, be they from the highest social circle or the lowliest hard-scrabble, that wasn't an absolute expert on what was wrong with the USA. Canadians were kind of like that distant Aunt that is nice enough but had definite opinions on why everyone else was a screw-up, and what they should be doing to correct the situation. So, I was at a junction, a fork in the road if you prefer. (Or a runcible spoon. . .sheesh. . . whatever.) I could take the 'Fox News' perspective and possibly alienate an entire Province, or I could enter into a rational, constructive, and productive conversation wherein this group of heartland Canadians and these motorcycle riding interlopers from THE STATES could find common ground, bridging the ideological divide and promoting peace, harmony and brotherhood amongst all North Americans.

As I sat there, running over conversational options and likely outcomes of differing tactics, Mom leaned over and whispered, "Don't do it."

I started to protest, but as our brethren across the pond are so fond of saying, 'it was a fair cop'. Finally I decided to stop all the silly games and answer honestly. "Yes. Thank God."

As a unit the Canadian's jaws dropped. As if someone had snuck behind the curtain and with a pair of scissors cut the strings to their mouths.

Oh that's right, pigeon-hole me will you? Yeah, that just happened. I blew your mind. Deal with it. Lao Tzu would have been proud of my skills at throwing the enemy off balance, of changing the rules of engagement without notice. I now had them wobbling. The question was, should I go for the coup de grace?

Carl began to smile and then checked himself. Evidently a thought had crossed his mind and before he could open up to these travelers he had to make sure he wasn't dealing with something worse than a Republican. For all he knew I might be a member of the John Birch society. (I have been noticing quite a few unmarked helicopters flying in formation lately and it troubles me.) Or something worse. . . . the ultimate horror - a member of the Green Party.

"So," Carl said, and looked to his family for support, "who are you gonna vote for?"

"The same person I always vote for Carl," I purred.

Carl and the family exchanged glances, looking for confirmation that they hadn't missed something in the conversation.

"Okay. And that would be . . . ???"

"Hitler."

Mom grabbed my thigh under the table and gave me a vicious squeeze.

Evidently my voice had carried a bit in the room for conversation stopped faster than traffic at a trailer-park yard sale. The family, whose preternatural telepathic connection was humming strong at this point, looked at each other with saucer eyes. Carl started to say something, thought better, started to say something else and stopped. He tried to mouth words soundlessly but in the end simply exhaled loudly.

Martha reached over and patted my hand and giggled. She looked at her sons and said, "Now that's funny."

Carl searched my face, looking for some glint of a smile, some twinkle in my eye that perhaps his mother had seen that went unnoticed by him.

Deadpan, I shook my head in the affirmative. "It's true. Hitler."

He leaned back in his chair and the arms immediately folded across his chest. This seemed to be his natural posture.

"Hitler?" he asked incredulously.

"Yes. I always vote for Hitler. I write his name in every election."

I grinned and looked around at my dinner companions. The spectrum of emotion was on display in full force. Delicious. We had Martha giggling, and her son Mark had still not closed his mouth.

I let the grin on my face die, as if I finally understood their horror, and replaced it with a look of great concern. "Oh. . .not THAT Hitler. Sorry. Abraham Hitler. He lives down the block from us. Never thought about it before, but that's a very unfortunate surname isn't it? Heck of a guy. Has some really good ideas concerning reformation of the current banking structure."

Blank expressions greeted me from all sides of the table, except Martha who was now laughing openly.

I drew my lips into thin lines, shrugged my shoulders and nodded my head in the negative. "Naw . . . I'm just futzing with ya. I'm voting for Obama."

While none of the family found it as amusing as Martha, I did at least get a grin from the two men.

Martha leaned over and bumped my shoulder with hers. "They have no sense of humor," she said apologetically. "I have no idea what happened to them. So serious all the time." She looked to her boys as if she expected an answer.

Just then our salads and a basket of piping-hot bread arrived, so the grand topic of conversation was put aside while we praised the salad and bread, and dove into our first course.

Mom leaned over and whispered "Really?"

"Babe," I said quietly, "you have to lighten up a bit. Stop being so nervous and relax. They're not going to kill us for making a joke."

"But really," she said, "you had to go straight to Hitler?"

"It's an old comedic artifice. Welcome to what I like to call the 'Dance of Satirical Intellectuals', or as the French say "Danse de la faiblesse d'esprit". That has a nice ring to it, don't you think?"

"I don't think that's what that phrase means," Mom said.

"What?"

"'Danse de la faiblesse d'esprit' translates roughly as 'Dance of the feeble-minded'."

What kind of an alien had I married?

"Since when do you speak French?"

Mom just shrugged her shoulders. Another one of her hidden stores of knowledge no doubt. Next thing I know, I'll have a miniature nuclear reactor sitting on the kitchen counter. Actually, that would be kind of cool. As long as we didn't go 'critical'. Then it would be a hoot!

"Had me goin' there for a minute, eh?" Mark smiled.

"Just trying to add a little humor. But seriously, I'm firmly planted in the Obama camp."

"But really," Mark said, jumping into the conversation, "do you think he has a chance?"

Now that took me aback. Of course he does. He's ahead in the polls, and from all indications the Republican party was scrambling to play the ever popular game 'Who is going to shoot us in the foot?.' The answer would come in a few short days. That answer was "all of them". No, I kid. The answer was Sarah Palin. I really, really, really wish that McCain had announced her as his running mate before we left Hidden Valley. Now that would have been fun.

I looked at your mom. She looked as confused as I felt.

"Oh, I think he has a very strong chance. I fully expect him to win come November."

Now it was Mark and Carl's turn to look confused. Mark said, "But you really think the US will elect," and here his tone became a bit sheepish, " . . . you know. A black man?"

Ah. There it was. Race seemed to be a very troubling topic for these Albertans. But come to think of it, it wasn't like we'd met anyone with even a suntan since leaving THE STATES. The coastal cities of Canada are quite international but evidently the plains were still the dominion of the white man. Well, if you didn't count all the First Nation people that had been slaughtered to make room.

"I think we're more than ready for a change, and while his race will certainly be an issue for some, I believe most of the US is ready to move beyond skin color."

I was very cautious of saying "America is ready to move beyond skin color," because that would have been like smearing sausage all over myself and jumping in the lion cage at the Zoo. Oh sure, it would be all fun and tongues for the first minute or so, then things would turn . . . toothy. See, while we in THE STATES (oh dear Lord now I'M doing it!) refer to our republic as 'America', them's fightin' words north and south of the border. You will be reminded lickety-split that be it Canada or Mexico they are Americans as well, dwelling on the North American continent as they do.

Personally, I think it's just an easy way to start a fight. Kind of like telling a bowler that it isn't a 'real' sport. Or, and this is one that is fun sometimes, telling anyone outside of our country that REAL football is what takes place in the good ol' US of A with helmets and padding and the occasional snapped neck. What the rest of the world calls 'football' is just soccer. With the absolutely bitchin' addition of hooligans, but soccer none the less. That's what we teach our kids to play in order to toughen them up for the gridiron. Proclaim that loudly enough at a World Cup and see how long it takes you to regain consciousness. One time at Safeco Field I tried to implement 'baseball hooliganism' at a Mariners game one fine summer afternoon, but it wouldn't seem to take. Stupid passive-aggressive Seattlites. You should have seen the looks I got whenever a member of the team came into home plate and I would jump up, raise my shirt and shout "GOOOOOOOOOOOOOOOAAAAAAAALLLLLLLLLLLLLLLLLLLLLLLL!" Then I would throw my beer in your Uncle Bob's face and punch him in the nose as hard as I could.

Ah . . . good times, good times. You know, and this ticks me off to no end, Safeco security has NO sense of humor whatsoever.

"Well that may be," Carl said, "but do you think he'll really *make* it to the White House? Or last long if he does"

I ignored the assassination angle.

"Funny that," I said. "Supposedly, if he's elected they are going to paint the White House on Jan. 19th, just before the inauguration. It will then be known as the 'Black House'." This statement was met with puzzled looks all around. "It's true. I read it on Wikipedia. The interwebs don't lie."

Martha giggled. The only one, but as you know it's more of a response than I usually get.

Mark grinned. "You know what Carl means."

I sighed. "I do. That is certainly a concern but hopefully it won't come to pass."

"I don't know. Just seems like you guys are pretty fast with the guns down there. And with race relations what they are, well. . . " he let his voice trail, as if the rest of what he was thinking didn't need to be said.

"Don't you think if he's elected there's going to be rioting?" Mark asked.

"Seems like you guys could tumble into a civil war pretty quickly."

Mom and I exchanged a glance. Rioting? Civil war? Just what kind of an impression did these Canadians have of our homeland? The guns maybe, but civil war? For a fleeting moment I panicked. What if these uber Canucks were right and we, too close to see the forest, were unaware that civil carnage was about to sweep our shining shores?

"I seriously doubt that. I'm sure there would be some unhappy campers, but civil war? No. I don't think so. That sounds like a lot of effort, and the lower 40 isn't that ambitious. Shoot, if we let Bush and Cheney steal the 2000 election without so much as a whimper from the general public, I don't think that electing Obama is going to cause chaos in the streets."

"But all those 'Red' states, eh?", Mark said, spreading his hands over the table as if he were referring to a map, "they aren't going to be happy are they? And with how it goes between blacks and whites, seems to me you guys would be ripe for problems."

"Those 'red' states are kind of a misnomer. A media construct. It's really more of a few hard-core Blue states, a few hard-core Red states, and the rest are varying shades of purple. But you don't hear that because absolutes make much better TV. And as for race relations . . . well, we've come a long, long way in the last twenty years. Even farther in the last 40. Are we there yet? No. But I don't think it's as big of an issue as you think."

"But the gangs," Mark said, "you can't tell me that's not a problem. We watch the news, we see what's going on. You have a problem with the blacks."

Wow. Now I was beginning to clue in. These people's perception of the US was gleaned from TV and movies. If you watched enough television, every young black man was a thug. A drug dealer. A killer. Every white person south of the Mason-Dixon, and more than a few north, were Confederate flag waving lynch-mobs with an average IQ of 67. It's amazing how much people's perceptions are based on hyped news reports and crime dramas. Both north and south of the border. Thank God not me. I'm much too smart for that. However I say that with one caveat - I will never visit Africa. Lions and tigers would eat me the moment I stepped off the plane. Plus, I hate the jungle. And cannibals. And a pith helmet is not flattering to my physique. Don't get me started on the kangaroos.

"The gangs are a function of youth, deteriorating familial structures, and economics. It's not just a black problem. It's Latinos, Asians, Whites, Blacks, exiles from the Dogon system - name a segment of the population and there's a gang associated. Shoot, I seriously considered forming my own gang, but", and I held up my cane, "the name 'Crips' was already taken. You can't have a good gang without a great name. I thought for awhile about calling it 'The Cripples', but that doesn't inspire fear and loathing, does it? I thought of the 'Handi C's', but again it's kind of lame." I turned to Martha, "Handi-capable my heiney."

Martha laughed and shook her head. Carl and Mark looked as if I had just knocked on their door and handed them a pamphlet concerning their immortal souls with a heavy dash of Jehovah thrown in for good measure. Or maybe the 'Book of Mormon'. Or, and this is a possibility, a religion entirely of my own creation. You know, like Catholicism.

I would like to say that the conversation ended here, but I can't. It went on, and on, and on, and a little further than that. The basic jest of the discussion followed the conflict between races. Then the Bush era. The Iraq War. George the father. George the son. Possibly George the Holy Ghost. The Gulf War. American imperialism - where I briefly suggested that the US quit screwing around and embrace Empire openly, take the continents and stop all the damn whining. This didn't go over nearly as well as one would imagine. Possibly because I suggested, in retrospect a bit too forcefully, that we start with Canada.

Martha listened to the ebb and flow of discussion without so much as a comment. Finally she looked at her sons, then back to me, (your mother had long since went to her 'happy place'), and said, "You know why we Canadians are so interested in what happens in THE STATES?"

See? Here's the problem: Never ask a smart-ass a question. We feel duty bound to offer an answer. How I managed to stifle myself I'll never know.

"It's because our politics are so dreadfully boring," she said, looking to her sons.

"Well, that's true eh? Can't even get worked up over this year's election up here," Carl chuckled.

"And the real reason we criticize THE STATES so much?" She looked around to see if anyone would answer. When no one did she continued, "Because we can. That's why. We all know that the US takes care of us, even if we don't want to admit it. We don't have to pour the money into defense that you do. We don't have to worry about invasion. We don't have to worry about locking up our borders. We don't have to worry about the world looking to us for solutions every time something goes wrong. Gives us a lot of time to bitch."

Mark, Carl, and their wives grinned like a kid caught downloading music. And that effectively ended the political discussion. At least with them.

The rest of the evening was spent the way I hoped it would in the beginning. We talked and compared histories and life stories. We celebrated our similarities; we dispelled misconceptions, and found the common ground of family and children. Your mom actually joined in and was laughing by the end of the night. I know! Miracles do happen.

The rest of the meal was uneventful, except for the food which was glorious. However, I did find one thing fascinating. Martha, during the course of conversation, shared that she lived on the outskirts of a small wheat farming

Albertan town of Vulcan. Unusual name, but Martha explained that it was named for the Roman God and that all of the streets in the town held the monikers of lesser Gods and Goddesses of the classical world. How cool is that? Canada has a knack with place names. Why can't we do something like that around here? Granted, the latest tacky-box development on the edge of town did name one of their streets 'Lois Lane', but I think that was by accident. I'm quite sure they, nor the city planners that approved the name, had a clue to the irony until it was pointed out to them.

The other remarkable tidbit regarding Vulcan, in true pioneering prairie spirit, was that the town had managed to take their unusual name and find a niche tourism market. How, you may ask, would a small agricultural town, with a population just shy of 2000 people, on the plains of Alberta profit from a name like Vulcan? Nary a volcano in sight. A rubber tire museum had been done to death. No, these hearty folks did the only sensible thing and decided to build a huge scale replica of the 'USS Enterprise' from Star Trek fame and declare themselves home-base for all things Spocky. I kid you not. They have treky themed murals, a museum and tourist center, (Oh that's right. . .that's an AMERICAN spelling so deal with it!), and once a year they hold a community wide celebration named VulCON / Spock Days / Galaxyfest. Take your pick. Upon further inquiry of my dear Martha, she summarized the entire process behind such a dedicated, albeit narrow, community identity - and the origins thereof - in one sentence:

"The winters are long and we tend to drink a lot."

Fair enough. But I don't care what you say, that takes some chutzpah.

As our dinner began to digest the need for sleep overtook the need for socialization. While it had now been 24 hours since nearly becoming an ursal snack, evidently you don't recover from a day like that immediately. Who knew? As the last of the stragglers finished their dessert, we excused ourselves and made our way back to the room, sans moose attack, and fell asleep almost immediately.

Tomorrow was another day. Who knew what that would bring?

October 4, 2008

Dear Amber,

I'm sending a few pictures along with this letter. Took them a couple of days ago and immediately thought of you.

Now that you've had a chance to look them over I have a question:

Does that look infected?

Love,
Daddio

Chapter 10

Of Bear Auras and BMWs

For some reason I didn't sleep all that well the second night. It may have been for any number of reasons, but the most likely cause was simple gluttony. I've noticed that as I get older the digestion of massive quantities of meat takes. . . longer. Oh the joys of the human body! It's like buying a shoddily built house - you keep patching it here and there and telling yourself that it's okay that the windows won't open and the doors are askew and the floor is buckled in the middle but all the time you're thinking, 'I can probably make this work. I can. . . I just. . . I need. . . Aw crap. I got screwed!'

When your mother woke me with a well placed poke to the ribs you'll understand I was a tad groggier than usual. It took me a minute to pry my eyes open and adjust to the early morning light pouring through the French doors from the deck. I was not a bit surprised to see that it was still raining. Bummer. I doubted that I could talk your mom into a ride today because every time I mentioned a short 'tour' of the area your mom would say 'No'. But not in so few words, and certainly not as politely as I thought she should. Still, there was that nagging thought tickling my brain. Flitting about my consciousness like sugar-dosed Ritalin kids at a Christmas party. The thought was this: I was determined to see another bear. Why, you might be asking yourself, would I want to place myself and your mom in a potentially dangerous situation on purpose?

Because I'm an idiot, and a man, and that's a dangerous combination. (Stop laughing. Not all men are idiots. In fact. . . okay. You're right. Men are idiots.) If it hadn't been for a genetic tendency towards lunacy we would never know what a bad idea it is to poke a badger with a stick. Or, if you prefer, try to control the Middle East. The point being I had convinced myself that my vacation wouldn't be complete unless I was able to witness once again the majesty of the largest North American carnivore in its natural environment.

Well, largest if you don't count Newt Gingrich.

"Get up sleepy head. Time for breakfast."

Gah. I didn't think I would ever eat again, but then . . . ummmmm . . . maybe there would be bacon!

Mom, who had evidently been up for some time, sat on the edge of the bed folding some clothes that had finally dried. "Did you hear an animal outside last night?"

"Umm. . . no. Did you hear one?"

"Well," Mom said, picking up a pile of shirts, "I could have sworn I heard growling and rumbling. Of course I was pretty out of it, so I might have been dreaming."

My stomach, realizing that the topic of conversation was drifting its way, seized the moment and let out a mighty roar. And when I say mighty, I mean that it rattled the lamps.

Mom looked at me, slightly disgusted. "Yeah. That was it."

"Sorry to disappoint babe. Although, if it makes you feel any better, it kind of was an animal growling. Albeit one that had been partially digested."

"Ew. Too early in the day for that image."

Who can argue with that logic?

"So," Mom said, "are you going to be up for breakfast?"

I yawned and stretched. "I could probably manage a little. I don't want to be rude you know."

"Oh heaven's no, you wouldn't want to appear rude," Mom said and threw a pillow at my head.

"Of course not," I said, throwing the pillow back at her and catching her square in the lower back. "We, my dear, are emissaries from a strange land. It's our duty to observe the local culture, to integrate with the natives and present our 'best side' as representatives of THE STATES. If that involves forcing myself to consume delicious meats and copious amounts of protein, well, I'm up for the job. Wouldn't want to offend, you know?"

Mom had made a slight 'gulp' when I hit her, and now she had armed herself with a pillow in each hand. She had one armed cocked over her head in what I was positive would be a vicious arc when released. Before she could let fly, I said, "Be warned. If you hit me with those pillows I will interpret this as an act of war and ---"

WHAP! WHAP!

I shall not recount the next ten minutes in detail, but I will say that as so often happens with pillow fighting, someone got a little carried away and tears were shed.

"Oh my God," Mom said. "Are you crying?"

"No," I sniffled.

"I didn't hit you that hard."

"I know. Will you help me look for my tooth?"

"You are such a drama queen," she said and walked into the bathroom.

I wanted to argue the point with her, but I had nothing. It was a statement that I could not refute. I would have preferred the term 'Drama King', but it doesn't have the same lyrical power as 'Drama Queen'. Really, I prefer the term 'positively emotionally engaged' but can I convince your mom to use that? No.

Even though I was bleeding profusely in my imagination, I managed to struggle to my feet and wander over to the window to take a peek at the moose party down below.

That's curious, the wallow was empty. Nary a moose or a deer or an elk or transient or unicorn or a gnome in sight. Evidently the day shift hadn't reported for duty as promised. Very unprofessional. But what do you expect from a bunch of animals? Still, I'm sure in some knothole or mossy cave there was a managerial chipmunk promising that 'heads would roll'.

"Hey Suz. Where are all the moose?"

Mom walked out of the bathroom, toothbrush in hand. "I saw one when I first got up but she wandered away. I haven't seen any since."

"Any other animals out today?"

Mom pulled the toothbrush partially from her mouth and spoke through the toothpaste. "Nah da I cuh see."

"We should turn on the radio. Get a traffic report for the trails. Might be a jack-knifed buck, or with the morning fog a multi-species pile-up. That can really cause a backup you know. Especially if you've got an incident with herbivores and carnivores. On the plus side if you give it enough time, it's self cleaning."

"Come on and get dressed."

I did as requested and before you knew it, we were once again trudging through a steady drizzle back towards a date with obesity.

"Let's take a quick detour and check on the bike," I said, turning towards the parking lot.

As we rounded a small stand of trees I saw our baby, alone, cold, and no doubt frightened. She hunkered just where we had parked her on the edge of the lot. She was quite a sight. The constant rain had left her with pools of water on her seat, and drips and beads everywhere else. She was dirty. I mean really dirty. Mud and dirt and bugs and God knows what else. Stuck between the front tire and the belly pan were the remains of something which I didn't want to look at too closely, at least until I found a proper stick to poke it with first. I think it may have been either a bunny or a partial Fairie. Later I would discover that it was nothing more than a huge ball of thistle-down which, and I'm sure you can relate to this, came as a relief. I didn't need a swarm of angry Fairies spoiling my day. (That would come later on an ill-fated trip to San Francisco.) The point being, she was a sad, sad, lonely sight.

"Aw, she looks lonely."

"She looks dirty and wet," Mom said.

"And lonely."

Mom considered this for a minute. "Mostly dirty."

"And scared. And lonely."

Mom looked at me. "Don't you think you're anthropomorphizing a bit?"

"No, no I don't think so. Look how she's squatting there. Her headlights look all droopy and her saddlebags are limp. No, she's lonely all right. Probably thinking we've abandoned her here in the wilderness, never to glide the smooth blacktop ever again."

"Right." Mom turned back towards the lodge. "Well, it looks like the bike is fine, so let's go have breakfast."

"Just a minute," I said. I walked over and patted her handlebars, and swept the pooling water off of her seats. "It's okay baby. We haven't forgotten you."

Mom fidgeted in the gravel. "Can we go now?"

I paused for a moment, patted her seat again and sighed as I turned to walk to your mother. "You know, we really should take her for a little ride. It wouldn't hurt us and would probably do her some good." I looked back over my shoulder. "She's just so . . . so . . . sad. And you know, we did promise her that we would show her Banff."

"Look," Mom said, "I'm not ruling out a ride. But if I never have to ride in the rain again I won't be disappointed. So let's just see what the day brings, okay?"

"Don't talk to me," I said, grabbing your mom's arm and locking it into mine, "I understand completely. Now you explain that to her."

Curiously enough your mom ignored me. I find that as the years progress that happens more and more. I blame the media and sugary snacks.

As we walked to the lodge Mom said, "I know you've got something up your sleeve, but for the life of me I can't figure out what it is."

"Sweetie, must you always jump right to the supposition that I'm up to something?"

"Mostly yes."

Of course she was right, but I had to act slightly peeved to throw her off the scent.

We had walked far enough towards the Lodge that I could see the other end of the parking lot. What I saw there between a vegan-colored VW bus - and by vegan-colored I mean that there was probably an original paint job in there somewhere but it was covered by so many "Visualize Whirled Peas", and "Support Your Local Economy", and "Karma Happens", and "Hemp Is Not A Four Letter Word" bumper stickers that the original color was long lost – anyway, next to the VW and a vehicle spattered with mud sat, and I don't know any other way to say this, a spanking new BMW motorcycle.

"Hey," I said, and pointed out the shiny, blue BMW dual sport to your mom, "well looky there."

"Aw crap."

I agreed with your mother as this was a fair assessment. Aw crap indeed. You know that to the outside world all motorcyclists are the same. But we in the community know that there are sport bikers, cruisers, dirters, cafe' racers, tourers, purists, the chopper and bobber crowd, and. . . BMW riders. BMW riders are a species all to their own. It's not that they are snobby, or elitist, it's just that they. . .I mean. . . when you. . . ah screw it. Most of them are complete ass-hats. But ass hats with hearts of gold so I am told. I wouldn't know. I've never gotten one to talk to me. I did have a guy tell me one time that the reason BMW owners are so standoffish is very simple: in their heads they are the only SANE, and REAL motorcycle riders on the face of the earth. The rest of us are poorly prepared, poorly dressed, and probably poorly educated. Probably just poor. These are lone wolfs, slipping between sloppy off-road and super-slab with nary a care in the world. It's possible, although I have no proof, that when you buy a BMW motorcycle, you must first attend a class titled 'Disdain 101'.

Before you think ill of me for picking on Beemer-boppers, you should know it's an intrinsic part of the nature of every one that rides on two wheels to quantify, categorize, and usually label as 'insane' anyone that rides differently. Hence, sport bikers look at the cruisers and tourers as 'geezer mobiles'. Cruisers look at the sport bikers, especially those under dressed, (and you know they have to be REALLY under dressed to draw derision from the bar-hopper set), as SQUIDS. (Stupidly Quick, Under dressed, Inevitably Dead) Choppers and bobbers insist that they are the REAL roots of motorcycling, and the rest of the biking world looks at them and says, "That's a nice looking bike. Comfortable?" To which they reply "Shut the hell up and help me find the exhaust which seems to have fallen off at some point."

The wonderful thing is that in a pinch we all stick together. If you see a bike by the side of the road you don't think about the brand before you offer help. We are a large, dysfunctional family, full of in-fighting and insult hurling. Much like the Austro-Hungarian Empire. And like any other dysfunctional family we can curse and yell and scream at each other all day long, but if you pick on one - you pick on all. Unfortunately not everyone knows that. The ONLY people that I've ever been completely, consistently, and pointedly snubbed by, are BMW riders. And scooter riders but they don't count. And Brazilians. Damn Brazilians. And your mom. I may be spotting a trend here.

"Well," Mom said, taking a deep breath, "to take a quote from you, this should be interesting."

Yes. Yes it should.

We walked into the Lodge and before you could say "Lorne Green", Stacy was at our side, taking your mom by the elbow and directing her to a table where sat another couple. The man was in his early to mid-forties. Average height, with a body that had at one time probably been quite athletic but now was getting used to an easier lifestyle. He had thick black hair trimmed neatly and parted on the side. His face boyish and smooth. His wife, and I was making an assumption at this point, was a few years younger than he. She had long, dark hair that framed an attractive face, her body slight but edging towards that evil mid-life spread.

"David, Suzanne. . . this is Robert and Jackie. They ride motorcycles too!" Stacy squealed.

Evidently this divine conjunction had made Stacy's day. What with there now being a couple with which we had something in common her job had become much, much easier. I wanted to tell her that we probably had more in common with the squirrels in the trees than this couple, but I didn't want to break her spirit so early in the day.

"Pleased to meet you," I said and offered my hand to Robert, which he promptly took and pumped out the very definition of a business handshake. Strong and with just the right amount of 'shaking'. You would be surprised what a vanishing art form the handshake has become. I myself am personally responsible for contributing to its demise by licking my palm before every shake. Nothing says 'business' like a wet, clammy hand. I also make my wrist and arm go limp. It's a joy to see the look of revulsion on a guy's face.

See sweetie, it's the simple things in life that make it all worthwhile.

"Nice to meet you," Robert said as your mom and his wife exchanged greetings.

We took our seats at the table, and busied ourselves with the ritual of morning. So far so good. They seemed like nice folks. It took me a bit to get seated and settled owing to the fact that I had been cold and wet a few days before, and now my joints were . . . protesting. I'd fire their asses, but it's so hard to get good cartilage these days. And here again was the issue of the biker with the cane. It's interesting to see people's reactions. Some act embarrassed by their own good health. Some go so far to ignore my condition that it becomes painfully obvious that they are ignoring my condition. Robert and Jackie looked embarrassed and empathetic. Good. I could work with that. See, they could refute our ride, but they couldn't refute the fact that whatever was going on with me physically, it obviously took a hell of a lot to crawl into that saddle each day. Something that most take for granted.

Ha! Two points for me!

"So," I said with a calculated and warm smile, "I take it that is your BMW in the parking lot. Very nice bike." Which I actually meant. His BMW was beautiful.

"Thanks. You're riding the. . .?"

"Victory Vision," I answered.

Robert nodded his head as if this was exactly what he would have said had he actually known the answer. My eyes narrowed. Perhaps I had found a worthy adversary. A soul from the opposite pole that would challenge me with wit and humor and carefully crafted conversation. Yes, I had high hopes for Robert. Let's just see from what mettle the man is made.

"What's a Victory Vision?" Jackie asked of Robert.

Robert opened his mouth to speak, then closed it, considered his response, opened his mouth and then closed it again.

I was a tad disappointed in my new found arch rival. However, having no interest in watching his fish impersonation, I jumped in and supplied an answer.

"It's a big touring bike. Very different styling. Very futuristic looking." My explanation was greeted with blank stares, so I continued. "It's kind of like a Goldwing, only more Buck Rodger-y. Or Jetson-y. Take your pick. You either love or hate the looks," I said with a shrug. "Personally Suz and I love it. She has an Art Deco ambiance."

"Oh," Jackie said, nonplussed. "Like a Goldwing."

That seemed to be all that Jackie needed. Every thing about her demeanor, from vocal tone to a flick of her hair said that the statement 'like a Goldwing' had quantified our placement in the motorcycle pecking order and it wasn't anywhere near the tier upon which the BMW roosted.

I turned back to Robert. "When did you guys get in? Last night?"

"No. We left early home this morning. We live in Calgary. Quite a trip on the bike, but it was beautiful. We didn't really hit any moisture until we turned off the road up into the hills. How about you guys? Where are you from? When did you get in?"

HA! Score another one for me. I had traveled much farther than he had. Pffftttt! A lousy 90 miles. Or, in Albertan, 36,000,000 decigrams. Mileage is the first filter with which riders measure each other. The second is . . . well, it could be a number of things. How much chrome you've bolted to your bike. How many electronic toys you have mounted to the bars. Or, in certain circles, the number of teeth you have in your mouth. Bonus points if they're real.

"We're from the Seattle area."

Chew on that Calgary BMW boy!"

"We came in late Monday night from a town just over the border from eastern Washington. Took us a bit longer than we thought it was going to," I said, and winked at your mom, which may have been a mistake.

Roberts eyes began to widen but he caught himself. "That's quite a trip."

Clearly he was impressed. Perhaps this rider was a different breed than the previous BMW owners to which I had been exposed. Or to put it in the vulgar, this guy might not be a jerk after all.

"Say, that was some road up here huh? Did you have any trouble? I doubt that you would, your bike is made for a ride like that."

He smiled and I knew what he was thinking. Perhaps this touring rider from THE STATES wasn't as big of an asshat as other cruiser-folk he'd known.

"No. Not really." Robert sipped his coffee, speaking over the rim of the cup. "I didn't think it was too bad."

I shook my head. "I've got to hand it to you. There were a couple of times I wasn't sure we were going to make it."

Robert just smiled. "Different equipment. As you said, my bike is made for this kind of environment."

"Well for us it wasn't that easy either," Jackie said. We slipped quite a bit in the gravel. I don't mind telling you that I was downright scared a couple of times."

She turned to your mom as she said this because as a fellow passenger she was convinced that Mom would understand. Which of course Mom did understand, owing to the fact that I had put her near death countless times in the last thirty years. However, Robert, being a male of the species, winced as she said this. It's one thing to admit vulnerability yourself, quite another to have your wife point it out to strangers. Evidently Robert had not been educating Jackie on the 'Man Rules' as I have your mother. Your mom knows how the rules work and would never, ever in a million years admit fear, or even concern to a stranger lest it tarnish my Alpha status.

Mom looked at me as she said, "I know exactly what you mean. I've been scared more on this trip than I have in my entire life. It seems as though it's been one hair-raising event after another."

Gah! Robert and I were both dinged with Man penalties. It was hard to tell who had the upper hand. I believe it was, as usual, our wives.

"Still", I said, pushing on and deciding for the moment to ignore those feminine observations, "those last switchbacks before the lake couldn't have been much fun."

"What?" Robert said.

"The switchbacks. Right before the lake with the road running next to the cliff?"

Robert looked at me first blankly, and then his eyes narrowed suspiciously.

What game was he playing? If he were trying to lull me into further admissions of my riding ability or choice of steed, there were going to be problems. Oh big problems. Huge problems. Problems of biblical proportion. Sure, I may never say anything out loud, and he may never know there is anything wrong, but in my head I wouldn't hesitate to give him a strongly worded tongue-lashing. Possibly a vocalized raspberry for good measure. Oh! And a stern wrinkling of my brow, which, owing to lots of free time and a mirror sitting next to my desk I have perfected into a thing of beauty. Not too harsh, for if you furrow your brow too intensely it looks not so much like you're peeved, but that you may be in need of laxatives. Too loose and it simply looks like you're suffering mild indigestion. Somewhere in the middle is just right.

Did I mention I have a lot of free time?

Back to the conversation.

"What?" Robert said.

"Umm . . ." and here I looked to your mom for support, "You know where the road climbs fast and turns back on itself - the switchbacks. Just before the lake at the top where you level off. Right before you have to navigate those vicious washboards on the uphill."

He paused here, studying me. It was his turn to figure out WHAT game I was playing.

"We didn't hit any switchbacks or wash-boarding to the degree you're describing. It was a little sloppy in the muddy gravel, but fairly smooth sailing once we turned off of the tarmac," he said, clearly puzzled. "And I don't recall a lake at all. Do you Jackie?"

"No. Not until we got to the valley. But that was a long time after we quit climbing. Right before we hit the lodge and it was a ways away. Not next to the road really."

It was time for a bit of humble pie. It was obvious that Robert was in fact probably used to these kinds of roads in this kind of weather. I suppose BMW riders have their reputation for a reason.

"Well," I said, "my hat's off to you. I thought it was pretty bad not long after passing the Nordic Center." I spelled it 'center', but I said it 'centre' so as not to be insensitive to the indigenous dialect.

Robert shook his head as if he were clearing a bad dream, or shaking free of a giant talon gripping his noggin. Take your pick. Personally, I prefer the latter.

"What Nordic Center?"

I eyed him suspiciously.

"The one on the outskirts of Carnack. After you leave the town proper, and right before you start the serious climb up here."

His face turned ashen. "Carnack?"

I nodded in the affirmative.

"You came up the Carnack side? On that big bike?"

"Well. . . yes. How else would we have gotten up here?"

"From Highway 40 like we did."

GAH! There it was again. I was beginning to think that there were, just possibly, two ways to Hidden Valley. A civilized approach and an insane approach. If so, I was a dead man walking. The minute that Mom and I were alone all Hell was going to break loose. Still, I felt a certain amount of relief in the thought that I might be able to get out of this place without having to retrace our previous route.

"Oh. I'll have to look at the map. Guess I didn't see that."

Robert studied me. "You really came up from Carnack?"

"Well, yeah."

We eyed each other, both calculating, both measuring, searching each other's souls. In the silence we came to an agreement. And just like that the battle was won with nary a shot fired. I had defeated Robert without even trying. We both realized one thing simultaneously - I was a cretin. No, that's not right. We realized that I had done something on a big-ass weird-looking touring motorcycle that he wouldn't have considered on a good day, let alone with the rain. He might have been tempted to test himself if he were riding solo, but not with his wife on the back. Yet your mom and I had done this - and lived. True, for us it wasn't really by choice, more of 'happy accident', but he didn't know that, nor did he need to know. And I did all of this WITH obvious physical limitations. I don't care how educated, liberated, or full of love you are, no one likes to be beat by a cripple. (Yes, I described myself as crippled. Make you wince? Good. That part of you that just died inside was the weak part. You'll be stronger now.) By the 'Man Rules' I was now his superior and nothing could ever change that.

"You mean we didn't have to come up that way? We could have taken an easier route?" Mom said with a voice full of sharp pokey things.

Well, nothing could change my man-status except your mom. I may have to pull the 'brain tumor' card from the hat to regain their respect and put the Universe back in balance. I'm not above it you know. Oh sure, the damn tumor is benign, and easily controlled, but really - does that matter in casual conversation? When someone says 'Hey, I have a brain tumor!' is the first question you ask 'Is it benign?' No. Owing to our dismal public education system the first question you ask is 'Is it contagious?' To which, if you have any sense at all, you answer 'Yes. (cough cough) Yes it is. May I have a sip of your drink?'

But I digress. Back to your mom's question.

"Evidently there is another way," I laughed. I raised my hands to my shoulders palms up, and grinned a grin full of love and forgiveness, "Who knew?"

You know the really bad-ass black-hat gun-slinging poker-player from every Western you've ever seen? Mom's look would have made them tinkle. Where the hell was Stacy with some hydroponically-grown-fair-trade-organic-carbon-footprint-offsetting-bran flakes when you needed her? Even though Robert and Jackie sat there silently through this exchange, in their heads they were jumping up and down, pointing at me singing 'Nanny-nanny-poo-poo you're in TROUBLE.

Mom shook her head. "Let's talk about this later."

No good ever came from a sentence that starts with "Let's talk about this later." Perhaps a short solo ride, immediately after breakfast and while there were still witnesses about was in order. Perhaps I would be lucky and a rogue grizzly would wander into the dining room and mistake my bald pate' for a giant marshmallow. I could hope.

Just then, a minute too late, Stacy and the staff began the breakfast service. I shan't recount the details because I'm sure you're getting tired of my gustatorial ramblings. Lord knows I am. Suffice it to say that it was all natural, all prime, and all delicious. Still no bacon. Bastards. If this kept up I may have to lodge a complaint.

Come to find out Robert and Jackie, like all of the people we've met in the land of warm beer and cold temperatures, were very nice people. We spent the next hour sharing stories, combing the fabric of each other's lives.

You would be proud - I didn't even flinch when I found out that Robert was a lawyer. We all make mistakes. I myself have made a few. (I know! Hard to believe but true.) Jackie and Mom hit it off rather well finding common ground in the 'why my husband is a lovable imbecile' thread of conversation. We discovered that they lived in Calgary, rode a good amount, and loved to hike in these mountains. They came for a trip each summer, taking a break from children and work to 're-discover each other'. I had no intention asking them to explain that, as several highly inappropriate images readily sprang to the front of my mind's eye and I was sure one of them was correct. I just hoped it wasn't the one involving badgers. But *chacun a son gout*, no? I know you speak Itallian, and not French, but come on. . . a Romance language is a Romance language. Okay fine, I'll translate - People are insane. Wait. . . that's not right. It's 'to each their own' or something very similar. I would look it up but that takes a lot of effort. Before you go criticizing me for intellectual laziness, might I remind you that we live in an age where news is fabricated, sources don't exist, and plagiarism is what all the cool kids are doing for fun. I should be different?

As the meal wound down, but before we made our box lunches, Stacy walked in and rang a small brass bell to get everyone's attention.

"Hey folks, just wanted to remind you that tonight in the library we have a special guest that I think you'll all enjoy. His name is Randy Dale, and he works in cooperation with the Parks Service to control the bear population in this section of the Park using Kaerlian Bear Dogs. He's worked here for the last 10 years and has some excellent stories to share as well as talk about basic bear behavior and how you can be safe in bear country. He's a great guy and very entertaining! So if you're staying with us tonight I would highly recommend that you come and listen to him talk."

Immediately my interest was piqued: Why would dogs be involved in paranormal photography and how would that help with problem bears? Would they photograph the bear's auras, and then point out spiritual deficiencies? How the hell would you get a bear to hold still, or actually cooperate with something like that? And that begs another question - just how strong are the bears belief in the metaphysical?

Oh, I was going to be at the talk alright. Wild hedgehogs couldn't keep me away. I had questions.

Jackie said, "Oh, that sounds like fun!"

All three of us agreed with her assessment. Our foursome then launched into a lengthy talk regarding every bear sighting, every bear encounter we'd ever had. This was kind of lopsided, because the only good and entertaining bear story of our own had happened just the day before. Well, that's not true. We once saw a bear on I-90 just outside of North Bend that ran like linebacker towards the freeway - then promptly smacked into a chain link fence, bounced off, and without so much as a pause, took off hell-bent-for-leather back into the woods. It was a Three Stooges moment in the wilderness. I can only imagine the bear trying to explain the chain-link fence pattern that was impressed on his face. If he were an adolescent bear, it would probably become fashionable amongst his peers and before you know it, a steady stream of black bear would be bouncing off fences all over the Northwest causing biologist all over the region to say, "WTF?" And who could blame them.

Anyway, Robert and Jackie had seen several local grizzlies in the wild, but nothing you could call close. Although to me, anything that didn't have a 12 inch plate glass window, or a 90 foot trench between me and said bear was 'close'. Since our encounter was not only very, very close but on a motorcycle to boot, I scored extra-bonus man-points. I tell you, it may not work for everyone, but stupidity has certainly done wonders for my social status. We then heard, for the 9000th time in two days, the story of the 'motorcycle hitting the grizzly' with the addition of the ominous, "and they were riding a cruiser" spoken in hushed tones by Jackie. I think if she'd had a flashlight she would have been holding it under her chin, shining the light up into her eye sockets and using a spooky voice.

Donny came around with a coffee pot and a tall pitcher of water for refills. He stopped at our table, refilled our cups and glasses, and said "So, David and Suzanne. . . you guys made it out for a ride yet?"

"Funny you should say that Donny. I was just telling Suzanne, oh, every five minutes or so, that it sure would be nice to take a little ride. See sweetie? Now I have confirmation."

Donny laughed and to my surprise your mom chuckled as well.

"I told David that I would love to go for a ride, but I think I'll wait until it dries up a bit. I don't mind riding in the rain if we are out and the weather changes, but starting out in the rain . . . ugh. I haven't rested enough for that."

Just then the sun broke through the clouds and painted the meadow, valley, and surrounding hills in the most brilliant light I've ever seen. The grass became neon, the stream a thin line of silver sparkles winding its way past the Lodge. Your mom looked outside, then at me, then outside and back to me again.

"Odd coincidence, wouldn't you say sweetie? I think the Universe wants you back on the bike for a bit."

The timing was so surreal that we all laughed.

"Donny, did you plan that?" Mom asked.

"Oh no. . . don't go lookin' at me. I had nuthin' to do with it," Donny said with a grin. "Now if you gentlemen and you lovely ladies will excuse me I'd better get back in the kitchen before I get into trouble with mah better half."

We sat and sipped coffee and asked what Jackie' and Robert's plans were for the day. They said they were going on a hike up to one of their favorite lakes. If they got back in time, maybe a short ride. They returned the inquiry and we told them that we were going to do the same thing we did yesterday - eat, read, eat, play cribbage and nap. They said they thought this sounded like a fine plan and they hoped they would see us at dinner. They then excused themselves and went to make their lunch.

After they'd gone, Mom and I sat alone at the table, marveling at the beauty of the mountains and the setting and thoroughly enjoying our tea and coffee. Especially since everyone else had scampered off to do whatever it was they had planned for the day.

Let's see if I could pull off this next bit with a straight face.

"So," I said, after a few measured beats, "what's up with the paranormal dogs?"

"What?"

"You know," I said, "the Kirlian Bear Dogs. What's up with that?"

"Honey, what are you talking about?"

"You know, the guy whose going to give the talk tonight. The Kirlian Bear Dogs."

Nothing. Blank stare. Not a hint of recognition on your mom's face. It was as if she had no understanding of what I was saying. There are times, not many, but a few when I wonder what happened to the woman I married. To discover such a basic deficiency in her *Scientia of Occultus* made me sad. Plus, it ruined the joke. Which was much more important. I could see it was going to be a long trip for a short bit of humor, but I had nothing else to do at the moment.

"Kirlian. Kirlian Photography. Now, how dogs do it, and how it relates to bears is a mystery. And one that I'm eager to solve."

"Okay," Mom said, "I'll bite. What is Kirlian Photography?"

"Surely, mon petite livre, you jest. How long have you lived with me now?"

Mom calculated in her head. "Thirty-two years. Did you just call me your 'little book'?"

"Possibly. Sometimes I speak in tongues. Back to the point. Have you paid me no attention in all that time?"

"Sweetie," she said, and put her arm around my shoulders, "I tend to scan if you know what I mean. I do listen. But after a while. . . ." she let her voice trail.

I thought about that for a minute. I started to build a fine indignation, a pout of mythic proportions, but then I put myself in her shoes. Suddenly, I knew exactly what she was saying. It wasn't a particularly nice realization.

"Point taken. Well Kirlian Photography was all the rage in the 1970's. I know, you're much too young to remember the 1970's, but for argument's sake let's pretend you do. Anyway, what they did was take a photographic plate, lay an object on top of it, like leaf or something, then charge that sucker with high voltage. In the resulting photo the leaf would glow around the edges with a visible aura. If you ripped a piece from the leaf, then photographed it again, you'd see the outline of the whole leaf. Kind of simplified but that the jest of the process. It was suggested that what was being photographed was the 'aura' or 'life force' of the object."

"And you think this has something to do with the talk tonight."

"Well. Maybe."

"About dogs and bears."

"I admit," I said, "it's a stretch. But not impossible. We're off the map here. We are in strange lands." I gave a quick glance right and left and said in a whisper "Here there be monsters."

"Excuse me just a moment," Mom said, and walked over to Stacy who was clearing tables. I couldn't tell what they were talking about because they were whispering. However, they did keep looking over in my direction. Each time they did I would smile and wave like a drunk Prom Queen on the Senior float. I figured your mom was explaining the basic photographic process to her. I supposed any minute they would both come to where I sat, seeking further illumination. They spoke in whispered tones for a long time. After a few minutes they both shook their heads and Mom returned to the table alone.

"It's not Kirlian, it's **Kaerlian**, and has nothing to do with the paranormal. It's the breed of dog." She looked at me blankly. "They come from Finland."

"Oh," I said. "I see."

"Yeah."

"Well damn it. That's a whole lot less interesting."

"No, Stacy says that it really is an entertaining talk. He brings a couple of the dogs in with him, and he has a ton of pictures of the dogs and various bears from the park."

"Still," I say, trying to hide my disappointment, "it's no study of bear aura, is it? No concrete proof of a universal force." I placed an exaggerated look of disappointment on my face. "The mysteries will have to remain. . . unseen."

Then for emphasis I hummed the theme from the Twilight Zone.

Mom's eye narrowed. "Wait a minute. You knew that all along, didn't you?"

"I know not of what you speak my dear."

Here Mom actually slugged me on the shoulder.

"God. I should have known. Good one there, Mr. Funny Guy."

Oh oh. I had crossed a line. I was being referred to as 'Mr. Funny Guy'. That comes right before 'Mr. Sleep On The Couch Guy', which in turn is followed by 'Mr. Dead In His Sleep Guy'. I put on my best smile. My look-at-how-cute-I-am-and-I-meant-no-harm-so-you-can't-be-mad-at-me smile. It didn't work.

"I want you to get up and walk to the door."

"Why would I do that?" I asked.

"So the entire Lodge can hear me shout 'Dead Man Walkin'!"

"Okay, now that's funny. I don't care who you are."

"It's a good thing I love you so much," Mom said, and leaned over to kiss my forehead.

"Honey," I said, leaning into the kiss, "I count my blessings every day."

* * *

We'd packed a lighter lunch than the day before because at this point in our stay I was dangerously close to not being able to fit into any of the clothes I'd brought on the trip. I tried to convince your mom that my rapid weight gain wasn't due to the massive amounts of food I was consuming, but actually a hold-over from our trip up here. I was simply swollen from the rain. All of the Moore men had a certain sponge-like quality I explained. She said she would believe that if I took three extra cookies so she wouldn't look like a complete pig. It seemed a small price to pay.

We returned to our room and settled into the morning. Mom sitting in her window, watching the birds and the squirrels, reading her book, and I on either the couch or the bed reaching out through cyberspace to see what I'd missed on Woot.

See, I'd been trying for a Woot 'Bag of Crap', or as we in the know say, a 'Bandilier of Carrots' - FOREVER - and a simple thing like being in the middle of the wilderness on a wireless connection in a foreign country wouldn't stop me. Shoot, I've sat up for two days straight trying to capture the elusive 'BOC', so this was nothing. As soon as I logged on I knew there was going to be trouble.

"Suz, listen to this. . ." I then played the "Woot Off" theme for her.

Your dear mother responded much better than I could have hoped.

"Oh, you have got to be frickin' kidding me! You are NOT going to spend the next two days in front of the computer so you can buy a box of broken crap for a buck."

"But sometimes there are good things - nay, great things inside that Bag of Crap! You want me to miss that?"

Here she paused for a moment, and it took me by surprise because I think she was actually weighing the pros and cons of watching me obsess for the next 24 hours. Finally she said, "You can do what you want, but there will be plenty of Woot-Offs to come." Here she paused and took a breath, "Having said that, if you want to spend your vacation refreshing a website every 30 seconds I won't stop you."

Oh damn you Woot! Damn you and your elusive Bag of Crap! How dare you infringe on my domestic harmony whilst on vacation? This called for a strongly worded letter to the Woot staff. A strongly worded letter indeed! Full of large words, and coherent ideas. And rhymes. Possibly some stick-figure crayon doodles in the margins with lots of 'Pew pew pews' and 'Krack!' and 'Plonk!!' to illustrate my disdain. But this was her vacation too, and despite what had transpired since we left home, I really did want it to be a good one. I, against all of my better judgments, closed the lid on the computer. "You're right. I must someday learn to break myself from fear-based consumerism. Might as well be today."

Mom laid her book by her side and came over to where I sat on the couch. "Thank you." She leaned over and kissed my forehead tenderly.

"Bah, like I need to spend more time on the interwebs."

Which actually I do because I'm way behind in my thesis on Memes, and whether they reflect a genuine cultural zeitgeist or are simply hilarious. Plus, as I've said before, and I know you can relate to this, I REALLY needed to find out if the walrus ever found his bucket. Poor thing. It was haunting me to no end.

Mom sat down beside me. I put my arm around her and she leaned in close to lay her head on my shoulder. We sat that way for quite a while, watching the brilliant yellow sunlight burst over the scenery from our window and then just as quickly fade to gray as the clouds moved in. It was mesmerizing. I have no idea how long we sat like that, but it wasn't long enough.

Mom stood and stretched. She walked over to the doors to the deck and looked down into the wallow. "You know it's funny. But there still aren't any moose or any other animals using the mud." Even though I couldn't see her face, I knew that her brow was furrowed with concern. "Do you think they're okay?"

"Who," I said, "the moose?"

"Yeah," Mom replied. "I just hope nothing has happened to them."

I could see where this was going and I needed to divert her attention ASAP. Otherwise, I would find myself on a moose rescue party, beating the woods and brush for a hint of dewlap. Now I'm not proud of this next fact but I think you'll appreciate where I was coming from. It was simple - Mom was worried about the moose. I wanted to take a ride and possibly, just possibly, see another bear. If I played my cards right I knew victory was in my grasp.

"Tell you what babe. If the weather holds maybe we'll pop out on the bike - just for a bit, and see if we can't find them. I'm sure they're around here somewhere."

Mom studied the clouds. "If it's not raining a little trip might be nice."

It was like taking candy from a baby.

I know! I'm a bastard. But a clever one.

Mostly.

October 5, 2008

Dear Amber,

Well, you're getting close. Only 9 more weeks to go. The hard part should be over. I imagine by now you and the rest of the Candidates have got this whole OCS thing down pat.

In my mind I picture you, the other Candidates, and the Drill Sergeants all sitting around in the evenings by a roaring campfire, toasting smores and swapping stories.

Mom says you get to go in a Helo Dunker this week. Is that like a doughnut shop on base or something?

Mmmm . . . doughnuts.

Why do they call them 'Helo'? Is that like the sub/grinder sandwich thing? An East Coast dialect thingee?

Mom also says that you are not looking forward to this experience. Hon, just get a bunch of glazed and start dunkin'. It'll be over before you can say 'Thank you Sir may I have another cruller?'

Love,
Daddio

P.S. It WAS infected. You were no help at all.

Chapter 11

Hikers - They're Not Just For Breakfast Anymore!

We were sitting in the fabulous "Moose Snot Roost" gearing up for what I hoped would be a fine adventure. I hadn't shared my hopes of running across another grizzly with your mom. Why, you may ask? Because I'm a coward. Plus, the disappearance of the animals in the wallow weighed heavily on her. She was becoming more agitated by the minute for lack of all things moosey. If I've said it once I've said it a thousand times, your mom's heart, when it comes to animals, knows no bounds. I feel the exact same way. Where your mom appreciates them in their natural environment, I prefer them between two slices of bread with some mayo. Yum!

"I mean," she said as she zipped her chaps, "that it's a little weird that yesterday there was a regular moose freeway outside our door, and today nothing!"

"Perhaps it's some high-holiday for our antlered friends. Possibly Rosh HaFauna. The day that God created the first furry, antlered, dewlap-ridden progenitor of the moosey race."

Mom paused mid zip. "Rosh HaFauna. Sure."

"I suppose they could be attending a convention, showing the latest in antler care and musk gland grooming. Or it could very well be that they're running motivational programs and self actualization courses for the lazier denizens of the woods. Like the Martin. Complete louts Martins. Slackers and knee-biters. Or, they could be negotiating a labor dispute twixt the beavers and the mountain sheep."

"That's a stretch, don't you think?"

"Not necessarily," I said. "Moose are known as the "Facilitators of the animal kingdom"."

"I did not know that."

"Oh yeah. Granted, they're not terribly good at facilitation, but hey. . . you know. . . moose. What do you expect?"

As we readied ourselves my pulse began to race. I had it all planned in my head and it was going to be spectacular! We would ride down the road a bit and there in the meadow, standing not too far, but certainly not too close, would be the majestic Grizzly. Your mom would spot the bear first, and we would stop in the road letting the bike idle. This giant, knowing that we meant her no harm, would continue with her routine, providing us a glimpse into the fascinating world of North America's largest carnivore. Oh, it was going to be glorious! We would snap pictures as if we were Paparazi for all things bearish. She would pose, a sly look on her muzzle as she turned this way and that, showing off her mighty physique. She would then in turn study us, wondering what manner of beast bore our weight. After both her and our curiosity had been satiated, we would trundle back down the road to the Lodge where we would sup gourmand and entertain our table mates with dashing tales of our ursal encounter.

I could hardly wait.

"Why is your face all flushed? Are you feeling okay?"

"Fine sweetie. Fine. Just a bit of excitement over taking a little ride. I didn't realize it, but I was coming down with a slight case of cabin fever."

"You know," Mom said as she slipped on her leather jacket, "I didn't want to say anything but I was more than ready to get out of our room for a while."

"Then M'lady," I said as I zipped up my own jacket, "your steed awaits." I bowed at the waist and pointed towards the door.

"Why thank you kind Sir," she said and opened the door into the gray afternoon.

We walked the short distance from the Lodge to where sat our baby. Did I detect a quiver, a slight shake of the handlebars as she anticipated release from this flat-gravel prison? I did my best to wipe the water from her seats but the effort was futile. I swiped most of it off, which was drier than it had been in three days, and that would have to do. I started her up, and did a quick inspection of all of the mechanics as I waited for the oil and motor to warm. Which would be a good thing, because it was frickin' cold. Not just a little cold, I mean really cold - like the temp gauge on the bike was hovering around 50 degrees. Suddenly my mesh jacket seemed a tad on the skimpy side.

"Where are we going to go?" Mom asked.

"Well, I thought we would head back the way we came in."

Mom's eyes widened. "If you're planning on going DOWN that hill, count me out. I'll ride it if I have no other choice but not for fun."

"Babe, let me assure you, I have no intention of riding back down that hill. We will turn around long before then. I thought we would ride down to where the meadow opened up. Just kind of take in the scenery. It was a little dark when we came through the other evening and I wouldn't mind getting a good gander at our surroundings."

"Yeah. A little dark AND a little scary."

"Well yes. Prolonged panic does tend to color your appreciation for beauty," I said.

Mom looked me dead in the eye. "Ya think?"

"I wouldn't know of course but I've heard rumors. I have nerves of steel myself. Solid as a rock."

"Yeah, a rock that screams like a little girl from time to time."

"My dear," I say to her, "that's not fear. That's the Tourettes." And here I gave a small 'squeak!' to hammer home my point.

"Does Tourettes make you scream and swoon when you see a spider?"

Gah! How dare she turn my own phobias against me?

"That's just prudent. It's a proven fact that arachnids are driven to utter terror by the sight of a middle-aged bald man yelling and hopping from one foot to the other as he cries for his wife. It's an aggression ritual. Much like the subtle interaction twixt men, I'm simply asserting my dominance."

She looked at me long and hard.

"If that's the story you tell yourself to get you through the day, it's fine by me sweetie," she said, kissing my cheek.

Superman has kryptonite. The Green Lantern has the color yellow. Hannity has Combs. And I, although I'm loath to admit it, have a little thing for spiders. It's not my fault. I was traumatized by these eight-legged devils as a child. Rogue groups of spiders would regularly beat me up for my lunch money. Then, to add insult to injury, laugh at my outdated shoes. Spiders have no morals. No compassion whatsoever. Frickin' spiders.

Anyway, we eventually got on the bike and I managed not to kill us getting out of the parking lot. Boo Yah! 100 kilo-yards from the Lodge and all was going fine until we hit the main road. Funny, and I'm just telling you this in case you find yourself in a similar situation, torrential rains on the gravel road had left it - squooshy. Oh, and slick. So when I turned the bike and we hit that wide gravel path, the back of the bike wanted to go north, while the front was headed east. Unfortunate really, because I wanted all of us to go west. After a few moments that your mom would later describe as 'some crazy slippin' and slidin'', I managed to get the bike fairly upright, mostly upright, and pointed generally in the right direction. The problem was that there were two narrow tracks, the width of a car tire, that were navigable. To either side was soft, soft gravel and certain death. No, I exaggerate. Soft, soft gravel and certain painful injury. So when I say I was careful, you know I mean that I was nail-biting, teeth-grinding, shoulder-cramping careful.

I managed to relax after a bit, hitting the rhythm of the bike and the road. The cold hardly bothered me at all. Hardly. Mostly. The sun had taken a permanent break long before we geared up, and now the day was not only gray but misty again. I suppose it would have been enchanting if I were in a car, with a heater. But alas, I was on a big-honkin' bike with a mesh jacket and a little woman behind me that at the first signs of me being frozen would lean forward and say, 'told you so.' Still, it was marginally better than staying in the room, and we did happen to spot moose butt slipping into the trees on the side of the road at one point, so. . . not a total loss.

We'd been cruising for a time when two things became apparent:

One - it was beginning to rain again.

Two - the road was getting worse the farther we traveled from the Lodge.

C - I was unable to feel anything below my neck.

I don't know how I managed to steer the bike. I have a theory. You know how they say when you lose one sense, the others become heightened and make up for it? Evidently since my entire body was numb, my psychic abilities had taken over, allowing me to corner and accelerate solely with THE POWER OF MY MIND.

"Honey, why don't we call it a day before you get so cold you can't remember your A B 7s" Mom asked. "Okay?"

What heresy was this? I had not yet seen a bear. Defeat was not in my vocabulary. But I was going to look it up and add it in as soon as we got home because I was really cold.

"Yeah. I guess we might as well. I was just hoping that we would get to see . . . more wildlife."

Mom leaned forward and wrapped her arms around my shoulders, clasping her hands below my neck. Her visor clinked on the back of my helmet. "You mean you wanted to see another bear."

I laughed. "Yeah I did. A little."

Had I been that obvious? After careful consideration I decided that more than likely I had. Subtlety was also not in my vocabulary. Hmmm . . . if you added those two 'not in my vocabulary' words together you would almost have a sentence. A subtle defeat. It's one where you lose but no one really notices. That's my kind of defeat right there.

Two. . . three . . . four . . . In this space you may insert an insult geared towards the French with my blessing. Way too easy for a pro such as myself.

"I'm sorry sweetie," she said patting me on the back. "Maybe next time."

See? This is why I adore your mother. How many women, after being on the journey I'd put your mom through, would even consider a 'next time'. That girl's got spunk I tell you! I think she's a keeper.

"Okay, as long as you promise you'll ride with me again once we are back home."

"Honey," she said, squeezing me tighter, "I'd ride with you to the far corners of the globe if that's what you wanted." She relaxed her arms and sat up, swiveling her head and looking in all directions. Oh wait," she said, "seems like I already have."

"Cute."

"Yes," she said, "yes I am."

After discussing your mother's own 'adorability quotient', which, we discovered, was nearly off the chart, I managed to get the bike turned around in the gravel through a combination of prayer and threats. Mostly threats. It seemed not only had the Elder Gods deserted me, but also the more conventional deities. Except for Loki or Coyote. This whole escapade stunk of their work.

With the road conditions deteriorating rapidly in the weather I had to be extra careful on the way back to the warmth of the Lodge. Driving, or trying to keep the bike on such a narrow track for such a long distance was exhausting, so when I saw a sign for "Annaminga Picnic Area", and a fine looking blacktop road going to these mythical picnic grounds, it was like a gigantic magnet for the Vision. Oh tarmac! Oh sweet, sweet blacktop! I didn't care if it only went a few hundred nanograms into the woods. For that brief time we would be cruising in the way we had become accustomed before entering these mountains, which is to say, full of sanity and hope. Why there was this lone blacktop road in a sea of crushed mountain didn't even register as a curiosity in my numbed cerebellum.

I leaned back my head and motioned for your mom to raise her visor. "Look! Blacktop! Mind if I point her in that direction? Just for a bit? Wouldn't it be nice to feel solid asphalt under the tires even for a few minutes? I've had enough of this slip-n-slide."

Mom didn't say anything but she gave me the 'thumbs up'. So, off the gravel we went and onto that loverly, loverly flat-black ribbon.

The road followed a small ravine cut through a hill. Steep gravel banks with small scrub trees framing the road on either side. I hadn't noticed how steep the road climbed but I also didn't really care. A steep slope on blacktop was no big deal. The road rose for probably a quarter mile, or about 76,000 liters, then crested the top and presumably went down the other side. Or, it may have dropped into a parallel dimension which would be. . . AWESOME!

I came to a stop at the turnoff with both wheels on that rich, black path long enough to wipe some fog from my visor and to figure out what the heck was going on with the three cars that were parked hodge-podge at the bottom. It looked as if they'd been dumped out of a bag, rather than parked with any thought, effectively creating a bottleneck to the picnic area. They had left just enough room to squeeze around them on the right side, and I was planning my path when I noticed something funny.

I leaned back and spoke to your mom. "Hey honey? Why do you think those cars are full of people? It looks like they are all just sitting there, waiting for something."

Mom peered around my shoulders. "That is kind of weird. Maybe they're hiking and sitting in the cars to warm up a bit?"

This made perfect sense. Although, why they were all waving frantically was beyond me. "They seem quite excited about something." I waved back at them with my gloved hand. "Probably never thought they'd see a bike like this up here in the middle of nowhere."

Mom said, "I'm not sure that's what's going on. They seem to be pointing at us, then somewhere to their right, then back to us."

"Well," I said, "I don't care how much I'd like to further international relations. I'm not going to amuse them by trying to climb a gravel hill on a touring bike. They can just forget that."

Although the thought flashed through my mind how cool this would actually be. Hill climbing on a Vision. Now that's old-school. I was positive I could make it. . . oh, ten feet or so before crashing spectacularly into a twisting ball of flame. The image was mighty appealing. At least I would be warm.

"I don't think that's it," Mom said, swiveling her head to look around.

"Then what the hell is. . . " And it was about that time I saw. . .

BEAR!

Big bear. Huge bear. Angry looking bear.

Here, before anything else came to mind, I thought, 'Self? What the hell were you thinking? You have voluntarily put yourself and your precious bride in danger- once again - all to satisfy some morbid curiosity flitting round your brain. Oh curse you gray matter! Oh curse your inquisitive soul! And while we are on the subject what have the two of you done with my common sense?'

I decided to explain this to your mom so that I could launch a preemptive apology before she saw the bear, saw how close it was, saw the general direction it was loping, and she chose to use any of her numerous weapons to 'teach the idiot that had put her in this situation a lesson'. Most likely stabby-stabby, but it could also be hitty-hitty, pokey-pokey, or my least favorite - burny-burny. I should have never given her that pocket blowtorch for her birthday. Never in my wildest dreams did I think it would be used against me. I was thinking a nice crème brouillette. Ah well. It was short, but a well lived life. I opened my mouth to explain the situation to your mom with calm and cool and composure, but what came out was. . . .

"Bear. Bear. BEAR!"

"Wha- . . ." her voice stopped mid word and then her brain digested what I'd said. ". . . bear? Where?" Her head swiveled in a lovely imitation of a woodland owl. "Where bear?"

"There bear." I pointed to a massive reddish-brown mass moving at an alarming gait, which I estimated to be just shy of the speed of light, down the hillside towards the cars, and unfortunately head-on towards your dear old Mum and Da.

"Gah!" Mom said.

So succinct. Such an economy of words. Yes. . . Gah, my dear. Gah indeed!

"Ummm. . ." I said. "MmmmGrrrk!"

Well that's odd, I thought. Evidently my ability to form actual words had been abandoned for a more primitive declaration of emotion.

"Oh my God. . . it's huge," Mom whispered, her helmet clinking against mine.

Without even thinking, and don't think less of me because you have to know this was an auto-response brought on by stress, my mouth opened and out came "That's what she said!"

"What?", Mom asked, genuinely befuddled.

"What?", I replied, staring at the beast, barely conscious of the fact that I had said anything at all.

Life never pauses as it does in the movies so you can take the time to discuss a situation to death. Before we could explore this conversational cul de sac, the bear stopped half-way down the hill. There she stood, surveying the bounty spread before her gigantic jaws in the form of thinly wrapped humans on a motorcycle.

I tried to look on the positive side. I was grateful there would be witnesses. If I couldn't live to tell the story myself, at least there would be others that would share the tale of our passing as a cautionary fable. We may even eclipse the 'motorcycle hits grizzly' anecdote and become legends of the Rockies. Two Bikers from THE STATES eaten by a bear. It would work on so many levels. It had all the elements. Foreigners. (Which immediately means they are stupid and unaware of the local ways.) Anti-Green. (For we had been riding a loud, gas-guzzling two wheeled death machine.) Stupid. (This would be self evident after we'd been eaten.) Put them together and you have a frame-work for a fine, fine morality tale. Foreigners. Anti-Green. Stupid. This is not exactly how I had pictured myself attaining fame, but beggars can't be choosers. If my 15 minutes came in the form of a Darwin Award, so be it.

Mom started poking me in the shoulder. First with her finger, then with her whole hand. "Go. Go. GO!"

While this was excellent advice, it was also easy for her to say. She wasn't in control of a huge piece of machinery pointing in the wrong direction. My reflexes kicked in. Without even thinking I pulled in the clutch with my left hand, braced my legs against the blacktop and pushed backwards with all my might away from the bear and away from the tangle of cars. If I could get enough room I would pull us around in the tightest u-turn possible given the length of the bike and the rake of the forks. As I've told you before usually when I back the bike up like this your mom likes to get off and watch from a safe distance. I fear this is a trust issue but I won't' get into that right now. I thought she probably wouldn't mind just holding on during this delicate maneuver so I didn't offer to let her off the back. Wise choice. The bike rolled back a bit and I once again braced my legs pushing with all my might. Sweat poured from my forehead. A few more feet and I would clear the cars. Spaceship bike my ass! Where in the hell was the 'hover' button on this thing anyway?

The whole time that I'm pushing backwards, balancing a five mega-ton machine to keep it upright, and worrying about your mom, I had one eye on the bear. My other eye, in a panic no doubt, had left the scene. That's what I thought at the time, but later realized that I was scrunching my face really hard as I pushed.

I saw the bear pause on the hillside, swaying back and forth on her front legs, no doubt wondering what Fairy Godmother had visited her unannounced and spread a smorgasbord of imbecilic tourists for her delight and could she finish it all at once or would she have to get a 'to-go' bag?

One more mighty push of my legs and we were clear. I caught a glimpse of a couple inside the car closest to us. A balding man with a scruffy growth of 'outdoor' beard. A woman with long dark hair. They waved and smiled like this was the most ordinary thing in the world. I managed a smile back but it may have been a bit lopsided owing to the fact of a tremendous burst of adrenaline rampaging through my body. You know, that much adrenaline makes me. . . twitchy. I turned my attention away from my new-found friends, possibly the last people with whom I would ever have any kind of human interaction, turned the handlebars on the bike as far as they would go to the left and continued to twist even after they came to a stop just shy of the gas tank. I thought maybe I could just keep pushing until matter gave way on the subatomic level and turned the bike inside out, surrendering to quantum gravitational forces that hopefully would spit us out of this Universe like a watermelon seed from a twelve-year old farm boy's mouth. Hopefully to a dimension where there were no bears.

Now, as anyone that rides will tell you, moving a motorcycle with the forks 'locked' in this manner at slow speeds is one of the most difficult maneuvers to accomplish on two wheels. Let me rephrase that - the most difficult maneuver to accomplish. . . successfully. It's quite easy to start that tight circle and then fall over. However, I was hoping to avoid the whole 'falling-on-the-ground-and-crying-like-a-baby-whilst-being-mauled-by-a-bear' thingee. I know. I put a lot of conditions on life, don't I? I had to accomplish this feat. If not for my sake, for your mom's. She was way too young to go to prison for killing her spouse. So, I revved the engine, and eased off the clutch as I threw my weight to the opposite side of the bike to counter-balance the turn. To my surprise, and with a 'whoosh!', the bike spun around like a well oiled top and before I knew what was happening we were upright and pointed AWAY from the bear. This, as Martha would say, was 'a good thing'.

It's amazing how quickly we can recover from a moment of terror. Now that the motorcycle was aimed in a direction that offered escape I relaxed a bit.

Not a lot, but enough so that I was breathing again. I glanced over my shoulder at the bear that was looking a little less angry and a little more confused as to what exactly was her part in this spectacle. First she looked like she was going to go back up the hill, and into the forest, then changed her mind and decided to continue down the slope towards the cars and ourselves.

"Let's GO!" Mom said, with no small amount of emergency in her voice.

"Just a minute. We can rocket off if we need to, let's just watch her for a bit. Get the camera. Take a picture. The kids are never going to believe us without factual documentation."

"Are you serious?"

"Babe, when will we get the chance to see a grizzly this close again?"

"That's what Zoos are for," Mom said through clenched teeth.

"Not the same," I reminded her.

"Good enough for me."

"Just one little picture to show the kids, then I promise we're tail-lights."

"Fine. But if I die I'm never going to let you forget it."

"Fair enough." I said.

During out little repartee' the bear, having reached a decision, was now making a beeline for the cars behind us. I increased the throttle, and eased out on the clutch until it barely grabbed, ready to take off down the road in a split-second if needed. True, the gravel was still soft and messy, but I was pretty sure given the circumstances I could set a world speed record no matter the surface.

Mom and I watched as the bear, having finished her descent ambled behind the cars, and when I say 'behind' the cars I mean she could have touched their "Will Hike For Food" bumper sticker with her nose. Now that the bear was closer I saw just how big she was. She made the Subaru Outback she walked behind, look like a go cart made from lawnmower parts and tinker toys.

Mom had managed to get the camera out of her pocket and I heard her snap a quick picture for posterity. Well, posterity and bragging rights. I was about to take our leave. . .

Then it happened. The most astonishing display of human behavior I have ever witnessed played out before our unbelieving eyes.

As the bear walked behind the cars, the couple that had been smiling at me flung open their car doors and jumped out to take a picture. Seriously. With the bear close enough to whack them with her paw should she desire.

Click click. Flash flash. Maul maul.

"Oh my God," Mom said, once again nailing the narrative square on.

I'm no biologist, but I was pretty sure that jumping out and surprising a slightly confused grizzly was a 'bad' idea. This is why you don't see many surprise parties for our Ursal cousins. I imagine it would go something like this:

Bear walks into a dark room.

'Click' goes the light switch.

"Surprise!" everyone shouts in unison.

Then. . . carnage!

Oh sure, there would be apologies later, but that doesn't really help if you've been bitten in two, now does it?

"What the hell are they thinking?" I asked of no one in particular.

The bear, now more confused than ever because she had no idea this was a photo opportunity, lumbered away from the back of the cars never taking her eyes off of the couple with the cameras. I swear, if they'd had crackers they would have held them out and cooed "Pretty bear want a treat?" as they stretched their arms forward to make it easier for this massive death machine to take not only the crackers, but also their upper torsos. And faces. And heads. You know how you read something in the paper and say to yourself, 'Now just how the Hell did that happen?' Just like this, that's how. In a way it kind of made me happy and sad at the same time. Sad because I didn't want to see anyone hurt. Happy for now Mom and I weren't the lowest fruit on the branch if you know what I mean. Ah, the sweet contradictions of life.

By this time the bear, having no desire to model, had made it over to the opposite side of the road and the base of the gravel bank. She paused there, clearly weighing the pros and cons of snacking. A moving bear is one thing. A stationary bear, and especially one that was having trouble making a decision, was quite another. I eased off the clutch and moved us the 15 feet to the edge of the blacktop.

"Let's go!"

"Okay, okay. Just give me a minute. . ."

The gravel road ran next to a swale. So, from our position we had about 30 feet of gravel in front of us, the width of the road, then a steep drop 12 feet into dense trees and brush. I give you this image so that you'll understand what follows.

As I began to move us away from the insanity, suddenly a hiker popped up the bank and onto the gravel shoulder. When I say 'popped' I mean it. Like he had been standing on a trampoline and took a mighty jump, vaulting himself out of the ether. This kid couldn't have been more than twenty-two or twenty-three at the most. His eyes were wide - I mean really wide - manhole cover wide - and his hair was matted from sweat making little ringlets on his forehead. One boot was untied and there was mud on his knees and what looked like a nasty bruise blooming on his forearm. He stumbled a few feet onto the road, and then - POP POP POP! Three more hikers followed. Another guy and two girls of about the same age, each one looking like they just crawled off the worst amusement park ride EVER.

"Oh!" I said, because that was the first thing that crawled from my throat. "Y hallo thar."

Some people reach for the bottle in times of crisis. Some to the bible. Me, I'll take a Meme or a LOL cat any day.

The youthful quartet huddled on the edge of the road for a minute, casting furtive glances over their shoulders. The leader, at least I assume he was the leader for he was the first one to scramble up the bank, walked a few paces towards me with a look of utter confusion on his face. Shell shocked in fact. I couldn't blame him. I mean really, think how it must have looked to them. They come out of the woods in the middle of God-knows-where to be greeted by two people on a spaceship like motorcycle with a tangled mess of tourists behind them. And behind that an agitated lump of muscle, teeth, and claw.

I made eye contact with the leader. He stared at me. I stared at him. He sized up me. I sized up him.

"Bear!" he breathed. His voice was barley a whisper, his breath flowing in delicate little wisps of mist.

"I know!" I pointed back over my shoulder, "She just came over the hill and . . . "

One of the girls stumbled over and joined him at his side. "Bear," she said. Although it came out as something between a question and a statement.

"Yeah," I said, "that's why were just about to. . . "

The other couple joined them. Suddenly I recognized the look in their eyes. This was the exact expression that teenage camp counselors wear right before the maniac with the knife ruins their day. If I heard ominous music then I would know we were truly screwed.

The group now milled about the middle of the road, clearly confused as to which direction to make their escape.

"BEAR!" the guy said.

What the hell? Was this a group for monosyllabic hikers? Possibly some support group exercise or wilderness vocabulary training?

"I KNOW!" I said, and again pointed to the bear behind us that had now ambled halfway up the hillside where she paused to inspect a small bush.

"What?" the leader said, confused.

Ah. I must use their language, their syntax to communicate. "BEAR!" I said, craning in my seat and pointing to said grizzly.

The boy shook his head as if shedding a dream. He looked to me, then to the bear, then back to me without a lot of comprehension cluttering his face.

"No," the boy said, "Bear. THERE!" He pointed back over his shoulder to the woods where they had emerged.

Now it was my turn for confusion. "You saw a bear on the trail?"

"Bear." The leader repeated. "Following us." He cast a nervous glance over his shoulder.

In a flash it became clear. We were being rounded up, herded if you will. The grizzles were the cowboys and we were naught but terrified sheep thundering dumbstruck through the woods. I'm pretty sure branding wasn't on their minds as we were now effectively the meat in a grizzly sandwich.

A thought drifted into my head. This might be the time to make our exit, stage left. Then another thought filled my head: right then I realized my quest had been fulfilled. A warm glow of satisfaction washed over me from head to toe. I had seen the mighty *Ursas arctos horribillus* in all its glory. Mission accomplished. I didn't need to see any more.

There arose a mighty din from behind us. Yelling and car doors and possibly a whimper. I had no interest in turning around. I didn't want to see what all the fuss was about. It couldn't be good. I doubt if the bear on the hill had popped into the tree line to retrieve her little hat, tutu, and unicycle to give us a show.

Mom, who had been strangely quiet during this last development leaned forward. "David. Let's get out of here." She cast quick glances right and left, then back to the group of young hikers who were now half hopping, half dancing in a state of modified panic. "This is utter madness."

Oh lord, why does she set me up like this? She knows I can't resist.

"Madness?" I pulled a mighty breath into my lungs and paused for dramatic effect. "Madness? THIS! IS! SPARTA!" I cried, and twisted the throttle to a roar as we lunged back onto the mushy road.

Mom leaned forward and shouted "What the *Hell* is wrong with you?"

"Long list or short list?" I shouted back.

"It was a rhetorical question," she said as she sat back in her seat, a remarkable amount of disdain clothed in her voice. Ah marriage. Even after all these years I never knew what was going to set your mother off.

We rode back to the lodge without further conversation or incident. It took everything I had to plow through the rain and mud, but I did so with a genuine feeling of satisfaction. We arrived a bit later at the Lodge. Cold, muddy, and the smell of sweat-fear permeating our clothes like stale smoke from a Rave. But most importantly unscathed, alive, and relatively unharmed. Well, unharmed if you don't factor in emotional damage.

As I stood by the bike, adjusting my cane and putting my gloves away, I caught movement out of the corner of my eye. "Hey! Look babe," I said, pointing to the woods beyond the parking lot, "your moose are back! Lucky, huh?"

Mom just shook her head.

Suddenly the adrenaline ran its course and I was exhausted. Legs of lead and all that. Time for a nap.

The question was, would your mom let me in the room?

Time would tell.

October 7, 2008

Dear Amber,

Well! I couldn't have been farther off on that 'Helo Dunker', now could I?

So, let me get this straight . . .

They strap you in the cabin of a helicopter, drop the box into a swimming pool as they rotate it upside down, make you escape the straps and buckles, and then you have to find your way out through a door or a window only to claw your way to the surface for air?

See? You thought I was just being cruel at your 9th birthday party. I knew those skills I taught you kids that warm summer afternoon would come in handy.

Love you,
Daddio

P.S. Called the base today. Marine Drill Sergeants aren't so bad. Very reasonable I thought, and quite pleasant on the phone. It took some convincing on my part, but by the end of the conversation your Sergeant promised me that you would receive 'special treatment' this week. You're welcome. It's what Dads are for.

Chapter 12

Why You Should Never Mention Quebec Outside of Quebec

Luckily, and with no small amount of pleading, Mom DID let me into the room, so evidently I was, if not forgiven, well on the way. We didn't discuss the bear incident. Which made me happy and nervous at the same time. See, in a marriage as long as ours nothing is ever truly forgotten. Oh, it may be shelved for a bit. It may appear that the topic shall never be broached again, but that ain't so. In my experience the longer between the incident and the discussion of the incident, the worse for me. See, your mom's logic which is excellent to begin with, becomes bullet-proof when she has time to stew. It's not fair. How am I supposed to weasel my way out of trouble, with a winning combination of cuteness and humor, when she's had time to think from all angles? There was no way I was going to let what had happened fester.

"So," I said, "that was something, huh?"

Mom dropped the book she was reading from in front of her eyes, just long enough to give me the look of death. The she raised the book again. It wasn't as if she were hiding behind the pages. It was more like she was behind a fortress. A fortress of literature. The strongest barrier known to mankind.

"We did get close, didn't we? I mean, wasn't she amazing?" I said. With no response from behind the book I took a chance. "It really wasn't that dangerous. I mean, we could leave at any minute." Still nothing. "Wait 'til we tell the kids. I bet they'll get a kick out of it."

Yes. I brought you and your sister into the mix. I played the 'child' card. It's a low ploy, but I was desperate. Oh, you have no idea how many difficult situations you and your sister have rescued me from over the years. Would this strategy bear fruit? Only time would tell.

Mom closed her book with a snap.

"Sweetie," I said, stalling for time, "before you say anything - - -"

"Oh will you be quiet," Mom said, cutting me off. "I'm not upset."

My hackles raised. My suspicions aroused. My interest piqued. It was quite painful. What game was this? What tact was she taking? What fresh Hell was I in now?

"Umm. . .," I said quietly. "Really?"

I wasn't about to let down my guard just yet. She could be hiding any number of weapons behind that book.

Mom stood up from the window bench and came to where I perched on the edge of the Lincoln-log bed. She sat beside me, putting her arm around my shoulder and drawing me close. I could smell the faint hint of freesia in her hair.

"Really," she said. Her hand crept up my back and stroked the smooth skin on my head. "Actually, now that I think back on it, it was kind of cool."

"It was, wasn't it? Quite an adrenaline rush!"

"Yeah, yeah it was," she smiled, patting my head. "Now we both know," she said, wrapping her arms around my shoulders, rocking me back and forth in a mock shaking, "that it probably wasn't the smartest thing to do. Agreed?"

"Agreed."

"And that we should have gotten out of there at the first sign of the bear, right?"

"Without a doubt," I said.

"AND we were REALLY lucky because that situation could have turned very ugly, very fast."

"We're so lucky we should go buy a Lottery ticket right now."

This made her chuckle. "But it was. . . actually pretty cool."

I pulled her close and kissed her. "Do you know how much I love you?"

"Enough to buy me massive amounts of chocolate once we get back home?

"My dear," I said, "I will buy you the flippin' Hershey's factory if that's what your heart desires."

"You couldn't afford that. I'll settle for a candy bar." She stood, cradling my head in her hands. "You know, you always think I'm ticked off at you. I'll let you in on a little secret." She bent and kissed me on the forehead. "Most of the time I'm not."

"Don't tell me that!"

"Why not?"

"Because," I said, "that's the only thing that keeps me in check most of the time."

"I did not know that. Well, if that's the way it is, then I'm an ogre. Shape up or feel my wrath."

That was better. Who does she think she is messing about with my fundamental perceptions? My reality is based on a series of observations that may, or may not, be real. But it's my reality and I'm fine with it.

"I shall give you a wide birth, oh master of all things ogre-y."

She laughed. "Ogre-y? Is that even a word?"

I thought about that for a minute. "It is now."

"Besides, who else would play the 'straight man' to your insanity?" And she kissed me again.

And just like that the issue was put to rest. Let me just say this unequivocally: Yer mom RAWKS. Rocks harder than a lapidary collection. Rocks more than gravel. Rocks more than a cradle. You get the picture.

"I am a little worried about those kids though."

"Yeah, I thought about that at the time. But really, what could we do? I've forgotten my circus training. The most I could pile on the bike was four. That still left two as bait. Besides, I'm sure the people in the cars offered them shelter."

"I certainly hope so."

"Sweetie, this is Canada. Where people are actually human."

"Good point," she said, "I keep forgetting that."

After a brief rest we returned to the Lodge for this afternoon's High Tea. We weren't terribly hungry, but a hot cup of coffee for me, and a nice cup of tea for your mom sounded like a grand idea. If certain pastries, meats, cheeses, caviar, and smoked goods happened to fall on our plates by 'accident', well, one has to do what one has to do. Sometimes we have the luxury of choosing our niche, sometimes not. As Red Green, the wise prophet of the north, states so well: "Remember, I'm pulling for you. We're all in this together." I have no idea what this has to do with me gorging myself on tasty, tasty tidbits, but somehow it seemed there was a connection in my mind. Oh curse you Canada! You have left me befuddled!

We walked into the dining room to a smattering of people sitting in twos and threes at the tables. The gray light of the afternoon pushing through the windows made the room feel heavy and ponderous. Outside the rain was raging in full force. The cloud cover had dropped low into the hills. We could see groups of hikers trudging the meadow trail back to the lodge. They plodded in their plastic ponchos, heads down, leaning their bodies into the weather.

We had barely sat down at a table against the window when Stacy greeted us with coffee and tea.

"Afternoon folks. How you doing today?"

"Stacy," I said, "we are doing wonderfully. How are you?" Catching myself I said "Wait - Suz? We are doing wonderfully, right?"

"We are," your mom said, smiling.

"We are. Yes. Good." With a nod of my head I turned to Stacy. "Sometimes I think we are doing great and I'm wrong. Never hurts to check. So how are you?"

Stacy giggled. Today she wore a denim dress with overall straps to compliment her bright pink pig-tails. The dress hung to just below her knees where it met the top of what appeared to be white tube socks. Her feet were adorned with 'waffle-stompers', so named for the pattern of their tread, or if you can't get your mind around that, then hiking boots if you prefer. There was a beaded hemp necklace dangling from her neck with matching earrings. Her fingers were a mess of rings and stones and doodads. On her this look worked. My God she was so cute I wanted to take her home and love her and feed her and get her shots and get her fixed.

Now that I write that, it sounds creepy. Really, I meant take her home like one would do with a kitten or a puppy. Not that I would keep a human as a pet.

Well. . . not again anyway. The prosecutor was quite adamant about that.

"I'm doing good! Are you folks enjoying your stay?"

"Yes we are. What a wonderful place you have here," Mom said, leisurely playing with the tea bag in her cup.

Stacy sighed. "I wish you folks had been here just a few days ago. The days were hot, the nights were clear. . . " her voice trailed off. "You should see the stars from here. It looks like they're close enough you could reach out and touch them."

"We seem to be storm bringers," I said. "The rain follows us. I suppose we could make a tidy income by visiting drought stricken areas."

"I think you're on to something," Stacy said. "So, did you guys get to go out for a ride? Explore the area a bit like you planned?"

We spent the next 10 minutes regaling Stacy of our encounter with bears and hikers and muddy roads. Mom had to keep correcting me on little details. Like the fact that I didn't stare the bear into submission, there were no UFOs, and I didn't have to fend off an attack by cloned hordes of Nordic warriors. Pfffttttt! Minor details.

"Oh my God!" Stacy said when we recounted the people jumping out of their cars to take a close-up picture of the grizzly. "People amaze me sometimes. What were they thinking?"

"I'm betting not much other than 'Hey! I'm pretty sure that wild animal six times my size, full of teeth and claw, wouldn't mind if I got really close and took a picture."

"You're probably right." She shook her head. "You know," she said, leaning close as if she were sharing a secret. "We had a similar thing happen here last summer with a couple from," she paused to think, "Germany? Is that right? Germany? Austria? Sweden?" She shrugged her shoulders. "Doesn't matter I guess. From somewhere in that part of the world. Anyway, we had this cougar hanging around the Lodge. . . "

Damn. Damn damn double-dog damn.

See, I'd known about the cougar because I'd spent quite a bit of time at Hidden Valley's website where they just happened to have over 9000 pictures of a HUGE mountain lion taking afternoon high-balls on the deck. And below the deck. And in the parking lot. And by the front door. And there may have been one of the cougar and the staff in a group picture, all hamming it up and making silly faces and sticking fingers in each other's ears but I may be confusing that with our family photo.

The problem here is that there really is only one animal that your mom is completely, thoroughly, and truly frightened of, on a primordial level. That's a cougar. She explains her fear thusly; "A cougar is really just a big cat. Right? Think about our cats. Little sweet kitties. Think about the way they behave. Now think about them weighing 150 pounds instead of 9 or 10. One moment they would be playing, the next they would kill and eat you. Eat you dead. Oh sure, they would feel bad afterwards, but they would still kill you and eat you just the same."

The problem is we all know she's 100 percent right.

Mom perked up immediately. "Did you say cougar?"

"Yeah," Stacy said. "A HUGE cougar. I mean, I've seen plenty of cats up here, but this one dwarfed them all."

Mom looked at me and I realized that this was probably one of the times that her look was dead serious.

"Anyway, this cougar kept hanging around the Lodge. Later we found out it was because it had killed a moose calf and buried it not 25 feet from where we're sitting." She pointed to a spot just off the outside deck. "But we didn't know that then. So, one morning we're having breakfast and we look outside and there's the cougar, just laying in the sun like it was a regular occurrence. Of course the guests and the staff all crowded around the windows to take a peek. I'd never seen one this close, you know? At least not in the wild. So we're standing there, oohing and ahhing over this gorgeous animal, when Donny looks out and sees there is this couple coming out from under the deck and WALKING RIGHT UP TO THE COUGAR! I mean right up! Like it was tame! Can you believe that?"

Okay, I'm an idiot, but not that big of an idiot. "Wow. That is completely insane. What did you guys do?"

"Well Donny made a bee-line for the door to the deck and opened his mouth to scream at the two to get the hell out of there, but thought better of it because he didn't want to startle the cat."

Yes. Good idea. The only thing worse than a cougar is a startled cougar. As I understand it, they don't take getting punked well. Not well at all. That's why you never see them on Ashton Kucher's show. Or at scary movies. Or at a GOP convention.

"So Donny," she continues, "in as gentle a voice as he can muster under the circumstances says 'What the hell are you doing?' to the couple. At this point, they're like 10 feet away and getting closer, cooing and saying things like 'nice kitty', 'pretty kitty'. It was unbelievable. They told Donny that it was okay, they weren't going to harm the cat." She stopped for a moment looking back and forth to your mom and me. "Really. That's what they said." She shook her head. You could tell that although she had probably told this story dozens of times it still shocked her. "We aren't going to harm the cat."

"What did Donny do?" I asked.

"Well, Donny is an old Navy boy. So he let loose with a string of words that would peel paint off the wall. I guess the last thing he said was, 'Fuck the cat. You guys are two seconds away from being shredded. Now back away slowly and get the hell out of there because I don't want to have to clean up the mess!' We watched them leave after that, although they seemed reluctant."

"People never cease to amaze me," Mom said.

"What did the cat do?" I asked.

"Just kind of yawned and stretched like it was bored with the whole thing. After about 5 minutes it got up and walked into the forest."

"Wow," Mom said.

"Yeah. It was intense." Stacy shook her head as if coming out of a dream. "Anyway, can I get you guys anything?"

"Nope," I replied, "I think we're good. Just bring the coffee around every once in a while. I'll be trouncing Suzanne in cribbage this afternoon, and I need to be alert."

Stacy smiled. "Okay, but take it easy on her now."

"Well, if I have too," I said.

"In your dreams mister," Mom added.

After Stacy was safely out of ear shot, Mom turned to me and said, "Cougar? Did you know about this?"

I studied her face. "Possibly."

She nodded her head up and down, but I don't think she was agreeing. "And you didn't tell me because. . .?"

"Umm. . . I was saving it for a surprise?"

"Try again," Mom said.

"I hit my head as we packed the bike and the only damage was to that one, tiny, little memory concerning the cougar?"

"Nope," she said, folding her arms over her chest.

"Wait, before we continue, is this a 'Oh David I'm so mad at you ha ha ha' situation, or a 'Oh David I'm going to kill you in your sleep' situation?"

"What do you think?"

"Umm. . . that I probably need more coffee?"

"That wouldn't be a bad idea. So really, why didn't you tell me about the cougar hanging around the Lodge?"

"Because I wanted you to come on the trip," I said, dropping my head in shame.

"Bingo. I thought that might have something to do with it."

"Babe," I said, "look - I know how you feel about cougars. But you and I both know that we probably pass by several a year just in the woods around our house without incident."

A look of panic flittered over your mom's face. "What?"

"Umm. Never mind. Forget I said that. Here, it's like this. You know how I am about spiders. I know they are all around us all the time but I lie to myself so that I don't go around in a constant state of the terminal willies. You know that about me. Do you tell me every time you come across one in the house?"

"Well, no," she said.

"And so why would I point out that over a year ago they had a cougar encounter at the Lodge? Would you tell me if you found out they had a spider in the dining room?"

"No, but that's different."

"How?" I asked.

"Because spiders rarely pounce on you, then carry you away to dine on later."

"Oh ho! Faulty logic there my dear. What if they're really big spiders?"

"Look, you can't compare spiders to cougars. Don't try to change the subject."

"Are you kidding me? Have you never watched any of those movies from the 1950's? The government is involved in a deep cover up. Deep I tell you! There are gigantic, venomous, atomic spiders all over the desert. That my dear, is why I refuse to visit Nevada." Here I put two curved fingers in front of my mouth simulating spider fangs. "Arrrgghhhh arrrggghhh."

"I'm ignoring that. Back to the original question. Why didn't you tell me?"

God I hate it when she demands the truth. Oh devil woman, why can't you be satisfied with carefully crafted delusions?

"Okay. I didn't tell you about the cougars because I didn't want you to worry and obsess the entire trip. If Stacy hadn't brought it up, you never would have known."

I thought about what I'd said for a minute then added, "But you know I mean obsess in the most positive, non-derogatory way. Really. In most people obsessing is a problem but you, oh when you do it, it's cute. And not full of insanity at all."

Mom chewed this over. I could see the wheels turning inside her head. Actually, it was quite exciting, like playing a slot machine. Would I get three cherries and everything would be okay, or would I have to mortgage the house in order to recoup my losses?

A smile crossed her face. "You know, you're right. I would have worried the whole trip."

Gah! This vacation was having a tremendous impact on your mom. When she slept tonight I would fingerprint her. Maybe take a dental impression, although she was a bit of a light sleeper for that. It seemed entirely possible that she, at some point on our trip, had been replaced by a doppelganger. Now the question was did this doppelganger have more money than Mom? This was relevant to my interests.

"Let's make a deal," Mom said. "You *tell* me about cougars, and I'll continue lying to you about spiders."

That seemed like an equitable arrangement to which I readily agreed.

We spent the next two hours eating way too many treats and drinking way too many cups of coffee and tea. I was on fire as far as cribbage was concerned. Yet, in order not to 'show up' your mother, I managed to allow her to win most of the games. We laughed. We talked. We watched the clouds drift through the valley like a river of cotton, the rain falling in sheets against the hills. At one point I happened to glance up from my cards and something about the quality of the rain caught my eye.

"Hey sweetie? Does that rain look a little 'thick' to you?"

"Thick?"

"Yeah. Thick. Semi-solid."

Mom squinted her eyes and looked outside. "It does look that way, yes. But it can't be snow, it's the middle of August."

"You're right. Must be a trick of the light," I said, and never gave it another thought.

*　　*　　*

Now I'm going to share with you something that even your mother doesn't know. Well, unless she's reading this that is.

After High Tea, and before dinner, I went out to check the oil level on the bike. We were leaving in the morning, and I didn't want to have to do it then. So, with a wary eye about for mooses and cougars and bears (oh my!), I walked the short distance to the bike and proceeded to take a gander at her vital fluids.

As I sat there with dipstick in hand, a horrible thought crossed my brain. An awful thought. An evil thought. A 'how could you do that?' thought.

Robert's bike was sitting so close, so very close . . .

I jumped off the bike and with the oily dipstick in hand, I went over to his BMW, and - oh so carefully - I placed 3 drops of oil on the ground underneath his bike's frame, directly below the motor. I spread them out a bit, in a trail, and I let a little puddle accumulate on the last one directly below the engine.

Yes. I realize I'm an evil, evil man.

For you see, nothing will shake a motorcycle rider faster than a little bit of oil under their bike. Especially a BMW rider. If Robert had been riding a Harley I wouldn't have bothered. Harleys leak oil all the time. A Harley rider would have looked at those three drops and wondered why there weren't more. The consensus amongst Harley riders is that it's not leaking oil - it's simply breathing.

But poor Robert, I knew, would spend hours trying to track down the leak. He would never find it of course, but it would haunt him for days. Weeks maybe.

Yes, your suspicions have been confirmed. I am a right bastard.

But a funny one.

Mostly.

*   *   *

The problem with spending a few days stuffing yourself on delicious food is that . . . okay I lied. There is no problem. Except the whole I-can't-button-my-pants-because-the-altitude-has-shrunk-the-waistband thingee. This was to be our last dinner at the Lodge and I was looking forward to the offering. After a bit of 'freshening up', and a nap, we returned to the dining room to once again stuff ourselves silly. I reasoned thusly: this was our last chance to sample the fare, and it would be 'poor form' to be anything but wildly enthusiastic about whatever they set before me. Gluttony may be a sin, but so was rudeness. Well, maybe rudeness is not a cardinal sin. More like a venal sin. Just a little sin. Oh, who am I kidding. This dinner was to be the spiritual equivalent of an atomic bomb. I intended to not only break all seven of the deadly sins, but also make up a few of my own.

What? You doubt me? How you may ask, at a simple dinner could I damn my eternal soul? It would take some work, but I was up to the challenge. To wit:

1. **Lust.**
    My anticipation of the feast to come was more than mere appetite. Oh, it was far beyond that. I had fantasized about dinner even as I was eating tasty treats at High Tea. I couldn't help myself. Really. Food. Arghlghlghrrrr.

2. **Gluttony.**

   Self explanatory. I would finish all on my plate, your mother's plate, and possibly the skinny little freaks sitting next to me. Bonus meats for me if they were Vegans!

3. **Greed.**

   Need I explain what would happen should someone take a fancy to something I had ordered? Whatever delicacy was presented before me was mine. MINE. And woe be to anyone that wanted 'just a taste' of anything on my plate. Or your mother's. Or, once again, to the skinny-ass vegan freak to my right.

4. **Sloth.**

   After such a grand dinner a nap would be in order. Due to my over-consumption, it would probably be best to have Donny wheel me to our room with a wheelbarrow. Or possibly piggyback. Something that wouldn't disturb me too much. I wanted to doze the 100 yards to my bed.

5. **Wrath.**

   Yeah. Just try to take my dessert. I dare ya. And if they were out of my favorite 'fair trade' coffee . . . Well, let's just say it wouldn't be pretty.

6. **Envy.**

   Dammit! I should have gone with the fowl like the skinny-ass freak next to me! It looks so much better than what I'm having!

7. **Pride.**

   After I had made it through such piggishness without a quick trip to the bathroom for a 'Roman Appetizer', I would be quite pleased with myself. Quite pleased indeed.

So, as you can see, I was on a path straight to Hell. A tasty, tasty path without a doubt, but one that ended with a date with Old Scratch himself. Quite sad really. No hope of redemption. And me, I can't even play a fiddle.

I mentioned this fact to your mother as we readied ourselves for dinner. "Honey, I have something to tell you. It won't be easy to say, and I'm afraid it's going to upset you terribly."

Mom sighed, braced her hands on the bathroom sink and looked at my reflection in the mirror. "Okay, I'll bite. What's so troubling?"

"I'm afraid I'm going straight to Hell. Do not pass GO. Do not collect $200."

Mom stared at me. After a bit she said, "Is that it?"

"Yes, I'm afraid so. There's naught that can be done. All is lost."

"And you're going to Hell because . . . ?"

Whereupon I recounted my reasoning concerning the Seven Deadly Sins, and the inevitability of my eternal damnation due to dinner.

"Oh sweetie," she said, standing and wrapping me in a tight hug. "you were cursed to Hell long before this."

I started to argue but we both know she was right. Somehow, this made me feel better. Hungry in fact. The road to Hell is paved with deliciousness. Umm . . . forbidden dinner. Yum!

Anyway, we walked into the dining room and the first thing that struck me was how empty the place seemed. It looked as if most of the guests had left. All of the people were sitting at one table near the windows at the back right side of the dining room.

At that table there were two empty chairs with place settings. This looked ominous. I glanced around the room and all the other tables were bare. Nary a spork nor a knife to be seen. Being somewhat quick on my feet I surmised that much like a Seder, the staff had left the settings empty so that the rest of the table could honor a pair of hikers that had been eaten earlier in the day. I wondered where we would sit? Because really, it had to be the Seder thing. If not, that meant that they intended Mom and I to sit there, and as I'm sure you know by now the only thing that would have made this situation worse for your mother, would be if one of the guests was a Cougar. Although, there was one lady sitting on the end that gave an unsettling look to the young men serving, but that's another story.

"David! Suzanne! Just in time," Leeza said, walking up behind us and putting her arms around our shoulders, gently steering us to what appeared to be our assigned places at the table. "Everyone? I'd like you to meet Suzanne and David," Leeza said. Then, almost as an afterthought she added "They rode their motorcycle up here from THE STATES!"

Two strikes and I hadn't even opened my mouth yet! This may be a new record. I noticed the group glance from my cane to my face as they processed the information. Oh, misguided conclusions abounded as to the nature of my disability! It couldn't have been plainer if you'd written on their foreheads in magic marker. Of course since I rode a motorcycle my obvious injury had come from a nasty meeting with the pavement. Would I correct them? Would I embellish a story confirming their suspicions? I could hardly wait to hear what I was going to say. You know how much I like surprises.

We took our place and pleasant greetings ensued. Leeza wandered back into the kitchen, leaving us alone with the tribe. We saw our BMW friends seated at the end of the table, close enough to chat but far enough away that you didn't feel a constant need to engage them in idle banter. They looked a little tired, a little worn. Their hike from earlier in the day had evidently taken a toll.

Next to them sat an older couple, probably in their mid-sixties. We would find out later that these were our Innkeepers, Bob and Linda. Next to them sat another couple of approximately the same age, and would turn out to be friends of the Innkeepers here on 'holiday' from the Canadian east coast. Really, is the word 'vacation' not adequate in these northerly climes? Is this a nod to the home Isles? Or just another in a series of 'this is why we are different from you so f' off'?

Continuing clockwise, in the next seats were a couple that appeared to be a few years younger than ourselves, a doctor and his wife up for a few days from Calgary. There were two middle-aged women on a yearly pilgrimage to 'the woods' as they put it. I really didn't want any more detail. Very "Goddess" looking, if you know what I mean.

Next to them sat a very interesting looking man and woman that we would discover were vacationing from Denmark. Three other couples of indeterminate middle-age rounded out the group. I would add more detail but they were sitting on the opposite side of the table so . . . they were 'fuzzy'. Which could only mean one of two things - either my eyesight was getting worse, or these folk were inter-dimensional beings having difficulty tuning to our frequency. Since I refuse to let my eyesight deteriorate any further - and my damn eyeballs know this - the obvious conclusion was that these wispy folks had to be from another world.

From my observations of these Canadians, these *Homo Canukus* if you will, from the shores of Galaway Bay to these lofty and majestic mountains, it was readily apparent that the entire population of the country was comprised of either shamans or psychonauts, just chock-full of dimensional capers. Oh you deceptively simple Multiverse! You never cease to amaze.

Come to think of it, it's entirely possible that Canada is the metaphysical attic of the North American continent. This would require further research and confirmation. I made a mental note to ask these ill-defined people sitting across from me if they had any 'Nozz-A-La Cola'. I've only had it once, yet no matter how I try I can't seem to get the damn taste, nor the craving, out of my brain. I didn't tell you about the Nozz-A-La Cola? What a night that was! Hopefully, even if these Brane-travelers had none of the divine nectar on their person, they could direct me to the nearest available thinnie. Perhaps I should stock up. We were almost done with our trip anyway and would be heading for home after breakfast in the morning. I could afford to jettison some socks and underwear for a few bottles of the forbidden beverage.

Back to the conversation. Now here comes my favorite part of non-chosen group communication - the 'easing in'. And by non-chosen, I mean a group of people, unknown to each other, thrown into a situation where they must interact. Oh, it's a veritable Rorschach Test coupled with some mighty fine Skinnerian interactions, then peppered liberally with a few down-home Pavlovian responses. Truly, people at their best. Who would dominate the group? Who would try and build consensus? Who would initiate conversation? Who would set themselves as the Authority? The Rebel? The Outsider? The Victim? The Negotiator? The Appeaser? I rubbed my hands together. This was going to be fun!

I looked at your mom. She now wore the expression of a woman facing a firing squad. Somehow she made the look work. Whilst waiting for this cavalcade of fun to begin in earnest, we spent the next few minutes chatting quietly with our partners, inspecting our place settings, generally avoiding eye contact. The tension was palpable and quite delicious. The dinner chatter would rise and fall in the natural sine wave of action, punctuated by long silences.

It was during one of these silences that Julie, the Doctor's wife, cleared her throat, turned to your mother and me, and spoke loud enough for the entire group to hear. "So you rode a motorcycle up here, huh?"

And here she was, the Instigator - The Authoritarian. The self-appointed spokesperson. I could smell a trap a mile away. What devious intentions did this woman have for calling us out? It couldn't be simple curiosity, I was sure of that. No, there was a subtext here, a definite unspoken opinion behind the question. The dominance gauntlet had been thrown. How dare she use the alpha-male ritual so early in the game? This was a serious breach of gender-etiquette and must be dealt with poste-haste. Swiftly I poured over my possible responses, sifting for just the right one.

"We're not the only ones!" I exclaimed in exaggerated defense, and pointed to our BMW buddies in an accusatory fashion, "they rode one too!"

Jaws dropped. God I love an inappropriate response. It just makes everything more interesting.

Julie's eyes first went wide with surprise, then narrowed into confusion. It was a short trip. Her face scrunched so hard that if you'd have held an orange to her eye-sockets OJ would have poured down her nose.

She looked from me to the Beemers, then back to me. "I'm sorry," she stammered, "I didn't mean anything. I just meant. . . I mean Leeza said . . . "

She looked around the table for allies, for confirmation that this situation had taken a weird turn. Wisely, no one was offering her anything in the way of support. Too dangerous to commit to any one person this early in the evening. What if they backed the wrong horse? That's a social risk few will take. Who said our forefathers learned nothing from Guy Fawkes and the Gunpowder

Plot? It's difficult to explain your way out of rebellion. No, best to hang on the periphery and the second that momentum swings to one side or the other, offer your support to the one with the numbers. Then claim that you've been with them all along. Much like any session of Congress.

Back to the situation at hand. Your mom however had spent the last 32 years with me, so her instincts as to where the conversation was headed were a tad sharper than our dinner partners'. She kicked my shin under the table. Hard. Good thing I was wearing my boots, that kick could have drawn blood.

"Don't pay any attention to him," she said looking at me, "he has a weird sense of humor."

I nodded in idiotic agreement.

"To answer your question, yes - we did ride a bike up here."

Mom studied Julie's face for some hint of relaxation. Finding none, she added "Did I mention he has a weird sense of humor?" She looked back to me, "And he's harmless?"

"Mostly," I corrected her.

Julie looked at your mom, then at me, then at the group, then back to me. I had rattled the poor dear. More than I had anticipated. I had to fix it before debilitating embarrassment set in. Never embarrass someone in front of a group unless you're looking to make an enemy. But you're my daughter. Bursting with inappropriateness of your own. I'm sure you've discovered this by now.

"It's true," I said smiling. "You really can't take anything I say too seriously." I paused, thinking about what I'd just said. "Even that statement needs to be taken with a grain of salt. Probably. Mostly." I grinned the grin of the seriously flawed. "I blame it on a public school education I received in THE STATES." I turned to the gentleman on my right, the man from Denmark. "Or possibly I shouldn't have drunk copious amounts of cough syrup in my youth. The jury is still out."

"Dat vould do it," he said nodding his head in the affirmative.

Damn, he looked familiar. For that matter so did his wife. I scoured my memory. Had I ever been to Denmark? I didn't think so, but there are several periods in my life I can't account for, so who knows? I did have that bizarre affection for all things Hans Christian Anderson-y. The pieces were all adding up. I'd have to check with your mother later. She'd know.

Now that it had been established - and people had been reassured - that I was a genial, and relatively harmless smart-ass, a chorus of giggles and smiles flowed around the table.

Even the corners of Julie's mouth turned up ever so slightly. She turned to the Beemers, "Did you guys really ride up here too?"

Robert grinned and smoothed his napkin. "We did."

"So," said Julie's husband the Doctor, whom we would later find out was named Terrence, "which one of you rides the BMW and which one of your rides . . . the other one?"

I looked at Robert. Robert looked at me. We both looked at Terrence.

"Ahh," Terrence said, "gotcha."

"That obvious?" I asked.

"Kind of." said Terrence.

Here was Robert, neatly attired in a dress shirt and slacks, his hair moussed into perfection. Here was I; bald, goateed, bulky, jean-clad and boot wearing.

"I would protest," I said to Terrence, "but it's a fair assessment."

"Just curious, but how did you manage to get that big . . . what's it called?"

"A Victory Vision. A Vivi, or a Vic if you prefer." I paused here, "Although, her actual name is Cindy. Cindy Loohoo. But I don't think you know her well enough to speak of her on such a personal level." I turned to his wife, "Strict southern upbringing," I explained, "very mannered. Birthed from genteel and polite society, if you know what I mean."

From the look on her face she didn't. Julie was going to have to get with the program or it was going to be a long, long night.

"Thanks," Terrence said, "a Victory. I was looking at it in the parking lot earlier. If you don't mind me asking, how did you ride that thing up here? It looks more like a street bike."

"Very, very carefully," I said.

Robert taped Terrence on the shoulder. "Ask him where he rode it from."

"What?" Terrence asked a bit confused.

"Ask him which way he came to the Lodge."

Oh this was wonderful! I had them speaking about me to my face! I was the Oracle at Delphi. I was the Sage. I was in - but not of - their world. I am Shaman! Cool. Then I realized that's also the way you speak to children, dogs, or the feeble-minded. That took a chunk out of the coolness.

Terrence studied me for a moment. Being a Doctor I assumed he was a reasoned man, a calculating thinker. He wasn't about to rush down any path without scouting the surroundings. He turned back to Robert. "Highway 40?"

"We," I interjected, "came up from Carnack."

Terrence studied me with a blank expression. Finally he said, "Why?"

"Good question," I answered. "I could dance around the issue, make lame excuses. Try to twist the facts. Sugar-coat the truth so as to make us seem better than we are. But I won't do that. I'll just speak it loud and clear for all to hear." I cleared my throat. "Suzanne tends to get lost." Then, in a stroke of pure genius I added, " A lot."

Your mom had been chatting, (I KNOW! Where was my anti-social bride? Oh Great White North - what have you done with her personality? You've taken her soul, isn't that enough?), with Julie and Jackie but turned her attention to me upon hearing her name. She's quite nosey like that. A character flaw that I've come to overlook.

"Are you talking about me?"

"He said you get lost. A lot," Terrence offered, then smiled at me.

Ah. A worthy adversary. Well played good Sir. Well played.

"It's okay honey, we're amongst friends. You won't be judged for your directional deficiencies." I patted her on the arm and looked at Robert and Terrence. "Women," I said, as if that explained everything.

Mom directed her attention to Julie and Jackie, and with a warm smile said, "Excuse me a moment while I kill my husband." She turned to me, then looked at Robert and Terrence. "Ask him who booked our trip and planned our route and was in charge of the GPS, as well as driving the bike."

I leaned close to the men and stage-whispered, "She gets confused quite easily poor thing."

Ignoring me, Terrance spoke directly to your mom, "I take it he did."

"Yes," Mom said, "yes he did."

She then recounted our afternoon, and our early evening journey to the Lodge three days hence. I didn't come out in the most positive light during her monologue but she had the basic facts straight. When she was done with her story, in all of its messy detail chock-full of near death experiences, the group, which had fallen silent as your mother spoke, now turned to study me.

I grinned, and brought my hands palm-up in front of my chest. With a shrug I said, "Whatcha gonna do?" Desperate to regain respect, I put on my best philosopher / old man face, narrowed my eyes and gently stroking my beard said, "Sometimes the only way out is through."

HA! Take that oh table' du Canadian. Chew on that bon-mot of irrefutable logic. Wrestle that paradox to the ground for an epiphany courtesy of this bald American biker! No need to thank me for enlightenment. You're welcome.

"Or sometimes," Terrence said, "sometimes the only way out is not to set on the path at all."

Gah! Evidently I had seriously underestimated Terrence. After filing that platitude away to later claim as my own I said, "But I think you'll agree, you cannot *travel* the path until you *become* the path."

Oh yeah, that just happened. I hurled The Buddha at you like a rotten tomato at the festival of La Tomitina in Bunyol, Spain.

Terrance chewed on this a bit. "Many are stubborn in the path they have chosen, few in pursuit of the goal."

Oh he did not just hit me upside the head with Nietzsche! This required a rapid and deliberate response. Go and get all existential on me, will you? I looked him square in the eye. "A well-beaten path does not always make the right road."

Refute that Mr. Man.

Although I had delivered what I thought was a killing blow, Terrence took a deep breath prepared his response. Damn. I was all out of quotes and proverbs concerning a path. If he answered I was going to have to start making up crap.

"The best path through life is a highway." Terrence tossed this into the conversation with ease. Pleased with himself he added "That's Henri Amiel."

I studied this man - this Doctor. The table, now thoroughly engaged in our little repartee turned to me as if they were watching ping-pong. Or tennis. Or a really bad duel. Damn. Double-dog damn. I scrambled. There was naught to be done but open my mouth and see what would spill out.

"The path is long and arduous, yet even the rat packs a lunch."

Terrence blinked. Once. Twice. Three times. Finally he said, "I have no idea what that means."

"Welcome to my world," I said. "I haven't a clue as to what I'm talking about three-fifths of the time."

Terrence laughed and I heard Robert giggle.

"That must be difficult."

Your mom, who had been following our tit-for-tat with mild amusement said, "You have no idea."

"Ah my dear," I said, putting an arm around Mom's shoulder, "what you call my ramblings, I call entertainment."

"Okay sweetie," Mom said, patting my arm.

The topic of conversation around the table now turned to your mom's and my encounter with the bear and moose. Everyone had a bear story.

Everyone.

Jackie cleared her throat and spoke. "You know what happened to us today? So there we were, hiking the 'Miner's Trail' up to Big Stone Gap. It was wet and rainy and cold and I don't know about Robert, but I'd had just about enough. So we turned around and were walking through this meadow when I looked off the trail and there was the HUGE bear eating berries! Right there!"

She looked around the table to see if people had comprehended the magnitude of what she was describing. "I almost freaked out but then realized that would be a bad thing to do."

"Yes," Robert added, "a very bad thing."

"Right," Jackie said, casting a not terribly appreciative glance at Robert, "not a good idea. So I just walked right on by as quietly as I could." Turning to Robert she said, " I don't think you even saw the bear until after I stopped you on the hill and pointed it out, did you?"

"Nope," Robert replied, "I can't believe it but I didn't even notice."

"And then," Jackie said, " we were standing there and I saw another couple on the trail behind us. Well, I had to warn them, right?"

"It was your duty," said Robert. "As we talked about later if something had happened and we hadn't tried to warn them, well. . .", he said, letting the group finish his sentence.

"Yeah," Jackie said, "how could you live with yourself? That would be horrible. Knowing that you could have prevented someone from getting hurt. Or killed."

Robert looked at her. "Well yeah. But there's also the risk of a liability lawsuit. If only one of them had survived, or maybe both just injured, I think a case could be made that we could be held liable. We had a legal obligation to alert them to danger."

Everyone had been following Jackie's story with interest, and now looked as if they had collectively hit a brick wall, with their faces, at about 30 kilometers a foot. (That's fast, right? Damn you metric system! You'll be my undoing yet!) Jackie looked disgusted, and Robert looked confused.

Taking command of the situation, I put my hand to the side of my mouth, blocking Robert from seeing my lips, and whispered WAY too loudly to the group "He's a law-yer," dragging out the last syllable and letting it fade to silence. I then shook my head up and down, confirming my own declaration.

Terrence regarded Robert with a cocked eyebrow. "I'm sorry," he said.

I was liking Terrence more and more as the minutes ticked by.

"A lawyer and a motorcycle rider. Yeah. There you go. Chew on that combination."

I sat back in my chair, full of satisfaction. "And you thought *I* was the scary one." To which we all chuckled heartily. Well all of us except for Robert. But even he managed a grin. "Sorry Robert. Cheap shot. Easy pickings and all that."

"It's okay," he said, "I'm used to it."

See? See what I mean? Congeniality flows through these northern lands like butter on a biscuit. Or like tears at a (insert your favorite Washington State sports team - college or professional -here) game. Or, like water in a urinal during dollar-beer night. Being in the Navy, I assume that the latter resonates quite well with you and creates an image with which you can connect. Although not the urinal part. Probably. And if it does - well kudos to you my dear.

"Back to the story," Jackie said, "I haven't even got to the good part yet."

Leeza came in with a cart, and began working her way around the table passing out salads and large bowls filled with steaming hot rolls.

"So there we were waving like lunatics. I didn't want to yell because I didn't want to startle the bear. The couple saw me because they waved back but they kept right on walking. I waved harder, and pointed to the bear that was still eating berries in just about the same spot as we'd left her. They waved back. Then they walked RIGHT BEHIND THE BEAR AND STOPPED TO WATCH IT! I mean, they just stood there, inches away from this HUGE animal and ---"

"Oh," the guy from Denmark said, "dat vas joo? We tought," he said turning to his wife, "dat joo vas just real friendly."

And right then and there I knew where I had seen this couple before. It wasn't in Denmark, that's for sure. No, this was the couple that jumped out of the car to take pictures during our bear encounter earlier in the day. How the hell did these people make it from the picnic area to the trail in such a short amount of time? Did they have some kind of Danish teleportation device that took them from grizzly to grizzly so they could taunt death and startle tourists? I mean sure, they were raised on a steady diet of Ingmar Bergman films, so death was like a weird old uncle, but really. (Okay. So Ingmar Bergman was Swedish and not Danish. It's close. It's like Seattle and Portland. Different towns, same tree-huggin' hippies. You lived in the U District. You know exactly what I mean.) Possibly they were the rarest of creatures: grizzly magnets. Not to be confused with 'chick magnets' unless you like your women toothy, hairy, and ill-tempered. If so, I once again refer you to Portland.

As Leeza leaned close, to pass me my salad, she whispered in my ear, "Oh my God. Now I remember them. They were the people that tried to pet the Cougar!" She straightened to return the cart, but I motioned her back down. Turning away from the group, I in turn whispered, "Oh my God! They were the ones trying to take a picture of the bear when we went for a ride!"

I stared at Leeza. Leeza stared at me. We turned in perfect synchronization and looked at the couple from Denmark. So did everyone else at the table.

"That was YOU?" Jackie asked.

The couple looked at each other for a moment, and the secret language flowed between the two like electric arcs on a Jacob's Ladder.

"Ya," he said with mild confusion. "Did ve do sumting wrong?" he asked the group.

Before, and probably for the best, I could say anything, Jackie said, "Well not *wrong*. It's just I was really worried about you. You guys stood really close to that bear for a long time."

"Oh ya. It vas a nice bear. Big rump." He smiled.

"Umm . . . ," I said, "weren't you a little worried?"

He wrinkled his brow. "Vat? About da bear?"

Dear lord. I think I just discovered what it's like to be on the other end of a conversation with me. I heartily apologize for your childhood. I looked around the table to see if anyone else was going to step up to the plate, but they were either shell-shocked by the casual attitude of the Danish man, or, more than likely, full on yellow-bellied chickens. Fine. If it was up to me then so be it.

"Well," I said, "Yeah. You know, inches from a grizzly and all that."

"Pffffttttt." said the woman from Denmark with a dismissive wave of her hand. "De bear knew ve vasn't going to hurt her." She looked around the table as if this statement should satisfy everyone's concern. "Am I right Eric?"

Evidently Eric was her husband's name. Good to know. Yet, in my heart he had firmly been established as 'Danish Man'. I'm sure that in years to come I will forget most of this episode and simply recall that I spent some time with a guy that made breakfast pastries in the shapes of bears. Memory is a funny thing. No wait! Not in the shape of bears - Bearclaws! That's it! Ah. . . mis-remembrances. It's never too late to have the past you want.

"Oh yeah. Ve see da bears all da time ven ve come to hike. Every summer." He looked around the table. "Ve don't bodder dem and dey don't bodder us."

"Still," I said, "you think it's wise to get that close? They are wild animals after all."

"Ah," said Eric's wife, whom we would later discover to be named Leah, "dey aren't so bad. Dey know vat you're tinking. Ve saw annuder one today at a picnic place. She vas a big girl! Ve got a picture of her as she walked by da car." She turned to me. "I tink jew vas dere on yer bike."

The residents of the table, now brimming with morbid curiosity, (Hey, Canadian or American, humans are humans), leaned forward with rapt attention, hanging on Leah's every word.

She appeared puzzled by our collective reaction. "Animals aren't da big bad creatures dat you tink." She looked to Eric for confirmation, which he gave with a nod of his head. "Last year ven ve vas here dere was a," she paused, searching for the right word. She turned to Erick. "Stor kat?"

"Beeg cat," he translated.

"Beeg cat. Dat's right. But the name. A. . ."

"Koogur," Eric supplied.

"Koogur. Yes, koogur. Anyvay, last year dere was a cougar right here at da lodge. Ve got a good look at her, didn't ve Eric?"

"Ya. Den da man yelled and made us come to da inside."

I looked over to where Leeza was peeking around the doorway to the kitchen, eavesdropping. Our eyes met. I don't know what mine looked like, but her's were open wide and her mouth hung agape.

"Ya," Leah agreed, "dere vasn't any problem. Ve veren't going to hurt her." She rolled her eyes.

"Nah," Eric said, "Ve luv da animals." He then looked around the table. As if his declaration cleared the situation up completely.

The table sat there in silence. Stunned. Incredulous. Horrified. It was delicious! Jackie in particular regarded the two with a look of disbelief bordering on anger. She was collecting herself to voice her opinion, and by the look on her face it would have been voiced quite forcefully, quite pointedly, and may have been couched in different terms, but was certain to boil down to 'what the Hell is wrong with you?'

However Robert, being a married man, saw this coming a mile away. "So," he said to the Danish couple, "it's Eric and Leah, is that right?"

They nodded in the affirmative.

"Eric and Leah, you said you guys come here every year?"

And as deftly as a ballerina transitioning from a pirouette to a entrechat, Robert had changed the subject completely. If they gave medals for husbands I would have nominated Robert for a silver cross. It was a thing of beauty. I was almost sad about the oil thingee.

Almost.

"Ya," Eric said, "ve save all our vacation and come over here for four or five weeks to hike in da mountains." He smiled. "Such beauty."

The table, with the possible exception of Jackie, were so grateful to Robert for ending a painful social situation that they literally bombarded the couple with questions concerning where they lived, what they did for a living, etc. Well, painful for them. For me? Shoot, this was good theater right here. Good theater indeed. I debated turning the conversation back to the subject of the bear, just for the lulz, but then decided that, in the man's world, this would be akin to kicking Robert in the dingles. Hard.

Protip: Never make an enemy of a lawyer, Canadian or not. It would be safer to toss rocks at a pack of pit-bulls on meth. Or Rush Limbaugh. Not on meth, he's a staunch, upstanding Republican for God's sake. So, no meth. OxyContin yes. Meth no.

Turns out that other than their bizarre relationship and beliefs concerning all things fangy, and the fact that it was only a matter of time before they were eaten - horribly, horribly eaten - Eric and Leah were very nice people.

Leeza, who had ushered the staff back into the dining room with piping hot plates of delicacies unknown even to Emeril Lagasse, cleared her throat and said, "Just want to remind you folks that at 7:00 we'll be hosting a fascinating talk with our resident bear expert, Randy Dale. Randy works in cooperation with the Park Service to control problem bears. He'll have his Karelian Bear Dogs with him, so stop by the library after dinner and join us. It should be," she said casting a quick glance at Eric and Leah, "a very informative evening."

Eric and Leah looked at each other in unison, and gave a slight shrug of their shoulders and roll of eyes.

The conversation died out a bit as we tucked in, and was replaced by single-word declarations; "Yum." "Oh!" "Wow.", as we dove into this night's gustatory offerings.

We spent the next twenty minutes making small talk. I learned several things. One, you can't grow roses in Calgary. Well, at least the people at the table agreed it was possible, but no one had ever done it successfully, at least outside of the Calgary Rose Society, who, it was agreed around the table, had made a pact with the dark ones in trade for a nice, bushy Cuthbert Grant.

Two, Terrence the Doctor took his kayak to work every day in the late spring and summer, where, on his lunch break, he would have someone drive him a few miles up the small river that ran behind his practice so that he could ride the frothy white back down in time for afternoon appointments. Now how cool is that?

Three, the friends of our hosts were actually from the Canadian side of Niagara Falls. He was a bicyclist, riding back and forth to work each day regardless of the weather. He said that he had actually missed only 4 days of riding the previous winter. Now usually the bicycle community, as I've explained, looks on the motorcycle community as their younger, dumber, drunk-ass brothers on the road. The motorcyclists regard the bicycle community as - - - well, obstacles. Something that you have to move over in the lane to keep from clipping and getting your bike all scratched. Anyway, this was one of the friendlier cyclists I'd encountered, and we actually chatted quite a bit about the road, and our experiences. I was quite taken with his ability and determination to ride year-round. He was impressed with my ability to speak in polysyllabic constructs. I think anyway. He may have been humoring me.

At one point during the evening I looked around at our dinner companions. Everyone was smiling, laughing, eating too much and drinking too much and generally having a great time. Even your mom was chatting freely with Jackie and Julie as well as others around the table. I'm sure you've drawn a mental picture. If you were to capture this exact moment in a snapshot, it would represent EXACTLY what I had hoped for in our vacation. As the staff cleared the dinner plates in preparation for coffee and desert I sat back and basked in the glow of the moment. Success. All was right with the world.

Now, if I could manage to navigate us back towards home in the morning life would be good.

"So, Terrence said, turning to me, "do you think Obama has a shot? Or are we going to get four more years of the same?"

Dammit. Really? Again? Couldn't we have just gone on down the rosy, cozy, safe path of banality? Must we enter into these dangerous waters fraught with international overtones and non-requested opinions? Fine. You want politics? Politics it is.

Mom, much to my surprise, jumped right in. "Obama has a good chance. A very good chance of being our next President."

The Canadians murmured. Or were whispering 'rhubarb rhubarb rhubarb'. My hearing isn't what it used to be since I stopped caring about most things.

"Really?" Robert asked. "Do you think that the US is ready for a black President?"

"I don't know how much being black has to do with it, but I know most of us are ready for a change," Mom said.

A wave of skepticism rose like the stink of dead fish on an old pier from our dinner mates.

Julie said, "But what about . . . you know, the south?"

"Oh," Mom said, "there are definitely pockets around the country that won't vote for him because he's black," and here she paused to look around the table, "but it's not everyone in the south, and you don't have to be in the south to think like that." Mom looked to me, "Shoot, there are places in the northwest where racism runs deep." Seeing that she wasn't making any converts, your mom continued. "I think you'll see both coasts vote for Obama, and enough in between to elect him come November."

One of the women at the other end of the table asked, "But aren't those the 'Red' States?"

"That's kind of a misnomer perpetuated by the media," I explained. "In reality there are four or five 'Blue' States, six or seven 'Red' States, and the rest are varying shades of purple." I said, repeating what I had said to our hiker friends earlier.

"That may be", Robert said, jumping into the conversation, "but what about Texas? He's not going to win there."

Texas again. What the hell? Then I realized that for those above the 49th parallel Texas was the epitome of all the gun-totin', whiskey-swillin, right-wing yahoo-ism that made America what it is today. Having a 'Bush' hail from there, (but he isn't really FROM Texas, now is he?), didn't help. Well, that and all the capital punishment. And the hats probably colored their opinion as well.

"Probably not," I agreed. "But Texas isn't necessarily the US."

No one spoke to this, they all just sat there, chewing what I'd said with their minds. Deciding whether to spit or swallow.

Finally, Niagara bicycle-guy said, "You have to admit though, that Texas might be the extreme, but it's where the country is headed."

"I'm not sure I'd agree with that," I said. "You know the funny thing about the US is that we're all one country, but it's really like we are a collection of separate and distinct sovereign nations. Kind of like the UK and her territories. Well, without the whole inbred Royal Family thing. I'm sure you know what I mean."

I looked around the gathering to see if what I said registered. Seeing that it didn't, I continued.

"Look, take the Pacific Northwest where we're from. In our State, Washington, you have the Cascade mountains running north and south bisecting the State into Western and Eastern Washington. Western Washington is known for our rain, our forests, our coast and fisheries, Seattle, and a liberal attitude." I looked to your mom to see if I was making sense, and she gave me a nod so I went on. "Eastern Washington is dry, agricultural, not nearly as densely populated as the west. They tend to be a bit more conservative on that side of the State. If you ask them what they have in common with the average person in Seattle, they're likely to respond 'Not much'.

You know that I was born in Tonasket, and our family was from the Okanogan, so I couldn't REALLY tell them what Eastsiders thought because . . . well, I didn't want to use that many curse words at once.

"Our area really has more in common with British Columbia and Western Oregon than we do with Wenatchee or Ritzville. There was even a movement a few years ago to break off the western portion of the two States into a new State called 'Cascadia'. I think northern California may have been in there too. Not a bad idea, but it never really caught on. And we are very different than Florida. Or Maine. Shoot, even Kansas and Iowa for that matter. So to say that Texas is representative of anything other than Texas isn't really right."

I was hoping I was getting through to them, because the effort of genuine communication, with nary a smart-ass remark nor highly amusing bon mot to pepper my speech was making me nauseated. It's not the way my brain works. I hope they appreciated the sacrifice I was making on their behalf to further international relations.

There were contemplative looks, confused looks, but none that I would really call convinced or even with a glimmer of understanding. Dammit! I would have to relate this in a more Canadian way if I wanted my point to be accepted.

"Look, here we are in Alberta. But do the people that live here have a ton in common with British Columbia?"

"Actually, quite a bit," Terrence said.

Oh Terrence, don't make me take back all those wonderful things I was thinking about you. Then inspiration struck! Oh, I knew exactly how to make myself clear! I had an ace up my sleeve.

"Okay, that may be. But how much do you share in common with. . . Quebeckers? You know, French Canadians?"

And then - as they say in the vulgar - boom went the dynamite.

This was no building of emotion. No small dissent that grew into a chorus of contempt. No, this was a gasoline tanker and I had opened the hatch and threw in a match. And a blowtorch. Then poured on lighter fluid for good measure. Our group went from polite, grinning, laid-back nature lovers to a raging mob. A mob complete with red faces, torches, pitchforks, and horrible pent-up resentment for difficult childhoods. The transformation happened in flash. About as fast as a Tele-evangelist repents when caught with his hoo-hoo somewhere it's not supposed to be. Rumblings and growls sprang fourth round the table like awful dandelions in spring. For a moment I thought we would have to flee the room, lest we become the target of their repressed northerly rage.

Bicycle guy, who I would later find out was named Charles, was the first to make his voice heard over the din.

"Fuck the Quebeckers!"

Whoa!

Rather than ostracize the man for dropping the f-bomb and having a non-politically correct viewpoint, everyone, much to your mom's and my surprise, jumped on the bandwagon.

"Oh God," Jackie said, "don't get me started on the Quebeckers."

Now I had always had a certain amount of disdain for the French Canadians because . . . well, I'm prone to carry a grudge and they're French. But I figured this was my own particular peccadillo, not one shared by - if this group was representative and I had no reason to doubt they weren't - the entirety of Canada outside of the city of Montreal and the Province of Quebec itself. I looked at your mom who sat there with a stunned expression on her face. Oh you Canadians! How dare you dash our deeply held stereotypes! Have you no shame? Where are the gentle, easy-going, polite people that we have made up in our heads? How dare you make us suspect that you are NOT the only sane nation on earth, but populated by humans just like everywhere else.

Oh Canada . . . our hopes had been so high.

"Wow," I said, "I've got to tell you that I'm a bit surprised by the reaction."

"Kind of a sore subject up here," Terrence said.

"Okay," I said, "let me understand this. If the rest of the country feels this way then why didn't you just let them secede back in . . . what, '97 or '98?

"Yeah, and years before that," Julie said.

"Oh, most of us want them out. Good riddance." Charles' wife said. This was met with a chorus of agreement.

Robert cleared his throat. "It's really not a matter of wanting them out, it's a constitutional matter. The issues that were raised and addressed during the Meech Lake Accord were ---"

But before poor Robert could further educate us as to the finer points of Canadian Constitutional law, he was drowned out by cries of 'I'm sorry, but I can't stand Francophones', and 'Who do they think they are?', and 'Do you know how much the government sends them every year? Do YOU!?', and 'They HATE the rest of Canada' and 'They can kiss my ass', and 'Fucktards!'. Although, to be quite honest that last one may have slipped past my own lips. I don't know. There was much shouting and pounding of fists and enough 'eh's and 'aboot's and 'hosers' thrown around to fill a three-penny opera. I kind of got caught up in the spirit of things.

Here's some advice: be wary of group-think. Next thing you know you're conquering neighboring villages for putting curses on your crops. Or, holed-up in a half-buried metal container somewhere in the hinterlands of Montana waiting for the end of the world, with 83 people dressed in spandex and praying to a four-slice toaster.

By the by, that was without a doubt the weirdest summer of my life.

So amongst the cumulative gnashing of teeth and eruptions of profanity, I was able to glean a few facts. I have no idea if these facts are true or not, because researching these particular accusations sounded . . . boring, so I took them as gospel. I mean really, would a Canadian lie? I think not. So, here is the skinny. A partial list of perturbances, slights, injustices and outrageous behavior wrought by the evil French Canadians against their much more civilized Anglo brothers and sisters:

1. A dangerous precedent had been set. Concessions were made by the Canadian Government to ensure that the Quebeckers did not secede from Canada proper, and all agreed that this was a bad idea and encouraged anti-Canadian behavior. Plus, it was pointed out Quebeckers whined a lot about everything.

2. Quebeckers were given way too many seats in the Canadian Parliament.

3. Quebeckers received a disproportionate amount of government money, which, if you ask any Francophone, was a perfectly reasonable thing to do. You see, according to our hosts, the Francophone position is that it was ALL theirs, and by the grace of their hearts and their superior intellect they allowed the rest of Canada to exist. Barely.

4. The Quebeckers wanted their culture represented well beyond Quebec itself, forcing their 'culture d'evil' upon the rest of Anglo-God fearing Canada, but don't you dare utter an English word in Quebec if you didn't want a nasty scolding. A nasty scolding indeed.

5. Way too many road and informational signs in French.

6. Apparently, they imprisoned Anglo children living in the borders of Quebec City, and the environs, and made them eat foie gras, smoke filterless

cigarettes, and watch director's cut DVDs of The Triplets of Belleville until they surrendered - then plopped these poor kids in public schools with tons of other soulless, broken children to be put into slave labor as clowns for Cirque.

7. The Quebeckers were, as a whole - and this seemed to be the one that stuck in the collective craw of our group - arrogant, antagonistic, and smelled funny. Plus they were bad tippers.

I sat listening to this outpouring of emotion for quite a while, deciding to let this little rant run its course. We all need to blow off steam now and then. This was probably healthy. It was definitely amusing.

I looked over to Eric who had been listening to the brouhaha as it unfolded. During a lull, he looked at me with a shrug and said with a casual tone, "Vat do you expect? Dey are French."

That summed it up perfectly. Yes, above all they are French. Nuff said. Eric's insight caused a slight pang of regret in my heart that such a perceptive soul would soon be devoured by any number of Canadian mammalia. But such is the circle of life.

Now came the personal stories. The 'friend of a friend of a friend' urban legends. Oh it was glorious! Half-truths. Rumor. Speculation. Outright lies. It had all the elements for the fermentation of a barely contained civil war. With the exception that while civil war was a definite possibility it was unanimously concurred that it wouldn't be much of a fight, because, once again, we were dealing with the French.

Just as things were winding down, Leeza come into the room and announced, "Everyone? We have about 15 minutes until Randy starts his talk in the Library. You're welcome to bring your drinks along. I think you're really going to enjoy what he has to say." Here she paused and looked at Eric and Leah. "Plus, he has some practical advice for wildlife encounters."

Eric and Leah looked at each other for a moment. Nothing was said, no change of facial expression, but I could tell exactly what communication had transpired twixt the two. They had better things to do with their time than sit and listen to some idiot talk about bears. They were content with their wildlife knowledge, and didn't need some fear-mongering khaki-clad interloper passing judgment on them.

Me? Oh, I couldn't wait. I still held out hope that there would be some paranormal overtones.

Plus, I had questions.

Lots and lots of questions.

October 10, 2008

Dear Amber,

Umm . . . sorry!

I guess that the Sergeant and I just have differing opinions as to what 'special treatment' entails.

You'll heal. Eventually. Probably.

On the bright side, you'll have some scars to show the other Pirates!!!

Now practice laughing and being dashing at the same time as you jump off tall thingd. Perfect that and you're all set.

Love you,
Daddio

P.S. Dammit! Slipped again. Do scars look good on a Pilot or does it cause concern with the passengers? I think it might make me question your aerial skills somewhat.

But on a Pirate they're a plus.
I'm just sayin'.

Chapter 13

Who Do You Have To Kill To Get This Job?

As the others at the table dispersed with 'Nice to meet you' and 'Take care' and 'Fuck the French', (man Charles was bitter), Mom and I made our way into the adjoining Library.

The Library. I don't know what I expected. I think there should be some rule, some governing body concerning the nomenclature of indoor spaces. You can't go bandying descriptors like 'library' or 'media room' or 'dungeon' about without something to back it up. A folding chair, pad, and pencil do not a studio make. A library should have books. Lots and lots of books and high-backed chairs and Meerschaum pipes. Huge Meerschaum pipes lying delicately on rich mahogany coffee tables that are arranged willy-nilly about the place. Oh! And a secret passage! And Grandfather clocks! Now that's a real library. That's a room that's ready for anything from a deep, confessional conversation, to a murder with a knife. Or a lead pipe. Oh! And there should be at least one candelabra!

I don't make the rules. These are the things you need for a proper library at an Inn in the mountains. Or so I've been conditioned to believe by copious amounts of television and the bastards at Milton Bradley. And a deer's head! Or moose. Or some poor hoofed creature mounted to the wall.

I know now why we hadn't visited the library before. I had seen the room, but mistaken it for a coat closet. No, I exaggerate. It wasn't that small, probably 10 by 15. It was crammed with so many over-stuffed couches and chairs that it looked like a summer deck party at a frat house. Or the front lawn of my neighbor. Or Ikea. As for reading material, there was one lonely bookshelf that had a few hardbacks, a number of paperbacks, a few board games and . . . well that was it. Shoot, your mom carries more reading material in her purse. Library indeed! Harumph! The rest of the room held some pictures of ducks, a few windows along the outer wall, and a rock fireplace that had a bladder problem. Although Mom explained to me that it was more than likely a serious problem with water leaking from the roof around the chimney. I remain unconvinced.

We took a seat near the entrance from the dining room on a large, brown leather couch. I wondered how many were going to show up for the talk. It seemed like everyone except your mom and I had made a beeline for their rooms as soon as Leeza made the announcement. The speaker hadn't arrived, or if he had he wasn't showing his face as yet, so Mom and I had the room to ourselves. I had a million ideas as to how we could occupy our time, but your mother thought this would be a good time, and I'm not making this up, to go over some 'ground rules' for the evening.

"First off," she said, "not one word about the paranormal, auras, or Kirlian photography. Okay?"

I studied her face. What sort of sacrilege was this? I was to edit myself?

"What if he brings up the subject first?"

"I don't think that's going to happen."

"You don't know that for sure," I said with a satisfied little grin.

Mom sighed. Man she does that a lot.

"I'm pretty sure."

"But what," I said, "if he's going along and talking about his adventures with the bears and then he narrows his eyes and whispers about the greatest bear he ever knew, Rotund Pete. He then would share the tragic tale of Rotund Pete and his untimely death one fine spring day from eating the wrong berries and how now his lost grizzly soul forever walks these woods, scaring the bejebus out of tourists? Am I allowed to pursue this angle should he broach the subject?"

"Rotund Pete? A bear ghost named Rotund Pete?"

"He was picked on in his youth by other cubs."

"And they named him 'Rotund Pete'?"

"Oh now, you know how cruel cubs can be. No, they called him fatty-fatty-fat-fat Pete. When he was older, he watched an episode of Oprah on personal empowerment and right then and there decided that no one would ever call him fatty-fatty-fat-fat Pete ever again. From then on he would be known as Rotund Pete, or by nothing. It was all very emotional and transformative."

"Why didn't he just call himself 'Pete'?"

"Self-esteem issues. Old wounds run deep," I explained. "Plus, he missed that episode of Oprah."

Mom sat there looking at me for a long, long time. I knew what she was thinking. She was thinking that turning in early was sounding better and better by the moment.

"Okay. If he talks about bear ghosts you have my permission to quiz his little head off. But ONLY if he brings up the subject first."

That sounded fair. I could probably steer the conversation in that direction without suffering your mother's wraith. I now had a goal. You know me, I like a challenge!

Just then we heard voices and laughter coming from the dining room and who should walk through the door but our BMW friends, Robert and Julie. They were followed by the Innkeepers, Bob and Linda and their friends, two couples that I had no idea where the hell they came from, and an older woman of about 60 with a defiant look in her eye and a hemp necklace. She wore, what I can only describe as a robe, and she was barefoot.

Ah, I had seen this species before. Disillusioned hippie. Jaded commune fodder. Angry post-menopausal environmentalist. She would take some watching. Her kind was unpredictable and more than likely slightly crazy. She stank of the fringe, if you know what I mean. My defenses were up immediately.

As we settled in I took a quick count of the room. Well, thirteen wasn't a bad turnout, not a bad number at all.

After a few moments a door - until now unnoticed by me as it was on the other side of the fireplace and partially out of view - opened and a man and a dog kind of sidled into the library. Very nonchalant.

The man was probably in his late 30's, flannel shirt, jeans and hiking boots. His face was soft, his eyes blue. I thought his hair was blondish, but on second look decided that he might be older than I had originally assumed as his hair was not blond but grey. His hands, arms, and neck were wind-burned and red, (couldn't be sunburn because as far as I was concerned the sun, this far north, was nothing but a rumor). He didn't say anything nor did he look at us, instead going about his business of getting his dog settled on a big comfy looking pillow by the chair he was evidently going to occupy. As you know I've done a fair amount of public speaking - some of it even requested - and I had to ding him right off the bat. He should have greeted us. Put us at ease. This is not the way to curry favor with your audience.

He futzed around for the next few minutes arranging his chair, trying various angles and positions until he found the sweet spot, whatever that was. Some fung shui no doubt. It was fascinating to watch. He was maneuvering around an area no larger than the footprint of a refrigerator. Perhaps he was looking to align his aura along a north-south axis. I don't know. Whatever it was he took so long doing it that the audience, small as it was, became anxious.

Finally he stepped behind his chair, and placing both hands on the back-plate he leaned slightly forward, and said, "Good evening. I'm Randy Dale, and this is Keesha," he reached down to stroke the dog's muzzle. It was a bit of a reach as she had her head on her forepaws, "She's a Karelian Bear Dog," he said as he gave her a quick scratch behind the ears which, from her expression, she tolerated. "Isn't that right Keesha?"

At the sound of her name her ears twitched and her eyes locked on Randy, looking for a hint of what he was going to do, ready for anything that was asked of her. With her head slightly cocked her eyes shone. Definitely an intelligent dog. You know how some dogs just seem to shine? Their spirit so bright that they appear to glow under their coats? That was Keesha. She was beautiful. Predominantly black with a white chest, belly, and front legs. Her head was squarish and blunt, with forward tipping ears and a stout snout that looked quite powerful. She didn't seem particularly large, not like a Newfie or even a large German Sheppard, but she wasn't small by any means and you could see the muscle ripple underneath her coat whenever she moved. When standing, her tail curved up over her back in a tight 'C' shape. She was a beauty and she knew it.

"And together," Randy said, rubbing his palms, "we handle the 'problem' bear population in this section of the Park."

Here he paused for a moment, as if his thoughts were slightly outpacing his actions, and he needed to collect them. I saw a slight blush creep across his cheeks, even through the wind burn. Ah. Now I understood. This was a man more comfortable with a dog and a trail than a roomful of bored tourists.

For the first time he glanced around the room. I felt bad for him. This was a sucky situation in which to be if you weren't used to speaking. See, a larger group would afford some anonymity, both for the speaker and the audience. A smaller group would lend itself to a more casual and conversational approach. But poor Randy was dealing with a beast that was just large enough, or small enough depending on how you looked at it, to be uncomfortable. For us as well as him.

Randy shook his head, as if coming out of a dream.

"Yeah. Okay." he said not quite under his breath but almost. "Okay. Well I guess I should start out by telling you a little bit about Keesha and her breed."

As soon as Randy started talking, you could see that this was a part of the talk with which he was very comfortable. Enthusiastic even. Now, I've been on enough stages, (once again, sometimes even invited!), and memorized enough lines to know when I'm hearing a monologue. And that's what this was - a monologue about his dog. Evidently Randy spoke in public more than I had assumed.

As Randy continued his patter, we learned that Keesha was about 7 years old and this would probably be her last year in service. Instead of Keesha being Randy's personal dog, as, once again I had assumed, it turns out that she was actually on loan from a breeding and training facility in Idaho. Randy, at the earliest sign of spring and way before the bears came out of hibernation, would travel down to the kennels in the States, spend two weeks training with his 'co-worker' for the season, and then return to the mountains.

He explained that Karelian Bear Dogs were a specific breed, originally from Finland - which would explain the thick, mid-length coat on the dog - truly a cold weather creature - and were known not only for their loyalty and hard work but their absolute fearlessness on the hunt.

We learned that the Karelian was a silent hunter, only barking when it had its prey cornered. They were absolutely wonderful with people, but not so much with other dogs unless they'd been raised with them. Even then, as a strong pack animal, they would fight for dominance and alpha status. They also completely understood their own worth, and it took a strong master to keep them in line. I would insert some line about your mom here but I think she might be monitoring these letters, so we'll just let it be for the moment.

Randy explained that Keesha loved nothing more than working the Park. She would often be up and ready long before Randy had his first cup of coffee. Keesha's job was to jump out of the truck at the appropriate time and bark, chase, and if need be, nip at the bear - all the while avoiding being eaten - until the bear, through sheer frustration, vacated the area.

Randy then paused again. "So . . . yeah."

I knew exactly what he was doing. He was following the script in his head. He had just finished section 1, and was now moving to a different topic. I thought this a little odd that his segues were so rough, but who the hell am I to criticize?

Randy scratched his chin, chewing something over in his head.

"Folks, I have to tell you, Keesha and I visit a lot of schools and classrooms through the year, so I'm not really used to speaking to adults. I'm sorry, just bear with me."

To which a chorus of reassurance flowed from the room like molasses in a microwave.

This encouragement seemed to relax him a bit, and he walked to the front of the chair and sat down, putting his hands on his knees.

"Okay. Well, since we're all adults here, I guess I can toss the classroom lecture and tell you what really goes on." A sly smile crept across his face as he said this. "I have the best job in the world. I get to drive around all day in a truck, and when I see a bear where no bear should be - you know, hanging around garbage cans, or hanging around the lodge here," he said, which elicited a hearty chuckle from our hosts in not an entirely positive way, " I get to shoot them in the ass with a paintball gun."

I repeated that in my head like the coolest mantra I'd ever heard. 'I get to shoot them in the ass with a paintball gun'.

Now there were several reactions to this statement. Some chuckles. Some shaking of heads. Some looks of incredulity from certain women in the group. I'm not pointing fingers, but old hemp-lady, as I had come to tag her, didn't look pleased at all. The men in the group? Their thoughts were painted on their faces as plainly as makeup on a televangelist's wife. It may have been phrased differently for all of us, but boiled down to this single notion:

Who the hell do we have to kill to get a job like that?

I mean really - you add a six-pack of beer, some cheese and crackers, and a Willie Nelson CD and you have every man's dream. Shooting grizzlies in the ass with a paintball gun from the safety of a truck and all sanctioned by the government! I mean really . . . what did he do? Find a Genie? Trade his sister? Flunk out of law school but not before he'd collected some embarrassing info on a Park Official?

After the hub-bub had settled a bit, Randy continued explaining to us that there really were no problem bears, it was people that created the problem and the bears were just doing what bears do, finding the most amount of food with the least amount of effort. Much like big business. So it had taken him years, but he'd finally managed to convince the Park Service and the concessions operating in the Park, like the Lodge, to implement a strict garbage containment program so as to remove temptation from the bear's path. No food - no bear. Simple as that.

This made perfect sense to me. I myself have been known to leave a party early when they take away the snacks. Which happens quite often. Quite often indeed. That's curious, isn't it? Strikes me as a bit odd anyway.

Back to the bears. The thought of a grizzly being addicted to garbage conjured up all sorts of images and scenarios in my head. Most of them involving a grizzly attending a 12-step program, sharing its pain, and then eating the group. It's like Grandma used to say; "You can take the Grizzly out of the woods, but you can't make him adhere to strictly defined social customs and mores."

Ah Grandma. She could really turn a phrase.

Randy then went on to elaborate that the grizzlies, being at the tippy-top of the food chain but not quite realizing it, although they had strong suspicions, weren't terribly afraid of humans. So, in their search for food they'd come to recognize that human = garbage and garbage = food. Oddly, he left out the part about human = food but we all knew that was a given. When the bears lost their fear of humans, Randy explained, that's when the problems really started. But most bears were shy and stayed out of people's way. But not all of them.

Ya. Well, I hated to disappoint Mr. Bear-man here, but the bears that I'd observed since entering the Park didn't seem to be especially wary of human activity. Curious yes. Frightened no.

"So," Randy said, "we'll get a call about a bear in a picnic area or campground, or shoot - sometimes in a parking lot at a trail head, and Keesha and I will jump in the truck, hunt her down, then POP POP POP," he said, mimicking holding a paintball gun, "right in the butt."

Hemp-lady scowled but no one besides me seemed to notice. I offered her a smile because, I've come to learn in all my years on this planet, that it's best not to taunt the deranged. Well, you can taunt them. Just not to the point of breaking. Otherwise next thing you know one minute you're standing in line at the Post Office making snarky comments to the lady behind the counter, and the next you're at the Gates of Hell with nary a clue as to how you arrived. Hemp-lady didn't return the smile. I didn't worry. I could see by the folds of her robe she wasn't packing, being a Canadian and all, and besides - I was pretty sure Mom could take her.

Julie, who had been squirming for the last few minutes, either in need of a bathroom or VERY impatient to ask a question, said, "And that does it? I mean the bears go away and don't come back?" She turned to Robert. "Paintballs don't hurt, do they?"

Randy laughed. "Oh, you have no idea how bad they hurt! Believe me, you get shot with one of these," he said, taking an orange ball out of his shirt pocket and handing it to the person on his right for inspection, "you're going to be feeling it for a couple of days. Go ahead and pass that around the room."

Robert nodded in agreement. "We used to go into the woods once a year for a Retreat with the staff. One of the activities was paintball. Believe me when I say that they definitely hurt. They leave quite a bruise."

"And I don't use just paintballs. We use a variety of non-lethal methods. See, we're not trying to hurt the bears. Far from it. But we are trying to harass them to the point where they associate people with minor pain and fear. Bears are highly intelligent as I said. I can't use the same method all the time because they come to understand that whatever it is we're doing isn't going to kill them, only cause a little bit of discomfort which, given enough time, they'll completely ignore. So we mix it up. Maybe paintballs one day. Keesha running around them, nipping at their heels the next. Then we'll shoot sandbags. Or firecrackers. You know, keep it fresh."

"Wow. They really get used to it that fast?" Mom asked.

I was a little surprised that your mom had jumped into the middle like this, she's usually not one for participation. Then I remembered we were talking about animals. If she began asking how much dry dog food you would need to keep a bear alive and did they like left over corn chips, then I would worry.

"Oh yeah," Randy replied, "I said they were smart creatures. A couple of years ago we were having a problem with a big female. No matter what I did, she would still come back to the same places over and over. But when I showed up I could never find her. Smart girl." He tapped his index finger to his temple. "Turns out that she'd picked up on the fact that we came in white pickups. That's what we'd been driving because that's what the Park supplied, and that's what the staff use all over the park. So a white truck meant something unpleasant to her, but a car, or a truck of a different color? That she would walk right up to. So that summer I found myself down in the town, renting a different car every few days for the next six weeks so she wouldn't know which car was which." He looked around the room to gauge our reaction. "I told you they were smart."

So he gets to play 'Secret Spy' AND shoot bears in the ass? Life is so unfair sometimes. Plus, and I'm just guessing here, he probably gets to stay up late on school nights.

Randy then went on to espouse in a grand fashion on the intelligence of the grizzly bear. Evidently if they had thumbs we would be screwed. Or more screwed. Doesn't matter. I wanted to ask him how they trained the bears for the "Bear Calvary" meme, and started to raise my hand but Mom stopped me before I could get a word out.

Randy pointed to me and asked, "Did you have a question?"

"No he didn't," Mom said, entirely too quickly. It was almost as if she'd just been waiting for something along these lines. That woman is eerie.

Randy then returned to his standard patter about the grizzly. Size - up to 1500 pounds. Territory - hundreds of miles. Diet - just about anything. Vegetation, roots, berries, fish, moose, elk, deer, hikers, you name it. Credit Score - in the low 500s but that's not really their fault. It's hard to get credit when you don't have a fixed address.

Randy then explained general bear behavior, hibernation, mating behavior (evidently Craigslist has become a very, very popular site in these woods), lifespan, and the various distinctions between the male and female. He explained that 98% of the bear encounters in the park are with females. Males are very solitary and stick to the high country, rarely journeying down this low. Although, I thought 7000 feet, or 88,000 hectograms was quite high, evidently the grizzly has different standards. Sense of smell - acute. Think of a grizzly as a very sensitive nose with an appetite attached. He cautioned about food, and food smells, and how to wrap your lunch so that you didn't lose a foot.

"So," Randy said, "let's talk about what you folks probably came to hear about. What should you do if you encounter a bear?"

No one said a thing. I, like the universe, abhor a vacuum. "Wet your pants?" I offered.

Randy chose to ignore my rather witty remark. Bastard.

Hemp-lady, who, because of my previous attempt to soothe her lunacy, leaned close and whispered to me. "This is ridiculous."

"Isn't it though?" I agreed, not having a clue as to what she was talking about but egging her on just the same. That's just the kind of guy I am.

This was what Julie had been waiting for. The poor thing was in quite a tizzy. "Well let me tell you what happened to US today," she said launching into a lengthy, and detailed, account of their bear encounter on the trail, as well as the 'idiot couple' that walked up to the bear. Those were her words, not mine. I liked the Danish couple. I felt the same way about them as I do a goldfish dropped into a tank of piranha. Julie finished with "But it was right on the trail! Do you understand? RIGHT ON THE TRAIL!"

It was painfully obvious to everyone that Julie had been driven completely insane by wildlife.

"Well," Randy said with a scratch of his chin, "you did the right thing.

Let the bear know that you're there. You don't want to startle them. Ever. Believe me. I can't stress that enough. DO - NOT – STARTLE - A - GRIZZLY. That's why you should sing or make plenty of noise when you're hiking. And you need to constantly be on the lookout for bear. And not just bear, but evidence of bear in the area. Look for footprints or scat. That's one of the best indicators of grizzly activity."

I guess that answers that question. Evidently a bear does do it in the woods.

"The thing to keep in mind," Randy continued, "is that grizzlies want to avoid human contact. They really are much shyer than you would think. In fact, for every bear you see on your hike you've probably passed right by another five or six and didn't even notice."

Poor Julie. That was about the last thing she needed to hear. She now had the visible willies. It was really quite remarkable. A small quiver started in her head, and gained momentum as it traveled down her spine and trunk, until it almost knocked her off the couch as it reached her thighs. Therapy would probably be in order after the vacation. Possibly electro-shock.

"Oh my God!" she said, punching Robert on the shoulder. And this wasn't a friendly, teasing punch. This was a punch intended to inflict some pain of its own. Good thing Julie didn't have a paintball gun, or there would be some serious behavior modification in Robert's future.

"That is the scariest thing I've heard. But what should we have done about the other couple? I mean, should we have yelled or waved our arms or what? Did we do right?"

Unbeknownst to me, Leeza had been half-leaning in the door beside the fireplace, listening to our talk. She darted into the room and whispered something in Randy's ear that washed all expression, and a good bit of color from his face. "That was THEM?"

Leeza nodded and chuckled, and stepped out of sight.

Randy shook his head and rolled his eyes. "Well, you did what you could do. There's no protecting everyone, you know?"

"Were they in serious danger?" Robert asked, "Or are we making too big of a deal out of this?"

Oh Robert, Robert, Robert. I deduct 10 points from your man score. Do not pass GO. Do not have a pleasant ride home. Believe me when I say that it can be a long, long ride with a woman kidney-punching you all the way. And yes, I speak from experience.

Julie, and every other woman in the room, glared. Not just glared, but glowered. Not just glowered, but seethed. Sucks to be you Robert. Sucks to be you. Of course Robert, being a man and being married, knew the minute he'd let his question fly that it was a mistake. I smelled jewelry in Julie's future.

"Well," Randy said, "the short answer is yes. Anytime you are anywhere near a grizzly you're in danger. They are wild, unpredictable animals. I've been doing this for a dozen years and they still surprise me." He turned to Robert who now was doing his best to ignore his wife lest she go for his throat. "Did that answer your question?"

"Um. Yeah," Robert said. "Thank you."

"So," I said and watched your mom wilt into the leather of the couch, "let me paint you a picture." I then proceeded to recount our dusky arrival of a few days before, and the bears we'd seen. And the Moose. And, for a brief moment before your mom poked me in the ribs, my theory on Viking cloning.

"Wow," Randy said, "that sounds like quite a story. Where did you say this happened?"

"Right after you pass the lake, or reservoir - whatever it is - on your way up from Carnack."

Randy shook his head and blinked. I wished people would stop doing that. It was beginning to erode my confidence.

"You rode a motorcycle up from Carnack? The one in the parking lot? How did the BMW handle that hill?"

"Umm . . . I have no idea. We were riding the Vic."

Randy looked at me. Stared at me. Then blinked his eyes once, twice, three times. "No shit?"

I looked at your mom. "Well yeah."

"On purpose?" Randy asked.

"Do we really ever do anything 'on purpose' Randy? Is our path, our journey predetermined---"

"Not on purpose," Mom interrupted.

"Right. Not entirely on purpose," I said. "Mostly. But not entirely." I paused here and exchanged a look with your mom. "Okay, accidently then."

With a jerk of her thumb towards me Mom said, "He gets lost. A lot."

Woman! Woman what have you done? Have you no shame? How could you out me like this in front of a group of my peers? Next thing you know you'll be telling them that we listened to the soundtrack from the "Sound of Music" on the way here, and my reputation will be shot. Shot like a dry bean out of a toddler's nose.

"Not a lot," I said. "Just . . . frequently. But you have to admit, that when we get lost we do it spectacularly. With flair!"

Mom chose to ignore this comment.

"Wow. Okay then," Randy said. "Did you see a tag on the bear's ear?"

I wanted to ask him how the hell I was supposed to see that much detail when my vision was occupied with my life flashing before my eyes, but I held my tongue.

"Don't know," I said. "I was kind of preoccupied with not dying."

"I'm just asking because we haven't had a report of a bear in that area in quite awhile. See, we sedate and tag all the problem bears - the REAL problem bears, the ones that the paintball and other techniques don't work on - so we can keep track of them. You didn't see a large, yellow tag on her ear?"

I searched my memory, replaying the incident in my head. I saw a lot of things on that bear. A magnificent rump. A patch of mottled fur. Teeth. Drool. What I'm sure were bits of flannel between her paws but definitely no tag. Possibly an expired Library card caught in her molars.

"Well that's a little worrisome," Randy said. "Keesha and I might have to look into that. How close was she?"

I pointed to the wall behind him. "And she didn't run?"

"Nope. Just kind of took her time walking across the road, then stopped and watched us. I don't know how long. I was trying not to look back, just trying to focus on the road ahead, you know?"

"That's not good. Not good at all," Randy said, furrowing his brow and talking more to himself than the group.

I decided to ignore this. "So anyway, back to my question. The grizzly can run . . . what, about 30 mph?"

"Miles per hour? Yeah, 30 or 35 for short bursts." He paused for a second, then added "That's right. You guys are from THE STATES."

Why yes, yes we are. Thank you for noticing.

"Yep, we are. Seattle area. Anyway, what should we have done in that situation? I mean, I would have thought that the sound of the bike would have scared her off."

"That's what's so worrisome," Randy said. I could feel your mom tense next to me. "As for what to do. . ." he raised his hands into the air, with a slight grin and a cocked head said, "I guess drive faster than 35 mph?"

Well that was less than helpful. He could have just as easily raised his hands and said 'Die?'. Which, come to think of it, might have been the subtext. As you know subtlety is not one of my strong points.

"I guess from your description she could have had some cubs. I haven't seen any in that area but it's not impossible." He looked around and addressed the group, "You don't under ANY circumstances want to get between a mother grizzly and her cubs. I probably should have said that first."

Like he's telling me? I've been to soccer games. I've bought more Girl Scout cookies than I could ever possibly consume strictly out of fear. You don't have to tell me twice.

Julie, who had been semi-catatonic through this exchange suddenly perked up. She clamped on to Robert's arm. "Do you think the bear WE saw had cubs?"

Randy, if you have an ounce of intelligence in your head, which, from all appearances you do, lie to the woman. Lie and tell her that there were no cubs. Lie like a used-car salesman at the end of the month with a broken-down hatchback and a quota to fill.

"I don't think so," Randy said, and Julie visibly relaxed.

"Oh," Julie said. "Okay then."

Randy turned back to me. "And then the moose blocked the road. That must have been tense."

"Pffffttt," I said. "All in a day's work for the adventure team. But it got me to thinking. Do you think that the bear and moose were in cahoots? You know, the moose trapped us while her friend the bear made the kill? I'm thinking the bear might cut her in for a share, but aren't moose strict vegans? Maybe the bear had a little dirt on the moose and was blackmailing her." I had addressed this observation to the rest of the group who were now looking at me as if I'd crossed some line. Changing tactics, I spoke directly to Robert, "It happens you know. Thuggery is rampant in these mountains. I blame the kids and their Rap music. Oh, and violent video games."

This elicited a few chuckles and half-hearted smiles. Randy, in his wisdom tried his best to ignore me. "Are there any other questions? I mean," he said looking at me, "any real questions?"

"What about the other bear?" I said.

Randy paused, chewing over what I'd just asked. Should he engage me in further conversation, or should he ignore me completely? "Okay I'll bite, what other bear?"

Ah curiosity. A horrible human foiable.

"Well there were two really. We saw another one this afternoon." I paused, "So I guess that makes three in total. I'll get to that one in a minute. I'm talking about the one Suzanne saw on our way in. It was after we had been cornered by the Moose Mafia, but before we reached the lodge." I turned to your mom, "You take it from here sweetie."

Randy, visibly relieved that he would be addressing the saner half of your parental units, raised his eyebrows questioningly.

"Well," Mom said, taking a deep breath, "like David said, it was after the moose. We were riding down the road and I looked up on this hillside. It was gravel and bushes for about 20 feet from the road to the top, then the tree line." She used her hands to show the incline of the bank and how it leveled into the trees at the top. "Something caught my eye, and I looked up the bank and right in front of the trees was a bear." Mom looked around the room to see if people were paying attention. "I watched it follow us for a while along the ridge. It was moving pretty fast, keeping up with us. Pacing us. It kind of popped in and out of the forest."

Randy made a sound much like Lucille Ball used to make, only not as funny. "EEEEeeeeeee!"

"EEEeeee?" Mom asked.

"So was this the same bear that you saw earlier?"

Well there was a thought that sent chills up my spine. I had considered it briefly, but thought I was just being paranoid. If it WERE the same bear, that means that at some time when we were stranded by the moose, Ms. Huge-butt had passed right by and traveled up the road ahead. One word came to mind. Ambush.

"I don't know. I didn't see the one that David saw."

"Can you describe it?"

"Well, it was big. And it was a bear." She shrugged her shoulders. "That's about it. It was the end of a very, very," and here she paused to look at me, "VERY long day. My brain was toast."

Randy looked at me and then shook his head in the affirmative at your mom, indicating he was pretty sure he knew EXACTLY what she meant. "That wasn't good. You don't want a bear following you like that."

"Why not?" Julie asked.

"Because," he said, raising his hands up to his chest in sock-puppet fashion, with the left hand slightly higher, "you know, predator," he said, bouncing his left hand, "and prey," he said, indicating his right. He then opened his left hand to mimic jaws, and clamped it quickly over his right hand, now curled into a fist. For good measure he made chewing sounds. "Arrrghllll bargel nom-nom-nom"

Mom looked at me and her eyes were wide. Wide and glassy.

"Oh," Julie said, and kind of collapsed back on the couch, leaning against Robert. It was then that I realized two things: One, after this trip Robert was never going to get Julie on the back of a motorcycle ever again. Two, Julie would never, ever commune with nature with the possible exception of a zoo or a documentary.

"This brings up a good point. Let's talk about the bear that doesn't run away. The one that isn't afraid or shy, for whatever reason."

Randy then went on to explain what to do if your bear hadn't read the manual. If a bear stops or alters its current behavior, you're too close and should back away slowly. If a bear comes running towards you, making loud sounds and slapping the ground with its paw, you should back away slowly. (Then change your pants. Randy didn't say that so it must be a given.) If a bear persistently follows or approaches you, without vocalizing, or paw swatting, change your direction. If the bear still follows, stand your ground. (Sure. And then I'll go slap Chuck Norris in the face and insult his mother.) If the bear gets closer, talk loudly or shout at it. Try to intimidate the bear. If you are with other people act together as a group. (For some reason this brought to mind performing a skit. Like at summer camp. I have no idea why, I'm just reporting what happened.) Make yourselves look as large as possible. (This is why everyone should wear puffy shirts when they hike.) Throw rocks. Whatever you do, don't run and don't turn away from the bear."

That last part, I'll have you know, goes against every single instinct I possess.

Hemp-lady looked at me while she said this. I couldn't make out exactly what she was saying, owing to the fact that I had lost interest in her about 10 minutes ago, but if I lip read correctly it was 'umphnd dephanertat'. She must be bilingual.

"One of the best things you can do is hike with a group. You're much safer with a group of people, than you are hiking by yourself or with a partner. Have you guys seen some of the rules posted on the trails around here?"

"You mean the ones that state the trail can't be hiked by less than a party of four, right?" Robert asked.

"Exactly," said Randy. "The incidence of a grizzly attacking a group of 4 or more is almost unheard of. So there really is safety in numbers."

Now this made perfect sense to me. Nobody wants trouble. This is why Mormons travel in packs.

Julie perked up at this, a slight ray of hope shone in her face. "There we go," she said to Robert, "all we have to do is bring my sister Carol and her husband Thomas on our next hike!"

While Robert didn't seem nearly as enthusiastic as Julie, he saw that if he wanted to visit anywhere with a tree ever again it would be best to be supportive. Being a man, and a married man at that, I read the smile-plastered-over-a-look-of-seasickness for what it was. There was no way in hell he would ever hike with her sister and brother-in-law, but he was probably going to have to do it anyway. Poor Robert, he was looking at this as a negative. I say take that bitter pill and coat it with enough sugar to get diabetes! If I were in his shoes I would find this a perfect opportunity to feed your Aunts and Uncles to the bears. Not that it would work. Our family is pretty scrappy. We survived the '70s. You don't think that took guts? I have three words for you: Bell-bottoms. Nixon. Disco. They would probably kick the bear's ass. So I would never hike with them, even if I could. I couldn't take the chance of having to listen to THAT story at every Thanksgiving until the day I die. There's only so much aggravation that can be covered up with pumpkin pie and gravy.

Randy began to wrap up his spiel. There was a bit more about bear behavior, but it basically boiled down to this: Take away the food and the bear goes away. Stay safe in the woods and don't go where the bear's food is. Which was Robert and Julie's mistake because they'd been walking through a berry patch. Julie poked Robert in the ribs when she heard this. Poor, poor Robert. Poor hen-pecked man. What, I wondered, must it feel like to have lost all shred of manhood and dignity at the hands of your wife. I was going to ask him what it felt like when your mom elbowed me in the ribs so I forgot about it pretty fast.

When Randy paused for a minute I jumped into the void. "Wait, we didn't tell you about the third bear. The one we saw this morning."

As you know I'm fairly astute when it comes to reading the body language of other people. I could tell from Randy's stance exactly what he was thinking, for I see this posture more than I would like to admit in my day-to-day life. Randy was thinking 'Can someone please make him stop?'

Silly Randy. Silly, silly man.

"Okay," Randy said with what I thought was an inordinate amount of resignation in his voice, "tell me about the third bear."

So as not to bore the rest of the group, and possibly so that I could gloss over some of the more embarrassing moments, I got straight to the point and gave Randy a concise, abbreviated version of this morning events. "We were down by. . . what's the name of that picnic area?" I asked your mom.

"Annaminga," she answered.

"Right. Annaminga. Well we were driving by and saw some cars parked at the entrance to the road. We pulled over and that's when we saw the bear." I continued on with the encounter describing how she came down the hill and how she acted. "But the most amazing part is that when the bear walked behind the car and. . . " here I paused, looking to make sure that our Danish friends were out of earshot. I saw that Leeza had at some point come to stand in the doorway behind us. She picked up on what I was doing and with a quick glance over her shoulder gave me a 'thumbs up' that the coast was clear. "And this couple jumped out and started taking pictures! It was the most amazing thing I'd ever seen."

"You're kidding, right?" Randy said.

"No. No I'm not," I said shaking my head.

"Well I don't know how to say this any other way but that was stupid."

"You'll never guess who it was," Leeza said with a grin.

Randy rubbed his temples. "You've GOT to be kidding me."

"Nope. Wish I was," Leeza chuckled.

Randy stood there for a bit shaking his head. "Wow. That's just scary."

"I know! I can't believe how casual people are about danger. I guess they are oblivious to the risk they're taking," I said.

Randy stared at me. "You do realize that you're riding a motorcycle in the middle of a fairly good size grizzly population, right? I mean you're riding right out there, not a window or door between you and the world?"

Oh I saw Randy's point. Pot and kettle and all that.

"LOL, I see wut you did thar," I replied in my best meme-speak but I think it was lost on this audience. "But it's different."

"Really? How so?"

"Because. It's me. And it's different for me." I flashed a huge grin around the room. "Oh, I know what it's like for other people, but for me - it's different."

Randy sucked on his front teeth, making a click. "Okay." Only he drew out the 'O' until it became an indictment of my judgment. I thought about getting all pissed for a minute, thought back over the conversation, and decided he was probably right.

Randy then quizzed us as to the size, color, and behavior exhibited by the bear. We talked about the young hikers, and the bear they saw. Man, he was into bears. Really, really into bears. Creepily into bears. We told him what we could, yet no matter how hard we scoured our memories it was still basically big, toothy, bearish.

After we'd exhausted this particular close encounter of the bear kind, Randy looked around the room and said, "Well, I think that about wraps it up. Are there any questions?"

I cleared my throat to speak and Mom pulled me close, rather abruptly I thought, and whispered in my ear one solitary word. A single word that might have only four letters and one syllable, but in actuality contained an encyclopedia of unspoken action.

"Don't."

I would protest that I knew not of what she spoke - but I knew exactly of what she spoke.

"It's okay," I whispered back, "this is a legitimate question."

Mom regarded me warily, but slowly released me from her grip.

"I have a question," I said and watched Randy tense. "You've certainly had your share of personal bear encounters. What was the one that frightened you most?"

Randy looked at me and blinked his eyes a couple of times. "That's actually a good question. I've been in some close spots with the bears but I've never been what I would call 'scared'. Concerned yes. Even pretty darn anxious. But when I'm out on the trails I'm planning ahead, practicing my bear-safe techniques. That's the trick. The best defense against a bear attack is avoiding the situation in the first place. So," he said, looking at me, "the most scared I've been on the job didn't come from a bear. It happened last year right here at the lodge with a cougar."

Oh oh. Crap and jehoobis! Wish I hadn't asked that question. I held out hope that this was going to turn out to be an uncomfortable incident with an older woman with a 'hankerin'' if you know what I mean, but I didn't think so. For one, Randy was way too old to be the plaything of a fading beauty. Plus I don't think that a hiking lodge in the Canadian Rockies is the natural habitat of that particular species of cougar. I think they prowl gyms. And discos. And high school football games. Sometimes cub scout meetings. You get the picture.

Your mom tensed every muscle in her body as well as a few in mine. She gripped my leg just above the knee and although I know she didn't realize what she was doing, dug her nails into my leg quite viciously.

On second thought perhaps she knew exactly what she was doing.

"Last year, what . . . was it mid-August? About this time of year?" he asked Leeza.

"Yeah. Just about."

"The lodge called me up and said that they had a cougar hanging around. That is really bad, as I'm sure you know, having a cougar claim your place as part of its territory is just asking for problems. People and cougars don't mix. Sooner or later the there will be a clash. So, we needed to get this cat away from here as quickly as we could. Wasn't as easy as you think. Cats don't stay in any one spot for very long. Every time there was a sighting and they called me, the cat would be long gone by the time I got here."

"It was really frustrating," Leeza added. "I mean, it was incredible to see this huge, beautiful animal, but we realized at the same time, the danger."

"Right," Randy said. "Leeza? Why don't you tell them the next part?"

"Sure." She stepped to the forefront and said, "I don't know if any of you have been around a cougar, but they make some bone-chilling sounds. Especially at night."

Oh yeah. We know that don't we? We've heard a few in the valley behind our house. I don't know which creeps me out worse, the sound of a baby crying in the woods at night or the sound of a woman screaming. Bah! Gives me the willies just thinking about that sound! You can't see it, but the hair on my arms is standing straight up.

"Well one night a bunch of guests and some of the staff were sitting outside enjoying the stars and the quiet." She turned to your mom and me. "Sorry guys. It really doesn't rain all the time. And when it's clear you can't believe how many stars there are in the sky."

"S'okay," I said, "we're from Seattle. We're used to it."

"Maybe you brought it with you," Robert offered.

"Possible. Seattle rain is notoriously needy. It might have gotten lonely and followed us here."

"Anyway," Leeza continued, "we were sitting out there when we heard one of the most disturbing sounds coming at us out of the darkness. And not very far away at all. Just out there in the meadow," she said, pointing through the room and out the dining room windows. "I won't go into details but the cat had caught and was in the process of killing a moose calf. It was horrible and heartbreaking at that same time. And those sounds. . . I don't think I'll ever forget the sounds. The cougar, the calf, and the mom." She turned to Randy. "It cleared the deck pretty fast."

"I'll bet it did."

"We didn't know it was a moose calf until the next morning when we could see in the light. We just knew that the cat had killed something. Blood, hair, the ground was tore up." She shivered. "The calf's body was gone but it wasn't hard to put two-and-two together. Yuck." Leeza here - for lack of a better term - made an ookey face. "That was scary enough, but then the next day we kept seeing the cat. All day long. It would just sit below the deck, or on the hill out back and watch. It wasn't scared and it wouldn't get scared. We tried all kinds of things but it wouldn't go away. It was really creepy. No one wanted to go outside. Well, almost no one," she said, rolling her eyes, "We had to do something, so of course we called Randy."

"And I got up here with about 15 minutes of daylight to spare. I'd been out all day and didn't get my messages until late that afternoon. We busted up here as fast as we could."

"And we appreciate that," Leeza reassured him.

"What I couldn't figure out is why the cat was here. Then when Leeza told me about the calf kill I figured out what was going on, or at least had my suspicions. After I got here it only took me a minute to confirm my fear. See, when a cat makes a kill, it likes to hide its prize from the rest of the world, going back to feed on it at its leisure. That's exactly what this one had done. I took a flashlight out and did a little scouting. Sure enough, right off the deck in back I found a fresh dig. This told me two things: One, the cat had claimed this area as its own - Lodge or no Lodge. Two, it was comfortable enough to bury its kill here. It had absolutely no fear of humans. And that," he said, "is really, really bad."

He paused, and I stole a glance at your mother. I wish I hadn't. I didn't need visual confirmation. I couldn't feel my leg below the knee. That was enough.

"It was too late to do anything with the cat, but I knew I had to do something," Randy continued. "So about the only thing I could do was get rid of the calf's carcass. Get rid of the cat's food. See?"

"And he came to ask me to help," Bob said, where he sat on the sofa beside his wife.

"I figured that if I was going to go out there I needed someone to hold a flashlight while I dug."

"Yeah," Bob said, "and watch out for the cat." He paused, then added. "It didn't hurt that I had a shotgun."

"No, that didn't hurt at all," Randy said. A small smile crossed his lips.

"Also, I didn't want to die alone in the dark." He turned back to the group, "So as you can see, fumbling about in the pitch-black, messing with a cougar's kill --- let's just say that it was more than a little scary. Bears are fairly predictable. Cats? Not so much."

"It's true," Bob said. "I don't know about Randy, but the whole time I was out there I expected to be pounced on by 70 kilos of angry kitty. It was," and he paused here, searching for just the right word, "intense."

"One way to put it," Randy replied. "I was scared out of my wits. Not kidding. Like Bob all I could imagine was the cat watching us from the darkness, and getting pissed because we were messing with dinner. You can believe I dug pretty fast, eh?"

Bob laughed. "That you did!"

Randy chuckled in return. "I was a maniac," he said, and mimicked digging a hole with a shovel at a pace just shy of a blur.

This elicited a few quiet laughs from the room.

"I couldn't believe how deep the cat had buried the calf. Usually they just kind of mound some dirt over the top. Pee around it to ward off any other predators and move on. But not this one. It seemed like I dug forever!"

"Wasn't that long," Bob said. "Just seemed like it was because we were both on the edge of panic. Every little noise and it was 'Whatsat? Whatsat?" he said, sitting up straight on the couch and whipping his head around as if he were hearing things in every direction.

"Finally," Randy said, "I reached the kill." He paused. "Well, not the whole kill. Just the head."

Now if Randy had set out to script a scenario, he could not have concocted one that would have disturbed your mother more. I finally had to pry her hands off my leg when her fingernails touched each other through my muscle. I had to give her credit. Substitute 'large carnivorous spider' for 'cougar', and I would have been in the middle of the room, jumping up and down, pounding on my head in a full state of 'willie-panic' faster than you could say Bob's yer uncle. Your mother had chosen to express her fear in a demure form of a slight sweat and a complete rigor. Oh well, I thought, at least it would be easier to carry her to the room with every muscle in her body taunt as a bungee cord on our bike. Light as a feather, heavy as stone and all that. I tried to give her a hug, but she whipped her head to look at me and her eyes said 'if-you-touch-me-I'm-going-to-go-all-primeval-on-your-ass-and-kill-you-with-your-own-arm-which-I-will-have-ripped-from-your-body'. As much as that sounds like fun I thought it best to give her some 'space' and retreated as far away as I possibly could, given the tight quarters.

"So. That was my most scary moment."

I had to say something. I had to try and cast a glimmer of hope over this whole affair or your mom would never step outside again. If I couldn't get through the fear I would have to have her boxed in the Lodge and shipped home at a later date. I would hope they would remember to poke some air-holes this time. It's one of those little details that's so obvious everyone thinks that someone else has surely taken care of it.

That reminds me. I miss your cousin Molly.

I cleared my throat. Mom didn't even react. Crap. This was more serious than I thought. "So, once you moved the head, did the cat stay away?"

"No," Randy said. "We wound up tranqing her a couple days later and re-locating her a long way away from here. Bears will generally learn to stay away. Cats, just like those little kitties you have at home, are creatures of habit. Once they get something in their head it's hard to get them to change their behavior."

Now, I hadn't realized that your mom hadn't been breathing until I heard a WHOOSH sound as she exhaled. She grabbed onto my arm and made a quiet sucking sound as she gulped the air into her lungs. Randy looked a bit surprised.

"So, once you re-located her, did she come back?" I asked, knowing full well what your mom needed to hear and praying that Randy would figure it out.

"Oh no," he said. "We never saw her again." He turned to Bob and Linda, "have you guys seen any more cats around here?"

"Don't think we have," Bob said, and looked to Linda for confirmation. She shook her head in agreement. "Saw one down on Highway 40 last year, and I've seen some tracks while we've been out and about but nothing close to the Lodge."

When she heard this, Mom sat back in her seat, the fear draining out of her like soapy water in a bathtub and taking most of the color in her face with it. I relaxed a bit as well. She was going to be fine. Such a trooper. I wouldn't have to carry her to the room after all. I believe it was right then, as your mom would explain later, that she developed the philosophy that would be her cornerstone, her rock, her guiding principal for the rest of her life. And that is this: large, carnivorous wildlife is best viewed from a window or on television. Her reasoning was that we had spent thousands of years getting AWAY from these predators and it would be rude and inconsiderate to our ancestors if we didn't take full advantage of all civilization had to offer. Things like doors and locks. Guns. Indoor plumbing. And, because she is your mom, chocolate.

Side note: For millions of years we, as a species, were on constant guard. But now, shoot – you have to work pretty darn hard to be eaten alive. It takes some energy to put yourself in a place where you might be food. And people say that things don't change. Pffffttt.

Those were the highlights of the talk anyway. After we chatted a bit more about the cougar it became apparent that Randy was getting a little tired so he wound things up shortly thereafter. He gathered his things, woke the sleeping Keesha, and shared one more thing with the group.

"Something I forgot to tell you. It might sound as if you're taking your life in your hands every time you step out the door around here. But you know what? Cougar attacks are rare. Really rare. There was a series of attacks in the town of Banff back in 2002, but that was attributed to a single cougar. Other than that, nada. And you know how many bear fatalities there have been?"

Oh, such a leading question. Such a set up. But, and you will be very proud of me, I held my tongue because I didn't want to break the spell. See, Mom was now hanging on Randy's every word. If your mom was going to find an iota of solace in any of this, she needed to hear out Randy without any silly diversions from me.

"Anyone?"

When no one answered Randy continued. "None. Not one single death from a grizzly. And here is another thing to think about. There are way more people injured by elk every year than there are by bear. The people that *have* been attacked haven't been following our 'bear smart' suggestions. So get out there and enjoy the trails and mountains but keep vigilant. Oh! And don't forget to have fun."

A round of applause and 'thank you' echoed in the room. With a smile and a wave, Randy and Keesha slipped out into the night.

I was sitting there, kind of digesting all the information from the evening. Mom stirred beside me and I knew that she was ready to call it a night. We had a long day of riding ahead of us tomorrow, and while we were taking a different route home, which was supposedly easier than the one we'd taken here, we still had no idea how long - or how hard - our day would be.

We were getting ready to go back to our room when Hemp-lady turned to me and said, "Do you know why no one was hurt?"

Now, I could have said any number of things but I was tired as well. Not firing on all cylinders, if you know what I mean. I'd picked up on the fact that hemp-lady hadn't totally agreed with what Randy was saying, mostly due to the heavy sighs and eye rolling, and I figured it was because the grizzly was probably her 'animal spirit guide' or something like that. Usually I would be chomping at the bit to discuss with this woman exactly why her particular philosophy was loopy, but it seemed like a lot of effort for very little amusement. So instead of offering some pithy insight, I simply shrugged.

"God," she said, and shook her head in an all-knowing creepy kind of way.

"Really?" I replied, before my brain could tell me to shut the hell up or I would be here all night.

"Oh definitely. See. . ." she said, and I understood that this was going to go on wayyyyyy longer than I had any interest in pursuing. Damn me and my auto responses! Damnable forced socialization!

"See God has a plan for all of us. That includes bears. If God wants you to be eaten, you'll be eaten. That's that."

She smiled at me.

Like spit on a hot griddle, the room cleared at the first hint of zealotry, leaving only Godly-hemp-lady, your mom, and me.

"So you're telling me," I said, "that you could walk out into the woods with twenty pounds of sausage strapped to your back and if God saw fit for you to live then you wouldn't be harmed?"

"Exactly. God has a plan for us all." She cocked her head to the side, "Are you a religious man?"

I wanted to say 'define religious'. As you know, my allegiance to any one deity wavers with the situation. My prayers are defined in accordance with my needs. Cthulu is wonderful for instilling insanity in my enemies. Vishnu really helps with the multi-tasking and technology. Buddha gets the chicks. Christ is kind of a catch-all. He's always good for a helping hand. As I've said many times I tend to identify more with the tricksters. Loki. Coyote. Glen Beck. Pan is just straight out a partier, so he covers things like the weather for weddings or group rides. I also adhere to the Greek and Roman Gods. One can't be too careful. The Sumerian holy-rollers figure prominently in the pantheon of my polytheism. Good ol' northern European Orthodox Paganism is a favorite. Oh! And I also like Pat Robertson and fundamental evangelists, but just for shits-n-giggles.

"Terribly religious." I shook my head in the positive. "Horribly religious," I smiled.

This seemed to puzzle her a bit, but she carried on. "I think the best defense against a cougar or bear attack is to pray and recite quotes from the Bible. It's the Lord's shield."

I had heard this term before. 'The Lord's shield'. Boring. Tell me about the 'Lord's socks', or the 'Lord's grocery list'. Then you'll have my attention.

"Are you versed in the bible?" She asked, raising her eyebrows.

Oh my dear, you have no idea. I study the bible regularly online. Perhaps not YOUR bible, but that's beside the point.

"I can site chapter and verse," I told her.

She looked me up and down again and regarded me skeptically. I caught your mom out of the corner of my eye. As you know, her growing up the daughter of a Southern Baptist Minister had left her a bit . . . jaded. She started to stand, in order to physically pull me away from the discussion but I motioned her back down with a slight movement of my hand.

"Really?" hemp-lady said and sniffed.

Sniff at me will you? Oh, that was the third strike for you hemp-Christ-lady! I don't care what anyone believes. Honestly. That is a personal matter for each and every one of us and is our right. Just as it is my right to think you bat-shit crazy. Just don't force your philosophy down my throat or there *will* be trouble.

A sly smile, full of righteousness and condemnation spread over her face like ice-cream on a warm laptop. "What's your favorite verse?"

"I'm more of an old-school, Old Testament kind of guy. I like my God angry, ruthless, and unapproachable."

"But that didn't answer my question," she said, believing that she'd caught me in a lie.

"You'd like me to quote some verse?"

"Please," she said.

I thought about just walking away, but you know I can't resist a fanatic. Even one covered in hemp.

"Genesis do ya?"

"That would be fine," she said, never wavering, never breaking eye contact.

"Fine. You want Genesis, you got Genesis. But you'll forgive me if I'm a bit rusty. A few lines or the whole first chapter?"

"Anyone can quote a few lines," she said.

Oh lady, lady, lady. This is going to be ridiculously fun! If I hadn't been the one talking I would have pulled up a chair and brought out the popcorn.

"Okay. Genesis it is." I cleared my throat. "You'll have to forgive my pronunciation. Some of the words are a little foreign to me. Here we go!"

> " Oh hai. In teh beginnin Ceiling Cat maded teh skiez An da Urfs, but he did not eated dem.
>
> Da Urfs no had shapez An haded dark face, An Ceiling Cat rode invisible bike over teh waterz.
>
> At start, no has lyte. An Ceiling Cat sayz, i can haz lite? An lite wuz.
>
> An Ceiling Cat sawed teh lite, to seez stuffs, An splitted teh lite from dark but taht wuz ok cuz kittehs can see in teh dark An not tripz over nethin.

Before I proceed let me just say that I had never been happier to have memorized something in my life. Oh sure, I'd originally committed the passage from the 'LOL Cat Bible' to memory simply to annoy the hell out of your Aunt Vicky, but should that be held against me? I think not. Just because you've got a hammer in your pocket and you used it to fix Mrs. Grammerfield's kitchen door, although the hammer was actually there because you were going to go downtown and 'modify' a few windows, should not invalidate the kind deed. Besides. There's always plenty of time for a little 'keeshh! keeshh!' later.

Anyway, I was supremely proud of myself. I grinned the grin of the heretic.

I have no idea why this woman didn't interrupt me. Or, more technically 'smote' my ass. I think she was thrown so far off balance that her brain simply froze. I wish I could describe the look that came across the robed prophet, but alas, words fail me. Let it suffice to say that it was an absolute tidal wave of expression. Confusion. Horror. Revulsion. Anger. Righteous indignation. Anger. Contempt. Anger. Resentment. Anger. Hate. Anger. You know, all those good Christian qualities I've come to know and love.

"THAT!" she spat, "is NOT Genesis!"

"Don't let Ceiling Cat hear you say that. He can be a dark and angry kitteh." I looked side to side conspiratorially, nodding my head in the affirmative. "He'll tak u 2 da bar."

She became quite calm - a little too calm - and whispered deadly even, "Blasphemer."

Note the distinction of her word choice. Not blasphemy. But 'blasphemer'. One pertains to an action, one to the person. This was turning out way better than I expected!

"Orly? I c wut u did thar. LOL."

Her hands, hanging loose by her sides, now knotted and unknotted like a ball of snakes in an electric current. "You are going to Hell," she sputtered with a grimace that would have made one of Randy's bears head for the hills.

"Probably. But before I go we need to talk about that skin color you've got going on and the uncontrollable shaking. I believe you may be possessed. Possessed by the spirit of Basement Cat. Tell me, have you had an uncontrollable urge to shred the curtains? Steal a cheeseburger? Eets a plant den barfs? Charge yer lazers? Where exactly do you stand on the theosophy of Longcat and Tacgnol? Do you agree that the battle is Epic?"

To give her credit she tried to think of something more to say. She sputtered and worked her mouth up and down like a dying fish in the bottom of a boat. Might have even spit a little. Finally her face went from deep red to purple, and she turned on her heel, and with nary another word, strode out of the room.

As she crossed the threshold I shouted "kthxbai!"

Mom, strangely quiet through this entire encounter, let out a sigh. "Really? Was that necessary?"

"Necessary? Probably not. Fun? Definitely. I totally pwned her. A conversation chock-full of win and fail. Delicious."

"You do know that you are a forty-eight year old man, right?"

"Of course I do."

"And you realize that lolcat isn't a real language, right?"

I eyed her carefully. "Blasphemer."

"Okay fine. Whatever. Let's go get some sleep. But when we get home I'm going to confiscate your laptop." She took my hand and started leading me to the door. "It's a good thing you have me."

"Duh. Like I don't know that. But why do you think that?"

She stopped dead in her tracks. "Because after thirty-two years even I don't know whether you're completely insane, or just partially. But I would defend you to the ends of the earth," she said and leaned over to kiss my face. She then opened the massive door and pulled me onto the darkness of the porch. "Let's run! I don't want to be eaten!" she giggled and dashed over to our door.

I followed her. A day like today had worn me completely to a nub. A nice shower and a soft bed was what I needed. Tomorrow, we would get up and pack the bike, have breakfast and hit the road for home. It was bittersweet.

And it would be good to get home, back where summer was still in full glory. Not here. Here it was freezing.

And when I say freezing, I mean freezing.

Tomorrow should be interesting. Interesting indeed.

October 11, 2008

Dear Amber,

Well, the neighbors are at it again.

Any chance that when you start flying you could 'accidently' drop a bomb or fire a missile at their house?

If you could that would be grand. It might keep me out of prison.

Love you,
Daddio

Chapter 14

We bid Adieu

I love the mornings. Well, I love the mornings if they don't come too early. Up here, in the Canadian Rockies, morning came in the middle of the night. So you'll understand why I was a bit flummoxed to awaken to the delicate trilling of . . .

"Crap. Crap crap crap. Double crap."

As I've explained, your mother has always had a unique way of rousing me, but this was a new one even for her. Perhaps in my sleep deprived state I was mistaking your mother for a disgruntled song-bird.

I yawned and stretched. "Morning sweetie."

I squinted and saw the silhouette of your mom against the windows of the French doors to the deck. My eyes weren't working terribly well yet. The older I get, the longer it takes to fire up the systems. I need an upgrade. David 2.0 to David 2.43 would be nice. Guess I should have purchased the extended warranty.

"Have you seen outside?" Mom asked.

I thought about this for a minute, not quite sure how she thought it was possible that I, in my sleep, had observed the great outdoors. Astral projection is not my strong suit. Or sure, I can get out of my body but then I usually end up stuck in the refrigerator, a sideboard, or between floors. Boring! I decided, and correctly so because it was the start of the day, not to pursue this slip of language and point out to your mother that until 90 seconds ago my eyes had been closed. But I knew what she meant. She meant 'get-your-patootie-over-here-and-look-outside-because-I-have-to-share-this-with-someone-or-I'm-going-to-bust'. Even in my addled, caffeine-starved state I comprehended that whatever she was looking at couldn't be good.

"Whattsamatta? Something wrong with the moose?"

Please let it be something with the moose and not a bear and a cougar with guns taking turns sitting on the bike.

"No. Just come over here."

It took me a minute because I had to convince my body that moving would be a good idea. All indications were that lying perfectly still would be the body's choice, but the body knows nothing of the ways of marriage. Finally I managed to stand and hobble-hopped over to where your mom stood scowling. As I got closer she stepped to the side, drawing back the curtain.

Well. Well fuck. Fuckity-fuck-fuck-fuckity-fuck. Would you look at that.

Snow.

And not just a skiff. Oh no, they do things big up here in the mountains and this bit of weather was no different. No, there was a good three inches covering the deck, the Lodge, the meadow and peaks surrounding the valley. The sky was clear as anything that morning. Bluer than I'd seen a sky in a long, long time. We used to have the bluest skies you'd ever seen in Seattle, but that was back when Perry Como was alive.

The sun, up until now naught but a rumor, was just beginning to rise over a horizon we couldn't see. The effect was the top of the mountains looked like they'd been lit by humongous electric lights. Kind of like the security lights on our neighbor Fred's garage. You know, the one that shines RIGHT IN OUR BEDROOM!!

Which reminds me, I need more BBs.

Just picture it - early dawn, the meadow and valley transitioning from dark to light, and these mountains blazing. Reflecting the fresh snow like beacons. It was breathtaking. I would have loved it more except for an eensie, weensie, little negative thought that had crawled to the forefront of my mind and stuck there like a piece of spinach on your blind-date's remaining front tooth. No way around it, we were going to have to ride the bike through this stuff. Ugh.

"Gah! Snow? Well of course. Of course we would wake up to snow on the day we're to leave." I rubbed my forehead. "No doubt the Park Service has also seen fit to release the pterodactyls and T-Rex on this fine morning as well." I banged my head lightly against the glass of the door. "It is beautiful though, isn't it? You know, in a kind of 'last thing you see before you die' kind of way.

"I have to admit it's incredible," Mom said as I pulled her into a hug.

"But what the Hell? It's August! And mid-August at that. Doesn't Canada adhere to the seasons?"

What kind of a rogue nation fiddles with the seasons? And then it hit me. Wily Canadians, you have suckered us once again with your hellish measurements! What we were experiencing were no doubt kilomonths. Or nanoyears. Or decadays. Bastards. They could warn you when you cross the border, you know?

"Maybe there's some flippin' Canadian season converter no one told us about. Sure, it's mid-August at our house but for all we know it could be late November up here."

That stopped her short. She looked at me with wide eyes. "I'm scared," Mom said.

"Because of the snow?"

"Well yeah. But mostly because you're beginning to make sense."

"It's awful, isn't it?"

"Yes. Yes it is," she replied.

Poor dear, it's not easy to realize you've stepped through the looking glass.

"So," she said, looking up and down the length of the meadow, "What are we going to do?"

Fine question that. As you've seen, your mother has this unique ability to distill any situation to its essence. It wasn't just the snow that had me worried. We were taking the mythical 'Highway 40' back to the flat-land and I had no idea what we were going to find. I mean, what if these people, in some perverted punishment for us being from THE STATES, had collectively lied about the quality of the road? It might shoot straight off a cliff for all I know. Don't laugh. I've seen several movies where this has happened. Hollywood doesn't lie. And on top of the 'unknown Highway', we had to add snow. Four wheels on snow was bad enough. Take that down to two. The words slippy-slippy crashy-crashy die-y die-y come to mind.

With a sigh I said, "Not much we can do babe. I guess the best thing is to go have breakfast and hope that when the sun rises high in the sky it will melt the snow off the roads. Might cut into our travel time, but I don't see that we have any choice."

"This has been some vacation, hasn't it?"

"That is has my dear, that it has." I turned away from the door and returned to sit on the end of the bed. "Go take a shower. We'll go grab something to eat and deal with whatever we have to deal with."

As Mom 'made herself presentable', I sat and pondered. I wish I could tell you I arrived at some wonderful realization. Some grand epiphany. But alas, as I sat there all I could think of was 'Well. Guess I'm driving in snow.'

We entered the dining room for breakfast, and there at the table sat Julie and Robert. We took a seat next to them. There were a few other people in the room, but not nearly as many as in the previous two days.

"So," Robert said, "you guys heading home today?" he said, and made a pointed move to look out the window at the snow, then back to me.

"Yeah." I answered and poured myself a cup of coffee. "You guys?"

"We have one more day here," Julie said.

Robert grinned. "How do you think that big machine of yours is going to handle in the snow?"

"Pretty well actually," I said as casually as I could. "I don't think we'll have to deploy the automatic chain system, but we may have to use the in-line sanders a bit."

Julie shook her head. "You have chains for your bike tires?"

Robert and I looked at her in unison, then at each other, then back to her.

"Oh. A joke. I get it."

"Hopefully it will melt before we hit the road. If not, I may catch a couple of moose and hitch them to the front of the bike. They get through the snow pretty well, don't they?"

"Probably," Robert replied.

For some reason the image of two moose roped to the front of the Vision was just about the funniest thing Julie had ever heard. When she stopped giggling she turned to your mom and said, "Oh he's so FUNNY!"

"Oh yeah," Mom said, and rubbed my bald head, a tad aggressively I thought, "it's a laugh-a-minute with David."

"Babe," I said, "that didn't sound entirely positive."

She just shrugged. I would have been upset but it was a fair statement. I don't know if you've ever noticed but I tend to find the humor in any situation. Even when it's not appropriate. As they say, it's always fun until someone loses an eye. Then it's hilarious.

Julie, with a true look of concern said, "Are you guys going to be able to stay warm?"

Mom looked at me. Evidently this was a question that she would like an answer to as well.

"I think we're going to be fine. The Vision has heated seats and grips. We'll layer on as much clothing as possible.." I smiled, but I thought of my mesh jacket and shivered.

I caught Robert grinning.

"At least we won't have to worry about breaking down or anything. The Vision is remarkably reliable. I don't think I've ever even seen a drop of oil from her."

For a brief instant intense concern rolled over Robert's face. Ah, another job well done. My work here was finished.

We sat back with our coffee and our tea and watched the sun fill the valley with light. It was GORGEOUS. Morning light on fresh snow - August or not - is a sight of which I never tire. Well, as long as I'm warm and inside a building with central heat. It gets pretty old pretty quick when you're viewing a wonderland like this from inside a helmet with nothing but summer clothes to keep you warm.

The rest of breakfast was uneventful. Delicious but uneventful. I would write an opus to the meats I devoured, a sonnet to the eggs, and a song about the toast but I think you get the point by now. Let's just say that I had fulfilled my grease quotient for the day, and possibly all the days until next March.

We ate and talked, laughed and joked, and when we had eaten the last piece of sausage and drank the last cup of coffee there was nothing to do but face the facts - it was time to hit the road. We said our farewells to Robert and Julie, closing with what every biker says to the other when they part. "Ride safe."

Although Julie had to add, "Be careful on Highway 40. A biker hit a bear down there last week."

Et tu, Julie?

Turned out that Robert and Julie weren't such bad people after all. You know, for BMW riders. And lawyer folk. And Canadian.

Leeza came and sat beside us at the table. "So, you picked a fine day to be heading home."

"We Moores seem to have a knack for that," I said. "I think it's genetic. My Great-grandfather was the same way."

"Really?"

"Oh yeah. Let's just say that if it weren't for Great-Grandpa Chester, the Donner Party would have waited until spring. But no. He just HAD to convince them that fall foliage in California was a 'must see' experience."

Mom put her arm around my shoulders and said, "That would also explain your love of . . . how would you say it? All things meaty?"

"True sweetie. Too true. Before you judge dear old Grandpa, it really wasn't his fault. See, he was also dyslexic. He'd been holding the map upside down. Thought they were going to Vermont."

"You two crack me up," Leeza said.

Oh, a dollar for every time I've heard that over the years! Sometimes it was even spoken with a positive slant.

"Do you guys want to pack a lunch before you go?"

"No thanks," Mom said. "Sometimes enticing him with food is the only way I can get off the bike."

"Well, you two have a safe trip back to THE STATES. We really enjoyed you guys staying with us. Did you have a good time? Was everything up to your expectations?"

Before I could answer Mom jumped in, "This has been one of the best vacations I've had. The food, the room . . . shoot, even the wildlife. It's been a great adventure. Hasn't it?", she said, looking at me.

"Well I thought so, but I also am a huge fan of train wrecks and shipping disasters, so I'm probably not a good barometer."

The rest of the staff wandered in and said their goodbyes. It's amazing how attached you can get to people in such a short time. Now that it was almost over I didn't want to go. And it had nothing to do with the snow.

See, I had learned something about Canadus Sapien in my stay here in the mountains. I'd learned that . . . ummm . . . I'd learned that . . . well, I'd learned that they could put up with me for three days, and that made them A-okay in my book. Shoot, even you and your sister can't do that.

Donny was the last to tell us goodbye. He shook my hand so hard I thought I was going to lose a filling.

"You folks take care now. And be careful. A biker hit a bear down on Highway 40 last week."

I thanked Donny for his concern, and Mom and I stepped out of the Lodge for the last time and into the bracing cold.

Back in our room, I turned to Mom and said, "I suggest that we put on as many layers as we can."

"Do you think we're going to be able to make it?"

"Oh, I don't think we'll have much problem, if the road back down is as good as they say. The snow is starting to melt. It should be off the roads in just a bit."

We put on our layers. And more layers. Then a couple more for good measure. Your mom looked like a puffy little snow-woman. I didn't point this out to her.

It's amazing how quickly you can pack the bike when you're *wearing* three-quarters of what you packed. Before you knew it we were in the saddle, the bike was running, and the sky was blue and stretching out before us like an inverted ocean. True, it was a little difficult to bend my arms at the elbow, and my legs had a tendency to stick out straight from the sides of the bike but those were minor details.

I brought the bike upright, and put the kickstand up. With a deep breath I said "You ready for this babe?"

"No."

"And I can't blame you for that. Just stay relaxed back there and we'll do fine."

"Okay," she said, but I could tell she was less than convinced.

"Before we go, answer me this: Can you feel your lips?"

She pondered that for a moment. "Not really. But it's okay. It will distract me from the fact that we may die at any moment."

I told you she was a trooper.

So with a twist of the throttle, and a mighty 'Heigh-Ho Vision!' I eased off the clutch and slowly rolled through the fresh snow of the parking lot. We stopped and took a last look at the Lodge, at Moose-snot Roost, at what we had come to call 'our valley'. As we sat there a moose walked down the road in front of us and disappeared over the bank to the wallow. The perfect ending.

We slipped a little as I pulled onto the main road but the bike soon recovered. The snow was breaking up as the day warmed, so it was really a layer of slush on top of the gravel. Not too bad for travel. I was a little nervous for the first half-mile or so, but soon was lost in the incredible scenery that surrounded us.

Mom leaned forward and said, "This is magical."

"The scenery or the whole trip?" I asked through a slightly fogged face shield.

"Mostly this."

I would like to be able to tell you that the road back down the hill was as horrible as the route we'd taken up to the Lodge, but that wasn't the case. The road was wide and level with nary a washboard or pothole. The descent was as gradual as a baby's butt, and just as smooth. We made good time and before I knew it there was nothing but small patches of snow here and there. Another ten minutes and the road was completely clear. Five more and we had reached the turn-off to the Highway and the wondrous sight of blacktop. Another ten minutes and I was pulling over to start shedding layers.

"Well, that was certainly easier than coming up the other side, eh?"

"Ya think?", Mom said.

"Well, easier, but think of all of the adventure you would have missed out on if we'd came up this way in the first place."

I don't know what was going on in your mom's head, but I'm sure that if I were privy to her exact thoughts I wouldn't be pleased. Not pleased at all.

Finally, she looked at me with a blank expression and said, "Sure."

We jumped back on the bike and headed for, what even I had come to refer to, as THE STATES.

The rest of the trip was pretty ordinary. The scenery was fantastic. As we went south, we broke out of the mountains, and for the next eighty miles - yes miles, I was heading home to the land of REAL measurement so I could revert to my native calculations - we drove along the east side of the Rockies. The dusting of snow highlighted every swirl, every ribbon of granite and crop of rock. Glorious. Rockies to our right, and with no transition prairie to the left. It was as if the prairie, on its way to the ocean, had hit a major block and erupted, throwing its contents into the air. We didn't see any more bears, or moose, or any other wildlife but we did see many an oil well pumping crude, and they do look a little prehistoric so it was all good.

As I drove, I thought back over our trip. The fun, the danger, the conversations. I sighed a little. How is it what seems so difficult at the time, later turns into our fondest memories?

Mom had been silent for quite some time. Finally she leaned forward and said, "You know, for everything we've been through this has been the best vacation. Thank you sweetie."

I reached behind and gave her knee a loving squeeze. "So, you're going to let me live?"

"For the time being," she said, and patted me on the shoulder.

She sat back in her seat and after a few minutes leaned forward and tapped me on the shoulder again.

"I'm thinking next year we go to Alaska. Ride the highway all the way down. We could take the ferry from Seattle, then cruise back home."

"Why stop at home? I've always wanted to see Mexico," I said through the wind.

"Well, if we go that far, we might as well go all the way."

"Tierra Del Fuego?"

"To the ends of the earth for you sweetie. The ends of the earth," she said, closing her shield and leaning back in her seat.

How could you not love a woman like that?

THE END

October 13, 2008

Dear Amber,

Well, there you have it. The whole, unvarnished, completely true story just as I promised way back in the beginning. I hope you've found some smiles tucked away in these pages and hopefully a bit of distraction as you make your way to becoming a Naval Officer.

Your mom, your sister the firefighter / EMT, and now you - a Navy Pilot. How the hell did I get so lucky? And how did you all turn out so well?

Must have been something in the water, eh? Maybe Mom was putting something in the drinks . . . OMG! That explains SO much.

Love you,
Daddio

P.S. I look great in my Pirate outfit! I captured and plundered three boats the other day! I would have had four, but the ride operator said that I was scaring the children. Pffftttttt! Like I haven't heard that a thousand times.

About The Author

David lives with his wife - quite nervously - in small town nestled in the foothills of an active volcano.

When he's not writing, you can find him piloting the Vision with Suzanne on the back, meandering through the hills and dales of Washington State.

And usually plotting world domination through tasty, tasty snacks.

Made in the USA
Charleston, SC
21 May 2011